ISBN 978-1-59182-799-3

5 0 9 9 9

9 781591 827993

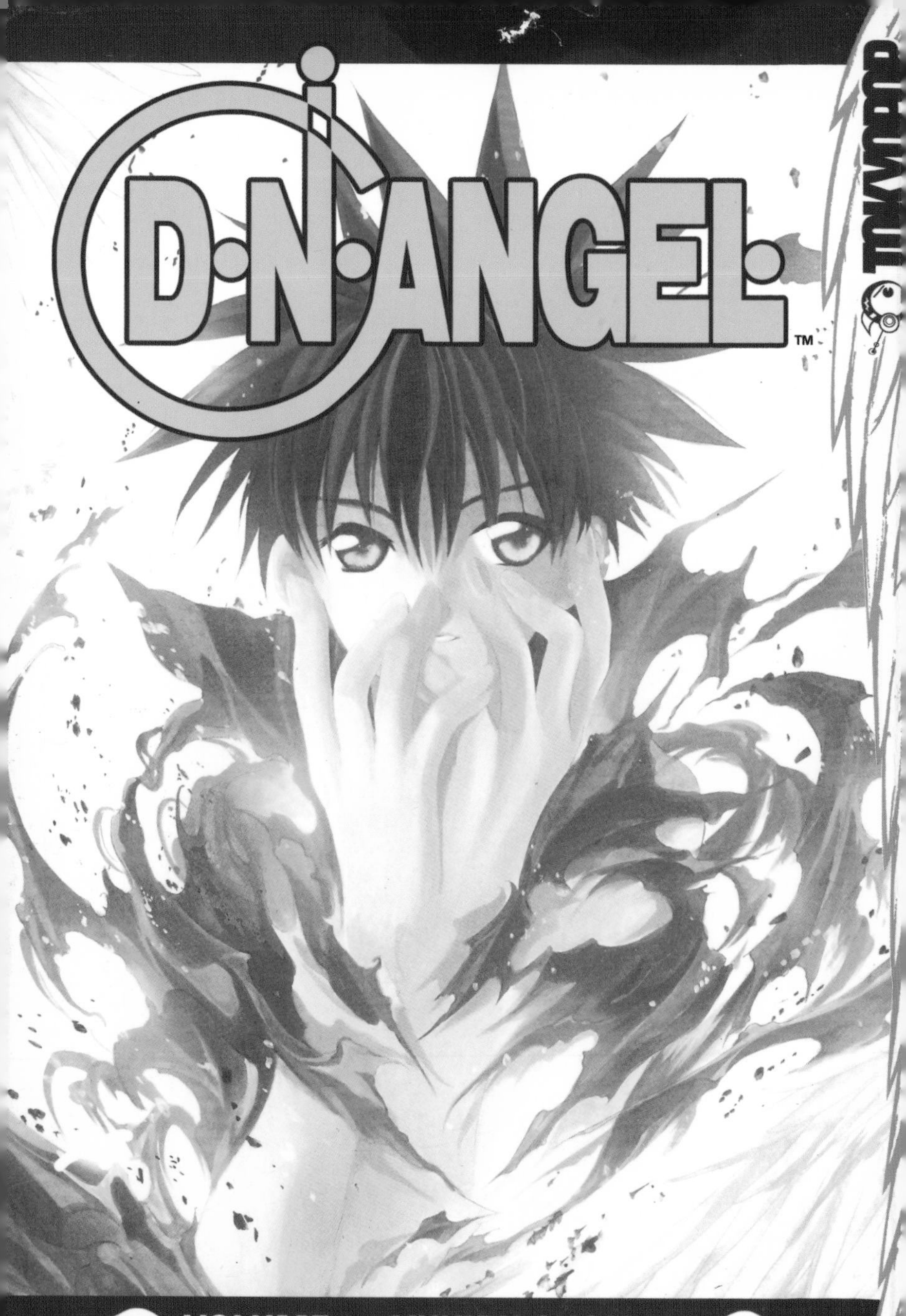
D·N·ANGEL™
TOKYOPOP

VOLUME 1 • YUKIRU SUGISAKI

# D•N•ANGEL

BY YUKIRU SUGISAKI

VOLUME 1

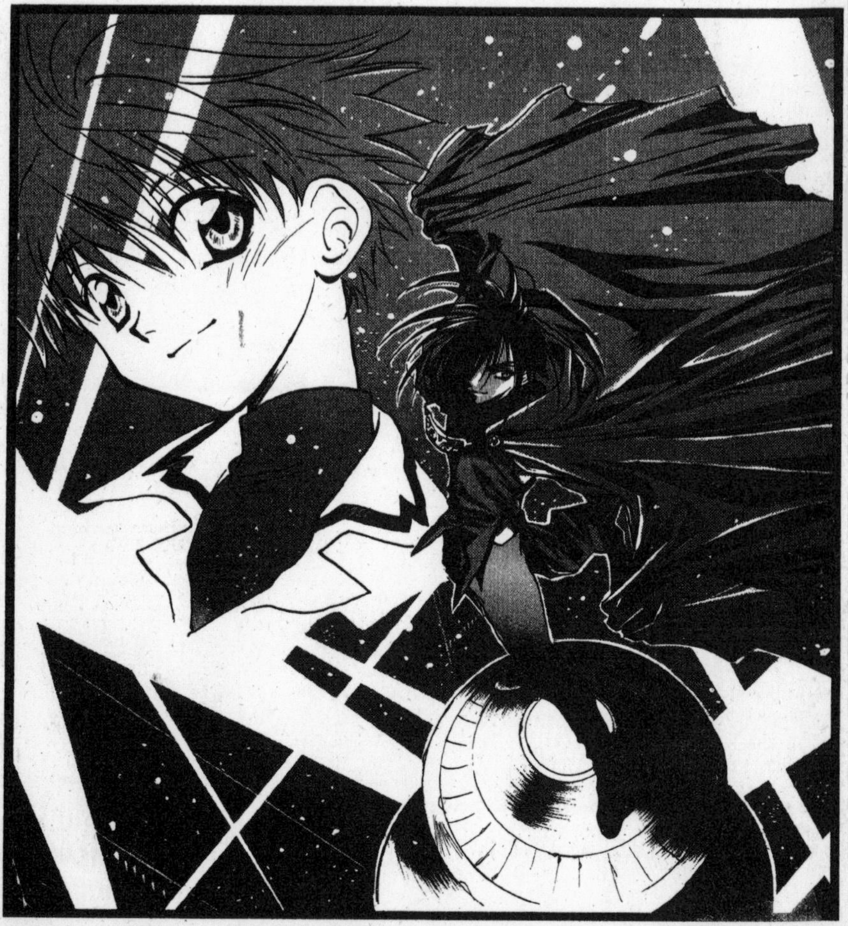

# ALSO AVAILABLE FROM ⟨⟩ TOKYOPOP®

# ALSO AVAILABLE FROM TOKYOPOP®

## MANGA

.HACK//LEGEND OF THE TWILIGHT
@LARGE
ABENOBASHI: MAGICAL SHOPPING ARCADE
A.I. LOVE YOU
AI YORI AOSHI
ANGELIC LAYER
ARM OF KANNON
BABY BIRTH
BATTLE ROYALE
BATTLE VIXENS
BOYS BE...
BRAIN POWERED
BRIGADOON
B'TX
CANDIDATE FOR GODDESS, THE
CARDCAPTOR SAKURA
CARDCAPTOR SAKURA - MASTER OF THE CLOW
CHOBITS
CHRONICLES OF THE CURSED SWORD
CLAMP SCHOOL DETECTIVES
CLOVER
COMIC PARTY
CONFIDENTIAL CONFESSIONS
CORRECTOR YUI
COWBOY BEBOP
COWBOY BEBOP: SHOOTING STAR
CRAZY LOVE STORY
CRESCENT MOON
CROSS
CULDCEPT
CYBORG 009
D•N•ANGEL
DEMON DIARY
DEMON ORORON, THE
DEUS VITAE
DIABOLO
DIGIMON
DIGIMON TAMERS
DIGIMON ZERO TWO
DOLL
DRAGON HUNTER
DRAGON KNIGHTS
DRAGON VOICE
DREAM SAGA
DUKLYON: CLAMP SCHOOL DEFENDERS
EERIE QUEERIE!
ERICA SAKURAZAWA: COLLECTED WORKS
ET CETERA
ETERNITY
EVIL'S RETURN
FAERIES' LANDING
FAKE
FLCL
FLOWER OF THE DEEP SLEEP
FORBIDDEN DANCE
FRUITS BASKET

G GUNDAM
GATEKEEPERS
GETBACKERS
GIRL GOT GAME
GIRLS EDUCATIONAL CHARTER
GRAVITATION
GTO
GUNDAM BLUE DESTINY
GUNDAM SEED ASTRAY
GUNDAM WING
GUNDAM WING: BATTLEFIELD OF PACIFISTS
GUNDAM WING: ENDLESS WALTZ
GUNDAM WING: THE LAST OUTPOST (G-UNIT)
HANDS OFF!
HAPPY MANIA
HARLEM BEAT
HYPER RUNE
I.N.V.U.
IMMORTAL RAIN
INITIAL D
INSTANT TEEN: JUST ADD NUTS
ISLAND
JING: KING OF BANDITS
JING: KING OF BANDITS - TWILIGHT TALES
JULINE
KARE KANO
KILL ME, KISS ME
KINDAICHI CASE FILES, THE
KING OF HELL
KODOCHA: SANA'S STAGE
LAMENT OF THE LAMB
LEGAL DRUG
LEGEND OF CHUN HYANG, THE
LES BIJOUX
LOVE HINA
LUPIN III
LUPIN III: WORLD'S MOST WANTED
MAGIC KNIGHT RAYEARTH I
MAGIC KNIGHT RAYEARTH II
MAHOROMATIC: AUTOMATIC MAIDEN
MAN OF MANY FACES
MARMALADE BOY
MARS
MARS: HORSE WITH NO NAME
MINK
MIRACLE GIRLS
MIYUKI-CHAN IN WONDERLAND
MODEL
MOURYOU KIDEN
MY LOVE
NECK AND NECK
ONE
ONE I LOVE, THE
PARADISE KISS
PARASYTE
PASSION FRUIT
PEACH GIRL
PEACH GIRL: CHANGE OF HEART

06.21.04T

## D•N•ANGEL Vol. 1
## Created by Yukiru Sugisaki

Translation - Alethea Nibley, Athena Nibley
English Adaptation - Sarah Dyer
Associate Editor - Katherine Schilling
Retouch and Lettering - Paul Tanck
Production Artist - John Lo
Cover Design - Gary Shum

Editor - Bryce P. Coleman
Digital Imaging Manager - Chris Buford
Pre-Press Manager - Antonio DePietro
Production Managers - Jennifer Miller and Mutsumi Miyazaki
Art Director - Matt Alford
Managing Editor - Jill Freshney
VP of Production - Ron Klamert
President and C.O.O. - John Parker
Publisher and C.E.O. - Stuart Levy

A  Manga

TOKYOPOP Inc.
5900 Wilshire Blvd. Suite 2000
Los Angeles, CA 90036

E-mail: info@TOKYOPOP.com
Come visit us online at www.TOKYOPOP.com

ISBN: 1-59182-799-X

First TOKYOPOP printing: April 2004
20  19  18  17  16  15
Printed in the USA

# Volume 1

## By
## Yukiru Sugisaki

HAMBURG // LONDON // LOS ANGELES // TOKYO

# CONTENTS

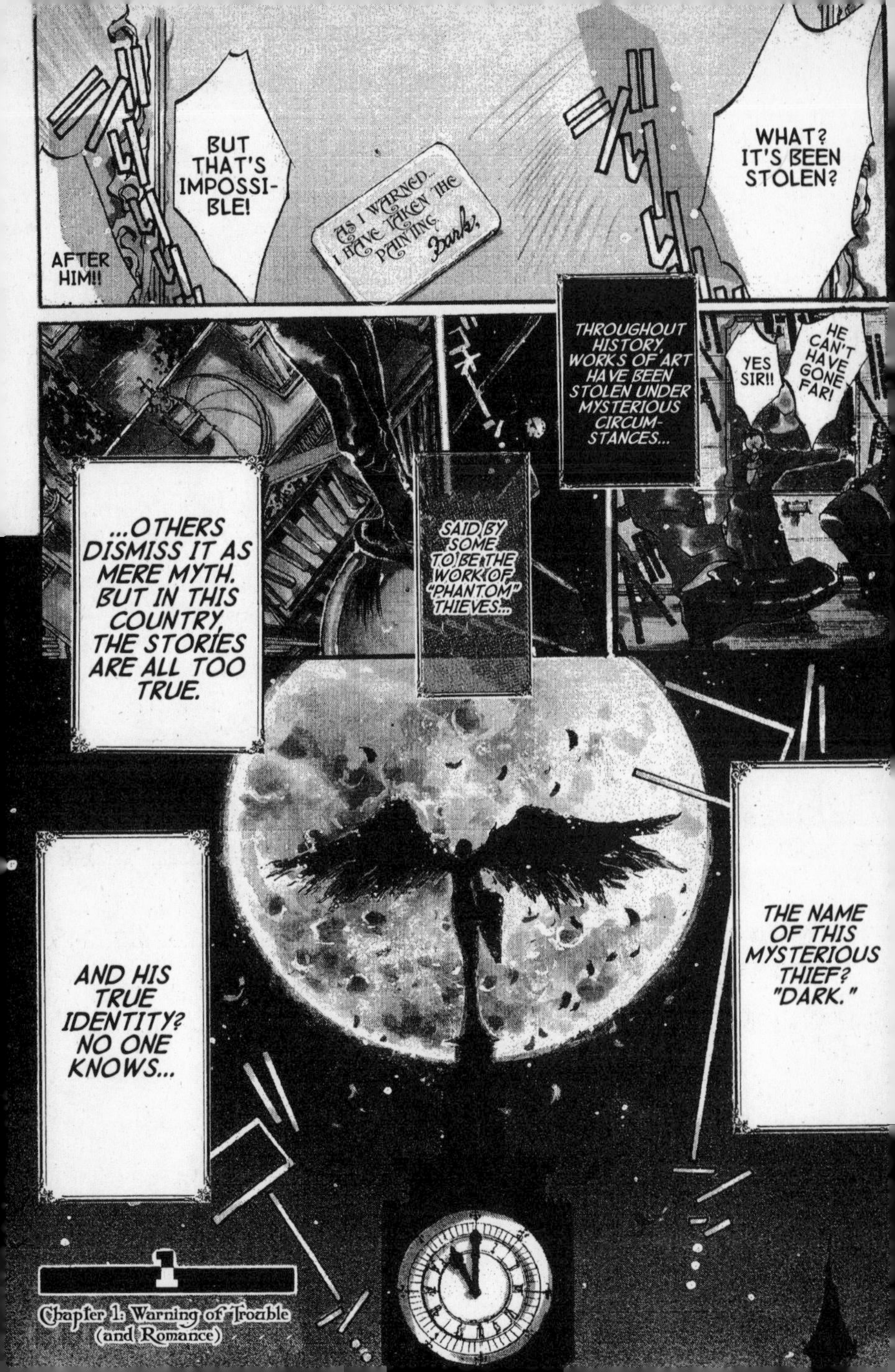

WHAT? IT'S BEEN STOLEN?
AS I WARNED... I HAVE TAKEN THE PAINTING. Dark
BUT THAT'S IMPOSSI-BLE!
AFTER HIM!!
HE CAN'T HAVE GONE FAR!
YES SIR!!
THROUGHOUT HISTORY, WORKS OF ART HAVE BEEN STOLEN UNDER MYSTERIOUS CIRCUM-STANCES...
SAID BY SOME TO BE THE WORK OF "PHANTOM" THIEVES...
...OTHERS DISMISS IT AS MERE MYTH. BUT IN THIS COUNTRY, THE STORIES ARE ALL TOO TRUE.
THE NAME OF THIS MYSTERIOUS THIEF? "DARK."
AND HIS TRUE IDENTITY? NO ONE KNOWS...
1
Chapter 1: Warning of Trouble (and Romance)

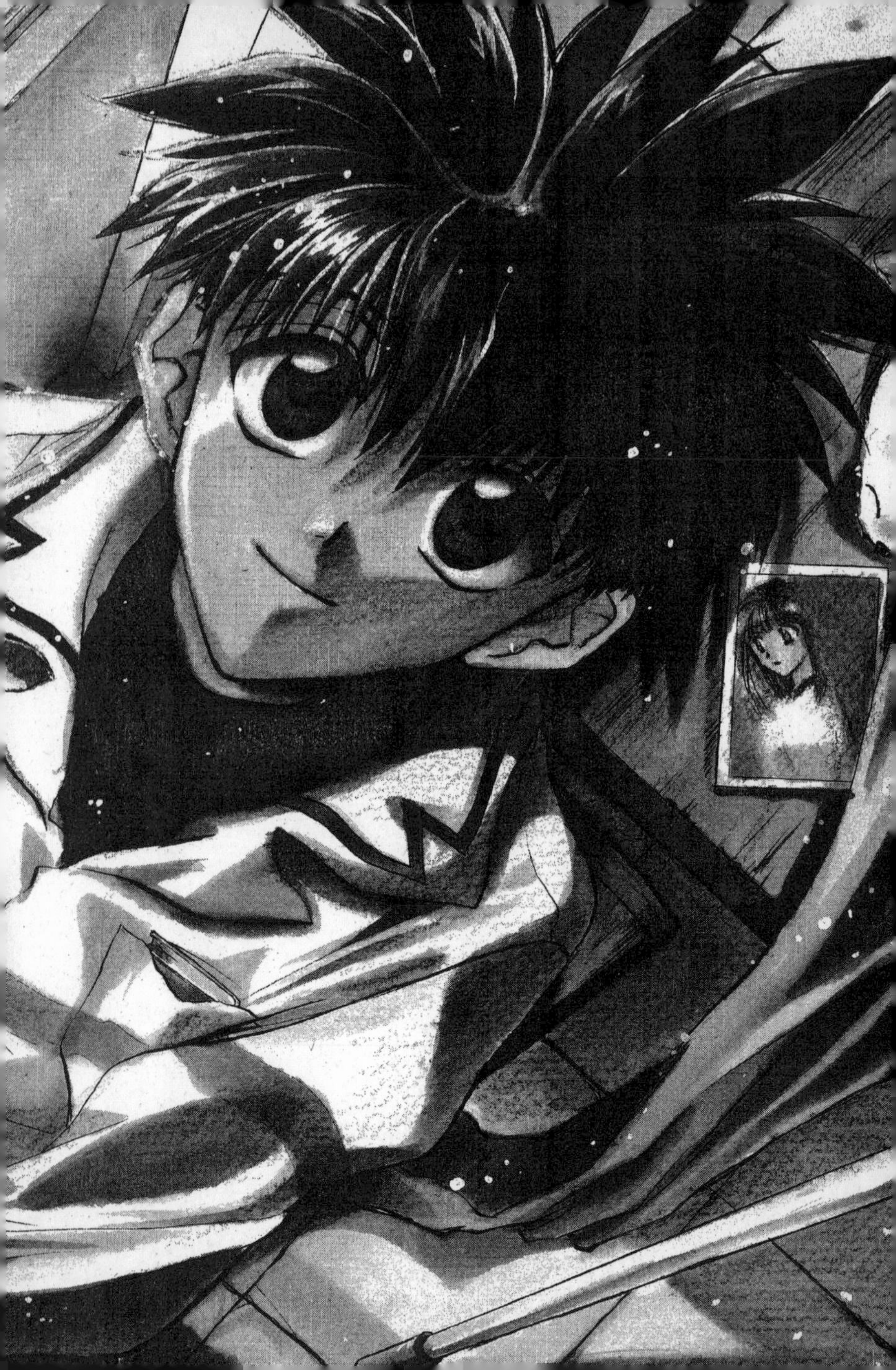

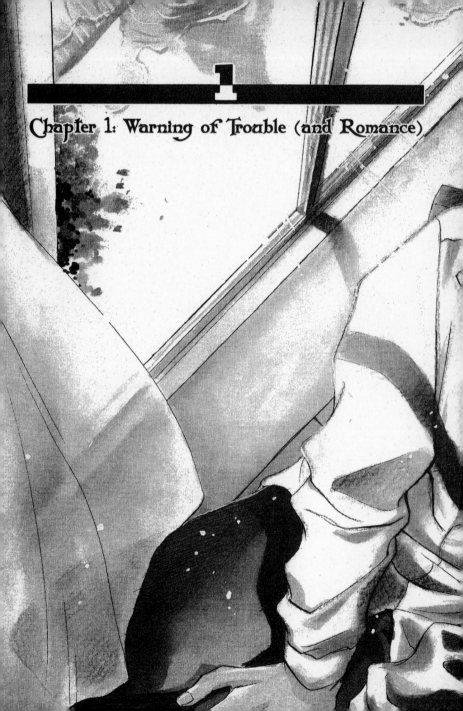

# 1

Chapter 1: Warning of Trouble (and Romance)

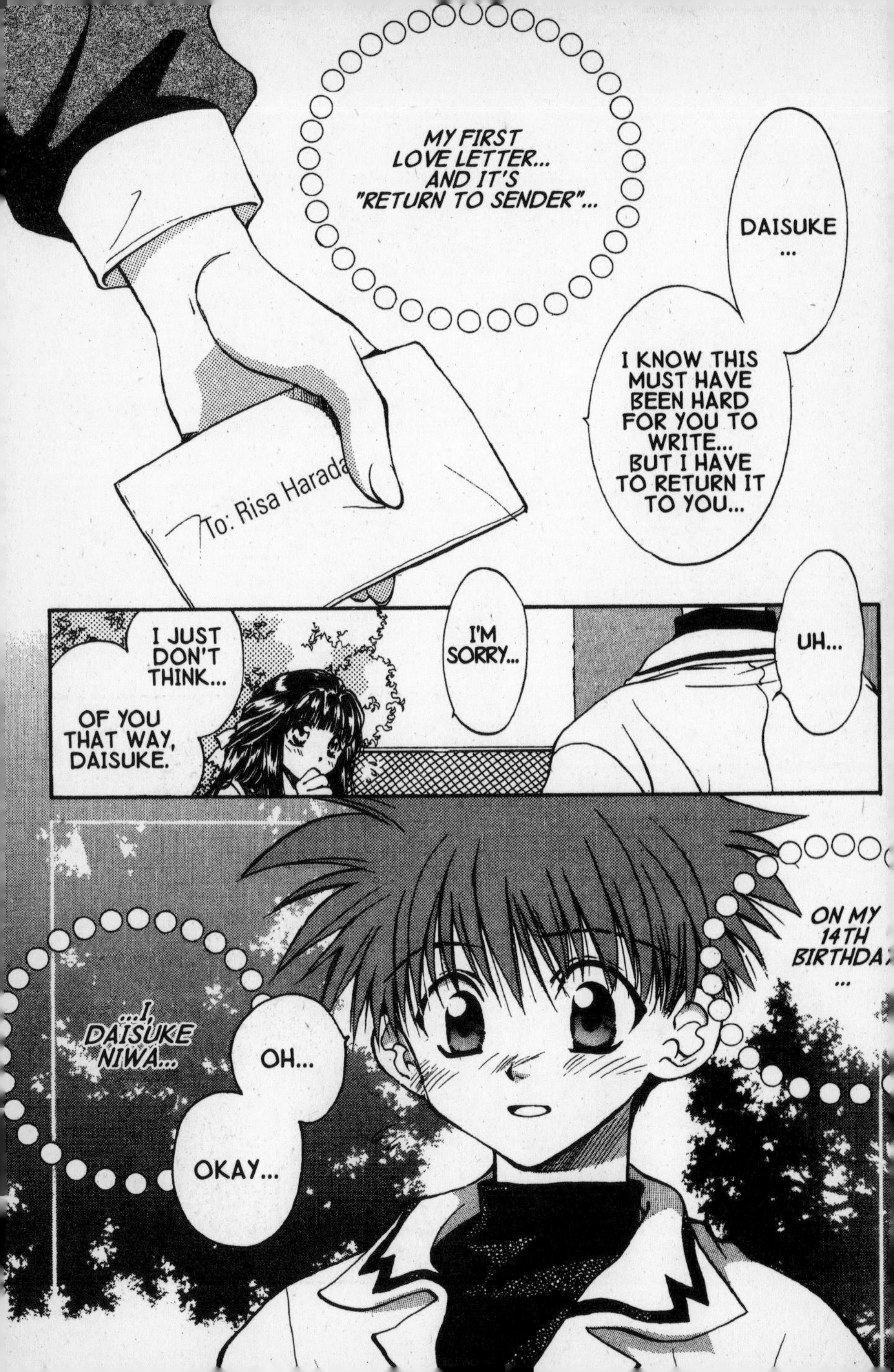
DAISUKE ...
I KNOW THIS MUST HAVE BEEN HARD FOR YOU TO WRITE... BUT I HAVE TO RETURN IT TO YOU...
MY FIRST LOVE LETTER... AND IT'S "RETURN TO SENDER"...
To: Risa Harada
UH...
I'M SORRY...
I JUST DON'T THINK...
OF YOU THAT WAY, DAISUKE.
ON MY 14TH BIRTHDA ...
...I, DAISUKE NIWA...
OH...
OKAY...

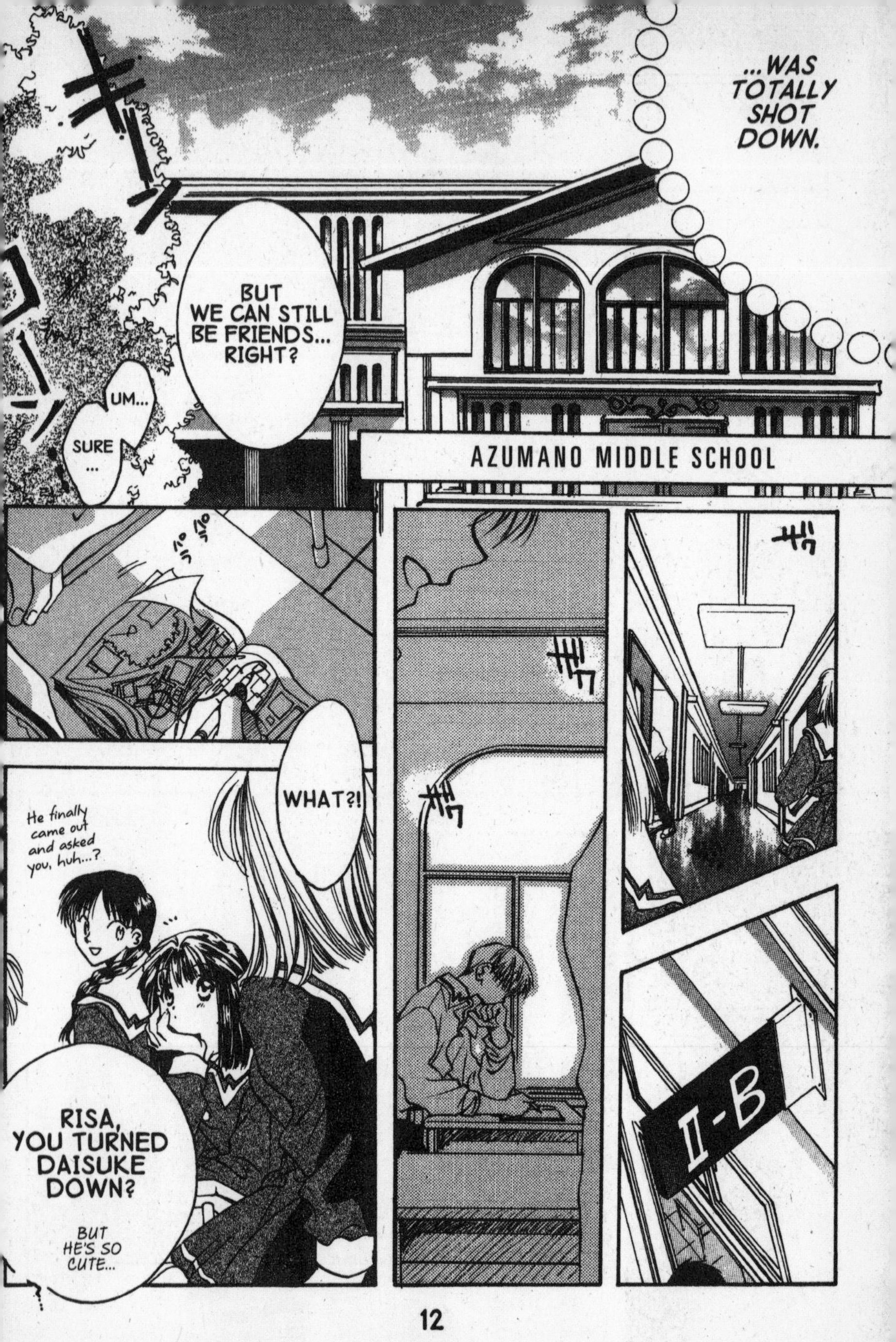
...WAS TOTALLY SHOT DOWN.
AZUMANO MIDDLE SCHOOL
BUT WE CAN STILL BE FRIENDS... RIGHT?
UM...
SURE ...
ギク
II-B
ギク
ギク
WHAT?!
He finally came out and asked you, huh...?
RISA, YOU TURNED DAISUKE DOWN?
BUT HE'S SO CUTE...

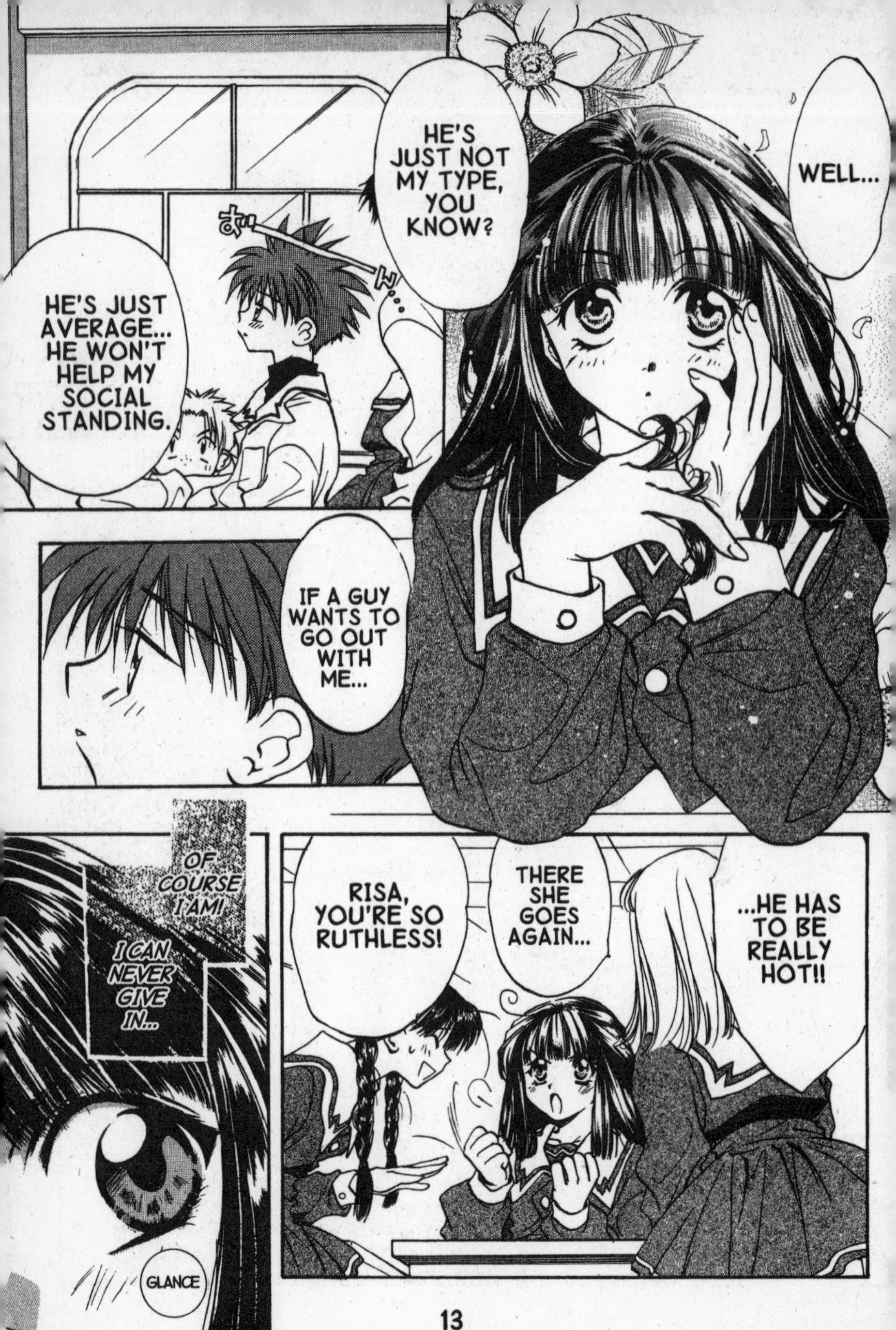
WELL...
HE'S JUST NOT MY TYPE, YOU KNOW?
HE'S JUST AVERAGE... HE WON'T HELP MY SOCIAL STANDING.
IF A GUY WANTS TO GO OUT WITH ME...
...HE HAS TO BE REALLY HOT!!
THERE SHE GOES AGAIN...
RISA, YOU'RE SO RUTHLESS!
OF COURSE I AM!
I CAN NEVER GIVE IN...
GLANCE

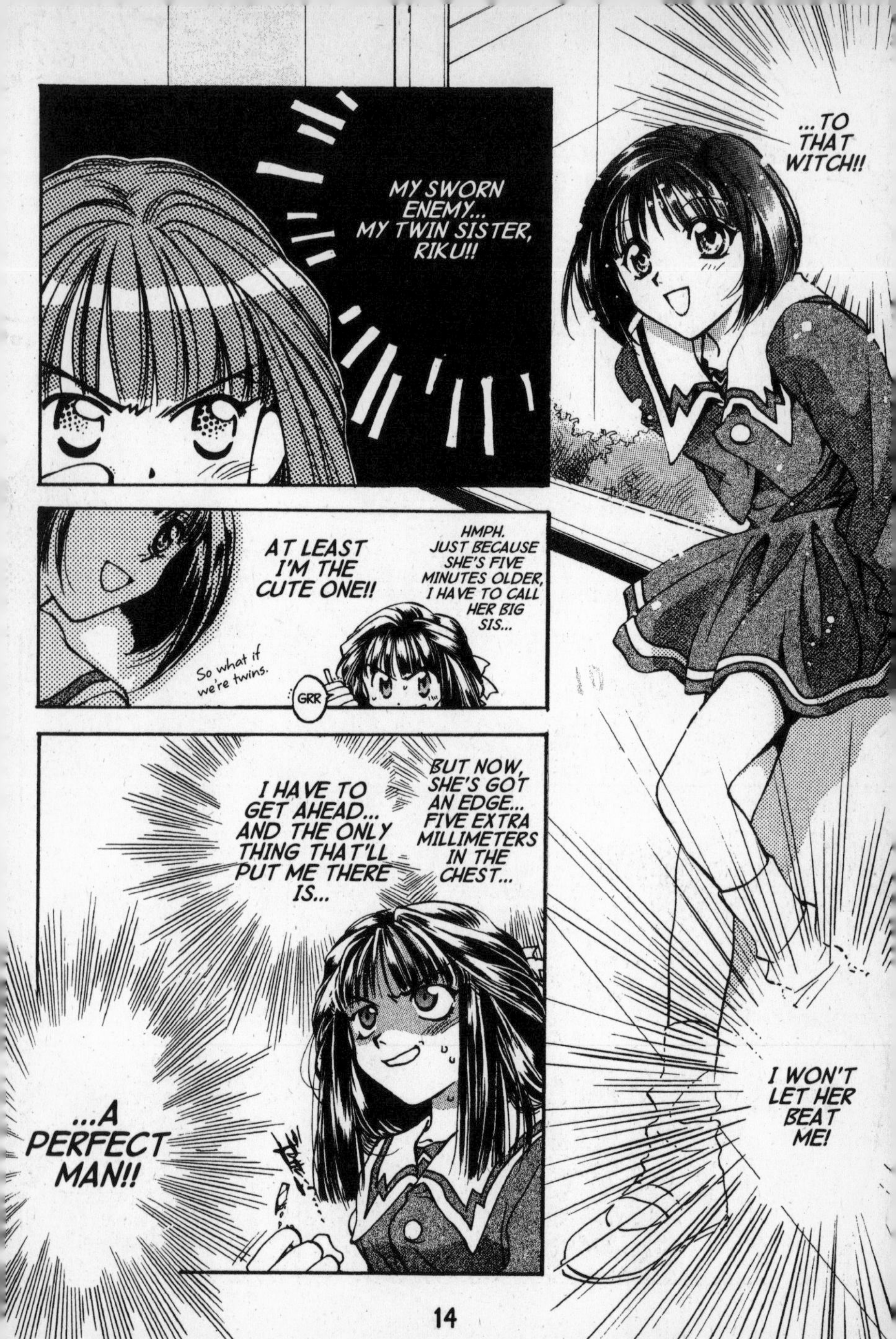
...TO THAT WITCH!!
I WON'T LET HER BEAT ME!
MY SWORN ENEMY... MY TWIN SISTER, RIKU!!
HMPH. JUST BECAUSE SHE'S FIVE MINUTES OLDER, I HAVE TO CALL HER BIG SIS...
AT LEAST I'M THE CUTE ONE!!
GRR
So what if we're twins.
BUT NOW, SHE'S GOT AN EDGE... FIVE EXTRA MILLIMETERS IN THE CHEST...
I HAVE TO GET AHEAD... AND THE ONLY THING THAT'LL PUT ME THERE IS...
...A PERFECT MAN!!

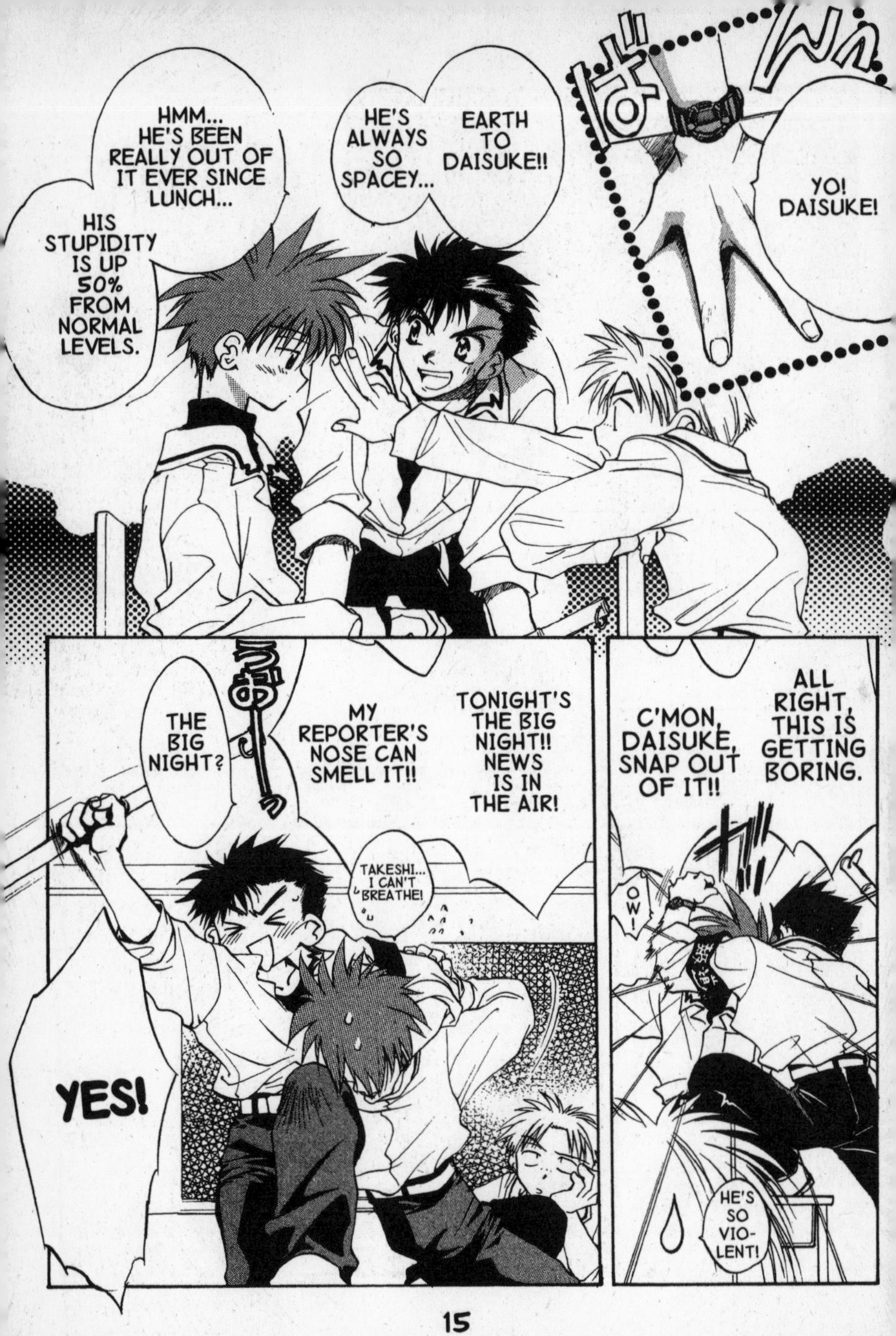
YO! DAISUKE!
EARTH TO DAISUKE!!
HE'S ALWAYS SO SPACEY...
HMM... HE'S BEEN REALLY OUT OF IT EVER SINCE LUNCH...
HIS STUPIDITY IS UP 50% FROM NORMAL LEVELS.
ALL RIGHT, THIS IS GETTING BORING.
C'MON, DAISUKE, SNAP OUT OF IT!!
OW!
HE'S SO VIO-LENT!
TONIGHT'S THE BIG NIGHT!! NEWS IS IN THE AIR!
MY REPORTER'S NOSE CAN SMELL IT!!
THE BIG NIGHT?
TAKESHI... I CAN'T BREATHE!
YES!

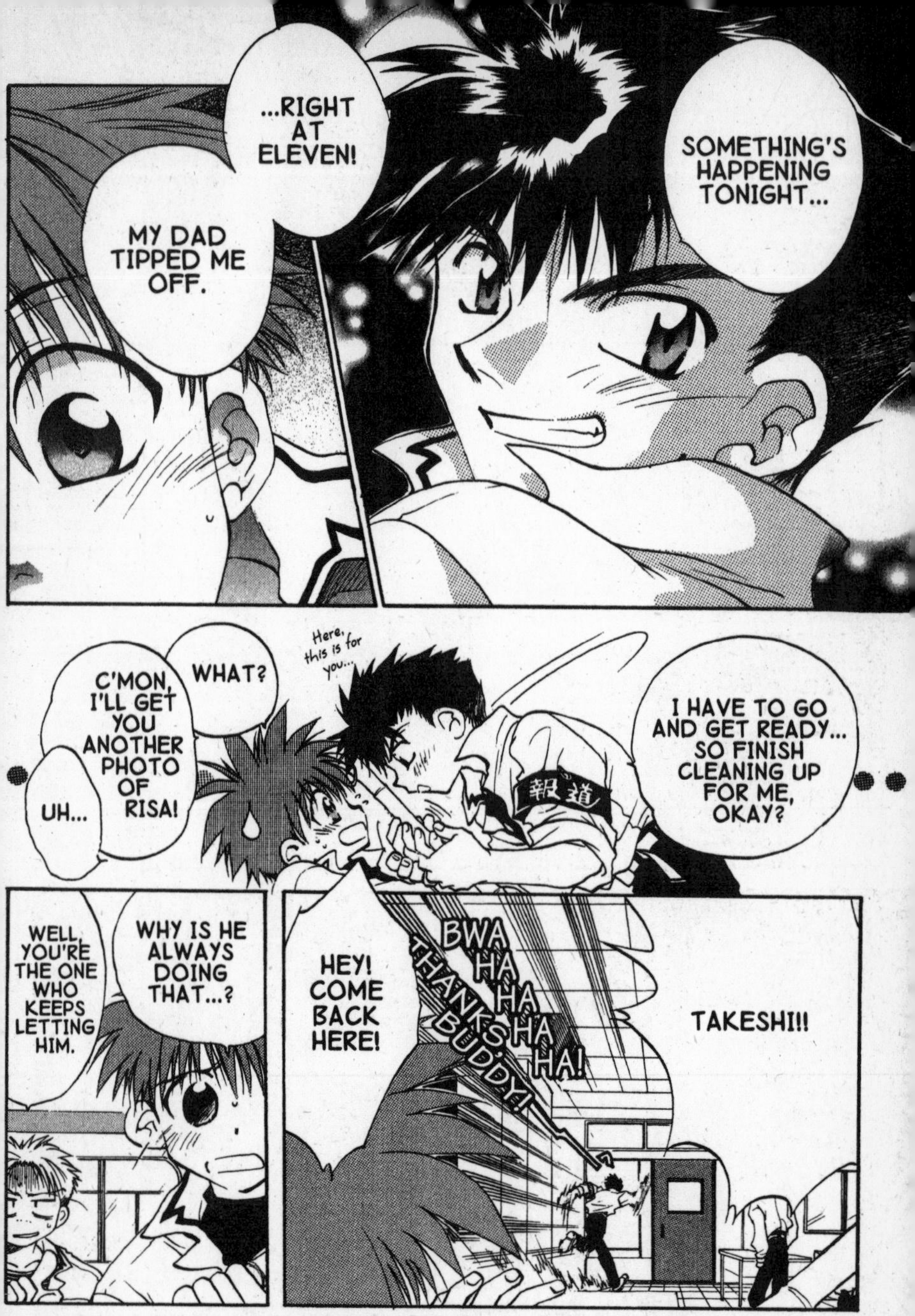
SOMETHING'S HAPPENING TONIGHT...
...RIGHT AT ELEVEN!
MY DAD TIPPED ME OFF.
I HAVE TO GO AND GET READY... SO FINISH CLEANING UP FOR ME, OKAY?
Here, this is for you...
WHAT?
C'MON, I'LL GET YOU ANOTHER PHOTO OF RISA!
UH...
TAKESHI!!
BWA HA HA HA HA!
THANKS BUDDY!
HEY! COME BACK HERE!
WHY IS HE ALWAYS DOING THAT...?
WELL YOU'RE THE ONE WHO KEEPS LETTING HIM.

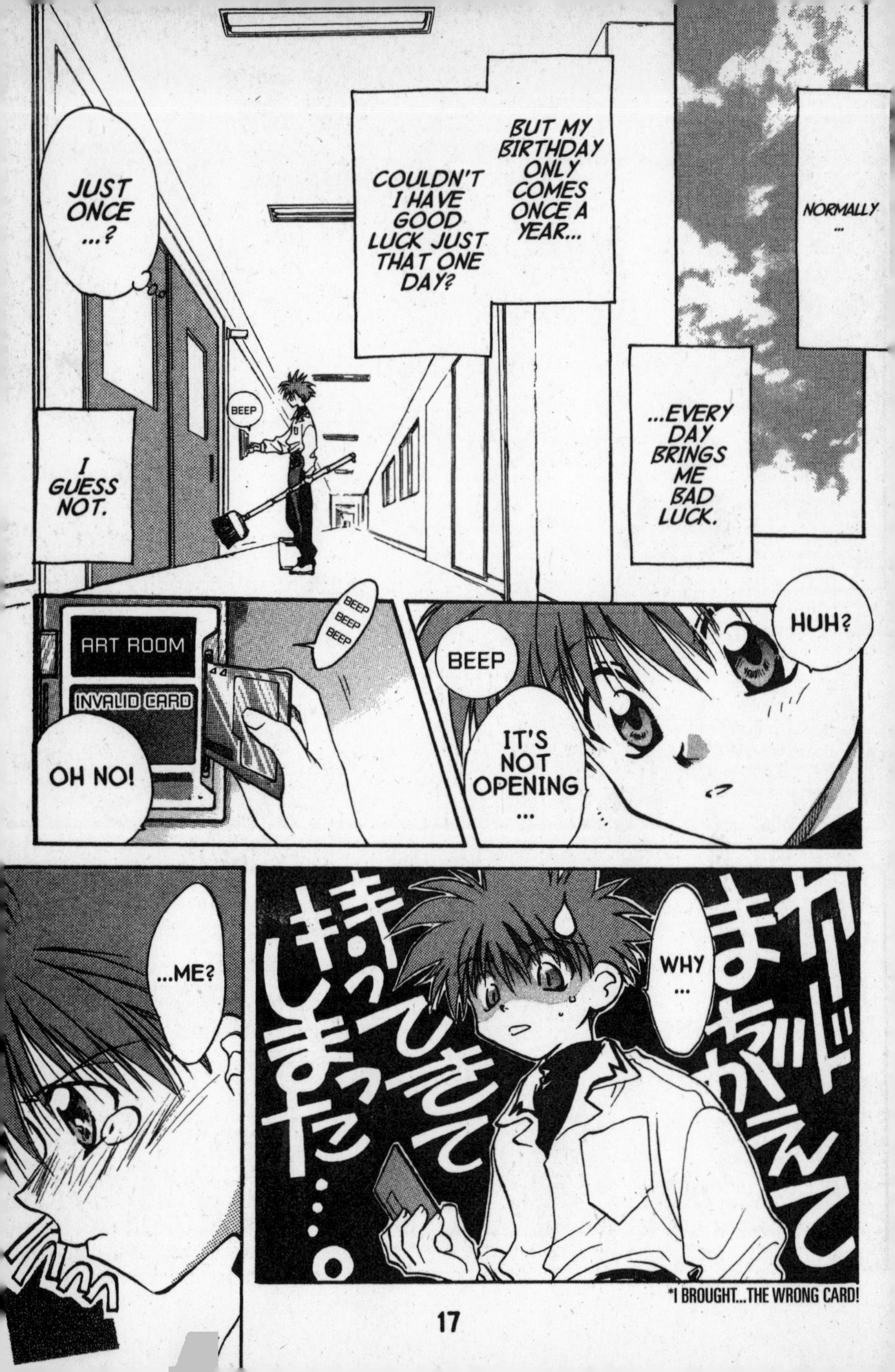
NORMALLY...
...EVERY DAY BRINGS ME BAD LUCK.
BUT MY BIRTHDAY ONLY COMES ONCE A YEAR...
COULDN'T I HAVE GOOD LUCK JUST THAT ONE DAY?
JUST ONCE...?
BEEP
I GUESS NOT.
HUH?
BEEP
IT'S NOT OPENING...
BEEP BEEP BEEP
ART ROOM
INVALID CARD
OH NO!
WHY...
カードまちがえて持ってきてしまった・・・。
...ME?

*I BROUGHT...THE WRONG CARD!

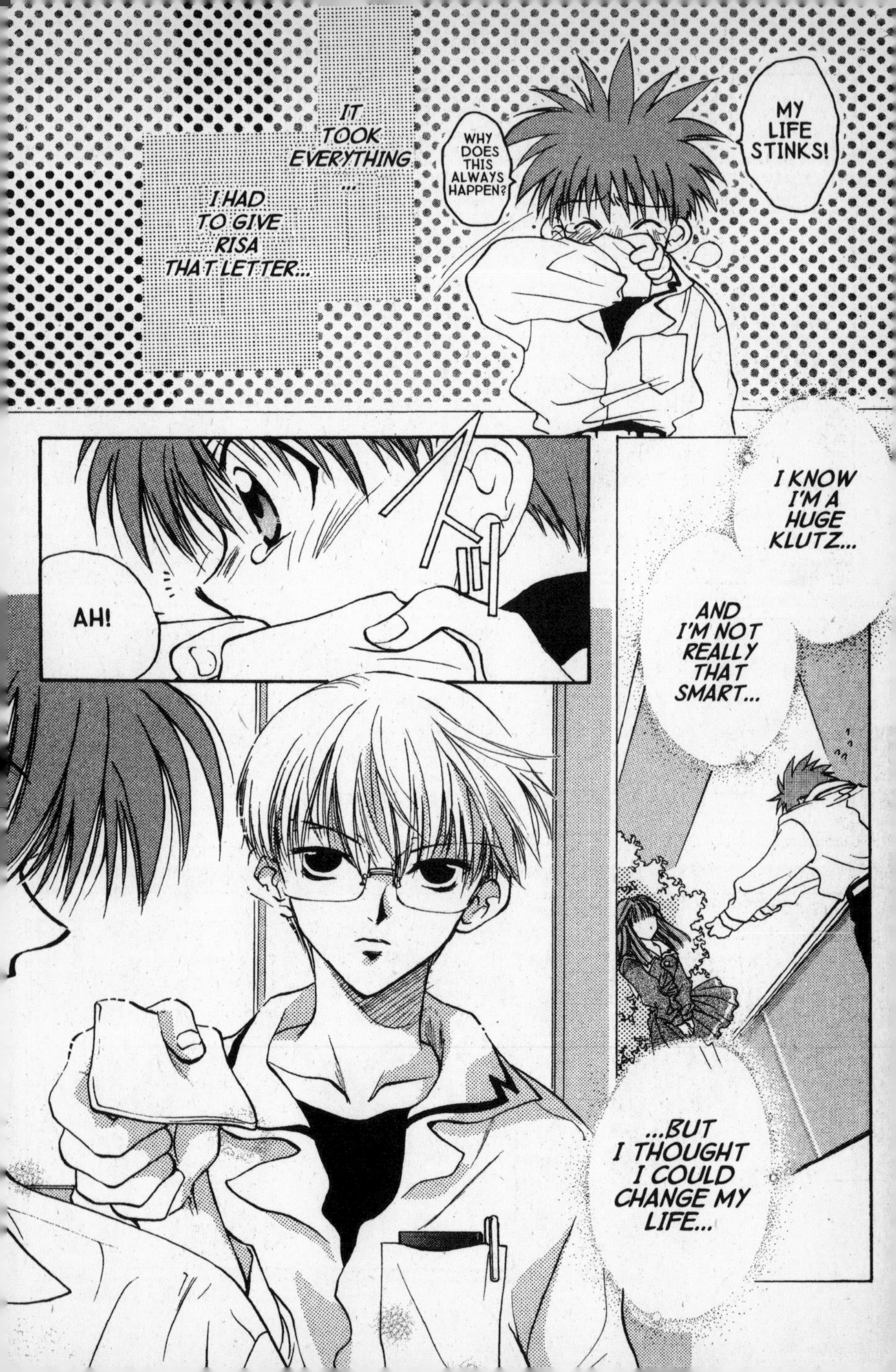
MY LIFE STINKS!
WHY DOES THIS ALWAYS HAPPEN?
IT TOOK EVERYTHING...
I HAD TO GIVE RISA THAT LETTER...
I KNOW I'M A HUGE KLUTZ...
AND I'M NOT REALLY THAT SMART...
...BUT I THOUGHT I COULD CHANGE MY LIFE...
AH!

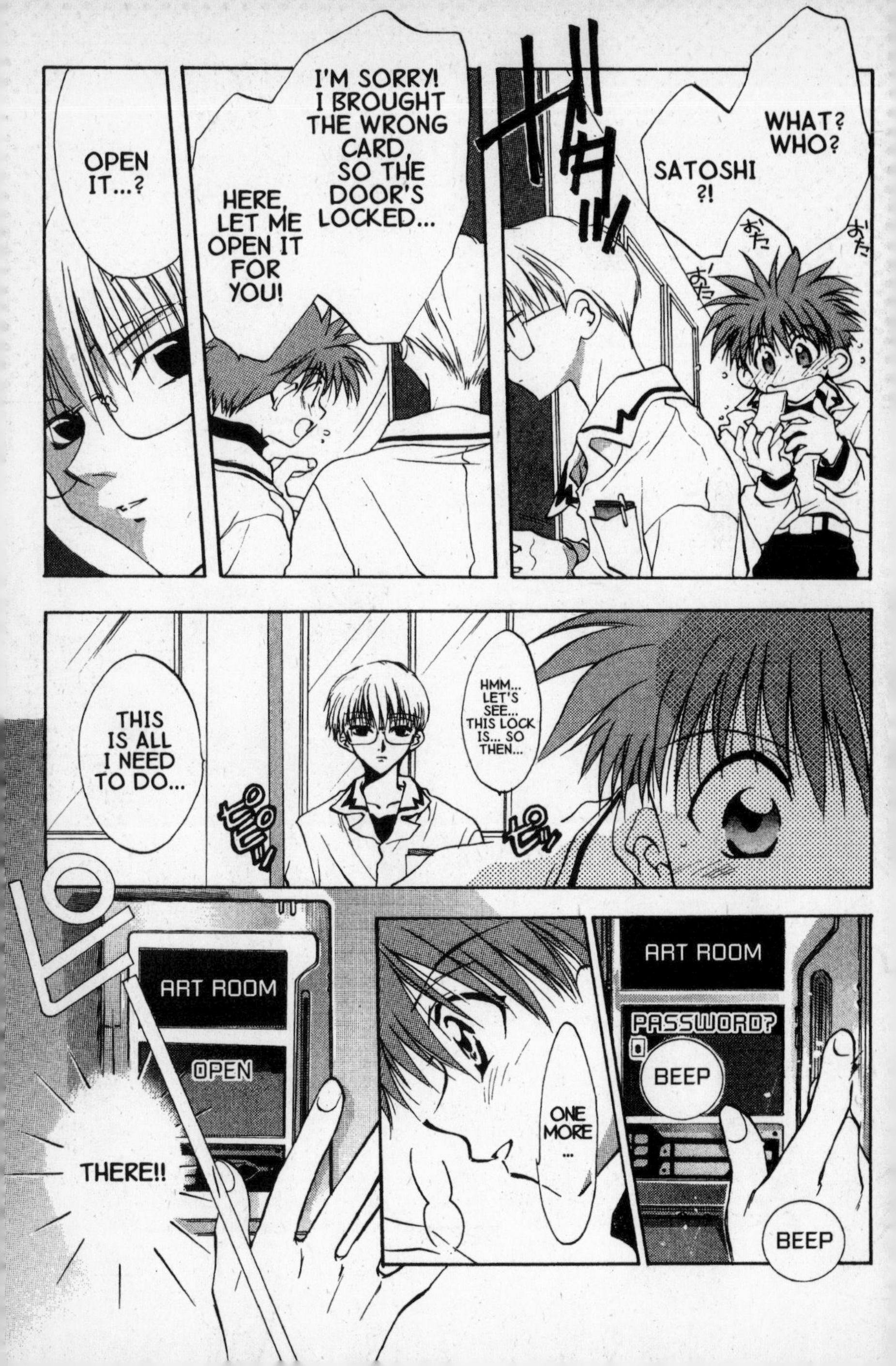
WHAT? WHO?
SATOSHI ?!
おた
おた
おた
ガタ
I'M SORRY! I BROUGHT THE WRONG CARD, SO THE DOOR'S LOCKED...
HERE, LET ME OPEN IT FOR YOU!
OPEN IT...?
HMM... LET'S SEE... THIS LOCK IS... SO THEN...
THIS IS ALL I NEED TO DO...
ART ROOM
PASSWORD?
BEEP
ONE MORE ...
BEEP
ART ROOM
OPEN
THERE!!

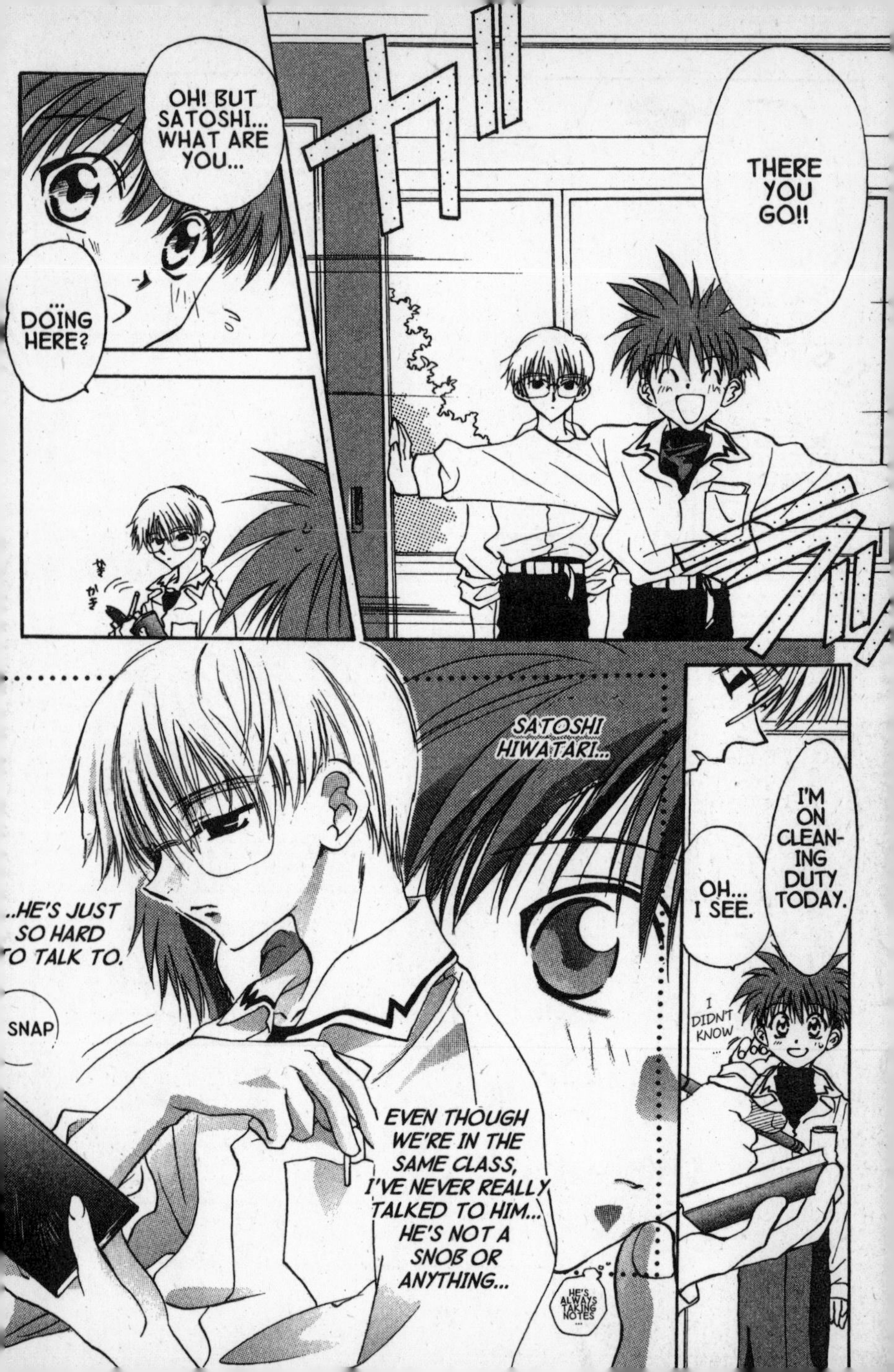
THERE YOU GO!!
OH! BUT SATOSHI... WHAT ARE YOU...
...DOING HERE?
かき かき
I'M ON CLEANING-DUTY TODAY.
OH... I SEE.
I DIDN'T KNOW...
SATOSHI HIWATARI...
...HE'S JUST SO HARD TO TALK TO.
SNAP
EVEN THOUGH WE'RE IN THE SAME CLASS, I'VE NEVER REALLY TALKED TO HIM... HE'S NOT A SNOB OR ANYTHING...
HE'S ALWAYS TAKING NOTES...

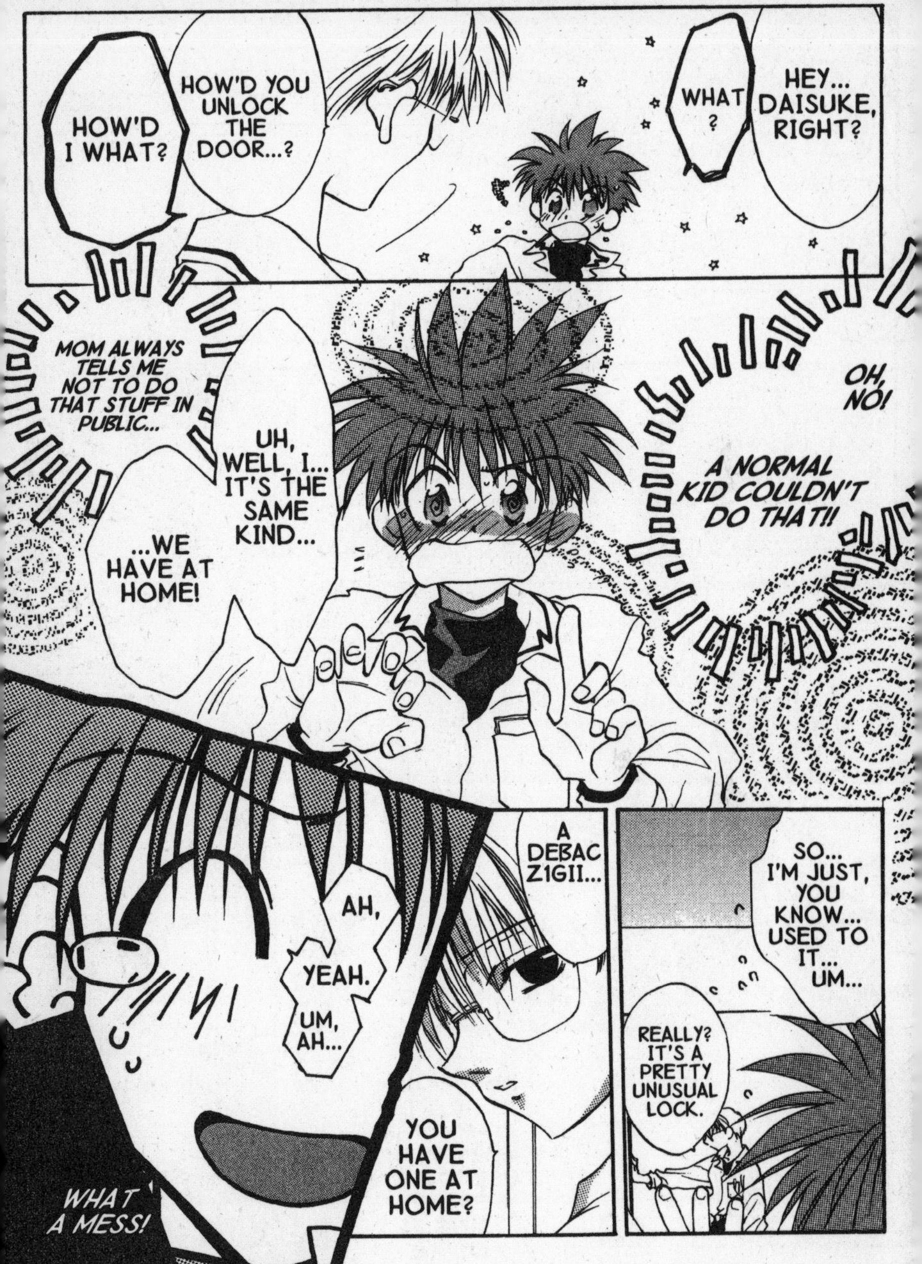
HEY... DAISUKE, RIGHT?
WHAT?
HOW'D YOU UNLOCK THE DOOR...?
HOW'D I WHAT?
OH, NO!
A NORMAL KID COULDN'T DO THAT!!
UH, WELL, I... IT'S THE SAME KIND...
...WE HAVE AT HOME!
MOM ALWAYS TELLS ME NOT TO DO THAT STUFF IN PUBLIC...
SO... I'M JUST, YOU KNOW... USED TO IT... UM...
REALLY? IT'S A PRETTY UNUSUAL LOCK.
A DEBAC Z1GII...
AH,
YEAH.
UM, AH...
YOU HAVE ONE AT HOME?
WHAT A MESS!

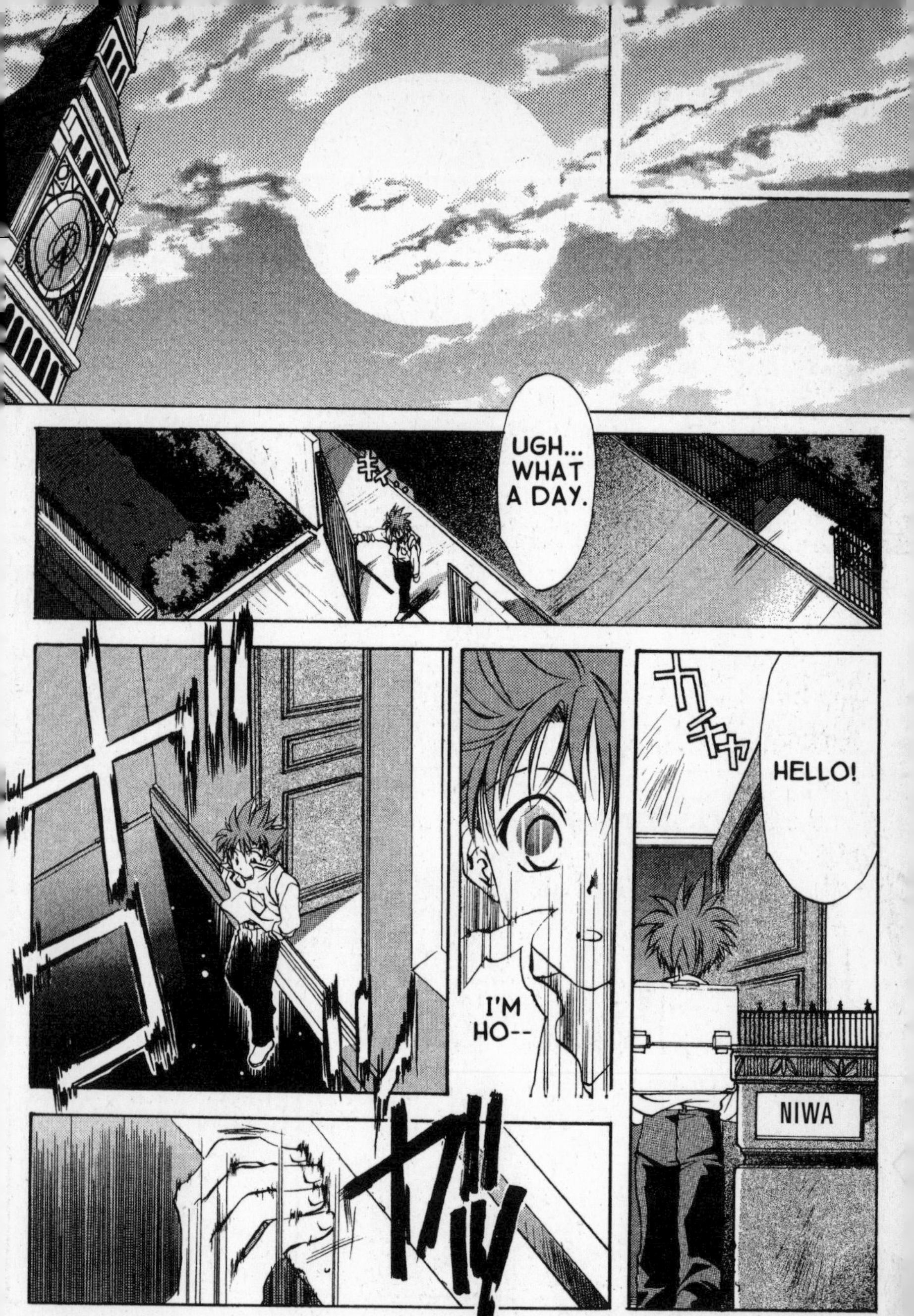

UGH... WHAT A DAY.
キィ…
カチャ
HELLO!
NIWA
I'M HO--

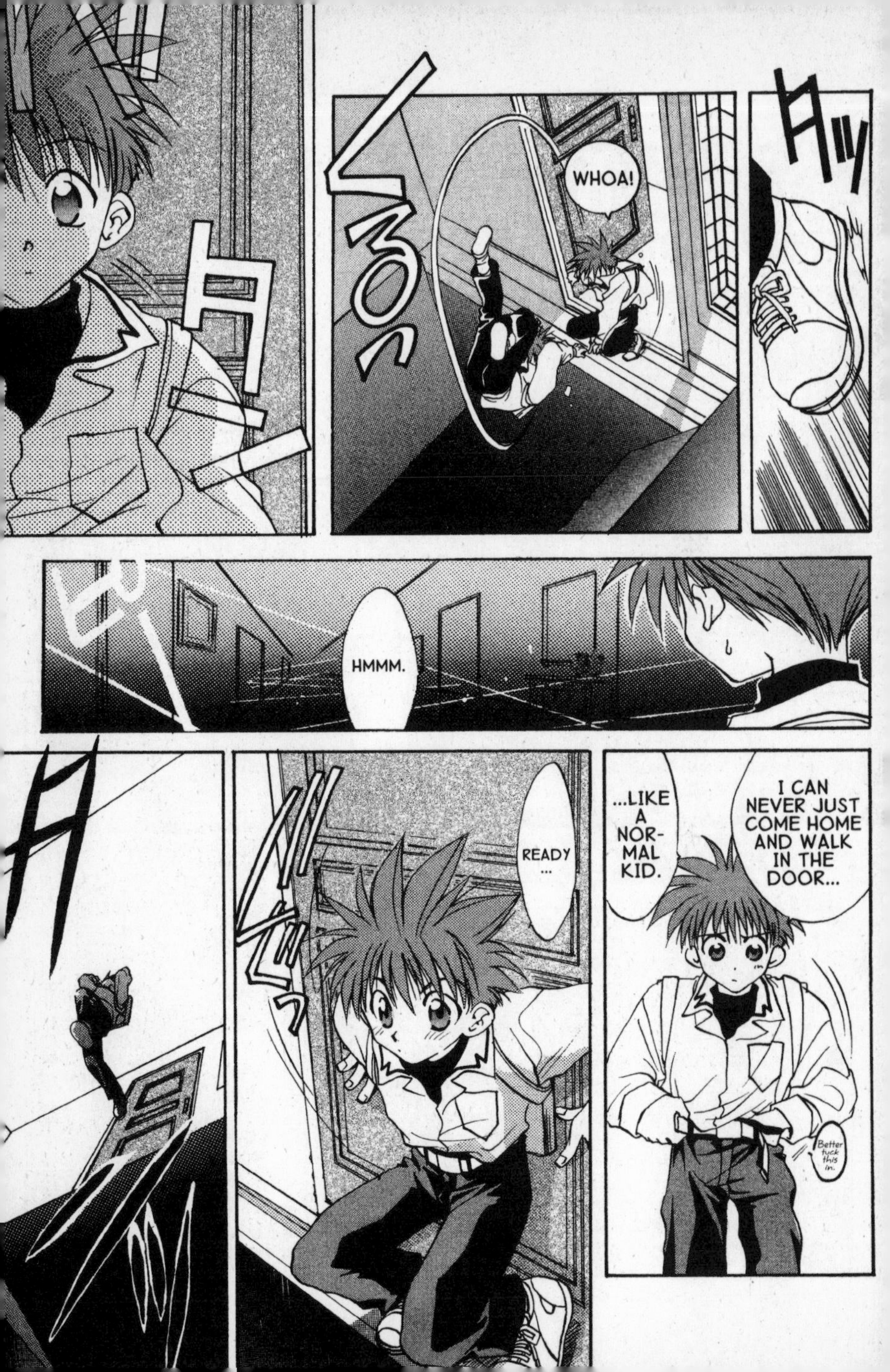

WHOA!
HMMM.
I CAN NEVER JUST COME HOME AND WALK IN THE DOOR...
...LIKE A NOR-MAL KID.
Better tuck this in.
READY...

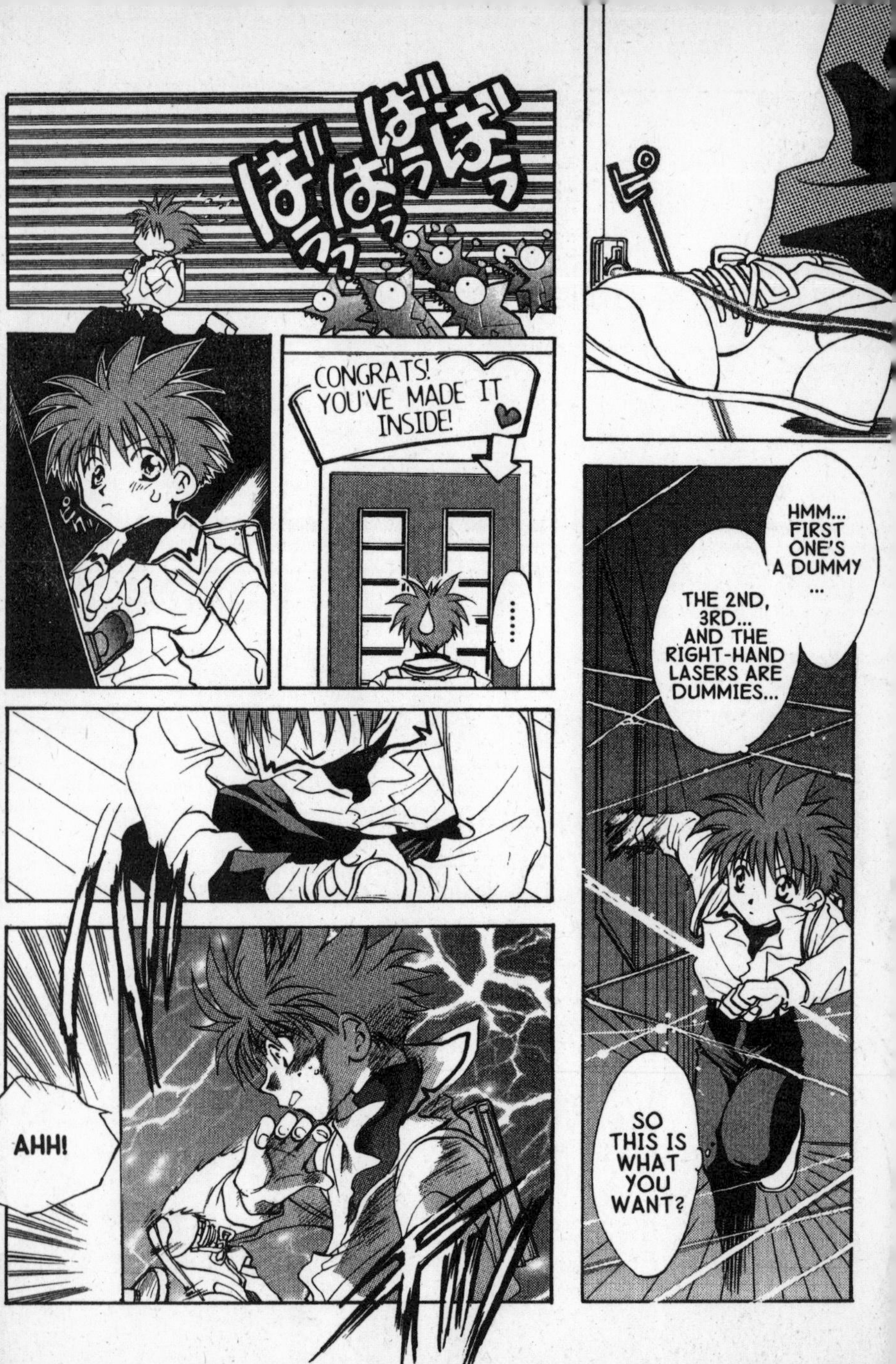
ぴ
ばぅ ばぅ ばぅ ばぅ
HMM... FIRST ONE'S A DUMMY ...
THE 2ND, 3RD... AND THE RIGHT-HAND LASERS ARE DUMMIES...
SO THIS IS WHAT YOU WANT?
CONGRATS! YOU'VE MADE IT INSIDE!
......
AHH!

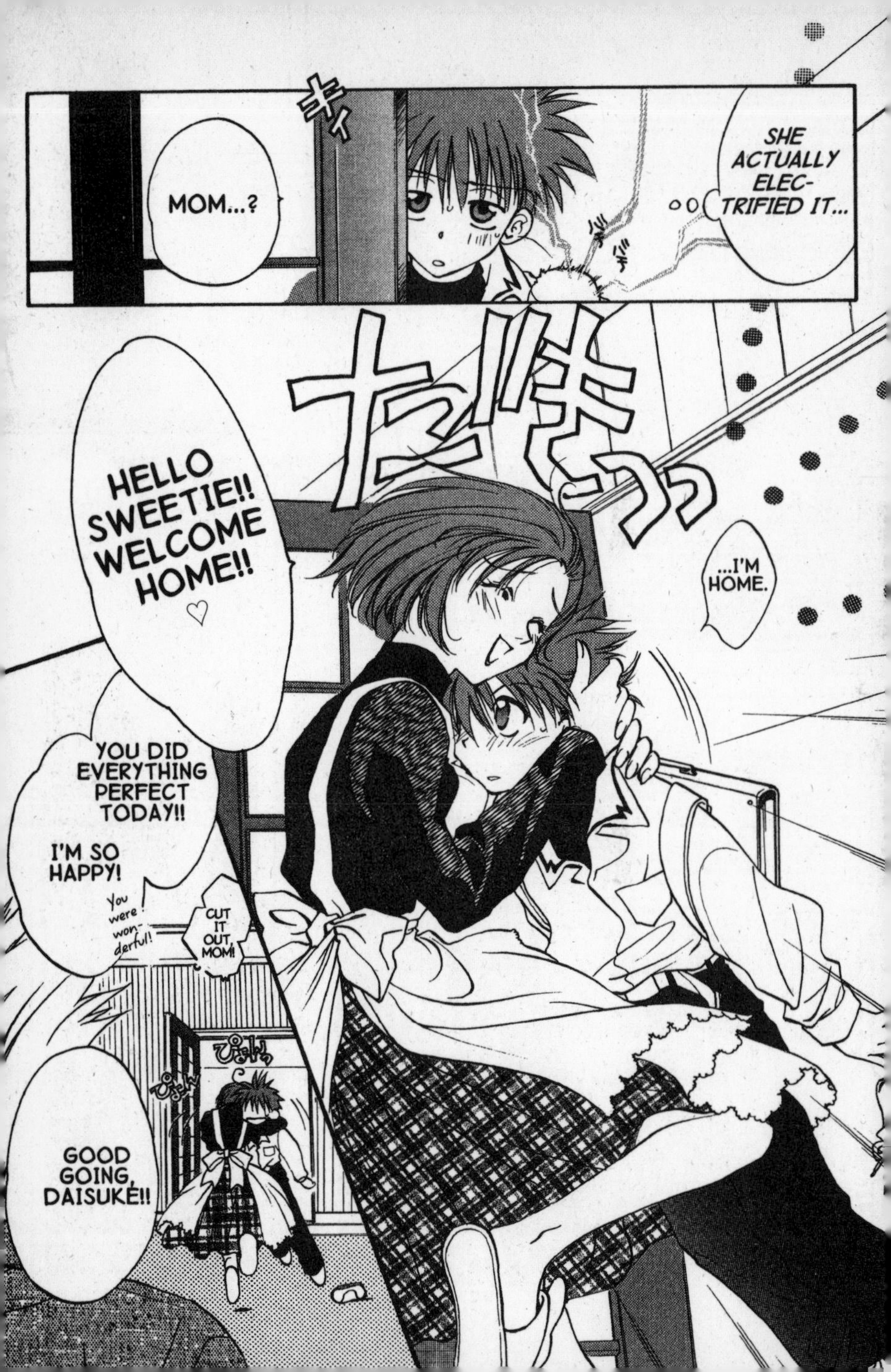
SHE ACTUALLY ELEC-TRIFIED IT...
MOM...?
...I'M HOME.
HELLO SWEETIE!! WELCOME HOME!! ♡
YOU DID EVERYTHING PERFECT TODAY!!
I'M SO HAPPY!
CUT IT OUT, MOM!
You were won-derful!
GOOD GOING, DAISUKE!!

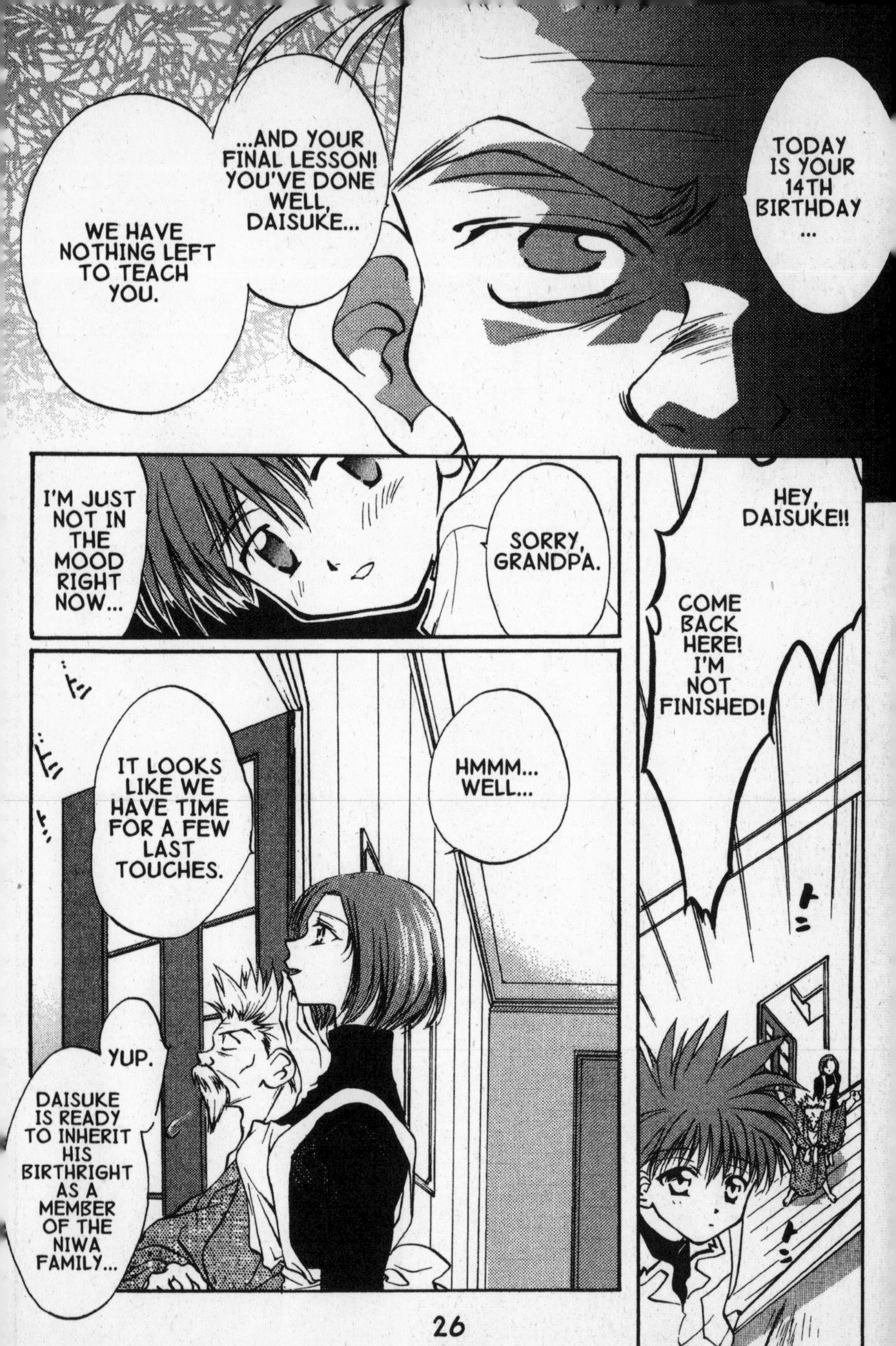
TODAY IS YOUR 14TH BIRTHDAY ...
...AND YOUR FINAL LESSON! YOU'VE DONE WELL, DAISUKE...
WE HAVE NOTHING LEFT TO TEACH YOU.
HEY, DAISUKE!!
COME BACK HERE! I'M NOT FINISHED!
SORRY, GRANDPA.
I'M JUST NOT IN THE MOOD RIGHT NOW...
HMMM... WELL...
IT LOOKS LIKE WE HAVE TIME FOR A FEW LAST TOUCHES.
YUP.
DAISUKE IS READY TO INHERIT HIS BIRTHRIGHT AS A MEMBER OF THE NIWA FAMILY...

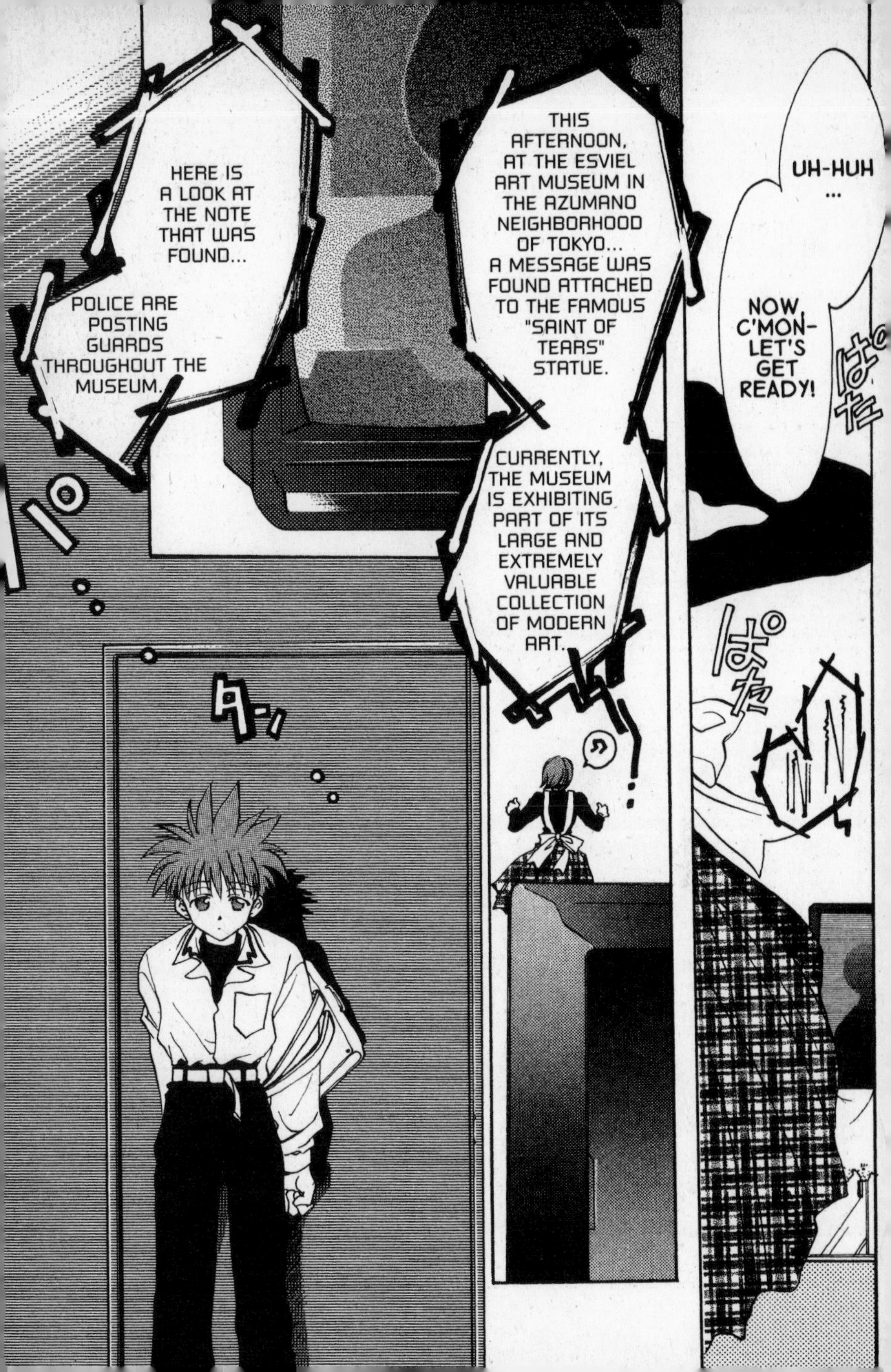

UH-HUH ...
NOW, C'MON-LET'S GET READY!
ぱた
ぱた
THIS AFTERNOON, AT THE ESVIEL ART MUSEUM IN THE AZUMANO NEIGHBORHOOD OF TOKYO... A MESSAGE WAS FOUND ATTACHED TO THE FAMOUS "SAINT OF TEARS" STATUE.
CURRENTLY, THE MUSEUM IS EXHIBITING PART OF ITS LARGE AND EXTREMELY VALUABLE COLLECTION OF MODERN ART.
HERE IS A LOOK AT THE NOTE THAT WAS FOUND...
POLICE ARE POSTING GUARDS THROUGHOUT THE MUSEUM.

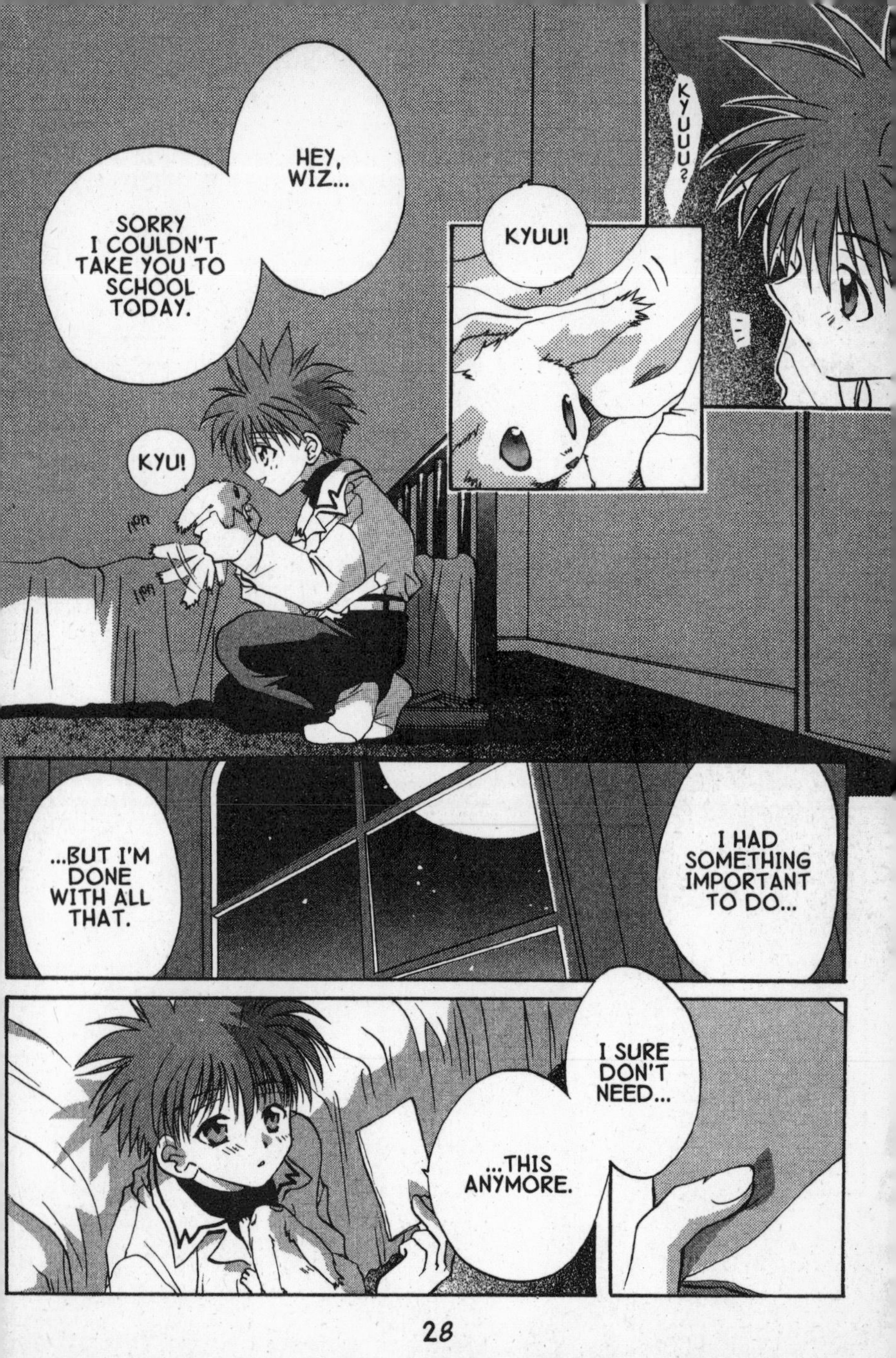
HEY, WIZ...
SORRY I COULDN'T TAKE YOU TO SCHOOL TODAY.
KYU!
KYUU!
KYUUU?
I HAD SOMETHING IMPORTANT TO DO...
...BUT I'M DONE WITH ALL THAT.
I SURE DON'T NEED...
...THIS ANYMORE.

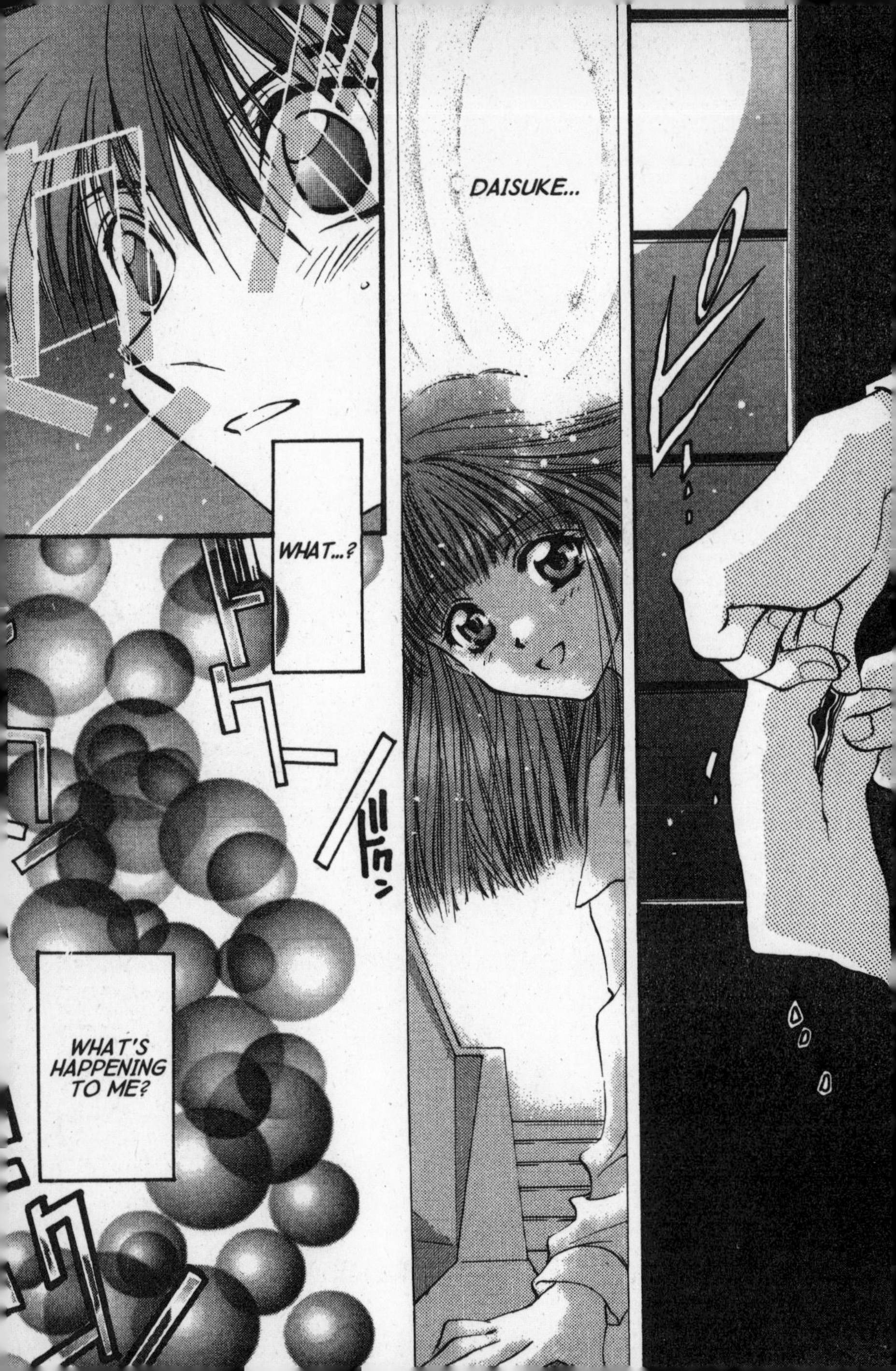
DAISUKE...
WHAT...?
ドクン
WHAT'S HAPPENING TO ME?

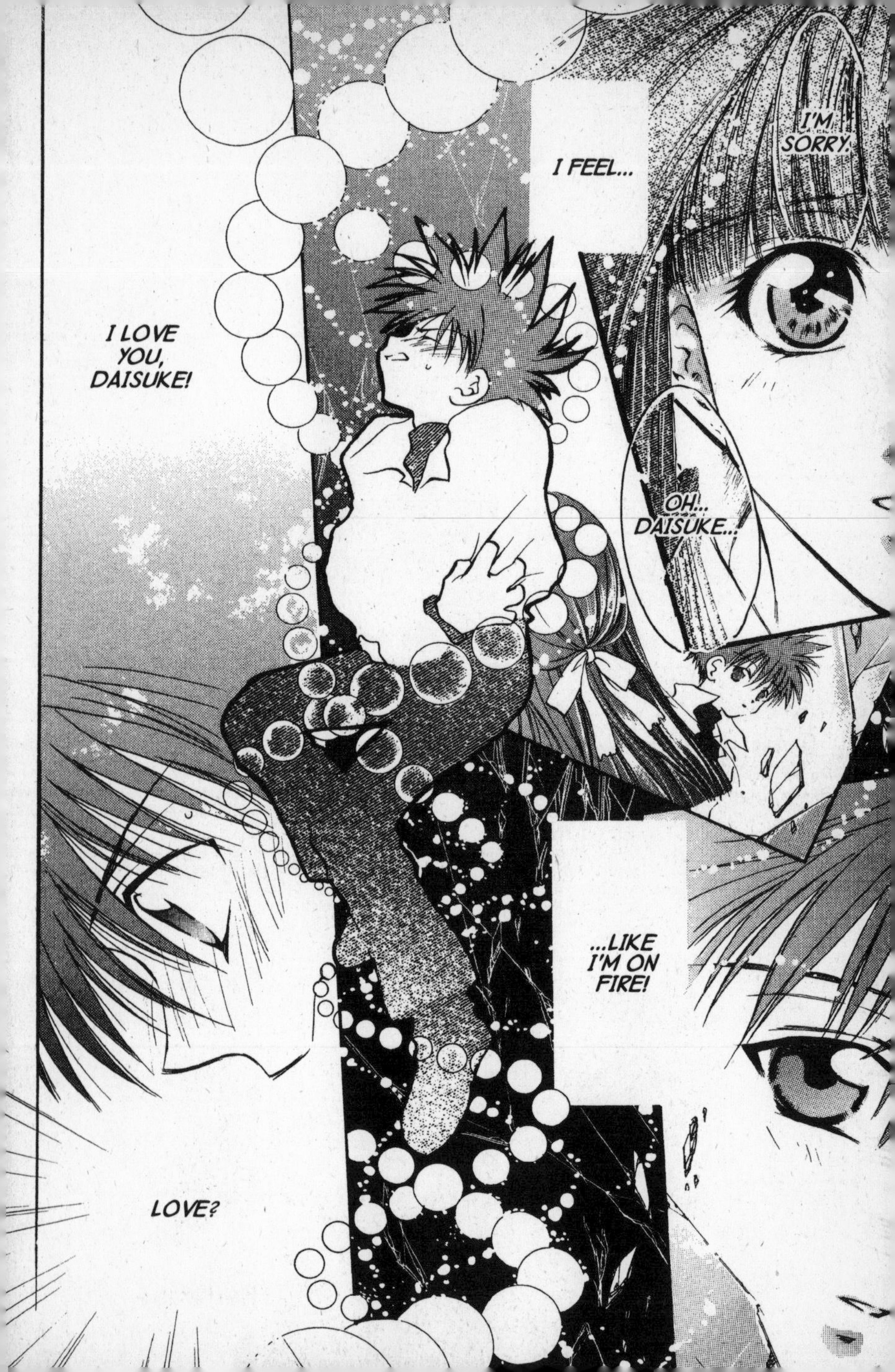
I'M SORRY.
I FEEL...
OH... DAISUKE...
...LIKE I'M ON FIRE!
I LOVE YOU, DAISUKE!
LOVE?

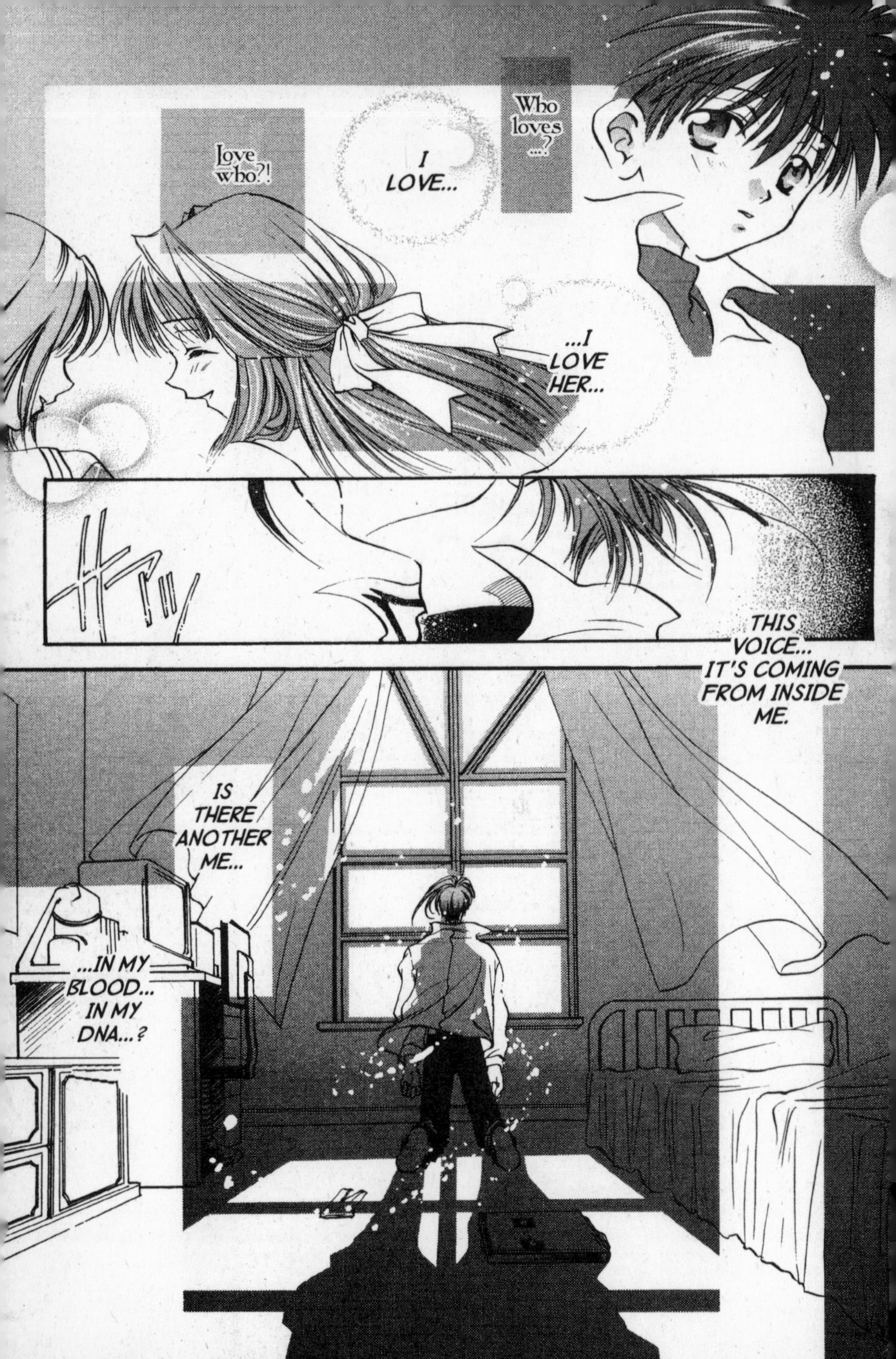
Who loves ...?
I LOVE...
Love who?!
...I LOVE HER...
THIS VOICE... IT'S COMING FROM INSIDE ME.
IS THERE ANOTHER ME...
...IN MY BLOOD... IN MY DNA...?

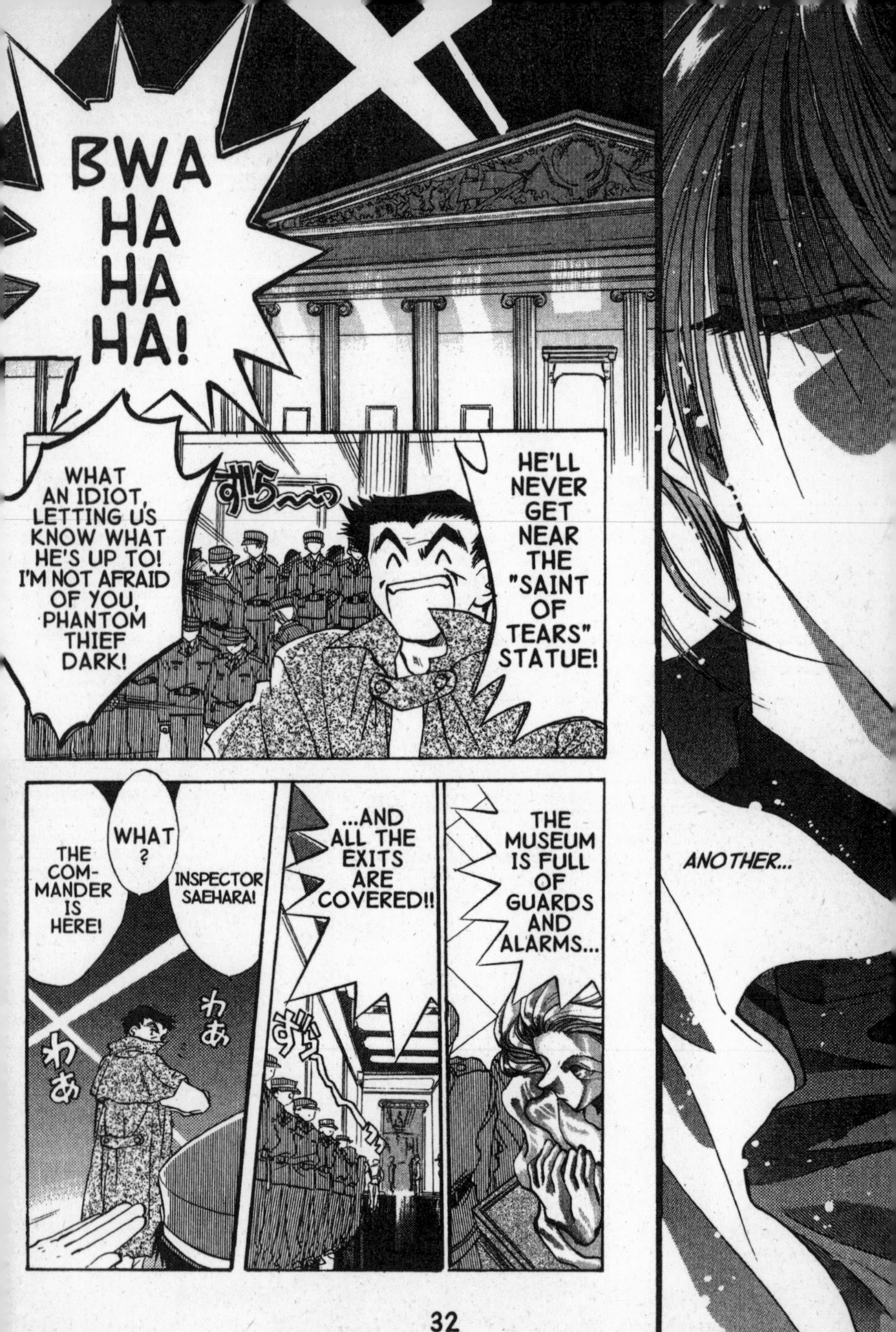
ANOTHER...
BWA HA HA HA!
HE'LL NEVER GET NEAR THE "SAINT OF TEARS" STATUE!
WHAT AN IDIOT, LETTING US KNOW WHAT HE'S UP TO! I'M NOT AFRAID OF YOU, PHANTOM THIEF DARK!
THE MUSEUM IS FULL OF GUARDS AND ALARMS...
...AND ALL THE EXITS ARE COVERED!!
INSPECTOR SAEHARA!
WHAT?
THE COM-MANDER IS HERE!
わあ
わあ

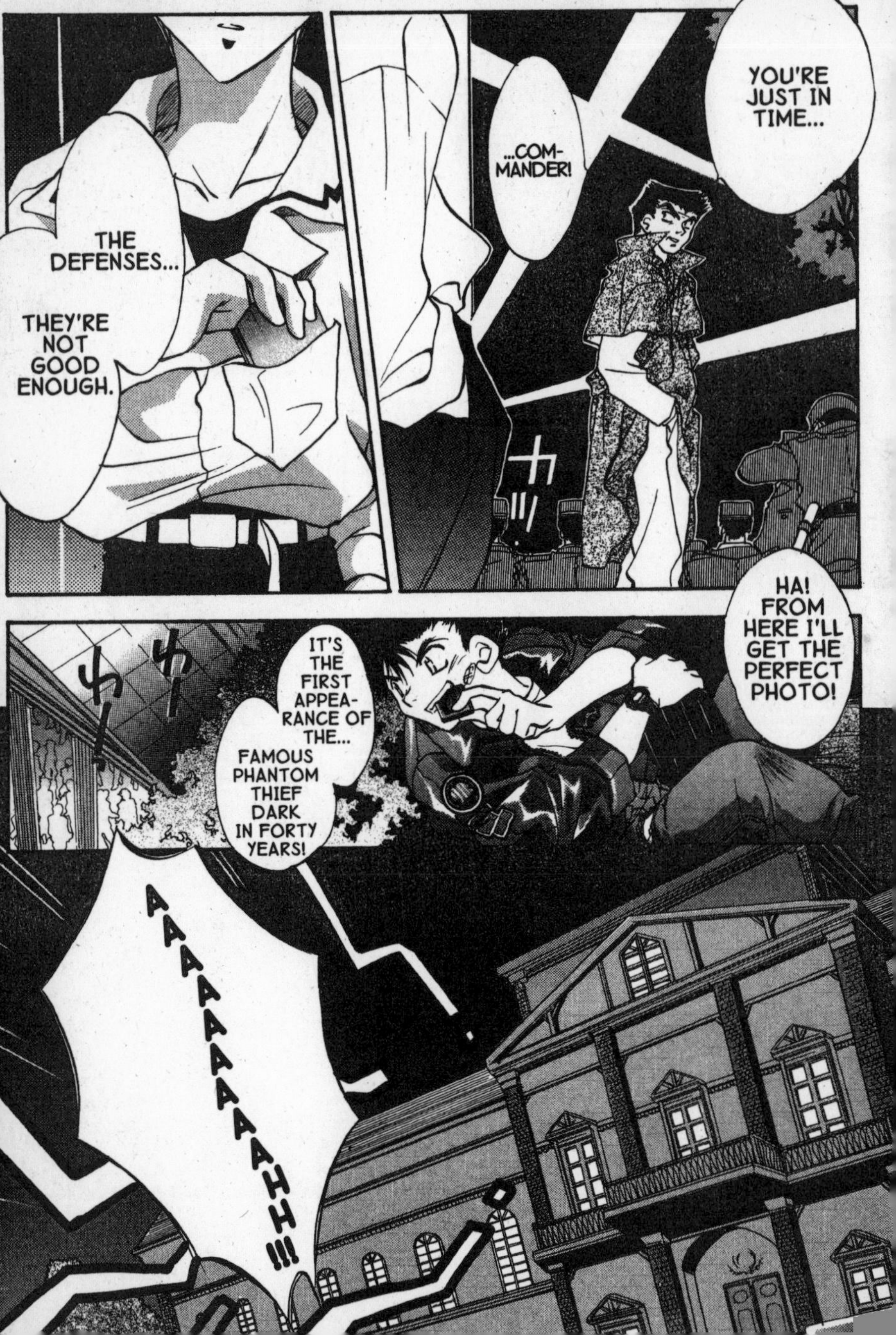
YOU'RE JUST IN TIME...
...COMMANDER!
THE DEFENSES...
THEY'RE NOT GOOD ENOUGH.
HA! FROM HERE I'LL GET THE PERFECT PHOTO!
IT'S THE FIRST APPEARANCE OF THE...
FAMOUS PHANTOM THIEF DARK IN FORTY YEARS!
AAAAAAAAAHH!!!

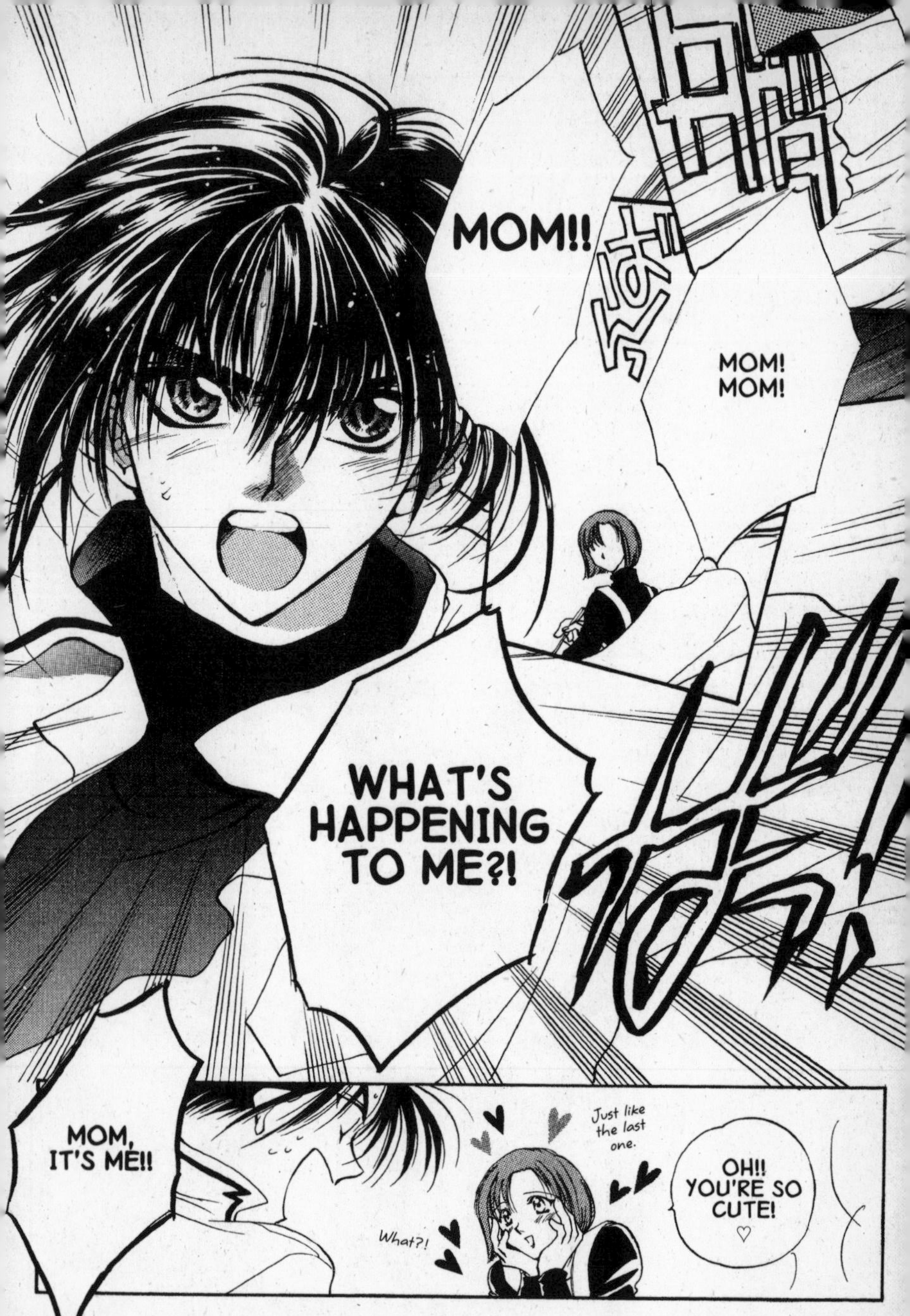
MOM! MOM!
MOM!!
WHAT'S HAPPENING TO ME?!
OH!! YOU'RE SO CUTE! ♡
Just like the last one.
What?!
MOM, IT'S ME!!

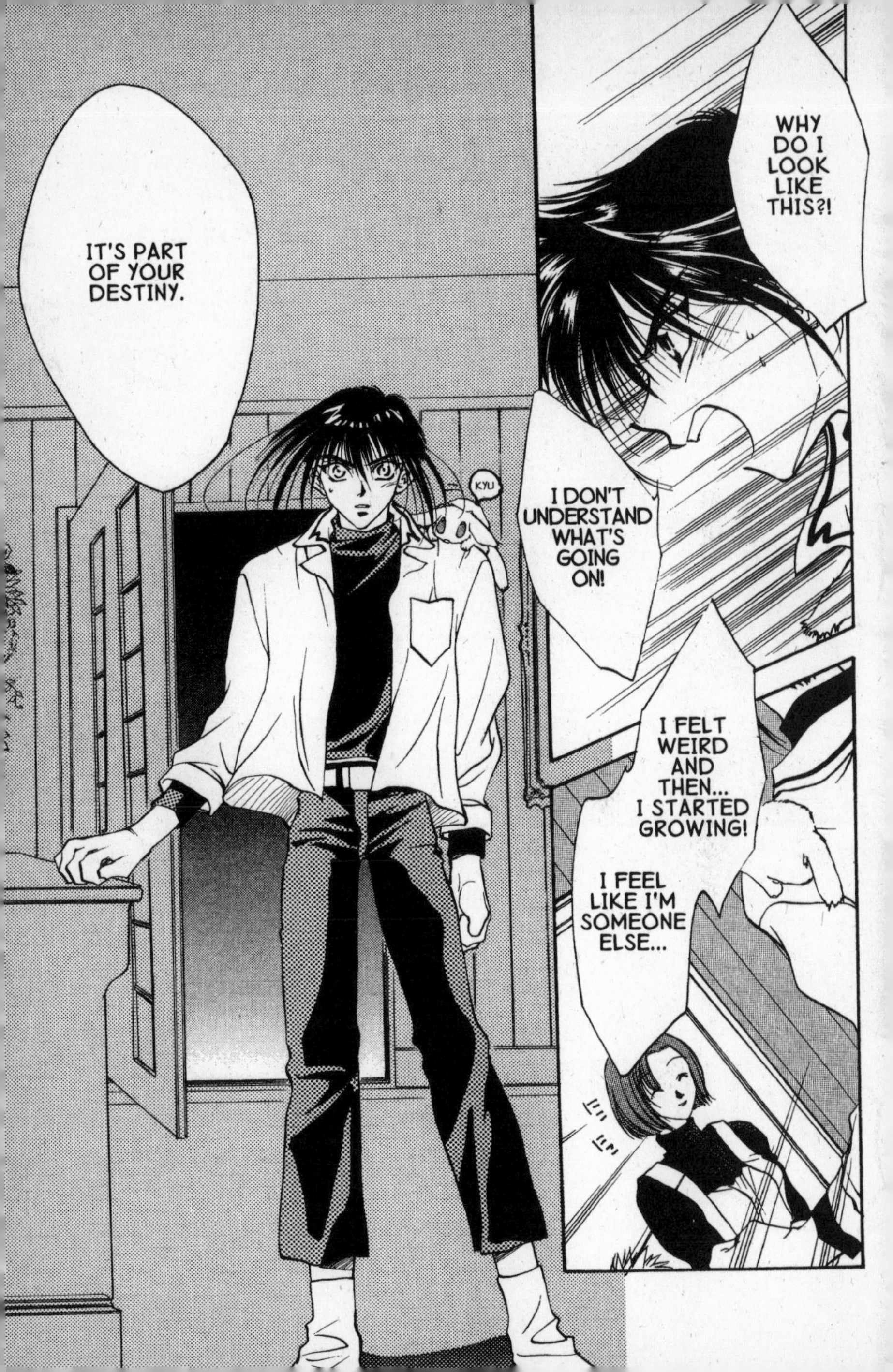
WHY DO I LOOK LIKE THIS?!
I DON'T UNDERSTAND WHAT'S GOING ON!
I FELT WEIRD AND THEN... I STARTED GROWING!
I FEEL LIKE I'M SOMEONE ELSE...
IT'S PART OF YOUR DESTINY.
KYU

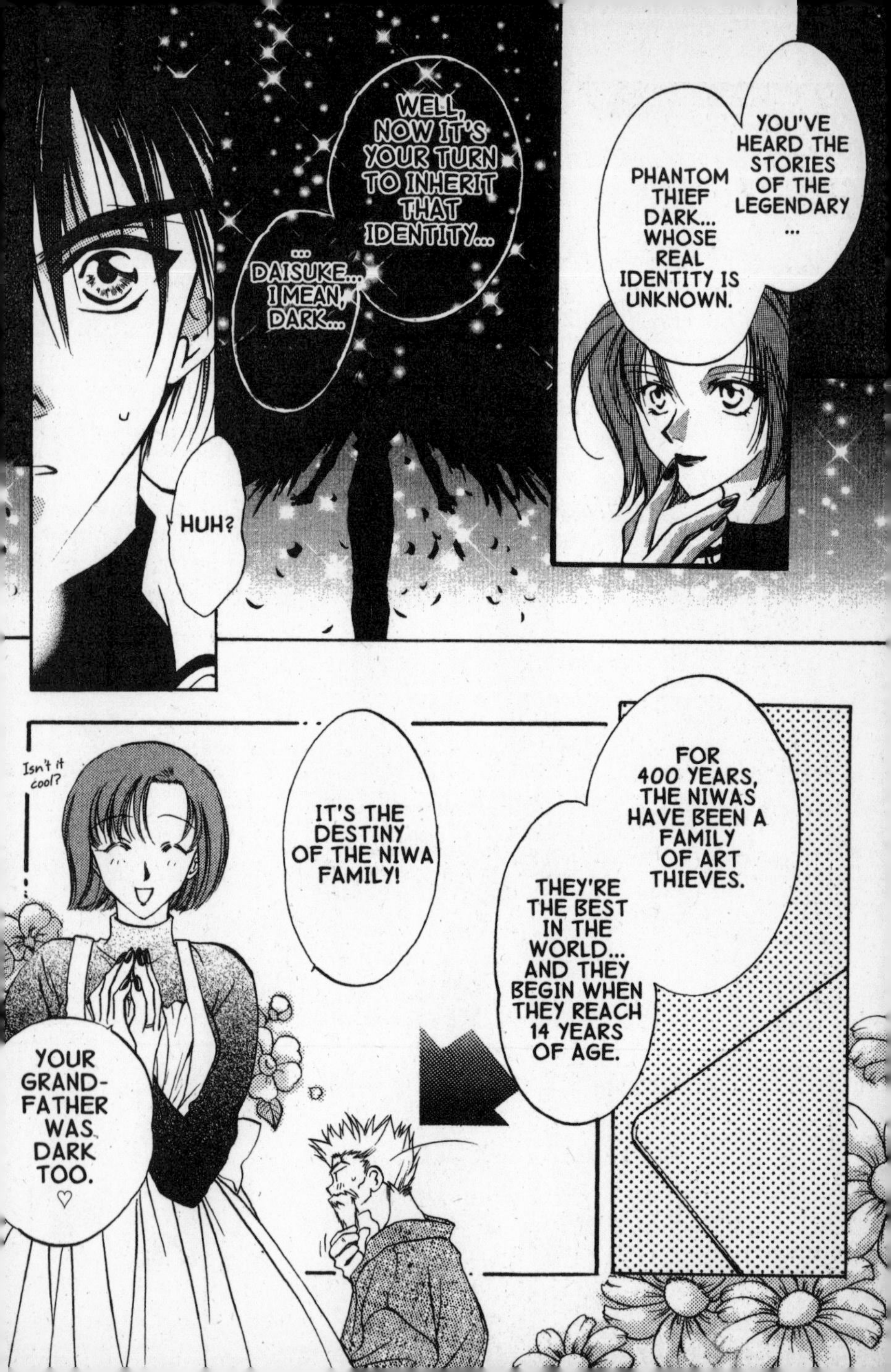
YOU'VE HEARD THE STORIES OF THE LEGENDARY ...
PHANTOM THIEF DARK... WHOSE REAL IDENTITY IS UNKNOWN.
WELL, NOW IT'S YOUR TURN TO INHERIT THAT IDENTITY...
... DAISUKE... I MEAN, DARK...
HUH?
FOR 400 YEARS, THE NIWAS HAVE BEEN A FAMILY OF ART THIEVES.
THEY'RE THE BEST IN THE WORLD... AND THEY BEGIN WHEN THEY REACH 14 YEARS OF AGE.
IT'S THE DESTINY OF THE NIWA FAMILY!
Isn't it cool?
YOUR GRAND-FATHER WAS DARK TOO. ♡

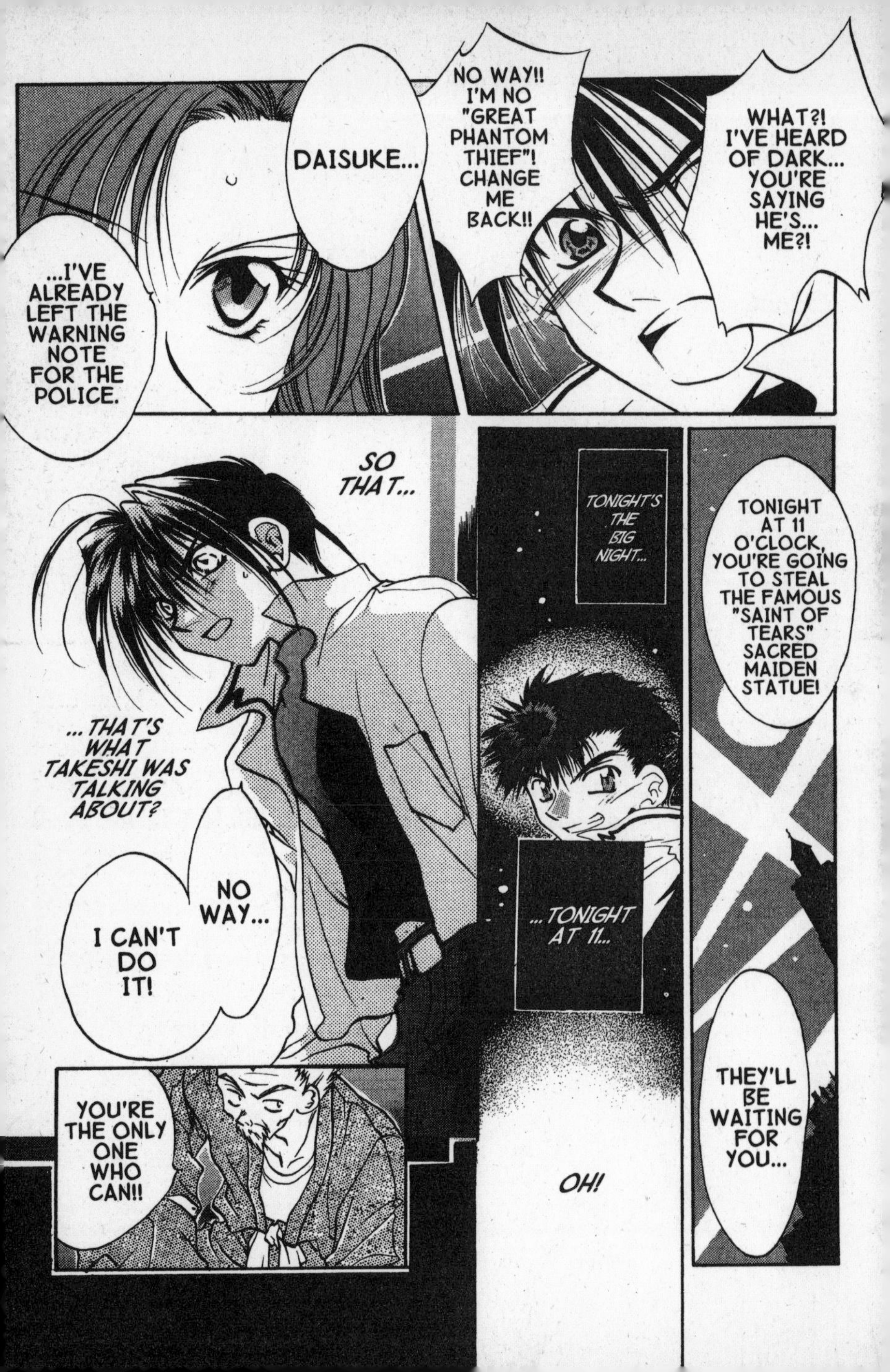
WHAT?! I'VE HEARD OF DARK... YOU'RE SAYING HE'S... ME?!
NO WAY!! I'M NO "GREAT PHANTOM THIEF"! CHANGE ME BACK!!
DAISUKE...
...I'VE ALREADY LEFT THE WARNING NOTE FOR THE POLICE.
TONIGHT AT 11 O'CLOCK, YOU'RE GOING TO STEAL THE FAMOUS "SAINT OF TEARS" SACRED MAIDEN STATUE!
THEY'LL BE WAITING FOR YOU...
TONIGHT'S THE BIG NIGHT...
...TONIGHT AT 11...
OH!
SO THAT...
...THAT'S WHAT TAKESHI WAS TALKING ABOUT?
NO WAY...
I CAN'T DO IT!
YOU'RE THE ONLY ONE WHO CAN!!

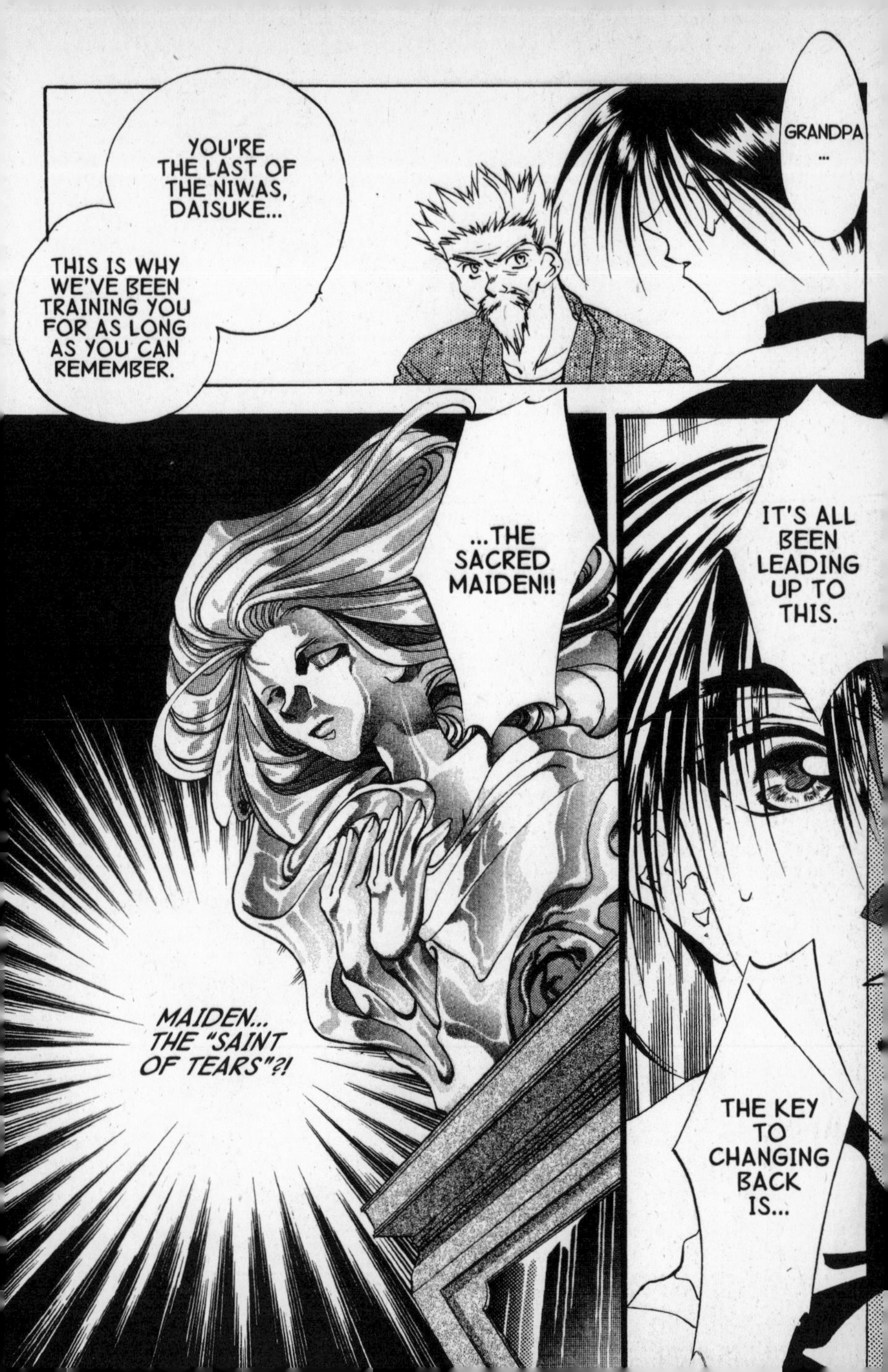
GRANDPA...
YOU'RE THE LAST OF THE NIWAS, DAISUKE...
THIS IS WHY WE'VE BEEN TRAINING YOU FOR AS LONG AS YOU CAN REMEMBER.
IT'S ALL BEEN LEADING UP TO THIS.
THE KEY TO CHANGING BACK IS...
...THE SACRED MAIDEN!!
MAIDEN... THE "SAINT OF TEARS"?!

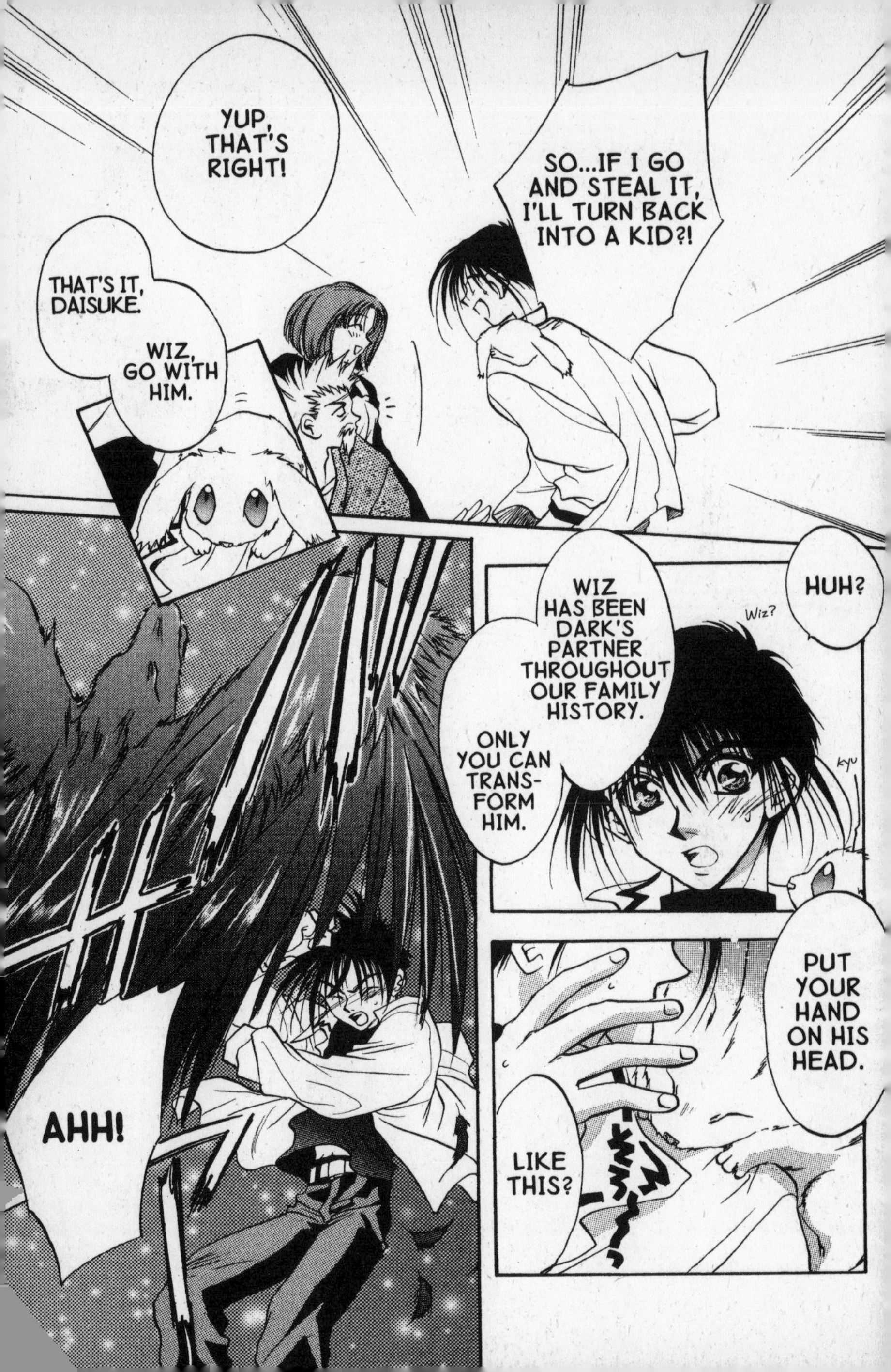
SO...IF I GO AND STEAL IT, I'LL TURN BACK INTO A KID?!
YUP, THAT'S RIGHT!
THAT'S IT, DAISUKE.
WIZ, GO WITH HIM.
HUH?
Wiz?
WIZ HAS BEEN DARK'S PARTNER THROUGHOUT OUR FAMILY HISTORY.
ONLY YOU CAN TRANS- FORM HIM.
kyu
PUT YOUR HAND ON HIS HEAD.
LIKE THIS?
AHH!

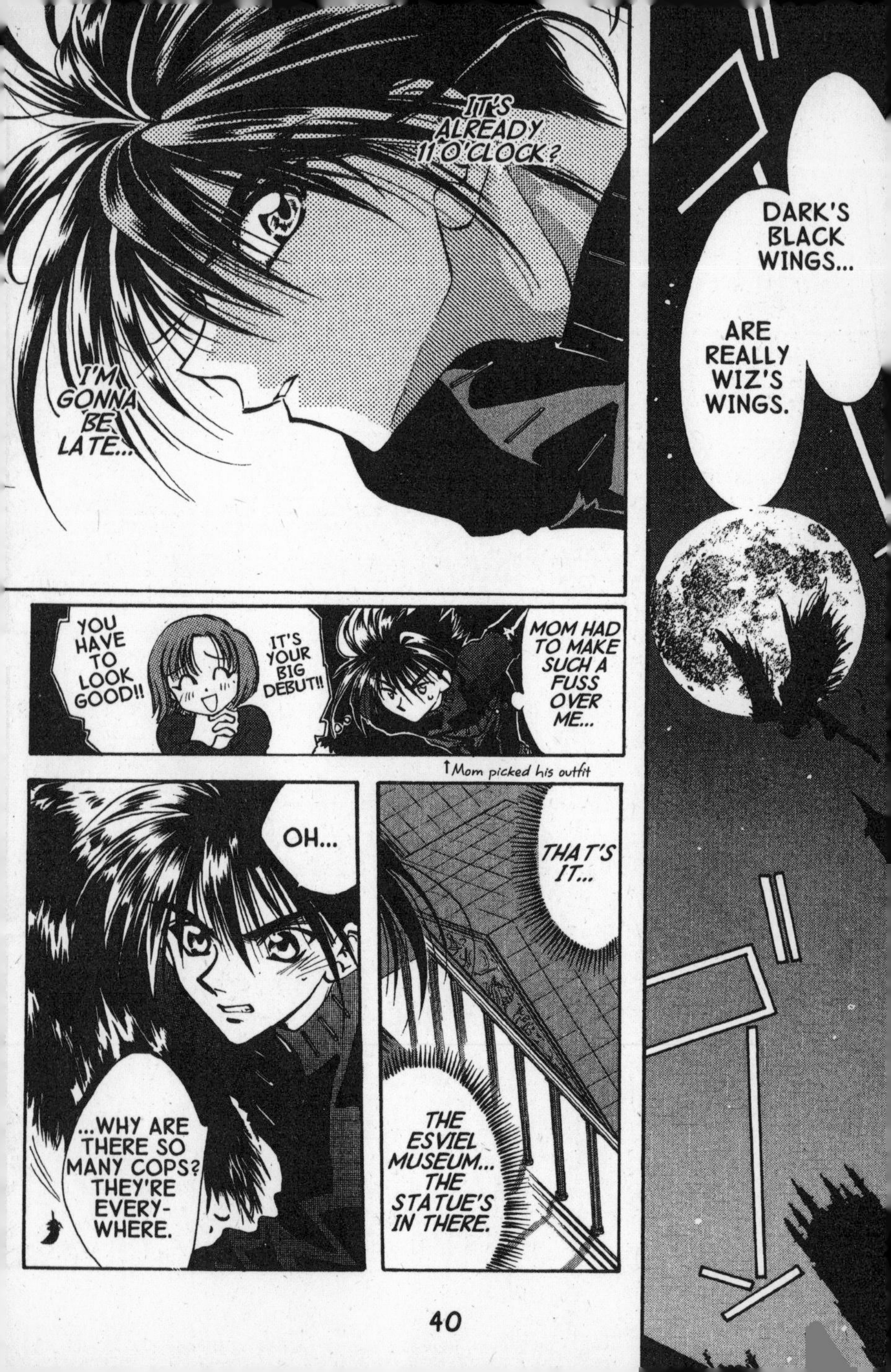
DARK'S BLACK WINGS...
ARE REALLY WIZ'S WINGS.
IT'S ALREADY 11 O'CLOCK?
I'M GONNA BE LATE...
MOM HAD TO MAKE SUCH A FUSS OVER ME...
IT'S YOUR BIG DEBUT!!
YOU HAVE TO LOOK GOOD!!
↑Mom picked his outfit
THAT'S IT...
THE ESVIEL MUSEUM... THE STATUE'S IN THERE.
OH...
...WHY ARE THERE SO MANY COPS? THEY'RE EVERY-WHERE.

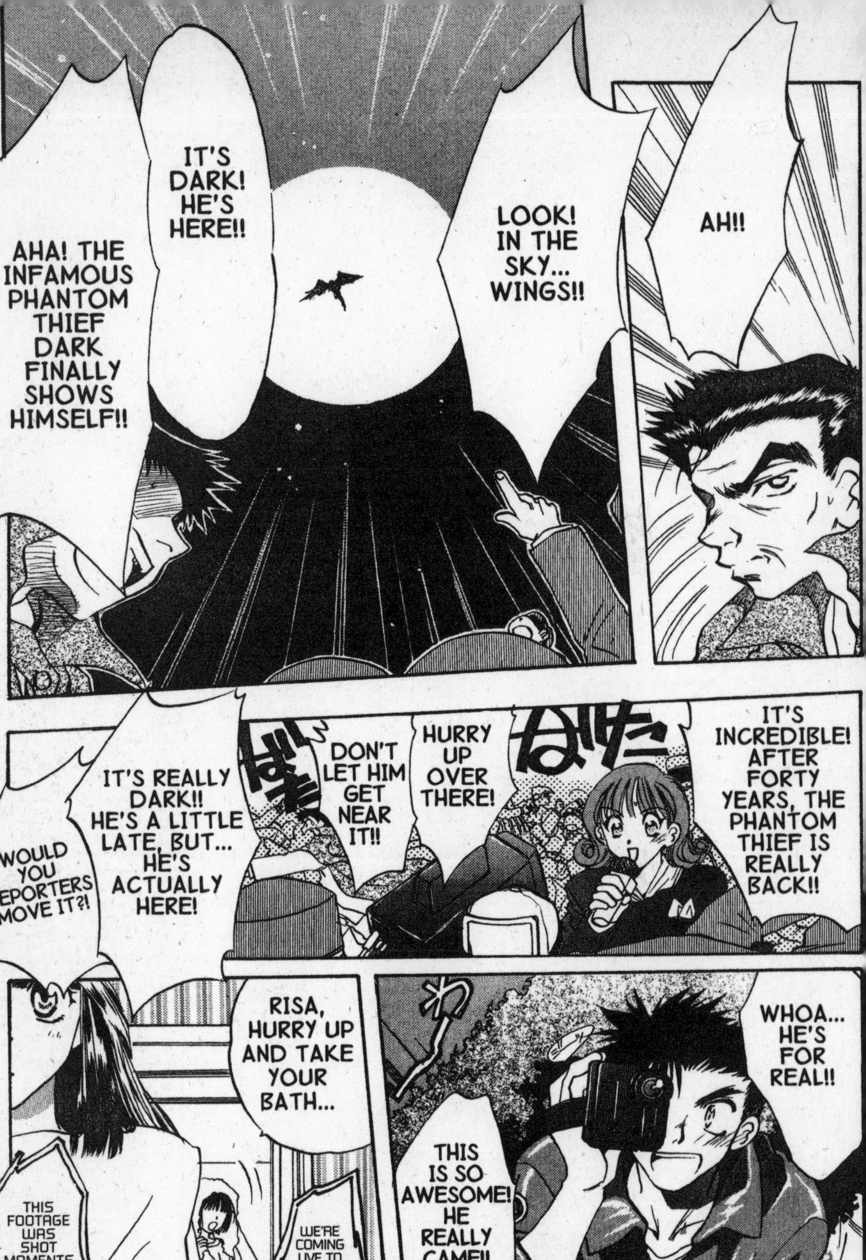
AH!!
LOOK! IN THE SKY... WINGS!!
IT'S DARK! HE'S HERE!!
AHA! THE INFAMOUS PHANTOM THIEF DARK FINALLY SHOWS HIMSELF!!
IT'S INCREDIBLE! AFTER FORTY YEARS, THE PHANTOM THIEF IS REALLY BACK!!
HURRY UP OVER THERE!
DON'T LET HIM GET NEAR IT!!
IT'S REALLY DARK!! HE'S A LITTLE LATE, BUT... HE'S ACTUALLY HERE!
WOULD YOU REPORTERS MOVE IT?!
WHOA... HE'S FOR REAL!!
THIS IS SO AWESOME! HE REALLY CAME!!
RISA, HURRY UP AND TAKE YOUR BATH...
WE'RE COMING LIVE TO YOU FROM THE SCENE!!
THIS FOOTAGE WAS SHOT MOMENTS AGO...

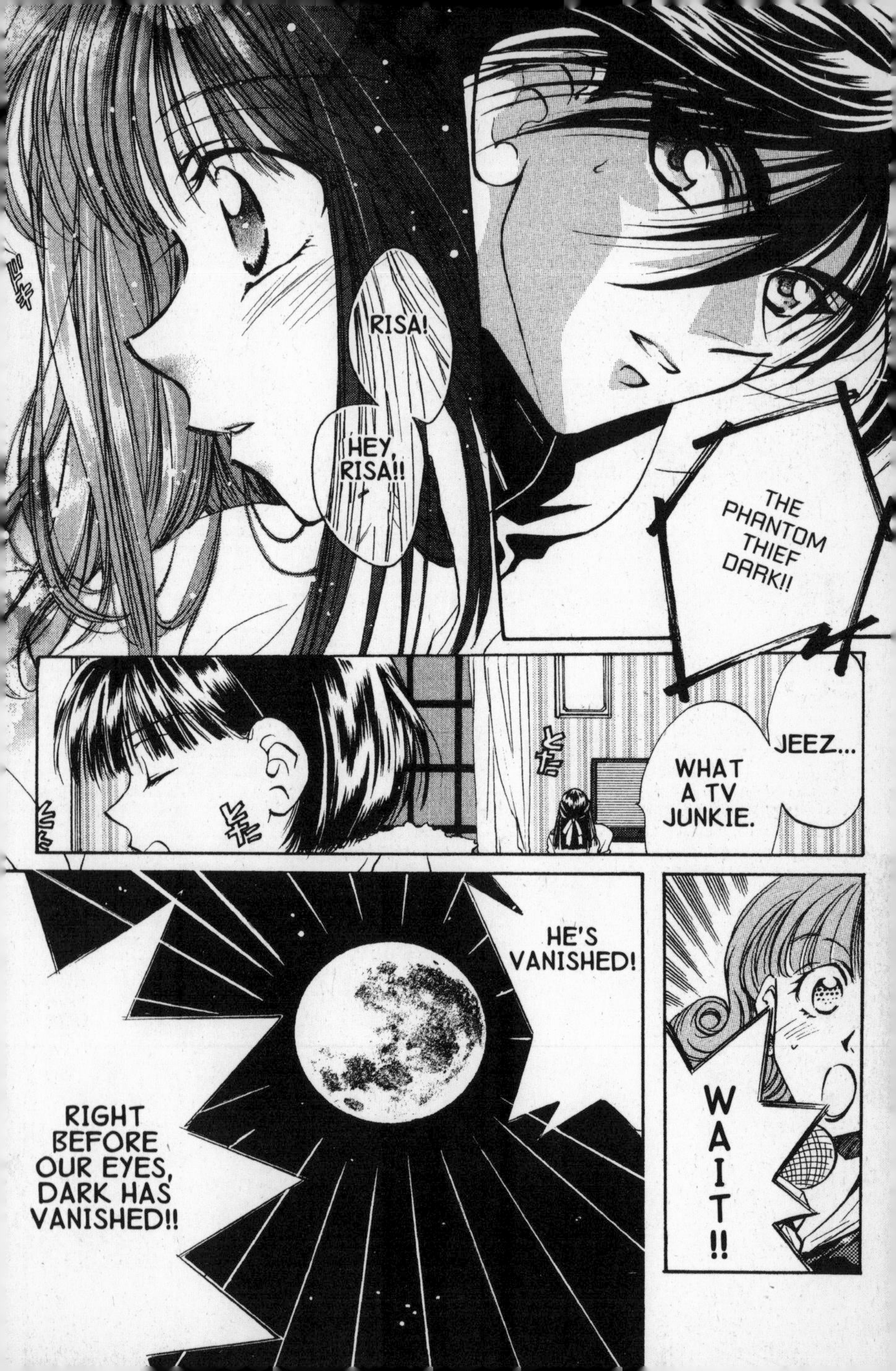
THE PHANTOM THIEF DARK!!
RISA!
HEY, RISA!!
JEEZ... WHAT A TV JUNKIE.
WAIT!!
HE'S VANISHED!
RIGHT BEFORE OUR EYES, DARK HAS VANISHED!!

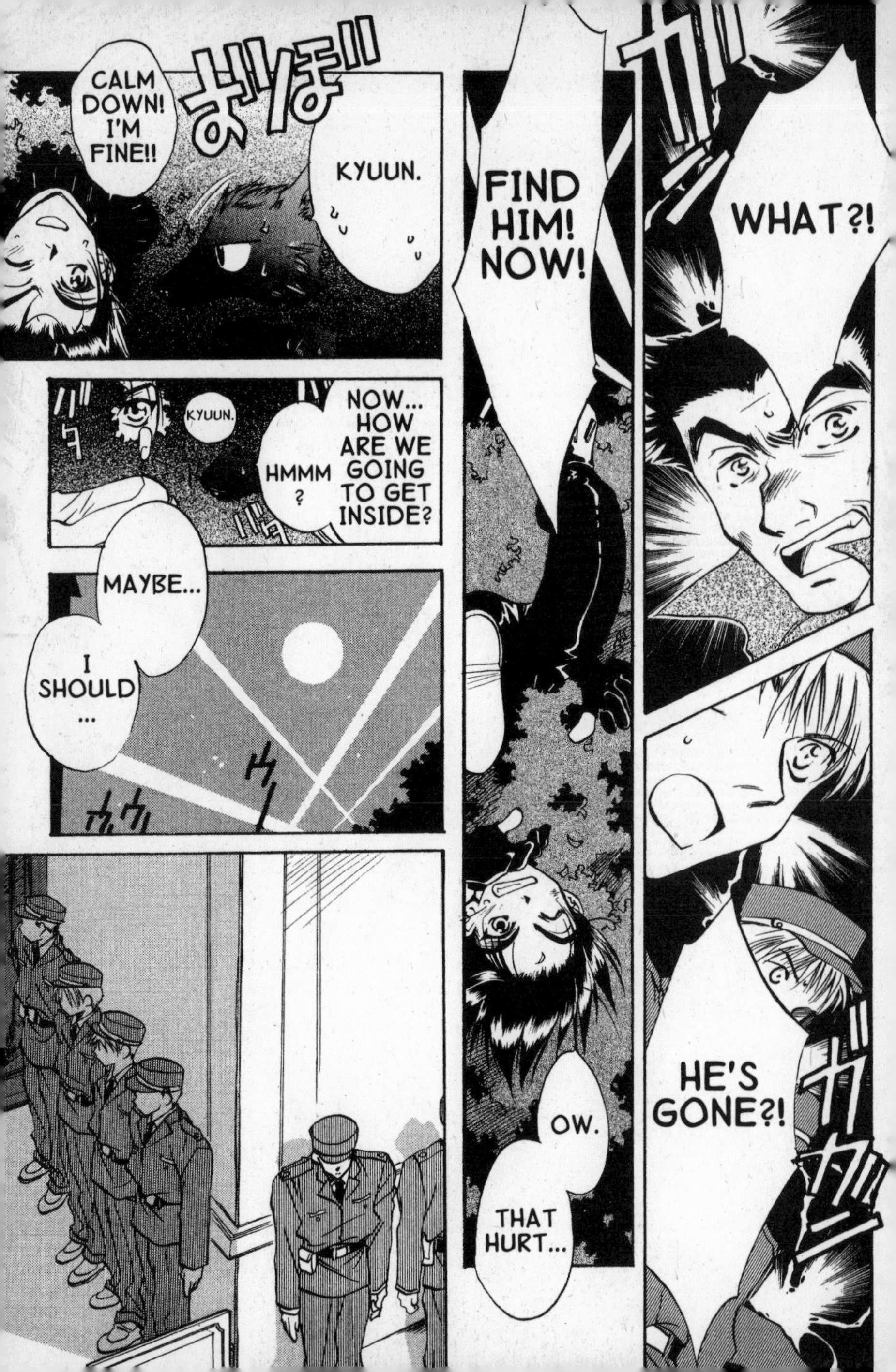
WHAT?!
HE'S GONE?!
FIND HIM! NOW!
OW.
THAT HURT...
KYUUN.
CALM DOWN! I'M FINE!!
NOW... HOW ARE WE GOING TO GET INSIDE?
HMMM?
KYUUN.
MAYBE...
I SHOULD...

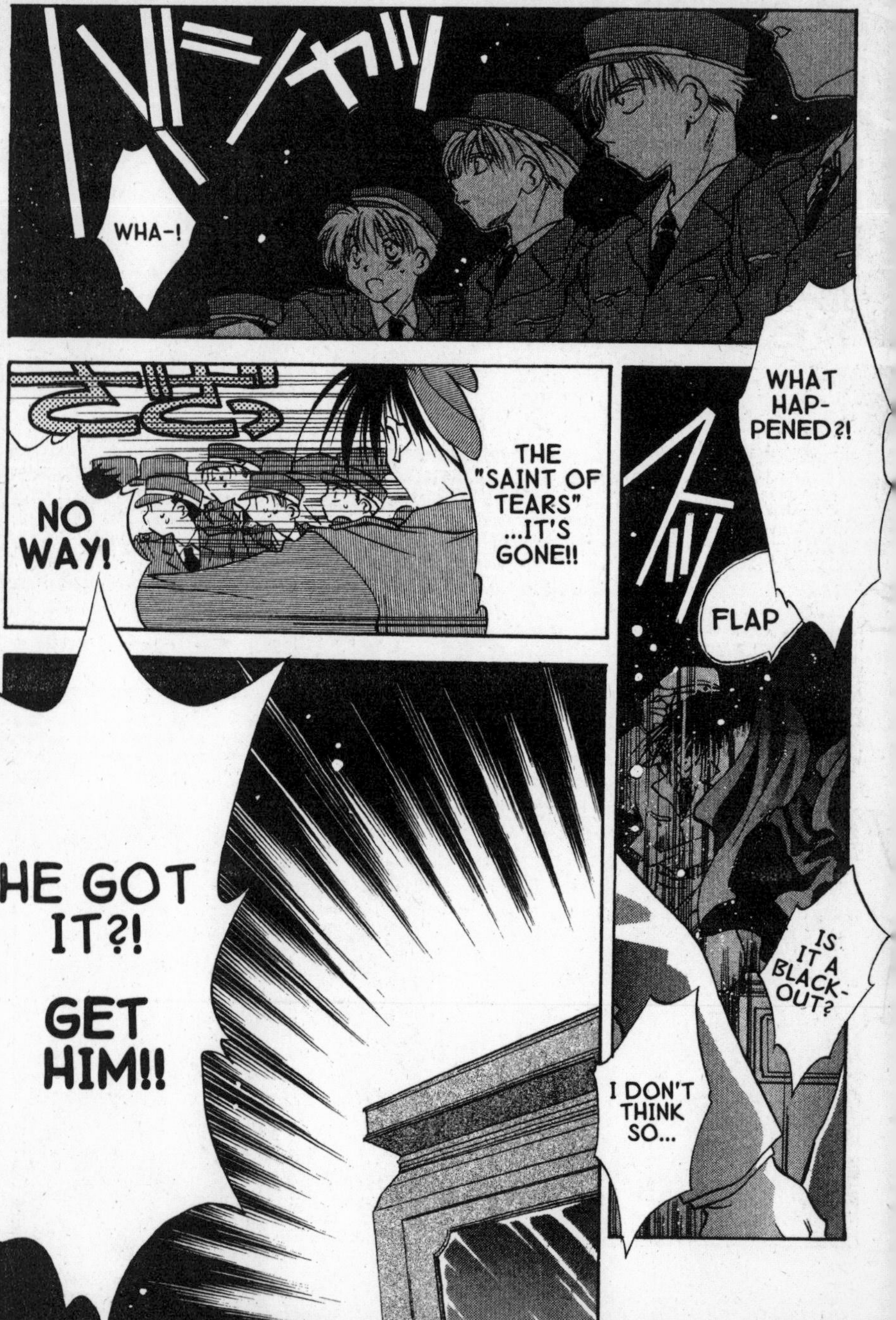
WHA-!
WHAT HAPPENED?!
FLAP
IS IT A BLACKOUT?
I DON'T THINK SO...
THE "SAINT OF TEARS" ...IT'S GONE!!
NO WAY!
HE GOT IT?!
GET HIM!!

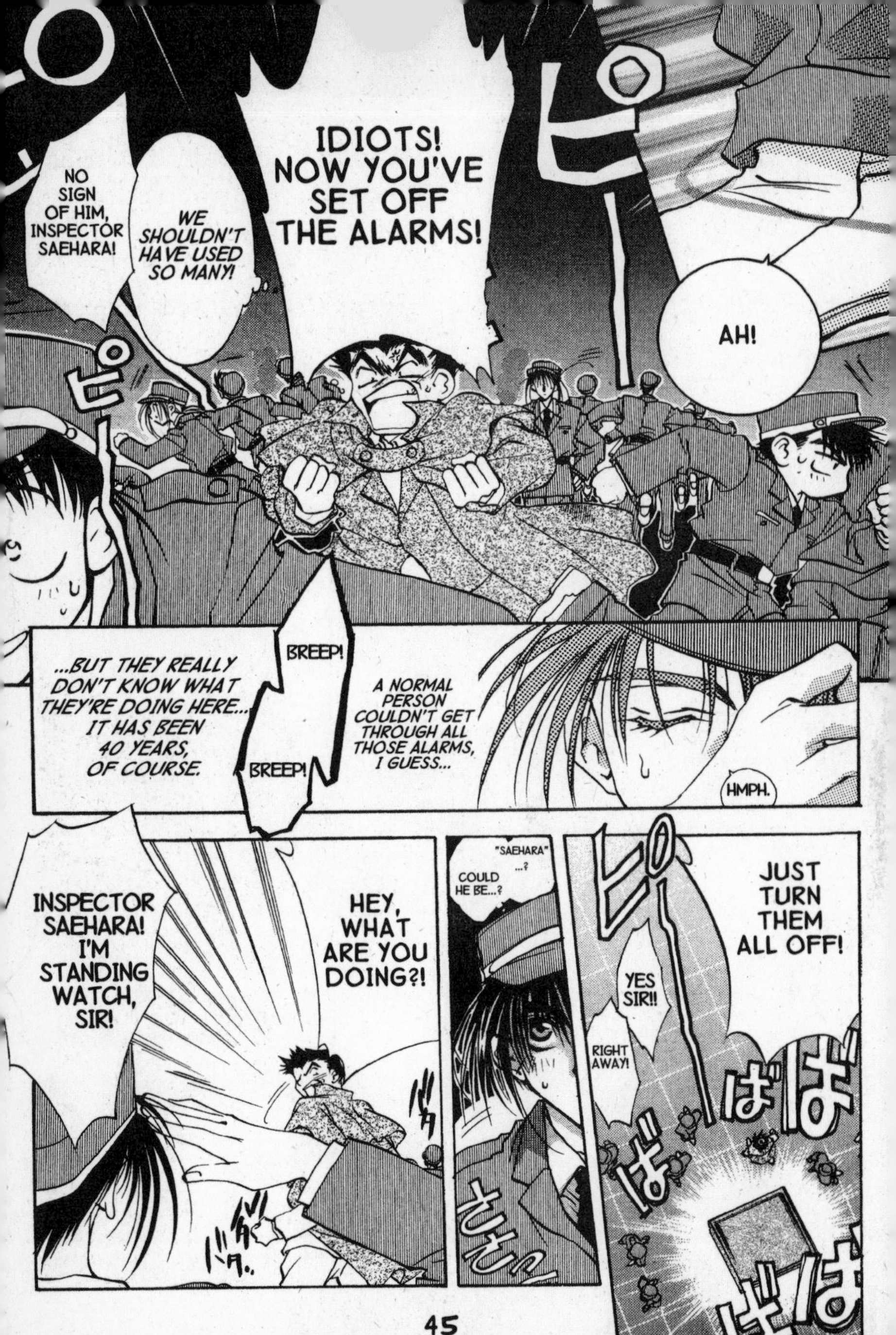
AH!
IDIOTS! NOW YOU'VE SET OFF THE ALARMS!
WE SHOULDN'T HAVE USED SO MANY!
NO SIGN OF HIM, INSPECTOR SAEHARA!
HMPH.
A NORMAL PERSON COULDN'T GET THROUGH ALL THOSE ALARMS, I GUESS...
BREEP!
BREEP!
...BUT THEY REALLY DON'T KNOW WHAT THEY'RE DOING HERE... IT HAS BEEN 40 YEARS, OF COURSE.
JUST TURN THEM ALL OFF!
YES SIR!!
RIGHT AWAY!
"SAEHARA" ...?
COULD HE BE...?
HEY, WHAT ARE YOU DOING?!
INSPECTOR SAEHARA! I'M STANDING WATCH, SIR!

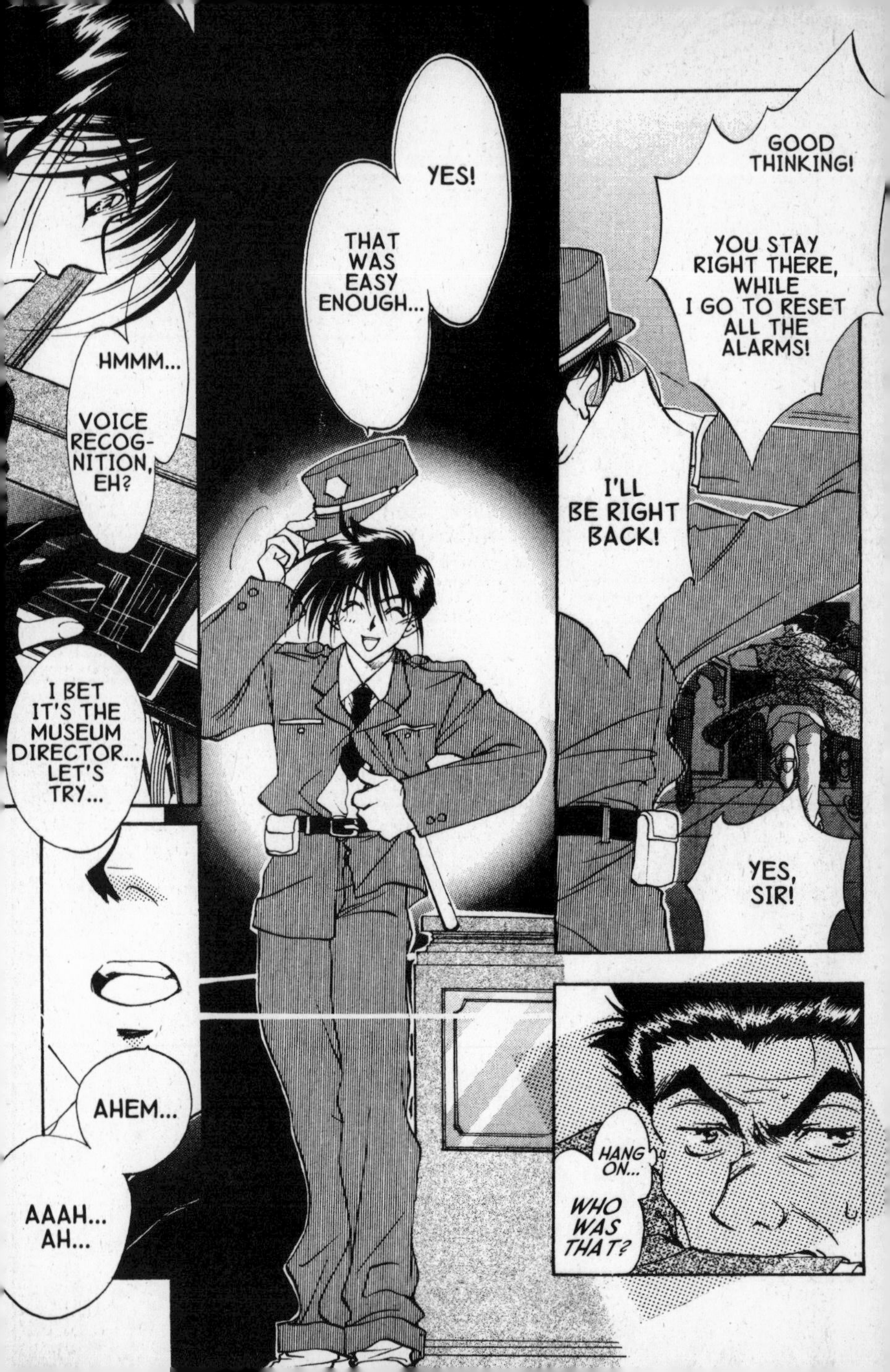
GOOD THINKING!
YOU STAY RIGHT THERE, WHILE I GO TO RESET ALL THE ALARMS!
I'LL BE RIGHT BACK!
YES, SIR!
HANG ON...
WHO WAS THAT?
YES!
THAT WAS EASY ENOUGH...
HMMM...
VOICE RECOG-NITION, EH?
I BET IT'S THE MUSEUM DIRECTOR... LET'S TRY...
AHEM...
AAAH... AH...

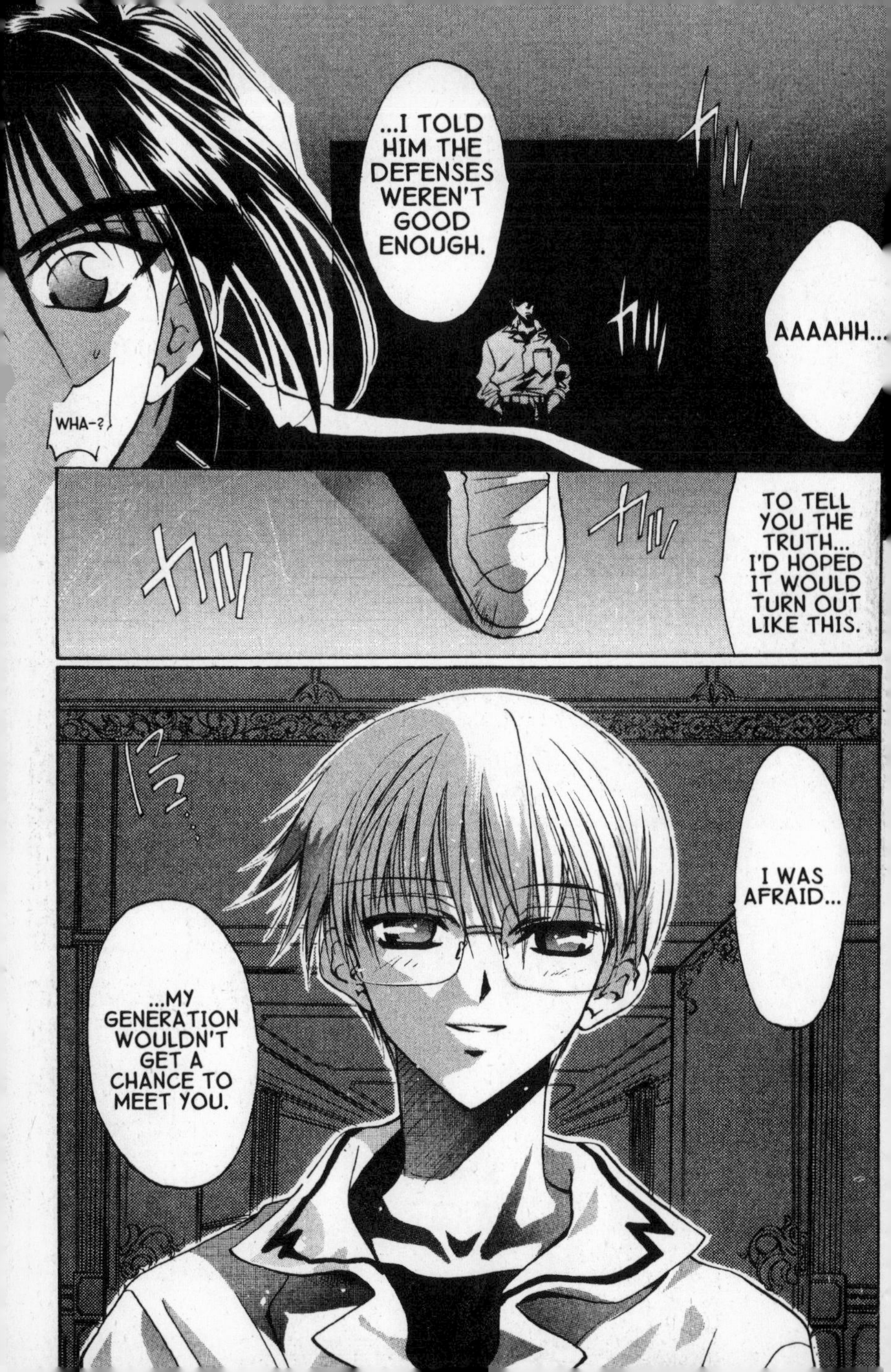
AAAAHH...
...I TOLD HIM THE DEFENSES WEREN'T GOOD ENOUGH.
WHA-?
TO TELL YOU THE TRUTH... I'D HOPED IT WOULD TURN OUT LIKE THIS.
I WAS AFRAID...
...MY GENERATION WOULDN'T GET A CHANCE TO MEET YOU.

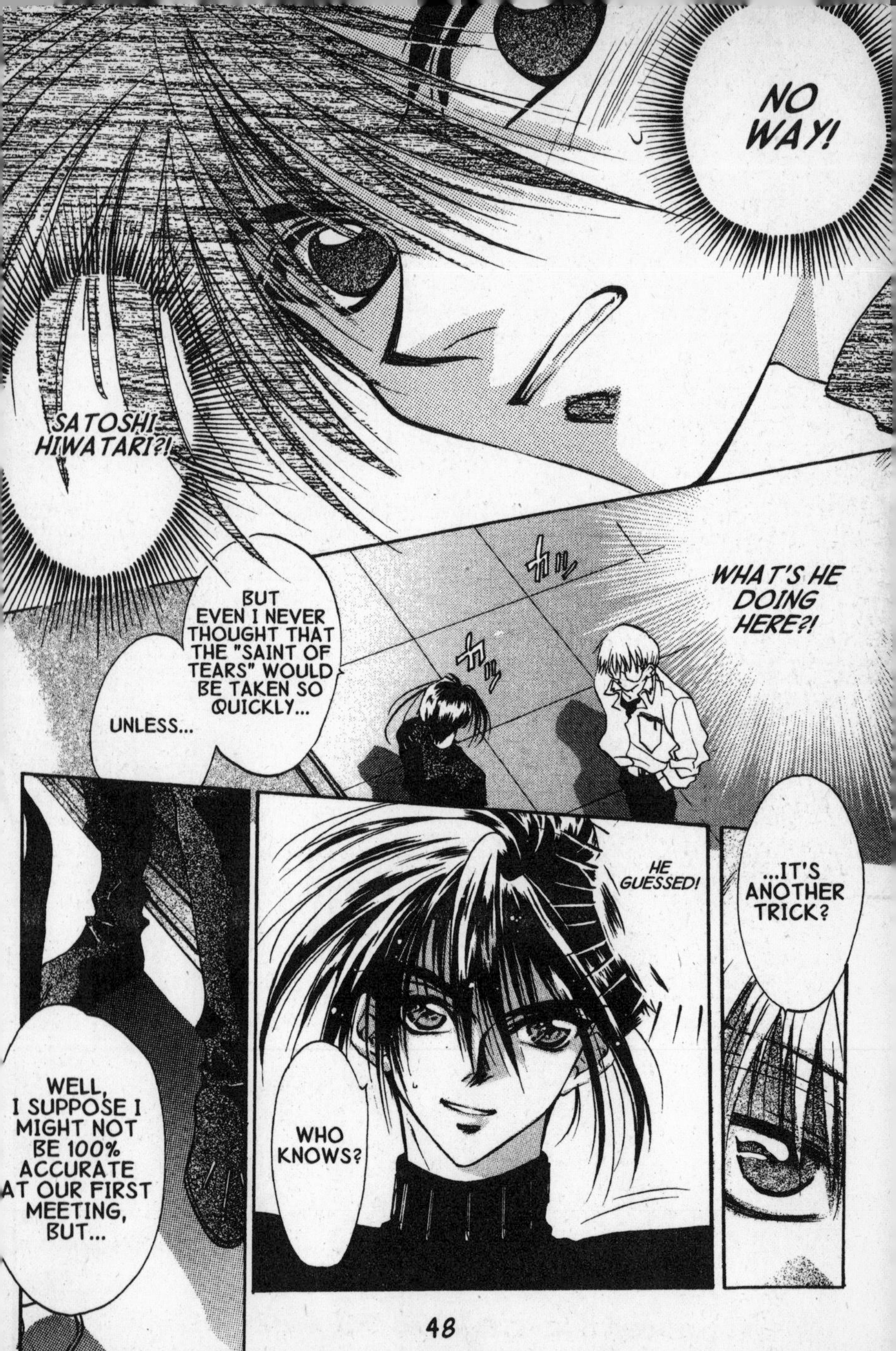
NO WAY!
SATOSHI HIWATARI?!
WHAT'S HE DOING HERE?!
BUT EVEN I NEVER THOUGHT THAT THE "SAINT OF TEARS" WOULD BE TAKEN SO QUICKLY...
UNLESS...
...IT'S ANOTHER TRICK?
HE GUESSED!
WHO KNOWS?
WELL, I SUPPOSE I MIGHT NOT BE 100% ACCURATE AT OUR FIRST MEETING, BUT...

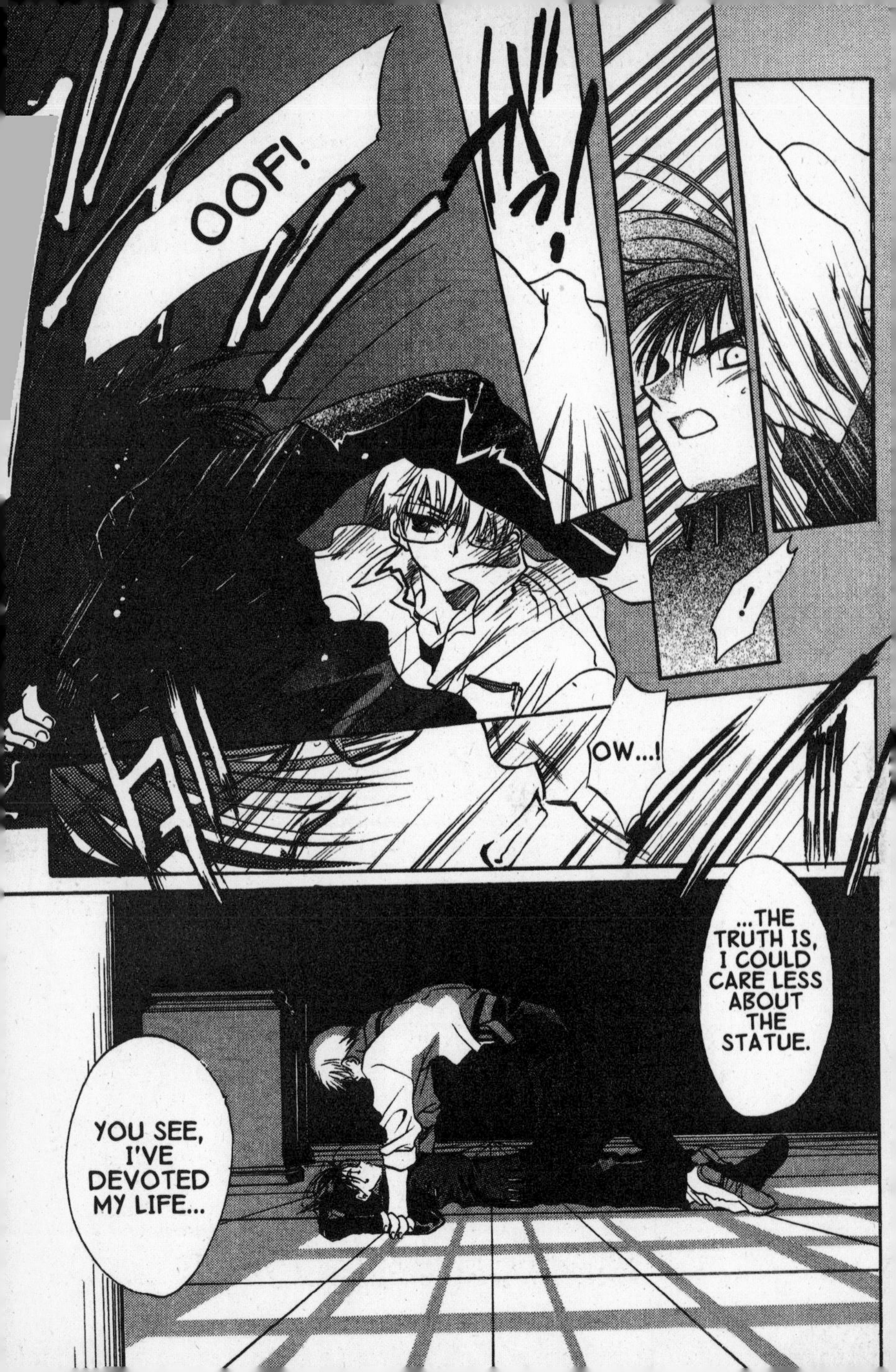

!
OOF!
OW...!
...THE TRUTH IS, I COULD CARE LESS ABOUT THE STATUE.
YOU SEE, I'VE DEVOTED MY LIFE...

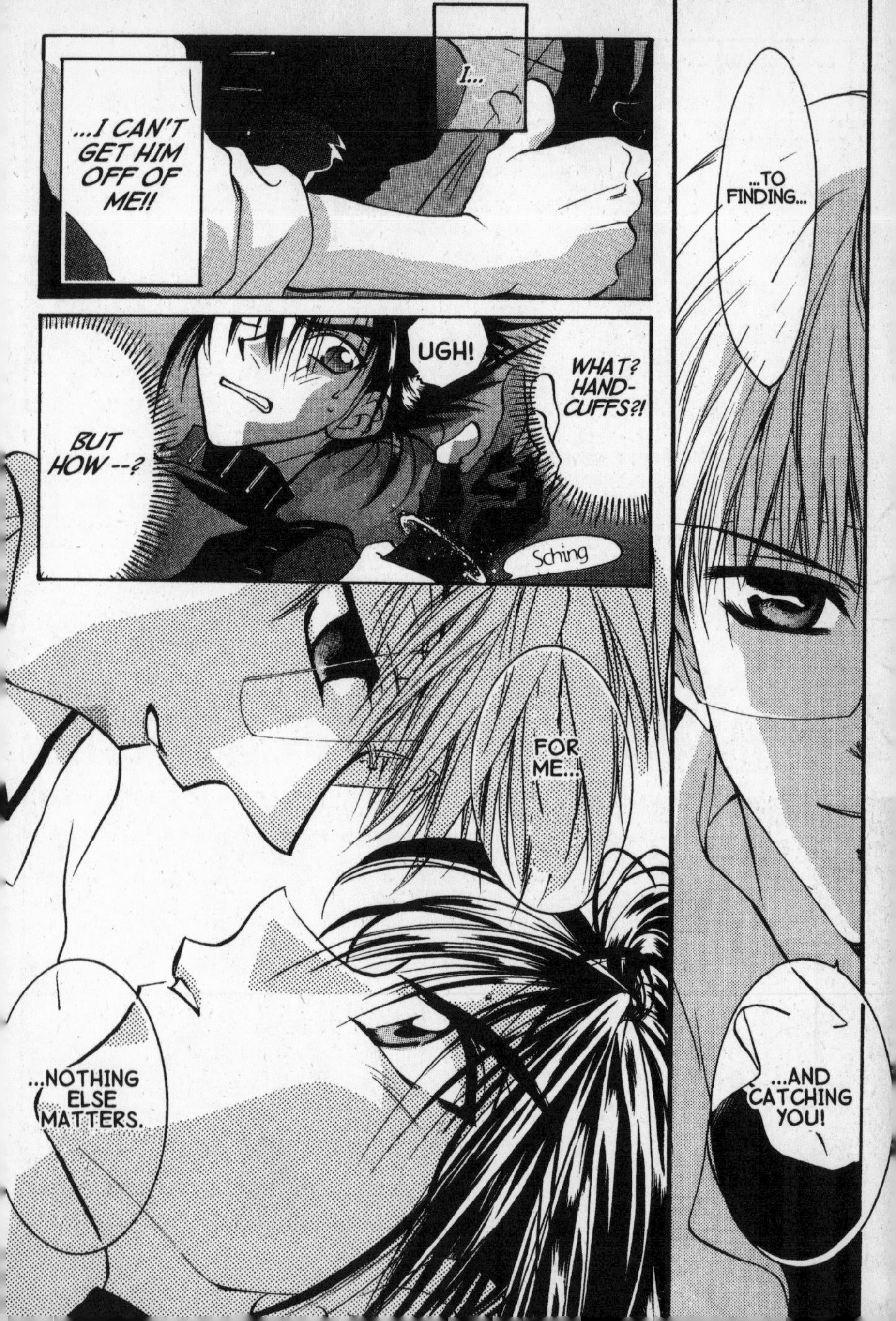
I...
...I CAN'T GET HIM OFF OF ME!!
UGH!
WHAT? HAND-CUFFS?!
BUT HOW --?
Sching
FOR ME...
...NOTHING ELSE MATTERS.
...TO FINDING...
...AND CATCHING YOU!

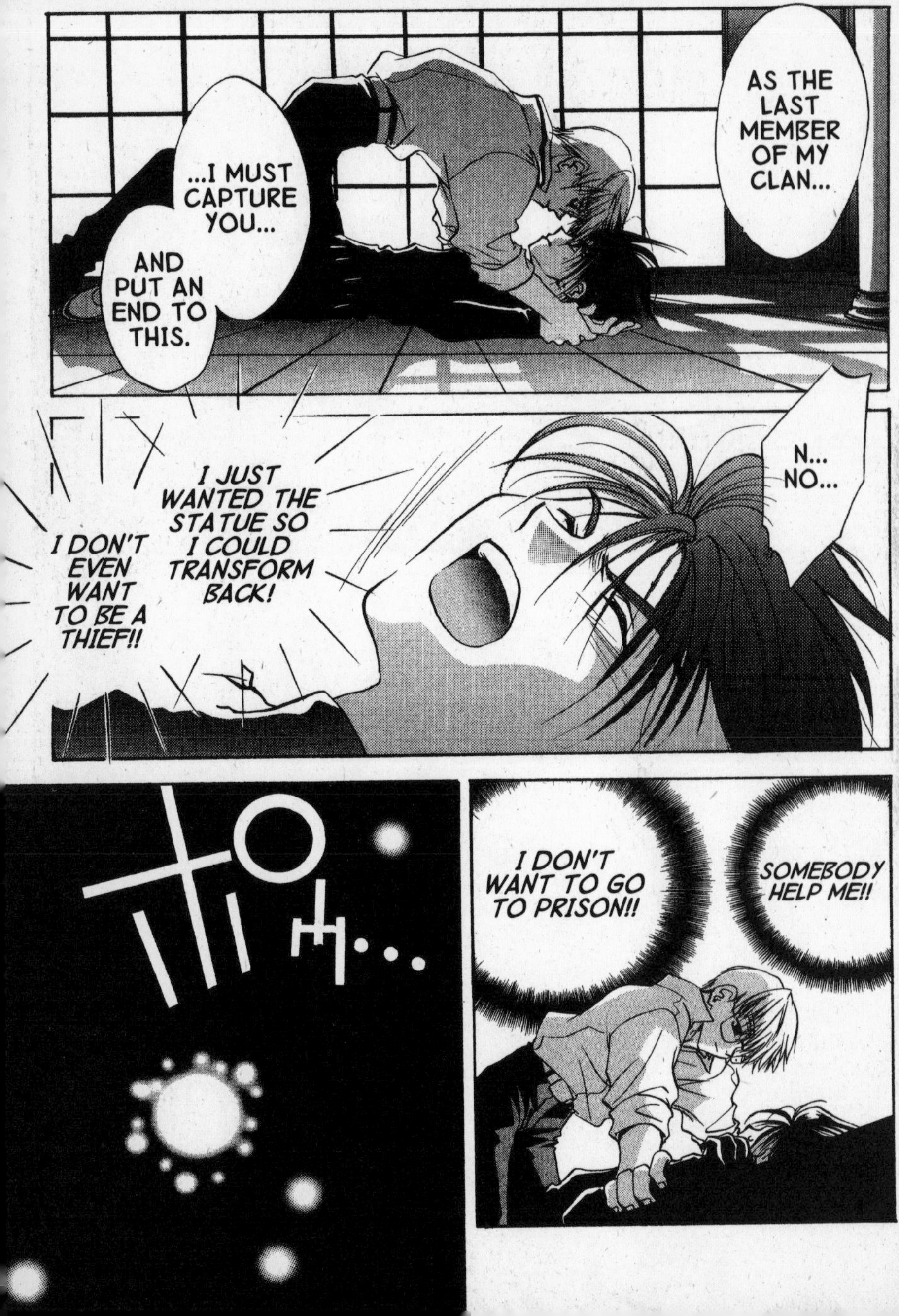
AS THE LAST MEMBER OF MY CLAN...
...I MUST CAPTURE YOU...
AND PUT AN END TO THIS.
N... NO...
I JUST WANTED THE STATUE SO I COULD TRANSFORM BACK!
I DON'T EVEN WANT TO BE A THIEF!!
SOMEBODY HELP ME!!
I DON'T WANT TO GO TO PRISON!!

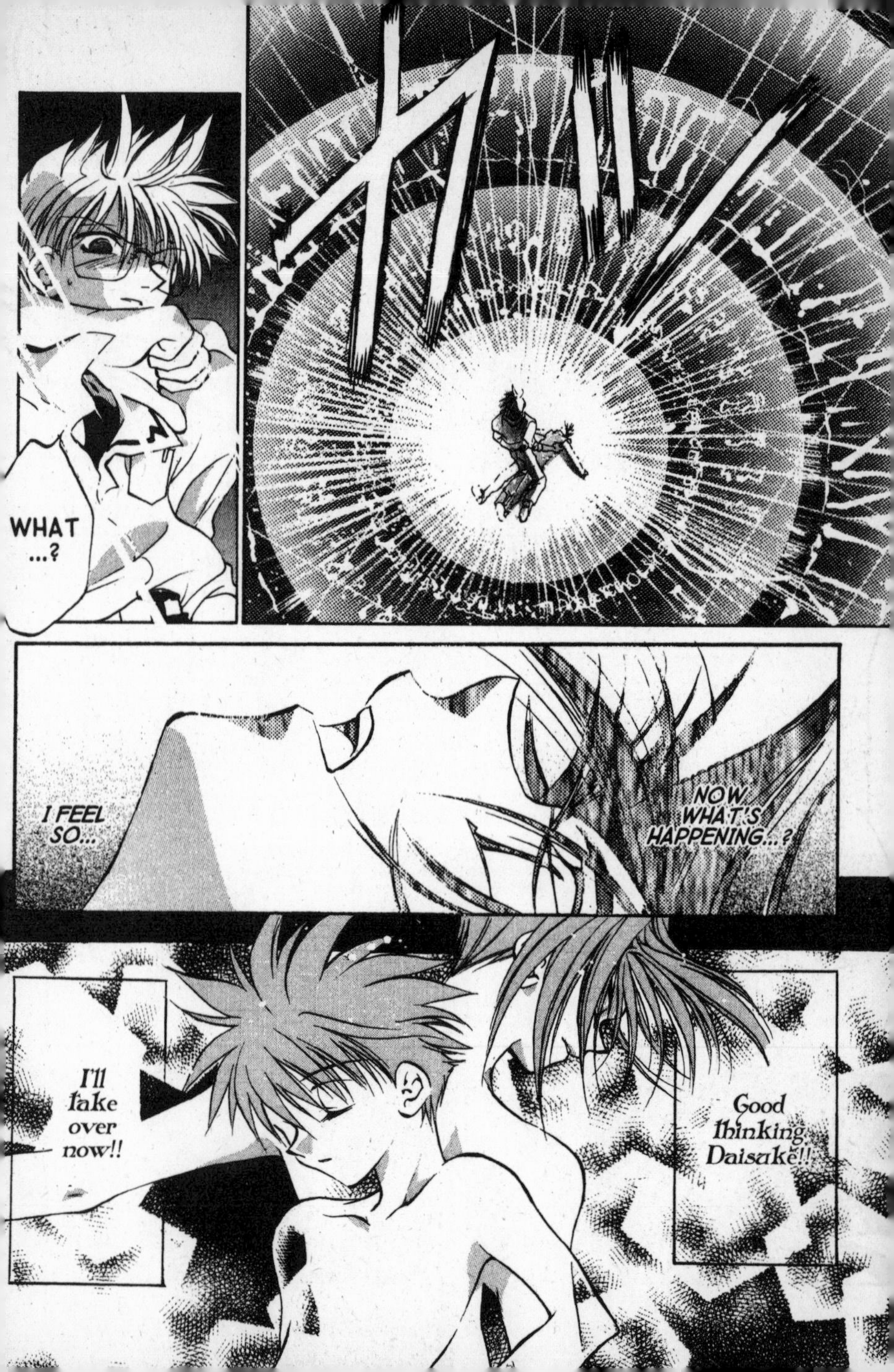
WHAT ...?
NOW WHAT'S HAPPENING...?
I FEEL SO...
Good thinking Daisuke!!
I'll take over now!!

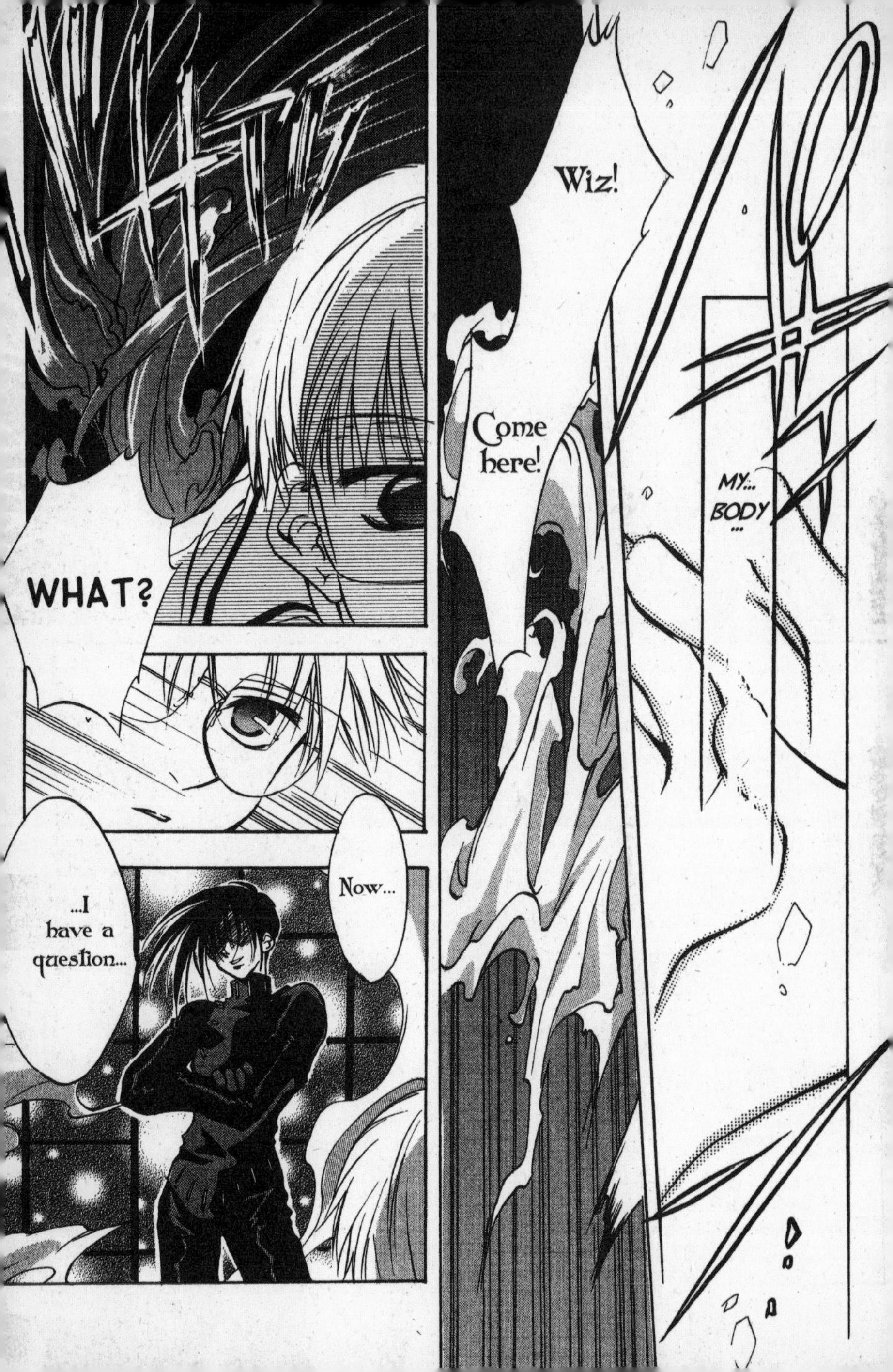
Wiz!
Come here!
MY... BODY ...
WHAT?
Now...
...I have a question...

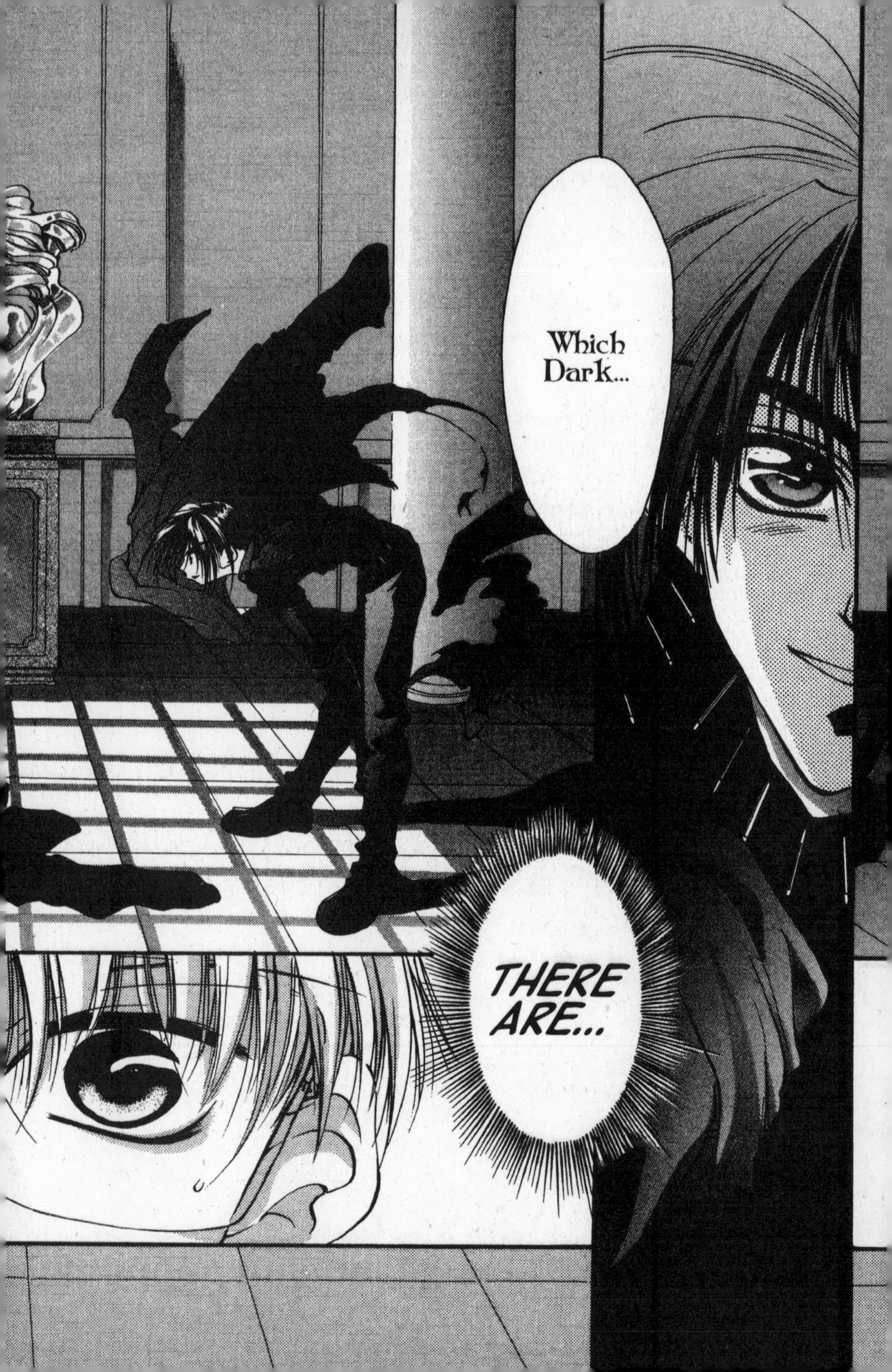
Which Dark...
THERE ARE...

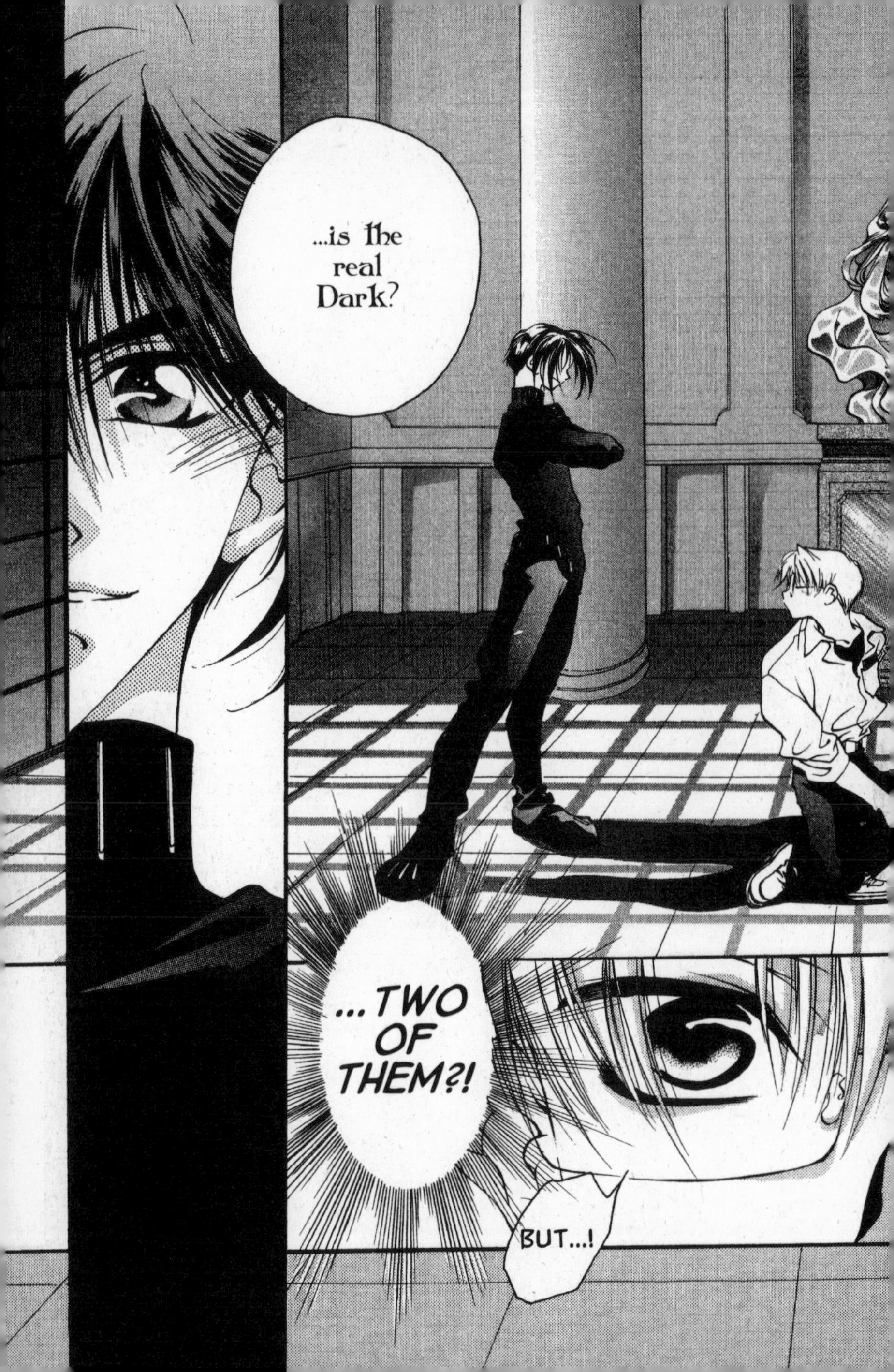
...is the real Dark?
...TWO OF THEM?!
BUT...!

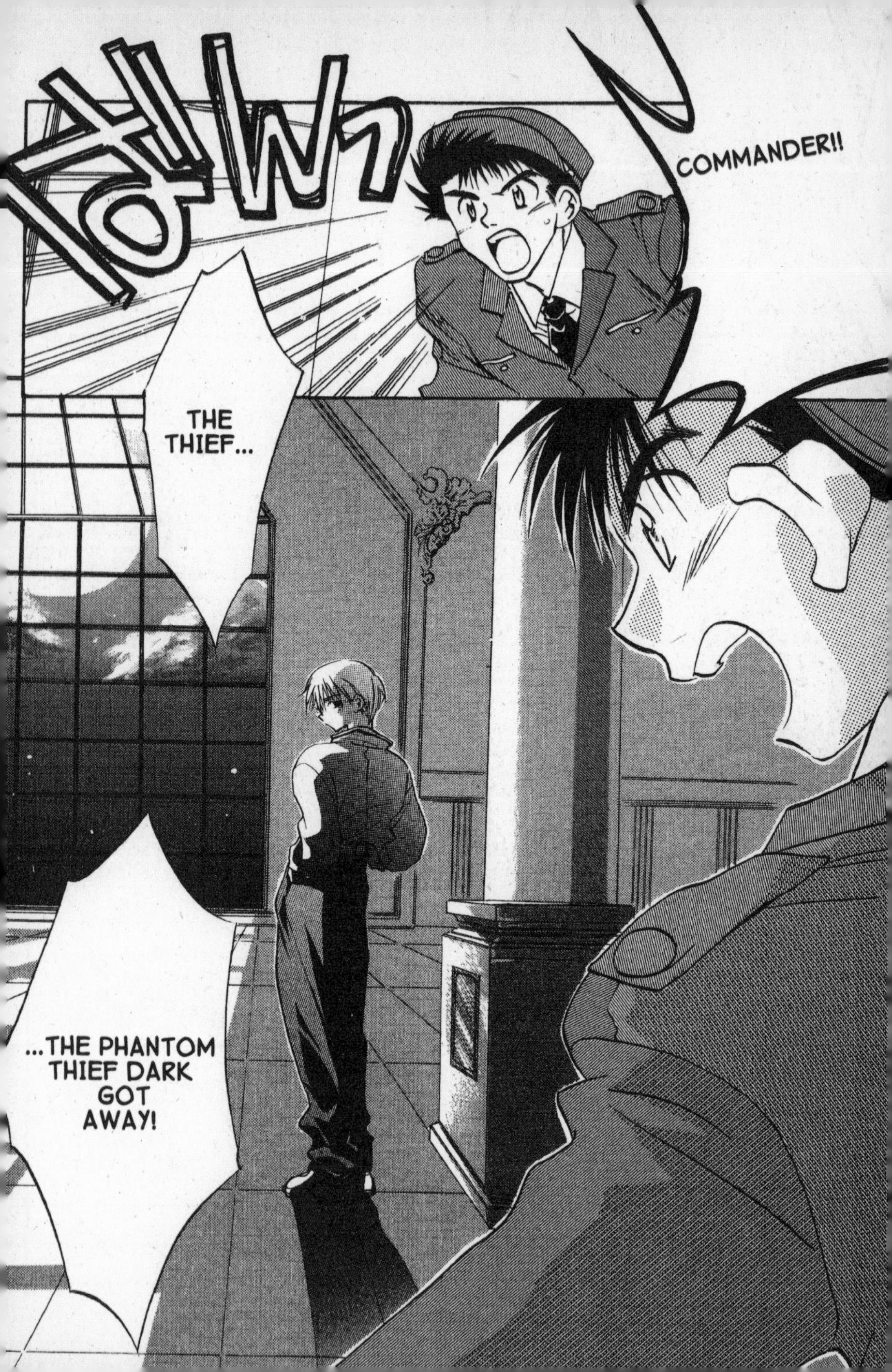
COMMANDER!!
THE THIEF...
...THE PHANTOM THIEF DARK GOT AWAY!

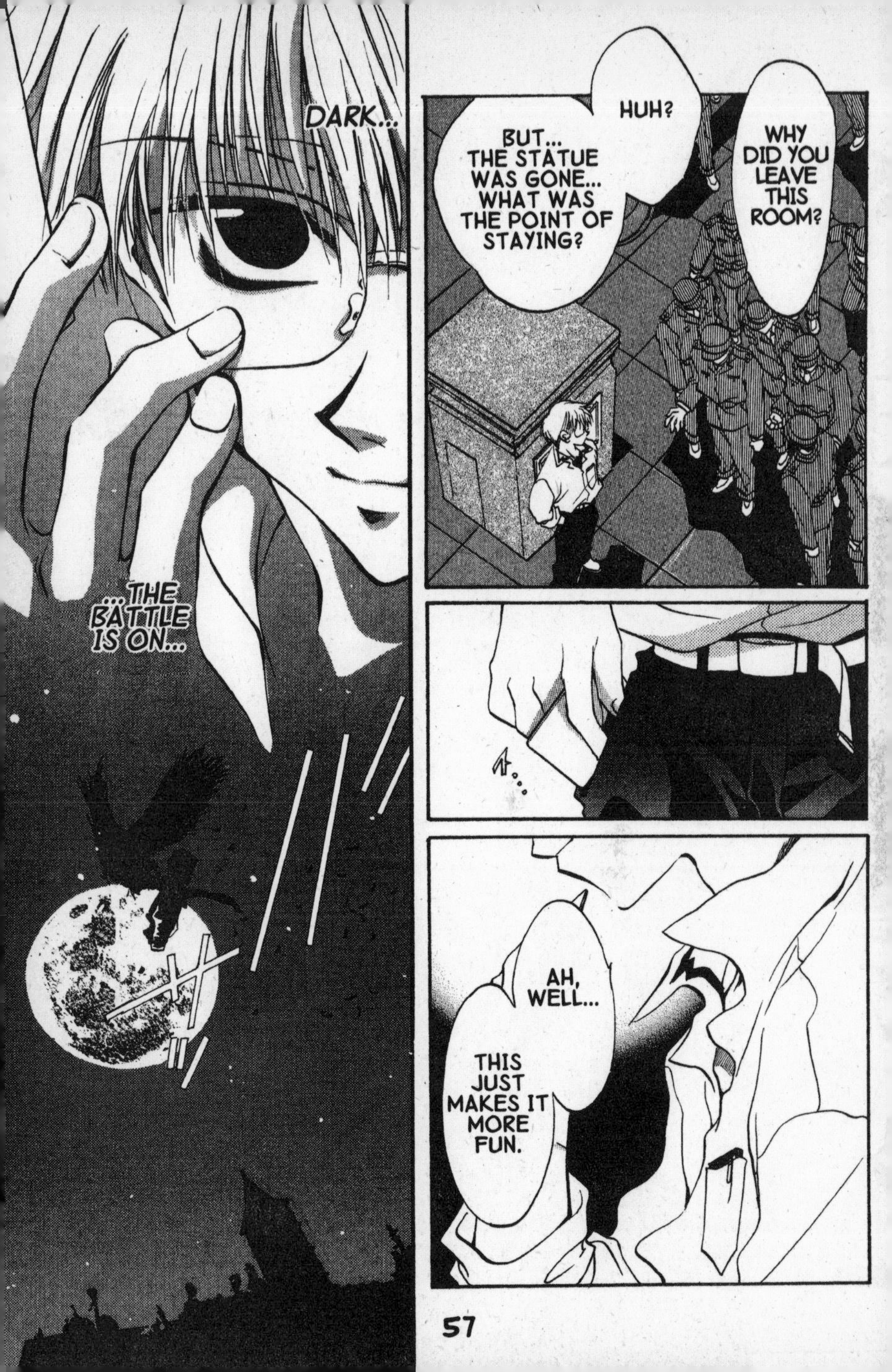
WHY DID YOU LEAVE THIS ROOM?
HUH?
BUT... THE STATUE WAS GONE... WHAT WAS THE POINT OF STAYING?
AH, WELL...
THIS JUST MAKES IT MORE FUN.
DARK...
...THE BATTLE IS ON...

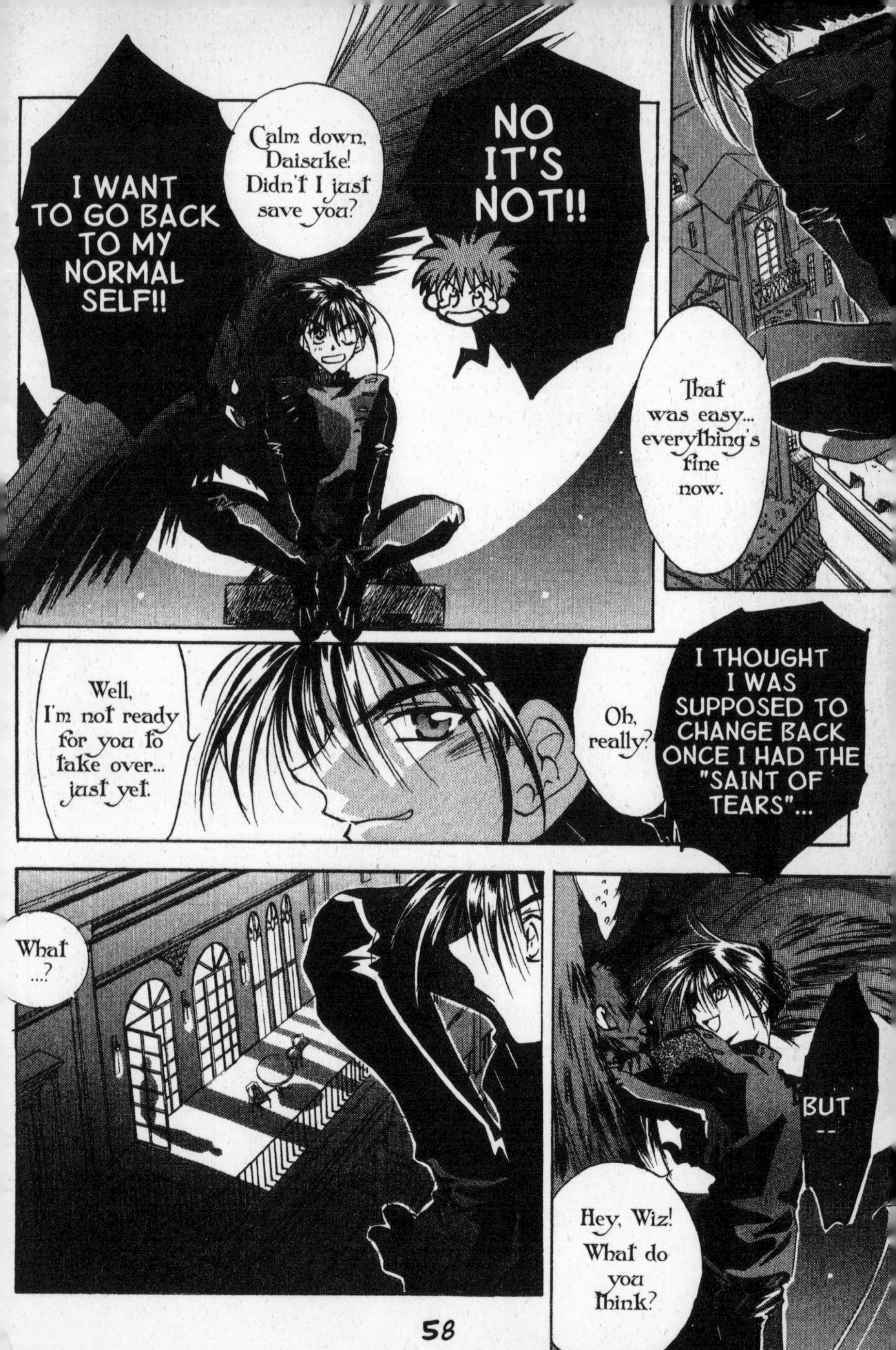
That was easy... everything's fine now.
NO IT'S NOT!!
Calm down, Daisuke! Didn't I just save you?
I WANT TO GO BACK TO MY NORMAL SELF!!
I THOUGHT I WAS SUPPOSED TO CHANGE BACK ONCE I HAD THE "SAINT OF TEARS"...
Oh, really?
Well, I'm not ready for you to take over... just yet.
BUT --
Hey, Wiz! What do you think?
What ...?

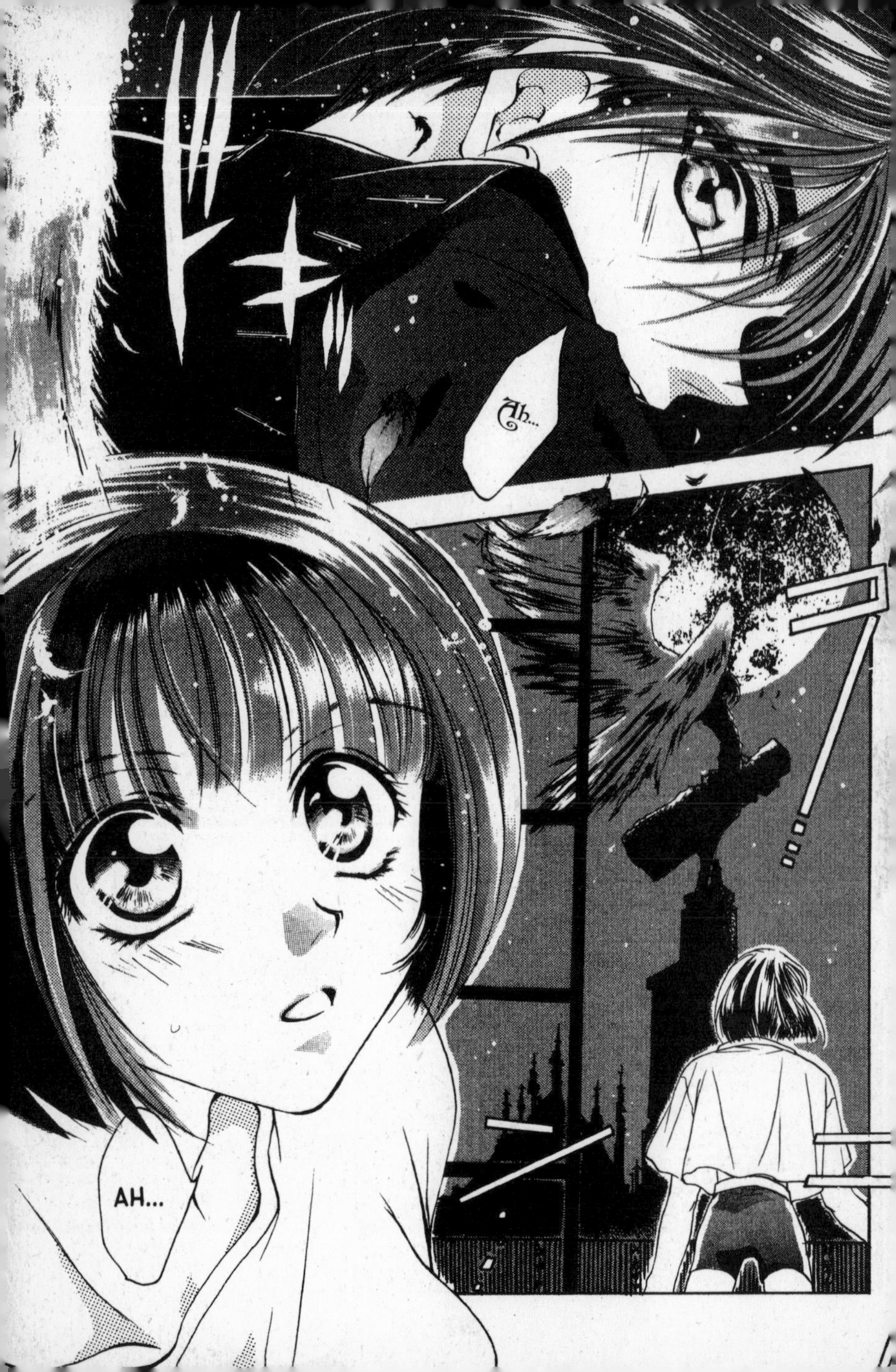
Ah...
AH...

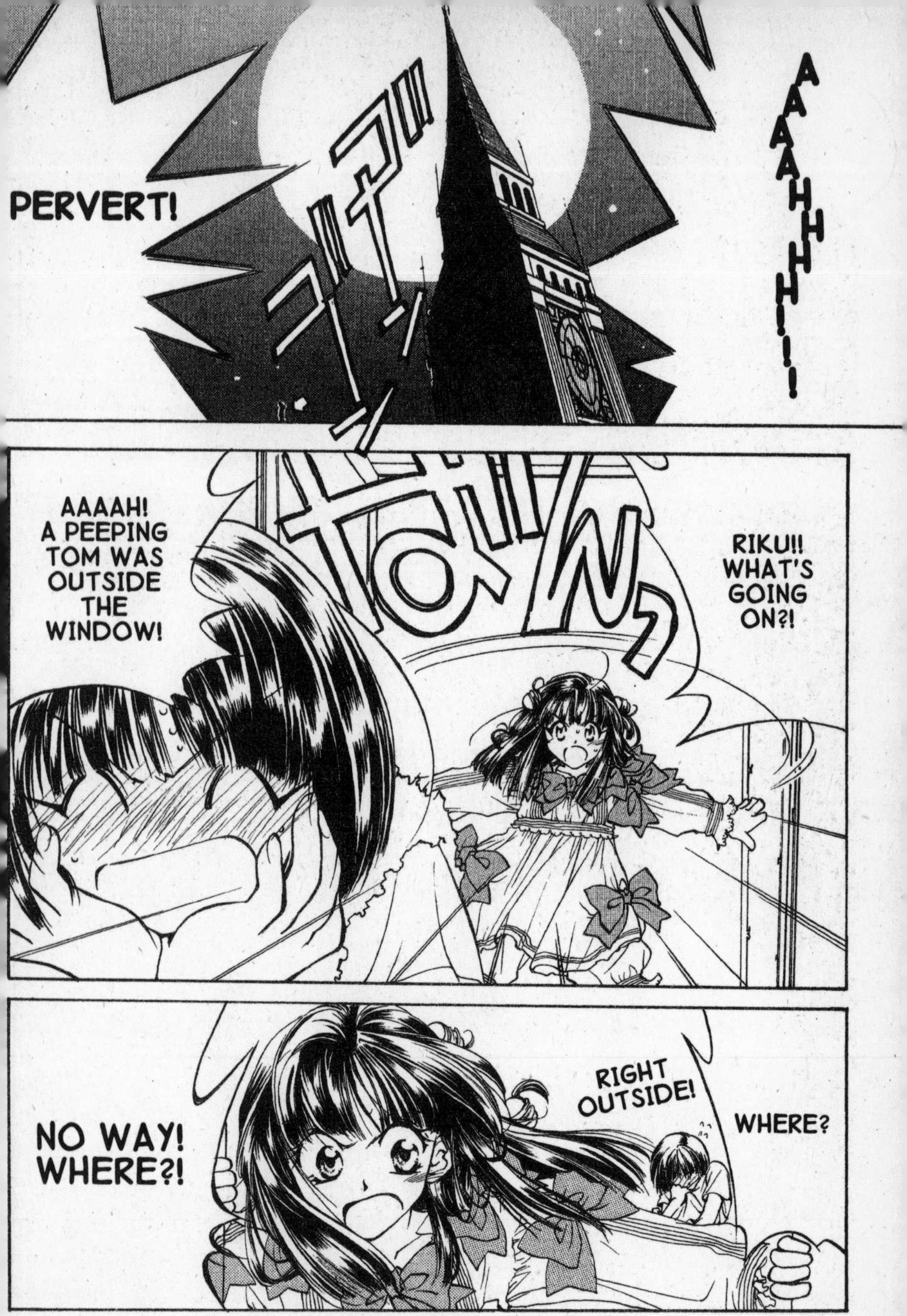
AAAAHHHH!!!!
PERVERT!
RIKU!! WHAT'S GOING ON?!
AAAAH! A PEEPING TOM WAS OUTSIDE THE WINDOW!
WHERE?
RIGHT OUTSIDE!
NO WAY! WHERE?!

OUCH...
OH.
I'M...
ME AGAIN.
I'M ME!!

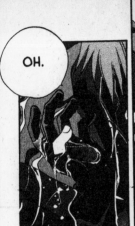

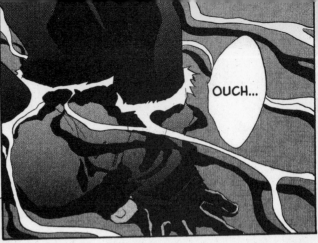

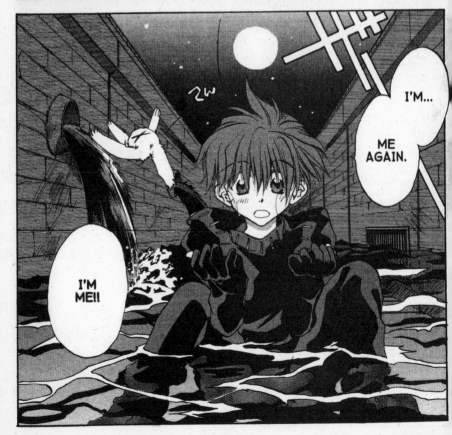

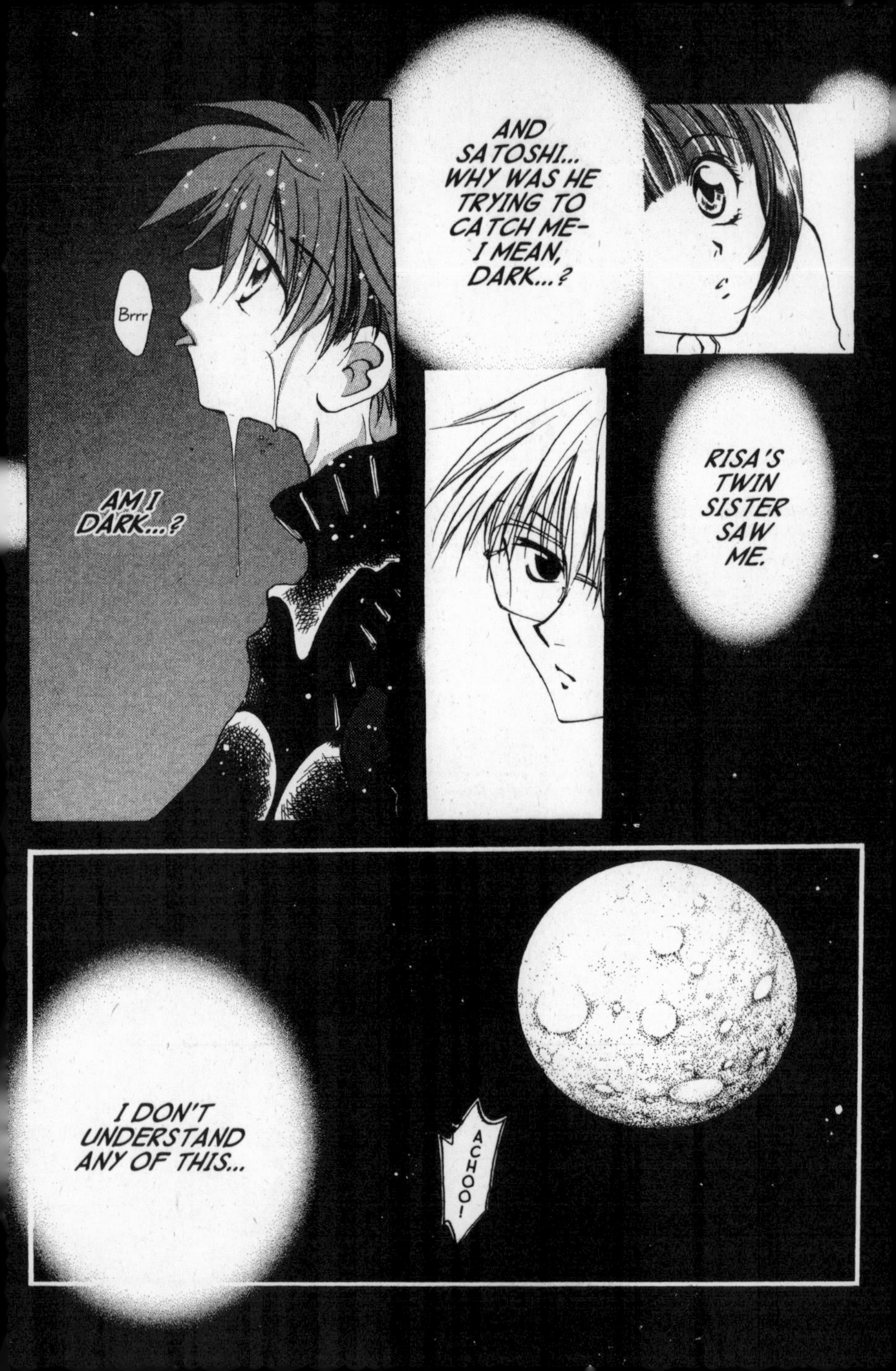
RISA'S TWIN SISTER SAW ME.
AND SATOSHI... WHY WAS HE TRYING TO CATCH ME- I MEAN, DARK...?
Brrr
AM I DARK...?
ACHOO!
I DON'T UNDERSTAND ANY OF THIS...

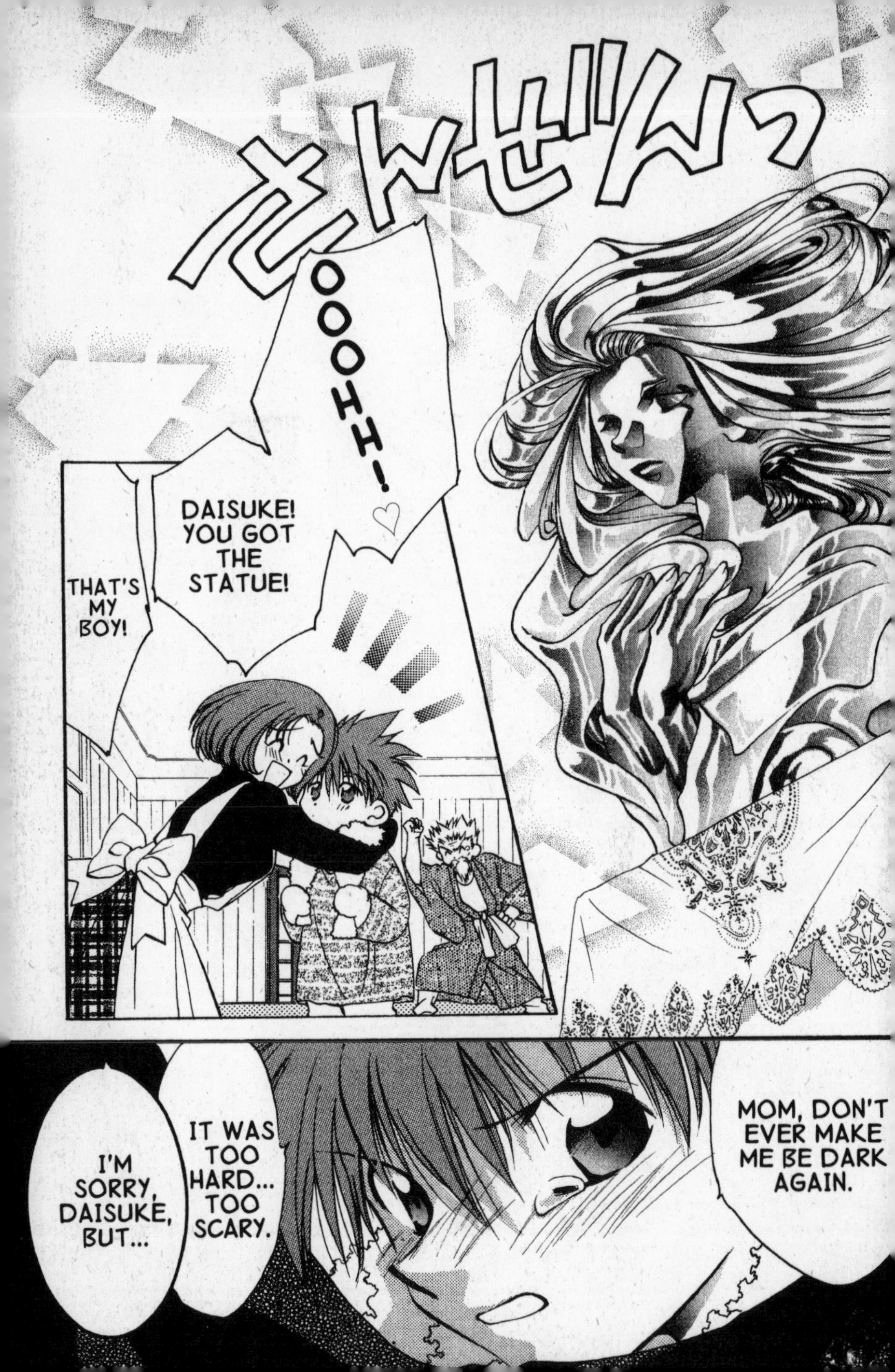

たんぜんっ
OOOOH! ♥
DAISUKE! YOU GOT THE STATUE!
THAT'S MY BOY!
MOM, DON'T EVER MAKE ME BE DARK AGAIN.
IT WAS TOO HARD... TOO SCARY.
I'M SORRY, DAISUKE, BUT...

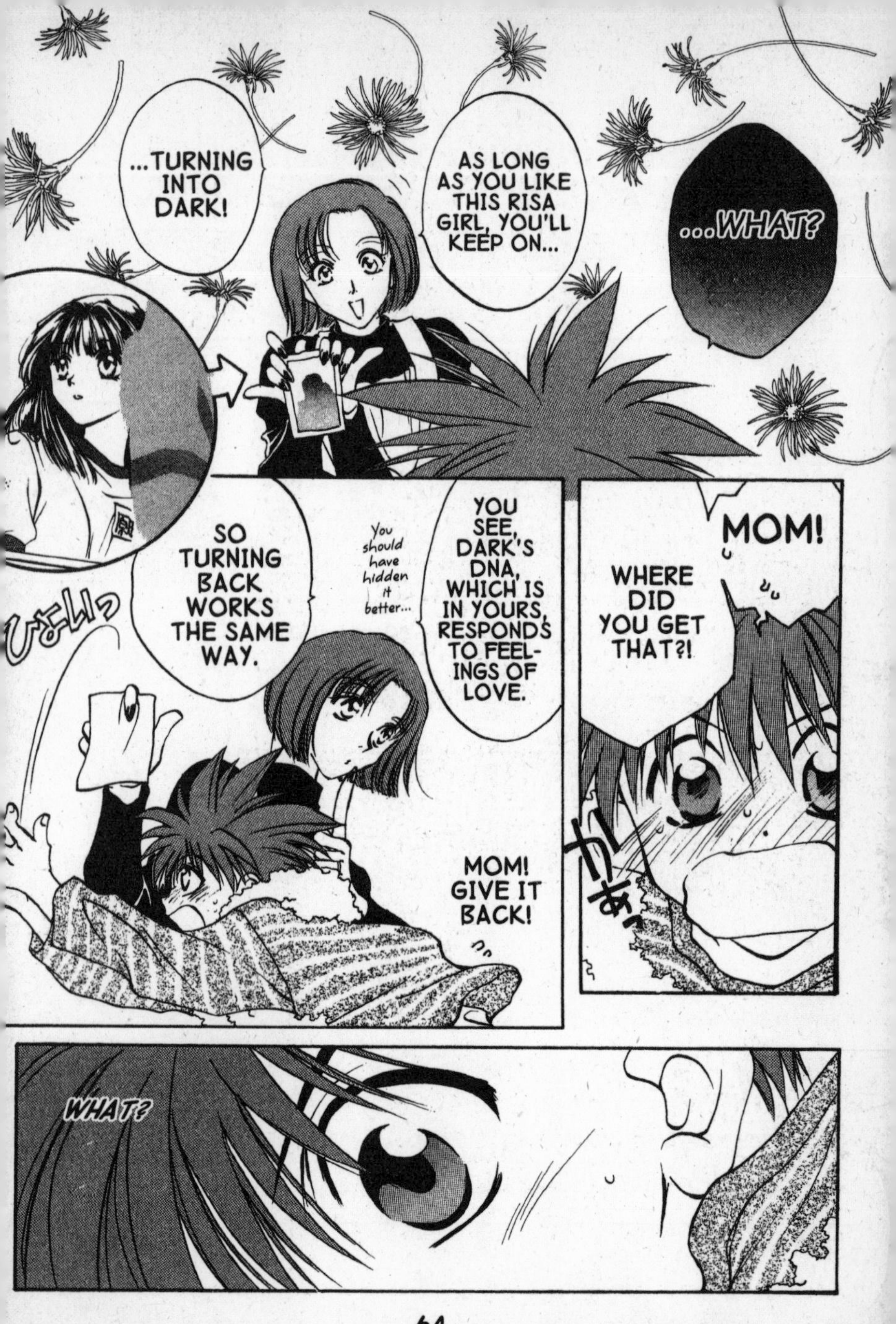
...WHAT?
AS LONG AS YOU LIKE THIS RISA GIRL, YOU'LL KEEP ON...
...TURNING INTO DARK!
MOM!
WHERE DID YOU GET THAT?!
YOU SEE, DARK'S DNA, WHICH IS IN YOURS, RESPONDS TO FEELINGS OF LOVE.
You should have hidden it better...
SO TURNING BACK WORKS THE SAME WAY.
MOM! GIVE IT BACK!
WHAT?

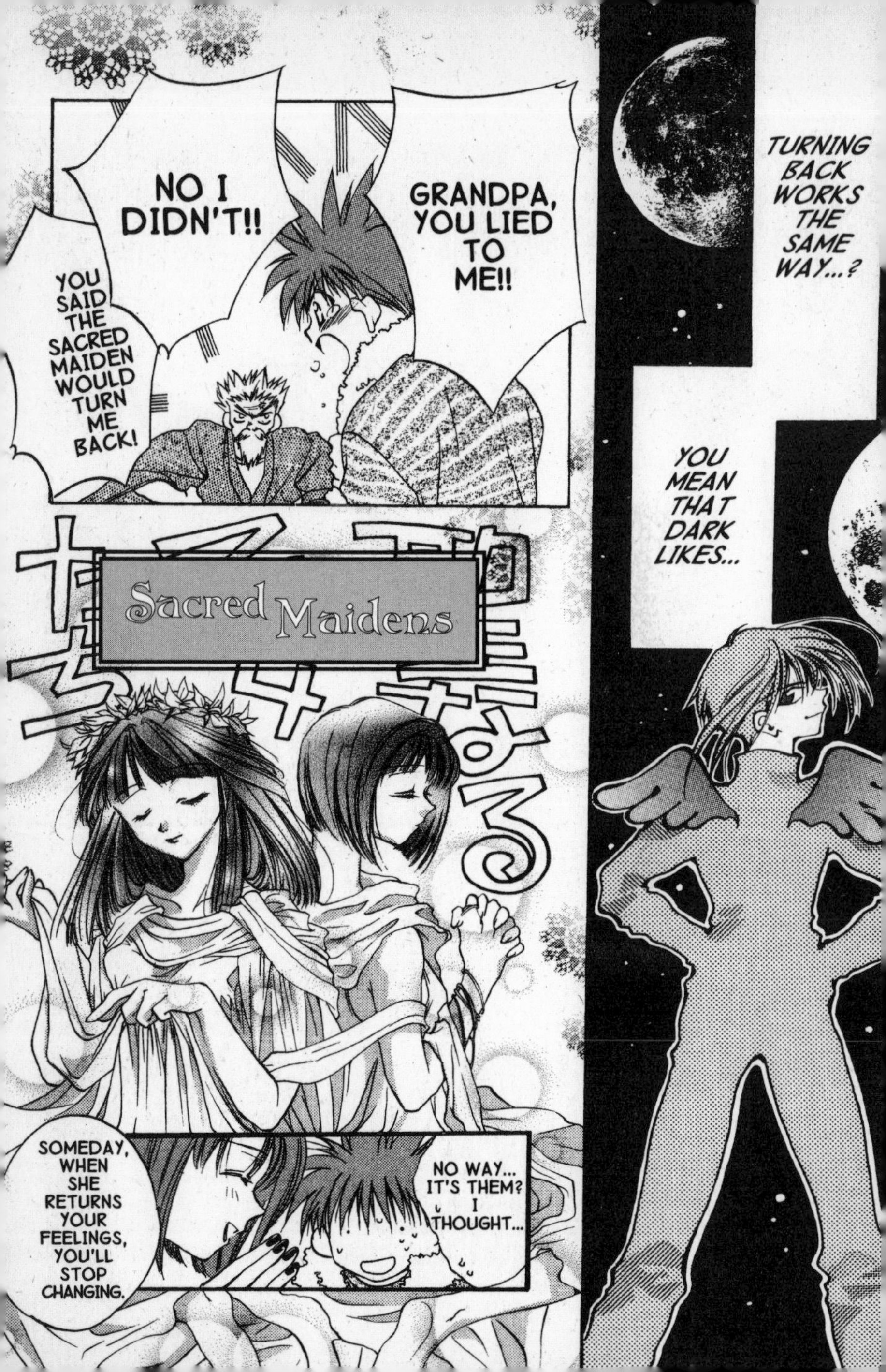
TURNING BACK WORKS THE SAME WAY...?
YOU MEAN THAT DARK LIKES...
GRANDPA, YOU LIED TO ME!!
NO I DIDN'T!!
YOU SAID THE SACRED MAIDEN WOULD TURN ME BACK!
Sacred Maidens
NO WAY... IT'S THEM? I THOUGHT...
SOMEDAY, WHEN SHE RETURNS YOUR FEELINGS, YOU'LL STOP CHANGING.

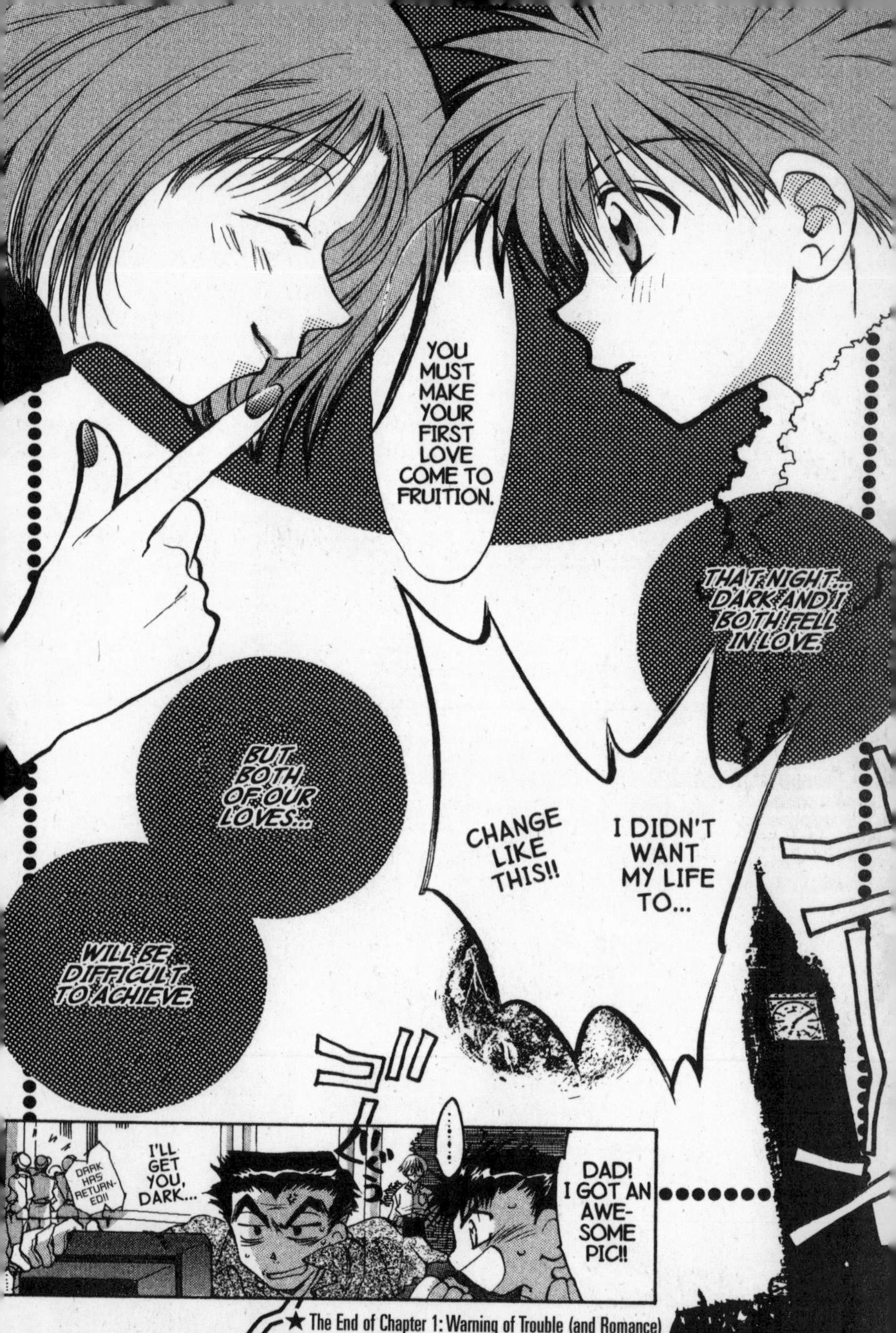
YOU MUST MAKE YOUR FIRST LOVE COME TO FRUITION.
THAT NIGHT... DARK AND I BOTH FELL IN LOVE.
I DIDN'T WANT MY LIFE TO...
CHANGE LIKE THIS!!
BUT BOTH OF OUR LOVES...
WILL BE DIFFICULT TO ACHIEVE.
DAD! I GOT AN AWE-SOME PIC!!
...!
I'LL GET YOU, DARK...
DARK HAS RETURN-ED!!

★The End of Chapter 1: Warning of Trouble (and Romance)

# 2

## Chapter 2: Warning of a Level Up (and Illusions)

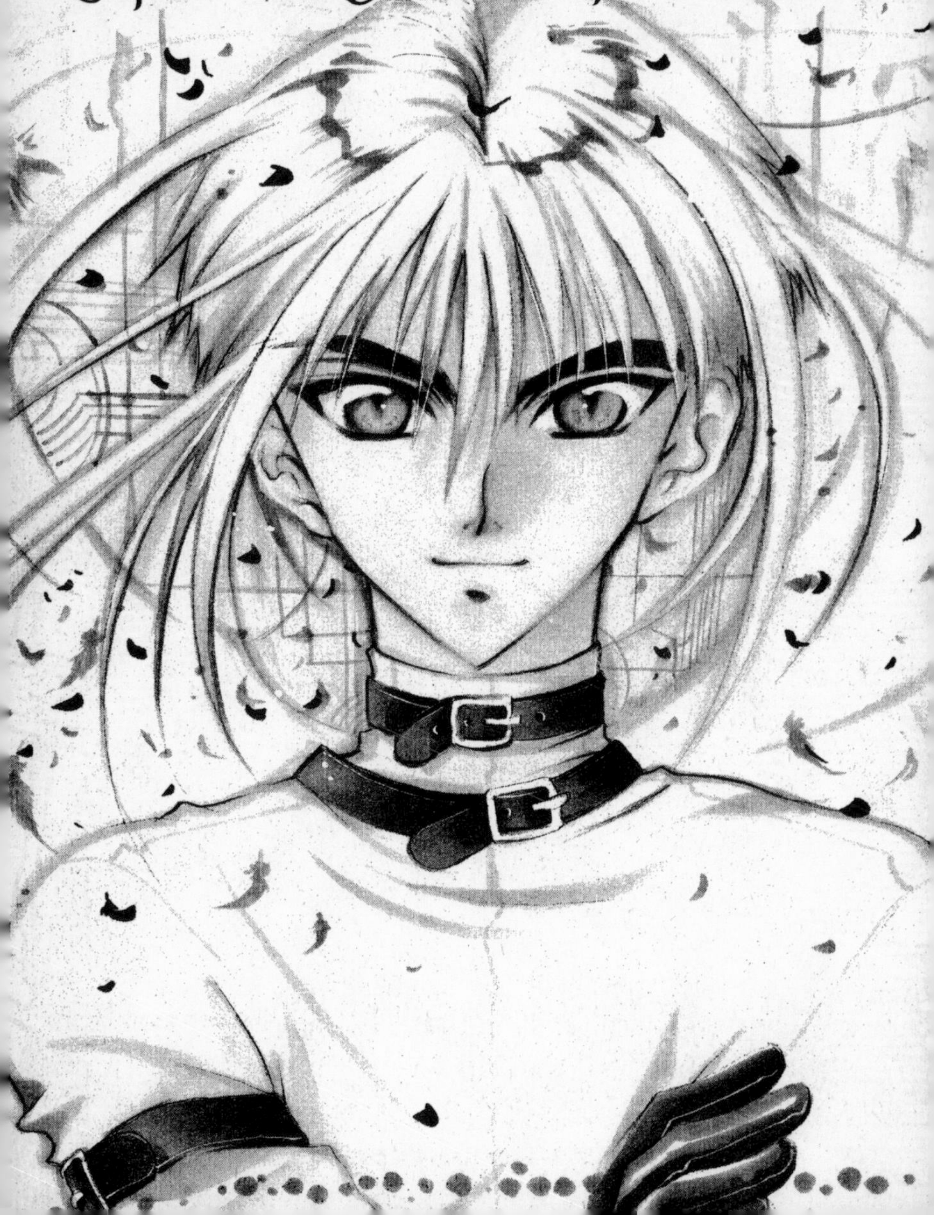

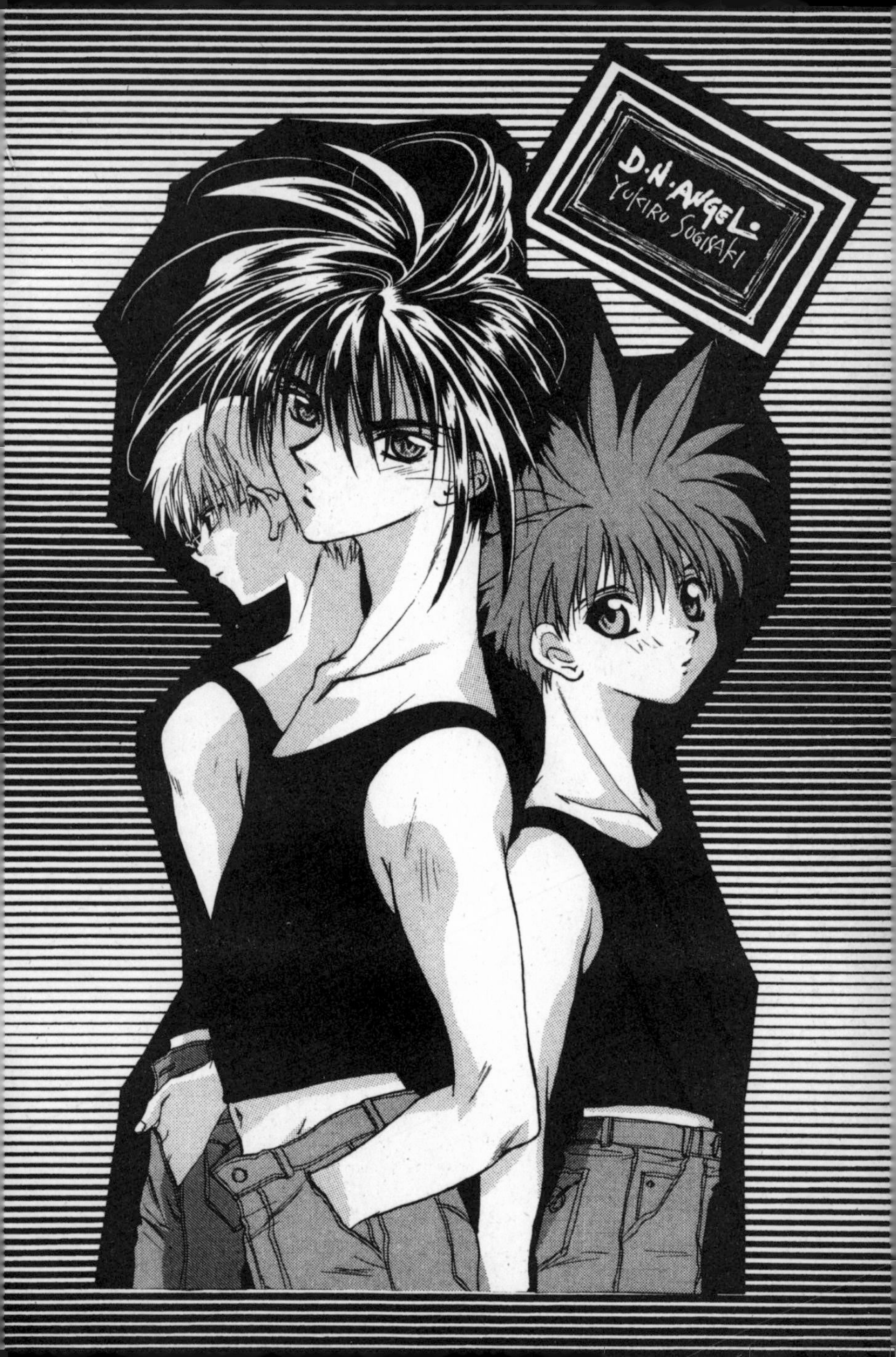
D·N·ANGEL·
YUKIRU SUGISAKI

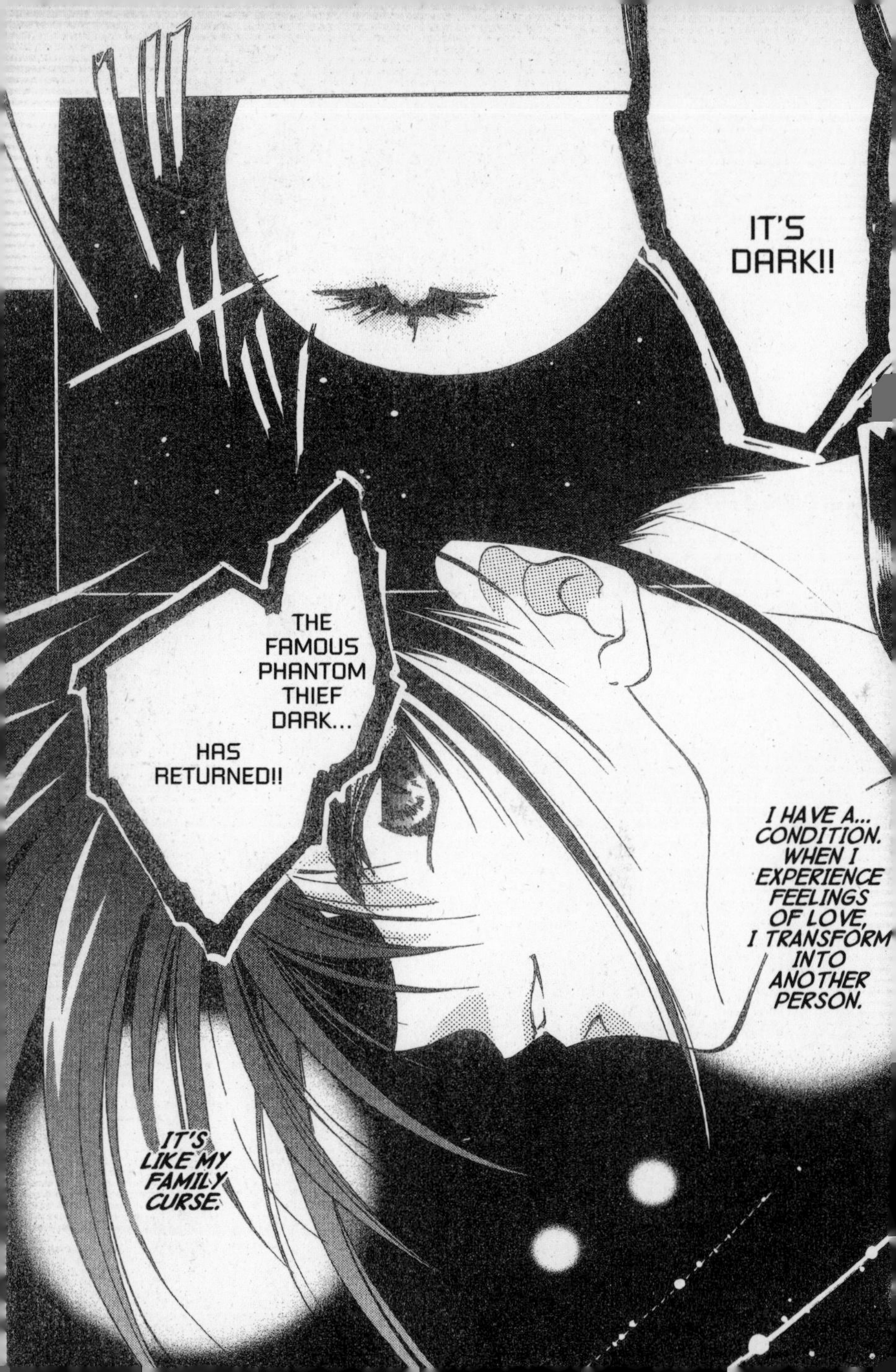
IT'S DARK!!
THE FAMOUS PHANTOM THIEF DARK...
HAS RETURNED!!
I HAVE A... CONDITION. WHEN I EXPERIENCE FEELINGS OF LOVE, I TRANSFORM INTO ANOTHER PERSON.
IT'S LIKE MY FAMILY CURSE.

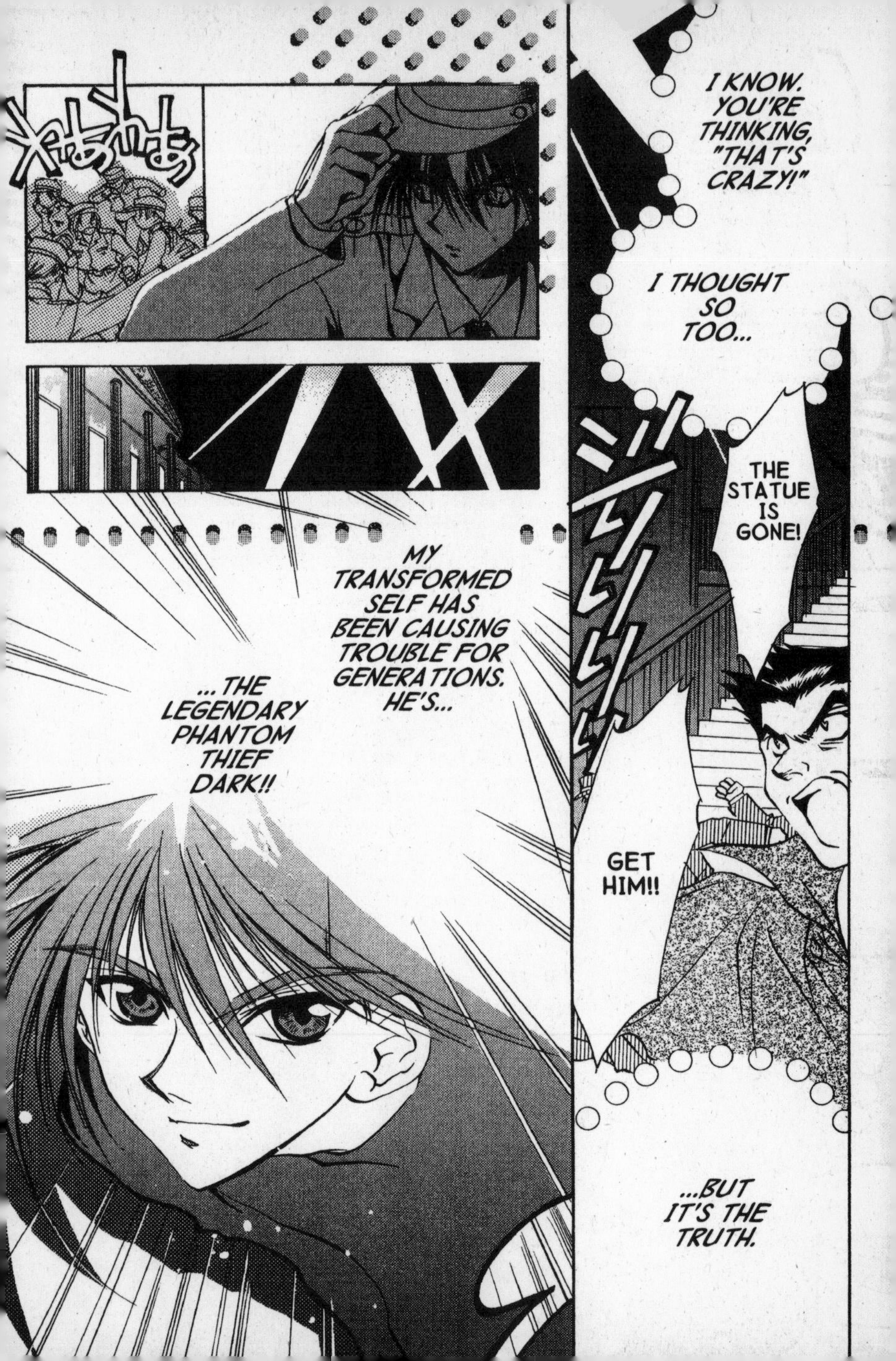
I KNOW. YOU'RE THINKING, "THAT'S CRAZY!"
I THOUGHT SO TOO...
THE STATUE IS GONE!
GET HIM!!
...BUT IT'S THE TRUTH.
MY TRANSFORMED SELF HAS BEEN CAUSING TROUBLE FOR GENERATIONS. HE'S...
...THE LEGENDARY PHANTOM THIEF DARK!!

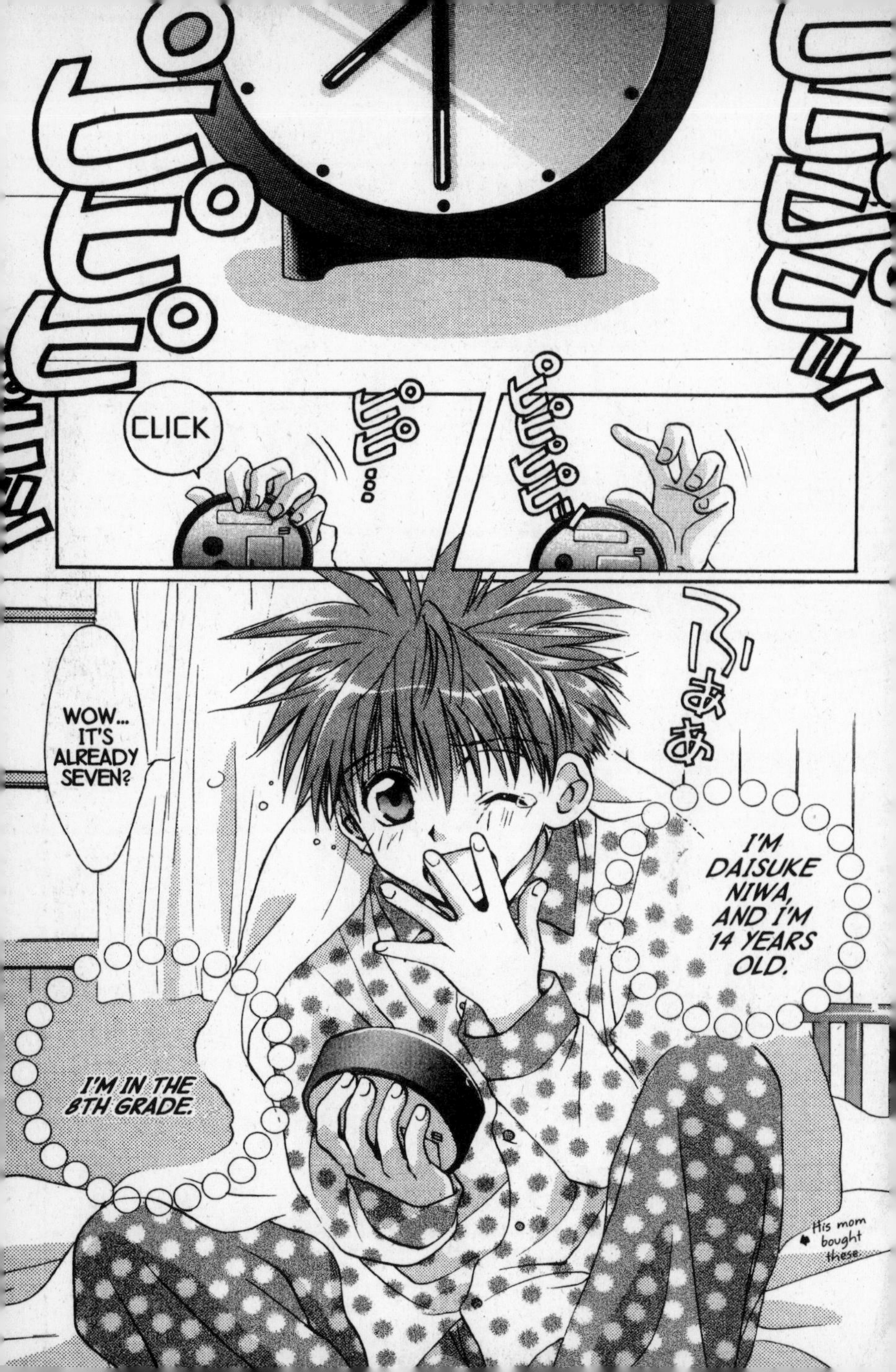
CLICK
I'M DAISUKE NIWA, AND I'M 14 YEARS OLD.
WOW... IT'S ALREADY SEVEN?
I'M IN THE 8TH GRADE.
His mom bought these.

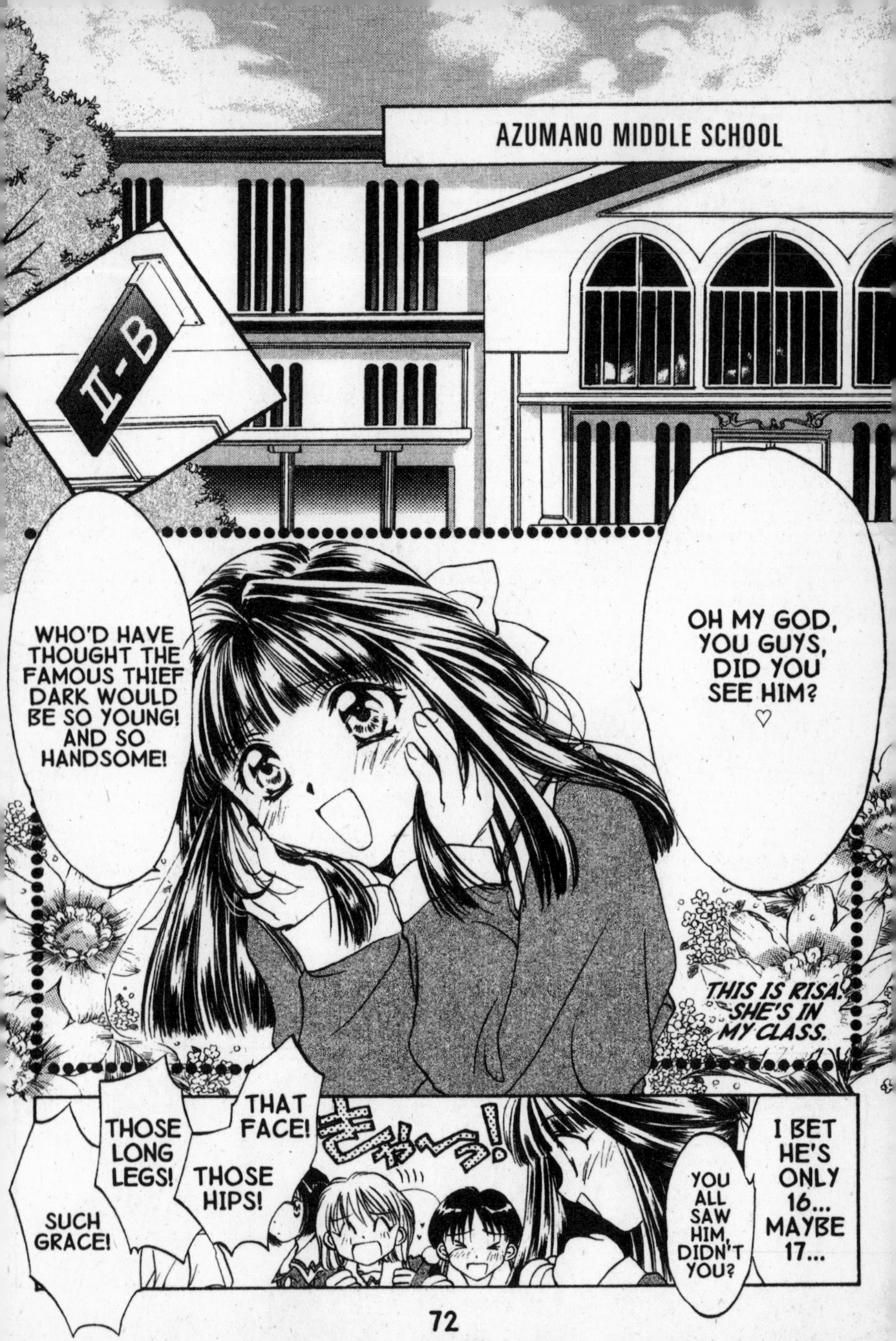
AZUMANO MIDDLE SCHOOL
II-B
OH MY GOD, YOU GUYS, DID YOU SEE HIM? ♡
WHO'D HAVE THOUGHT THE FAMOUS THIEF DARK WOULD BE SO YOUNG! AND SO HANDSOME!
THIS IS RISA. SHE'S IN MY CLASS.
I BET HE'S ONLY 16... MAYBE 17...
YOU ALL SAW HIM, DIDN'T YOU?
THAT FACE!
THOSE HIPS!
THOSE LONG LEGS!
SUCH GRACE!

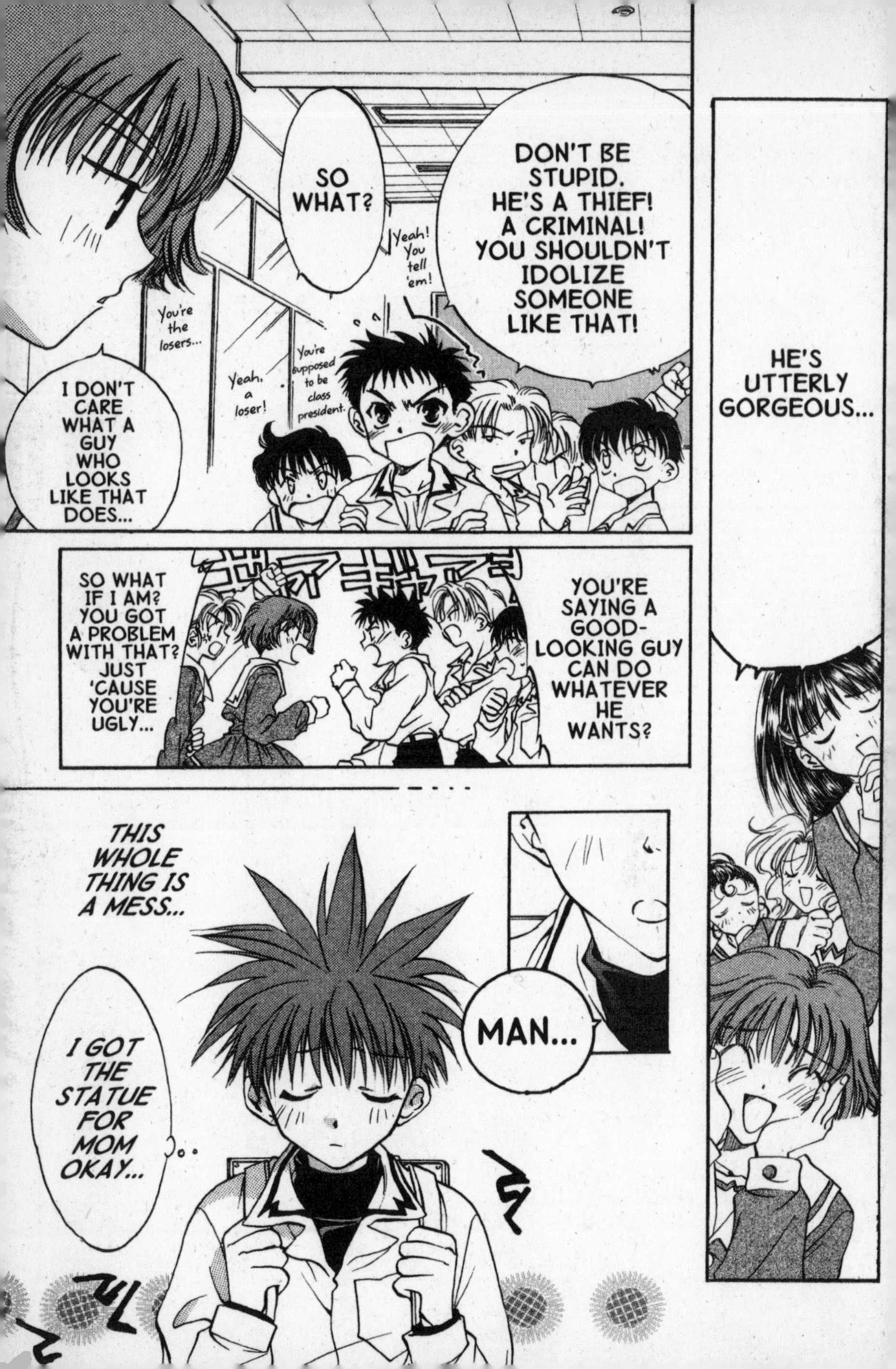
HE'S UTTERLY GORGEOUS...
DON'T BE STUPID. HE'S A THIEF! A CRIMINAL! YOU SHOULDN'T IDOLIZE SOMEONE LIKE THAT!
SO WHAT?
Yeah! You tell 'em!
You're supposed to be class president.
Yeah, a loser!
You're the losers...
I DON'T CARE WHAT A GUY WHO LOOKS LIKE THAT DOES...
YOU'RE SAYING A GOOD-LOOKING GUY CAN DO WHATEVER HE WANTS?
SO WHAT IF I AM? YOU GOT A PROBLEM WITH THAT? JUST 'CAUSE YOU'RE UGLY...
MAN...
THIS WHOLE THING IS A MESS...
I GOT THE STATUE FOR MOM OKAY...

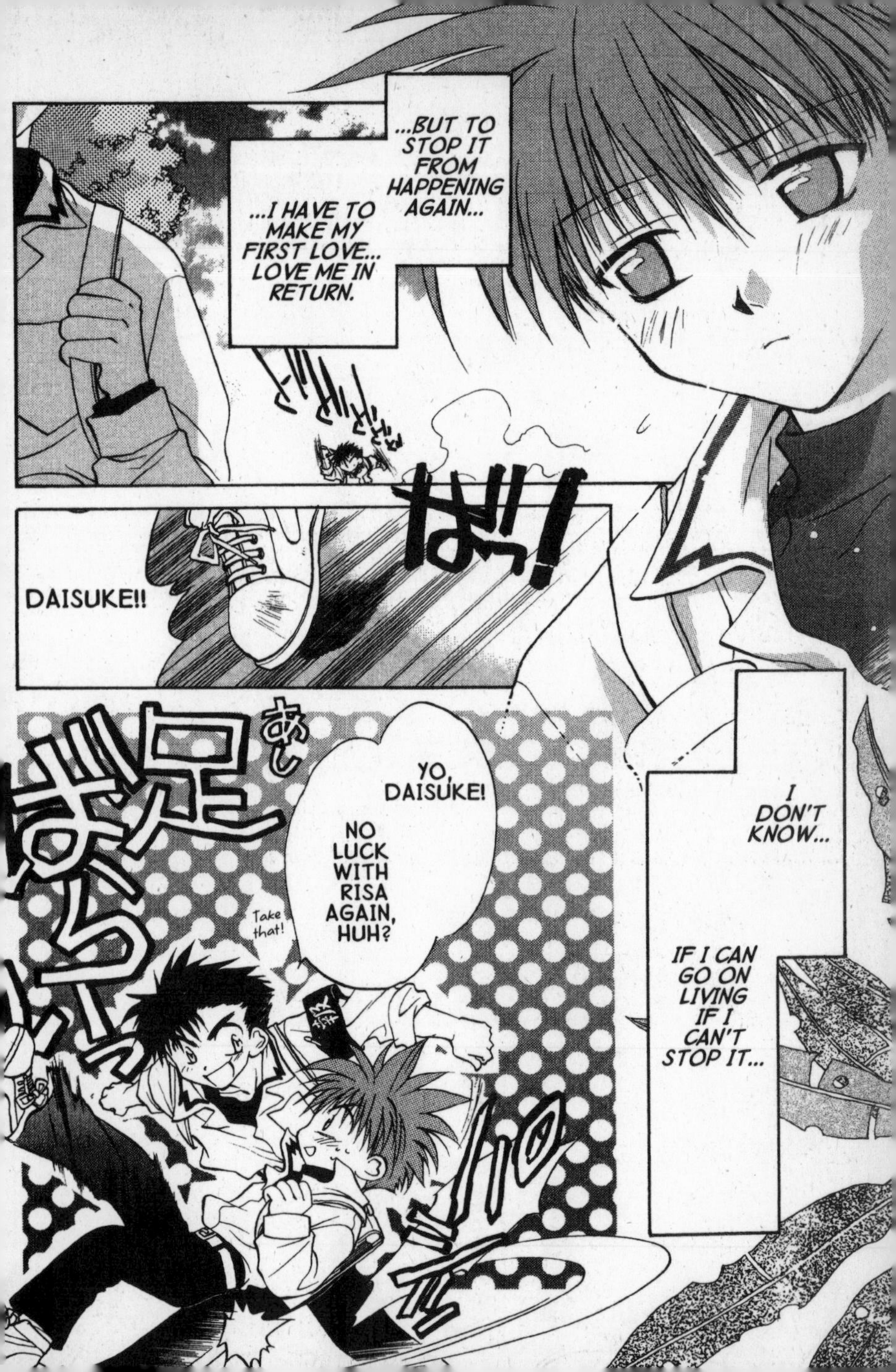
...BUT TO STOP IT FROM HAPPENING AGAIN...
...I HAVE TO MAKE MY FIRST LOVE... LOVE ME IN RETURN.
DAISUKE!!
I DON'T KNOW...
IF I CAN GO ON LIVING IF I CAN'T STOP IT...
YO, DAISUKE!
NO LUCK WITH RISA AGAIN, HUH?
Take that!

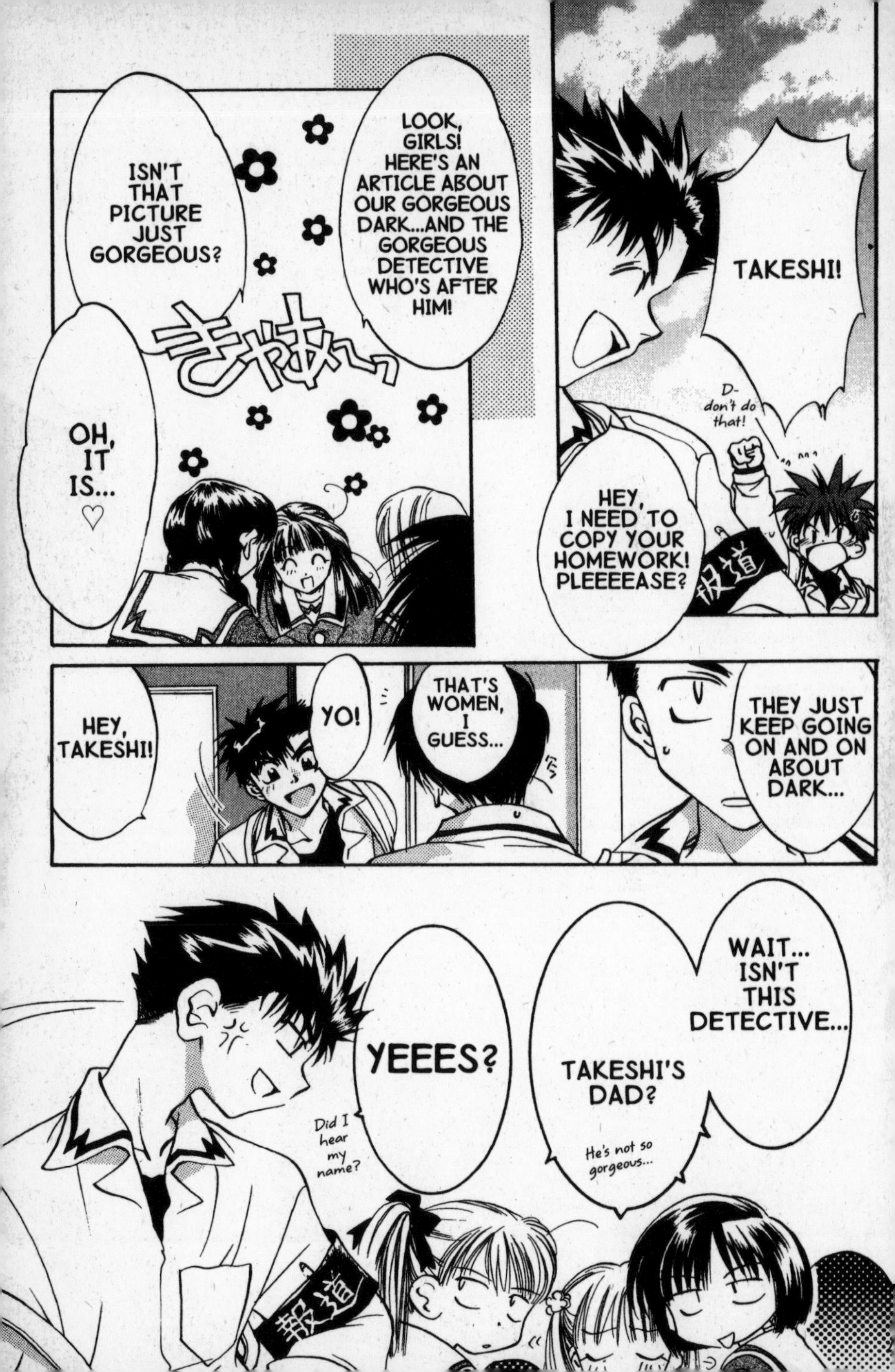
TAKESHI!
D-don't do that!
HEY, I NEED TO COPY YOUR HOMEWORK! PLEEEEASE?
LOOK, GIRLS! HERE'S AN ARTICLE ABOUT OUR GORGEOUS DARK...AND THE GORGEOUS DETECTIVE WHO'S AFTER HIM!
ISN'T THAT PICTURE JUST GORGEOUS?
きゃあ〜っ
OH, IT IS... ♡
THEY JUST KEEP GOING ON AND ON ABOUT DARK...
THAT'S WOMEN, I GUESS...
YO!
HEY, TAKESHI!
WAIT... ISN'T THIS DETECTIVE...
TAKESHI'S DAD?
He's not so gorgeous...
YEEES?
Did I hear my name?

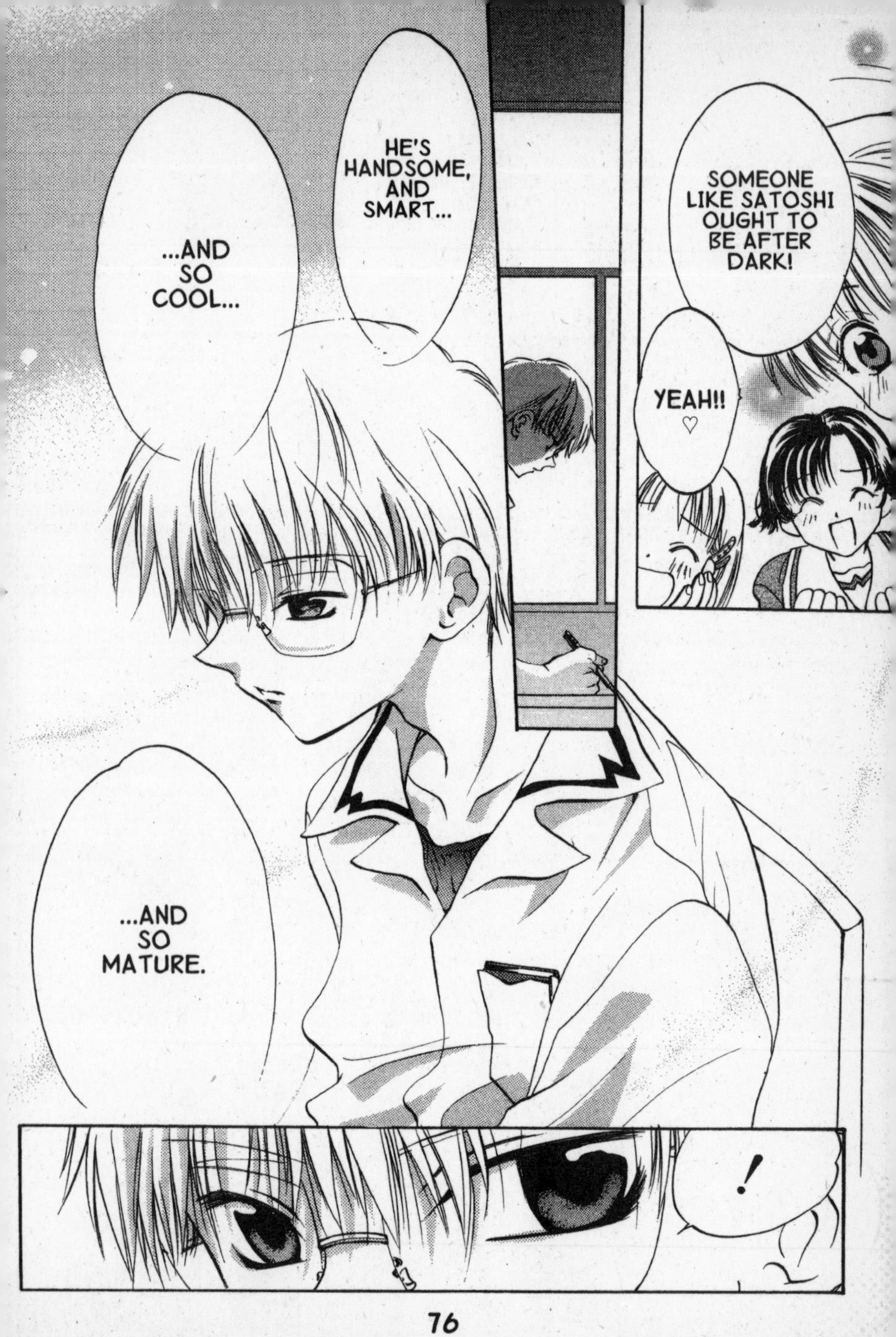

SOMEONE LIKE SATOSHI OUGHT TO BE AFTER DARK!
YEAH!! ♡
HE'S HANDSOME, AND SMART...
...AND SO COOL...
...AND SO MATURE.
!

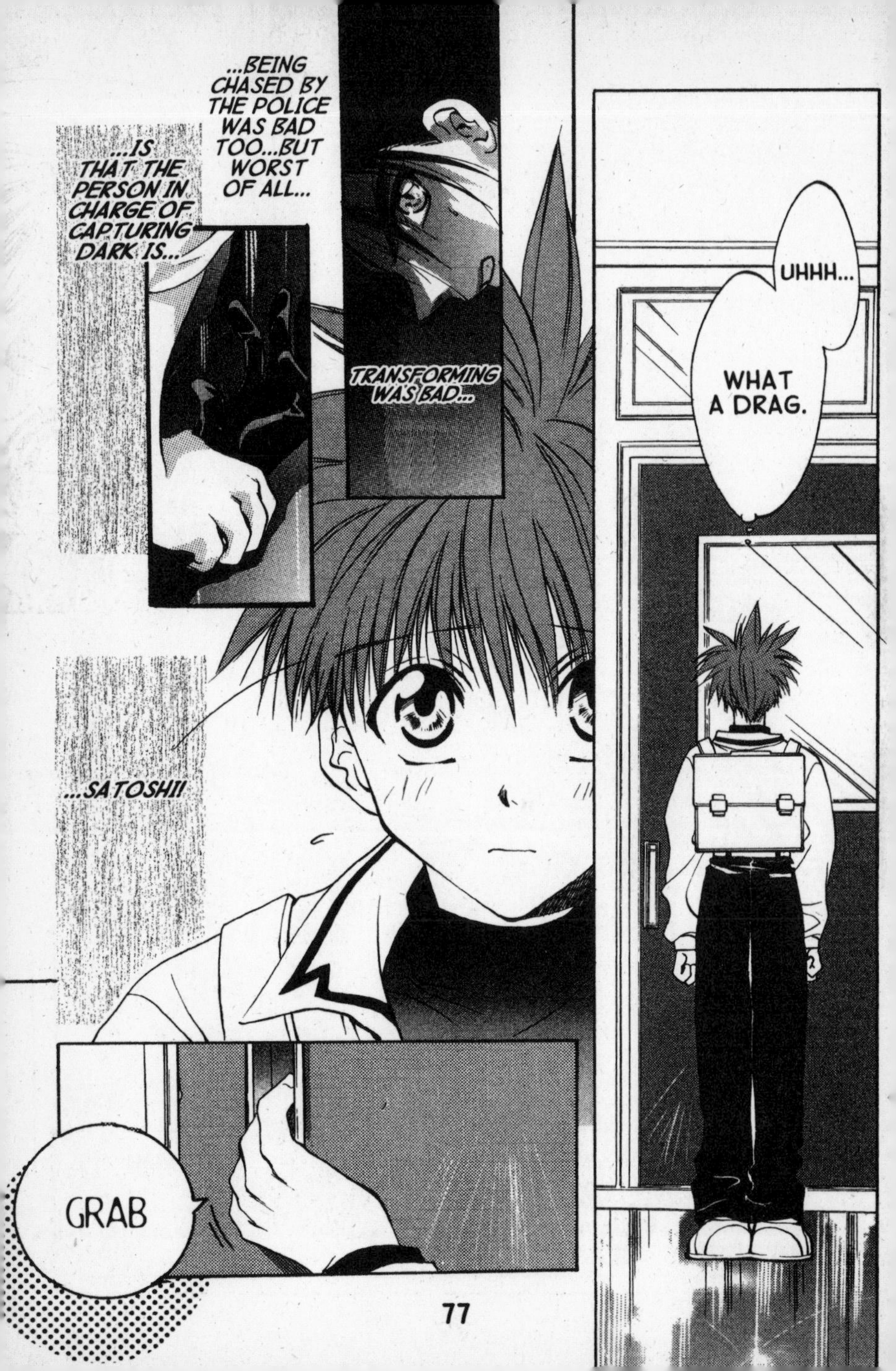
UHHH...
WHAT A DRAG.
TRANSFORMING WAS BAD...
...BEING CHASED BY THE POLICE WAS BAD TOO...BUT WORST OF ALL...
...IS THAT THE PERSON IN CHARGE OF CAPTURING DARK IS...
...SATOSHI!!
GRAB

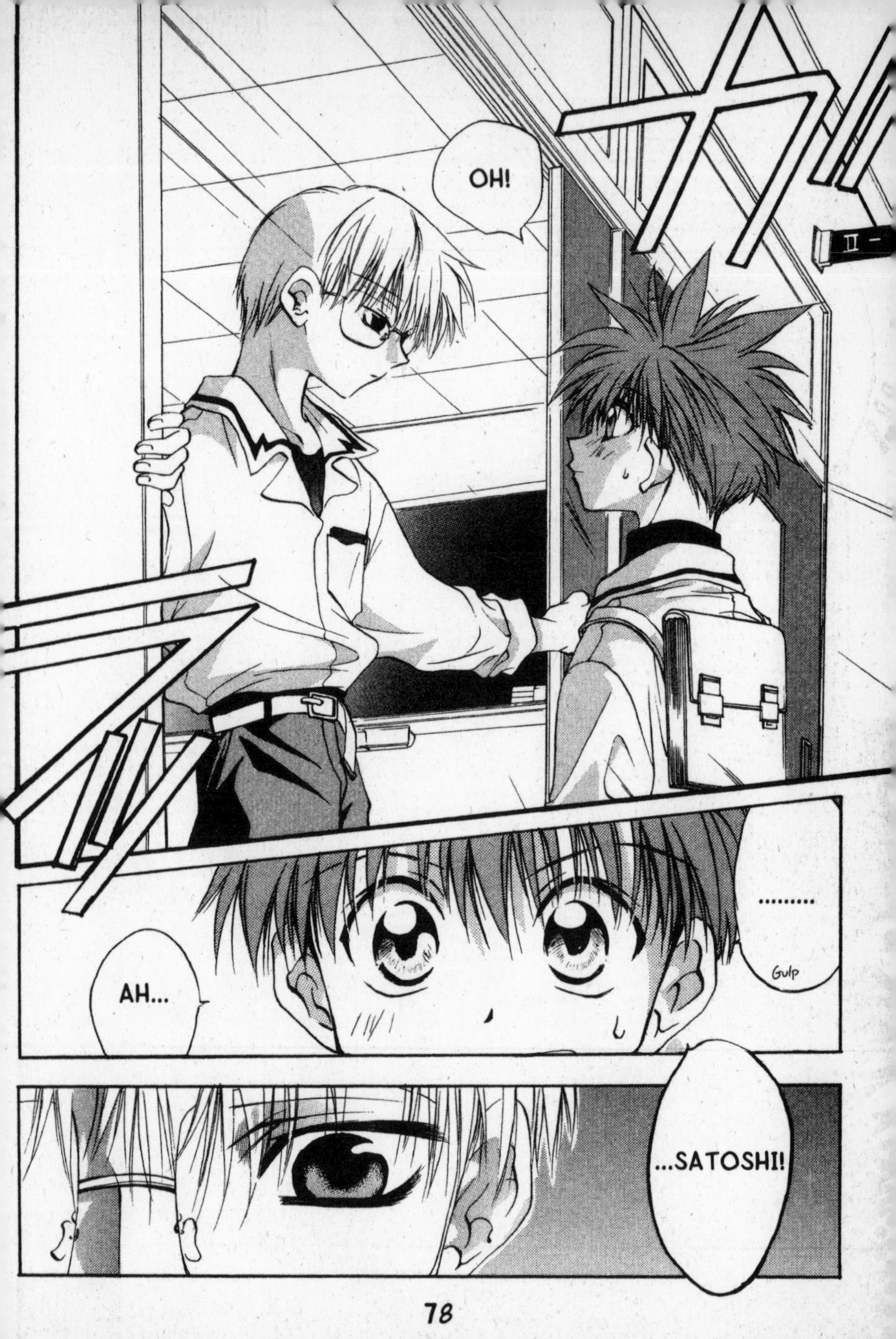
OH!
.........
Gulp
AH...
...SATOSHI!

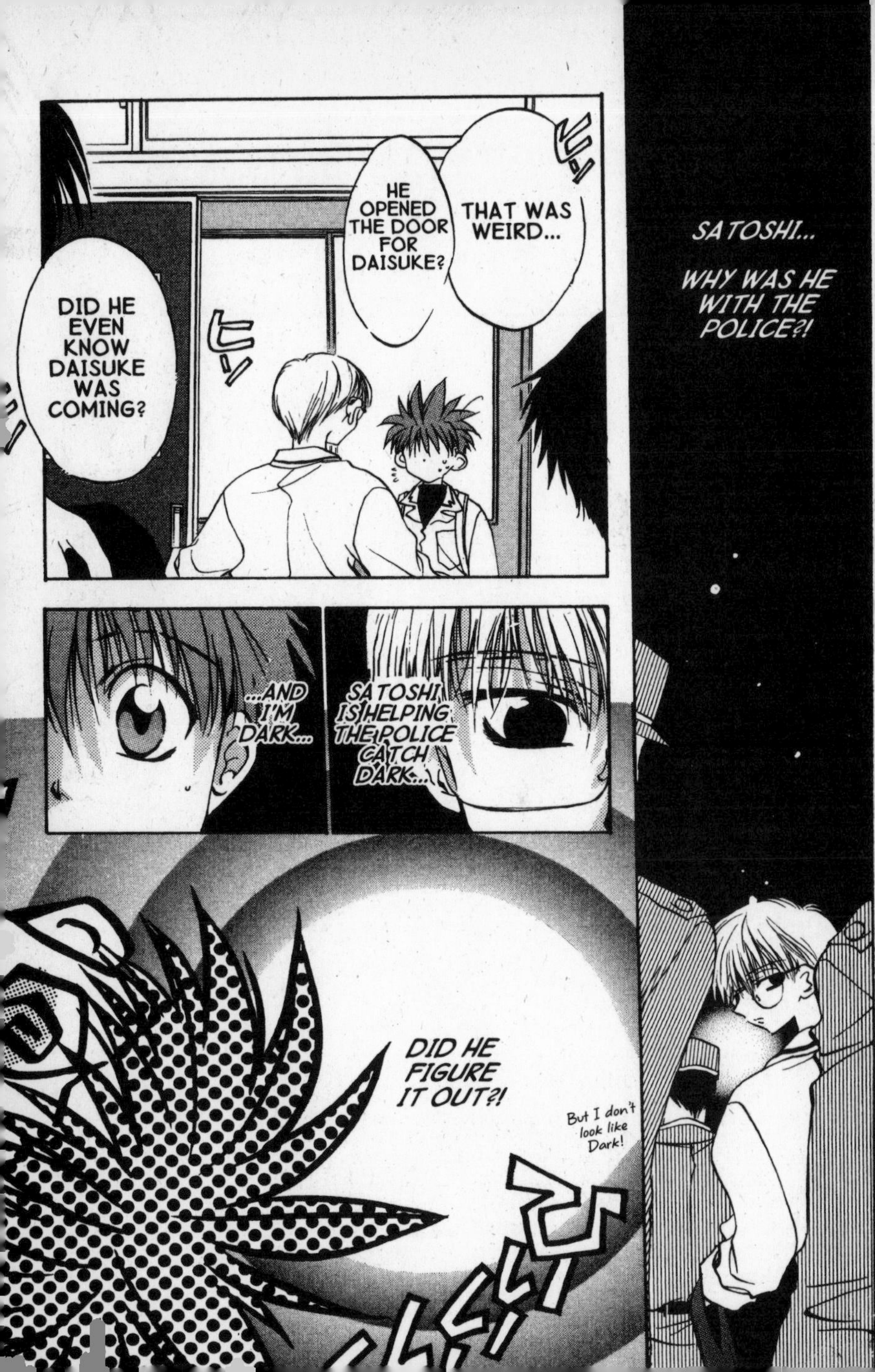
SATOSHI...
WHY WAS HE WITH THE POLICE?!
THAT WAS WEIRD...
HE OPENED THE DOOR FOR DAISUKE?
DID HE EVEN KNOW DAISUKE WAS COMING?
SATOSHI IS HELPING THE POLICE CATCH DARK...
...AND I'M DARK...
DID HE FIGURE IT OUT?!
But I don't look like Dark!

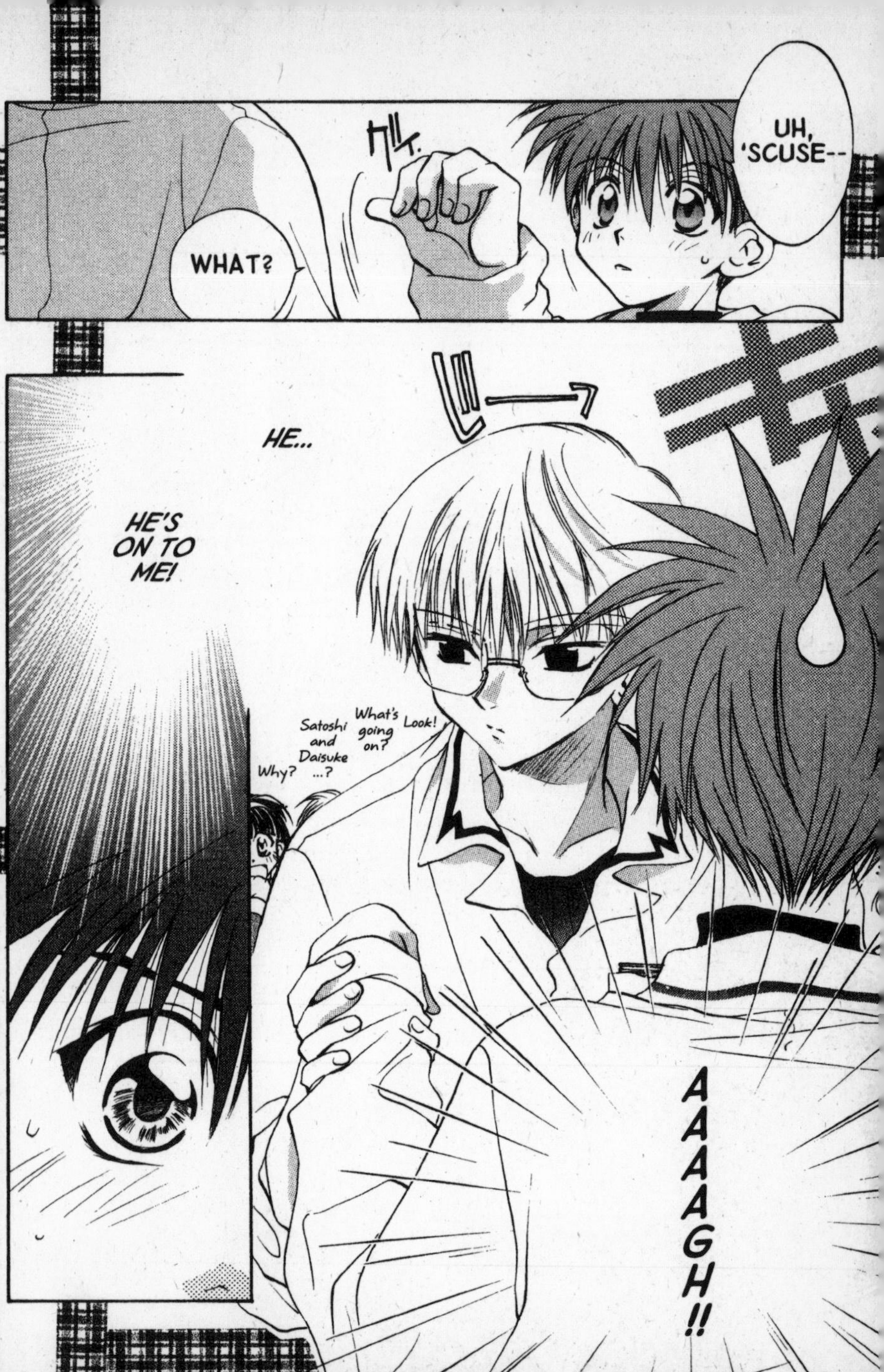
UH, 'SCUSE--
WHAT?
Look!
What's going on?
Satoshi and Daisuke ...?
Why?
AAAAGH!!
HE...
HE'S ON TO ME!

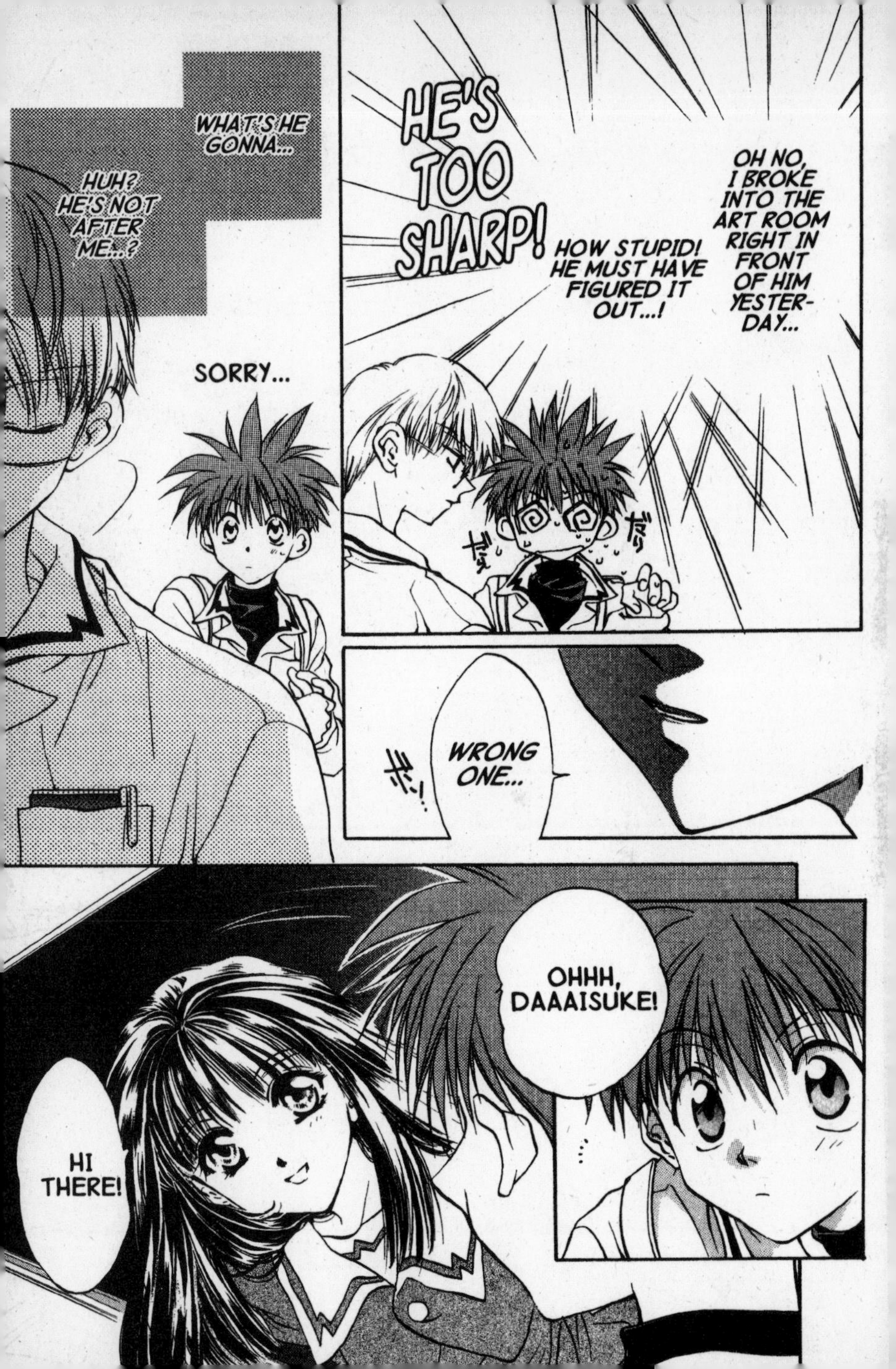
OH NO, I BROKE INTO THE ART ROOM RIGHT IN FRONT OF HIM YESTER-DAY...
HOW STUPID! HE MUST HAVE FIGURED IT OUT...!
HE'S TOO SHARP!
WRONG ONE...
WHAT'S HE GONNA...
HUH? HE'S NOT AFTER ME...?
SORRY...
OHHH, DAAAISUKE!
...
HI THERE!

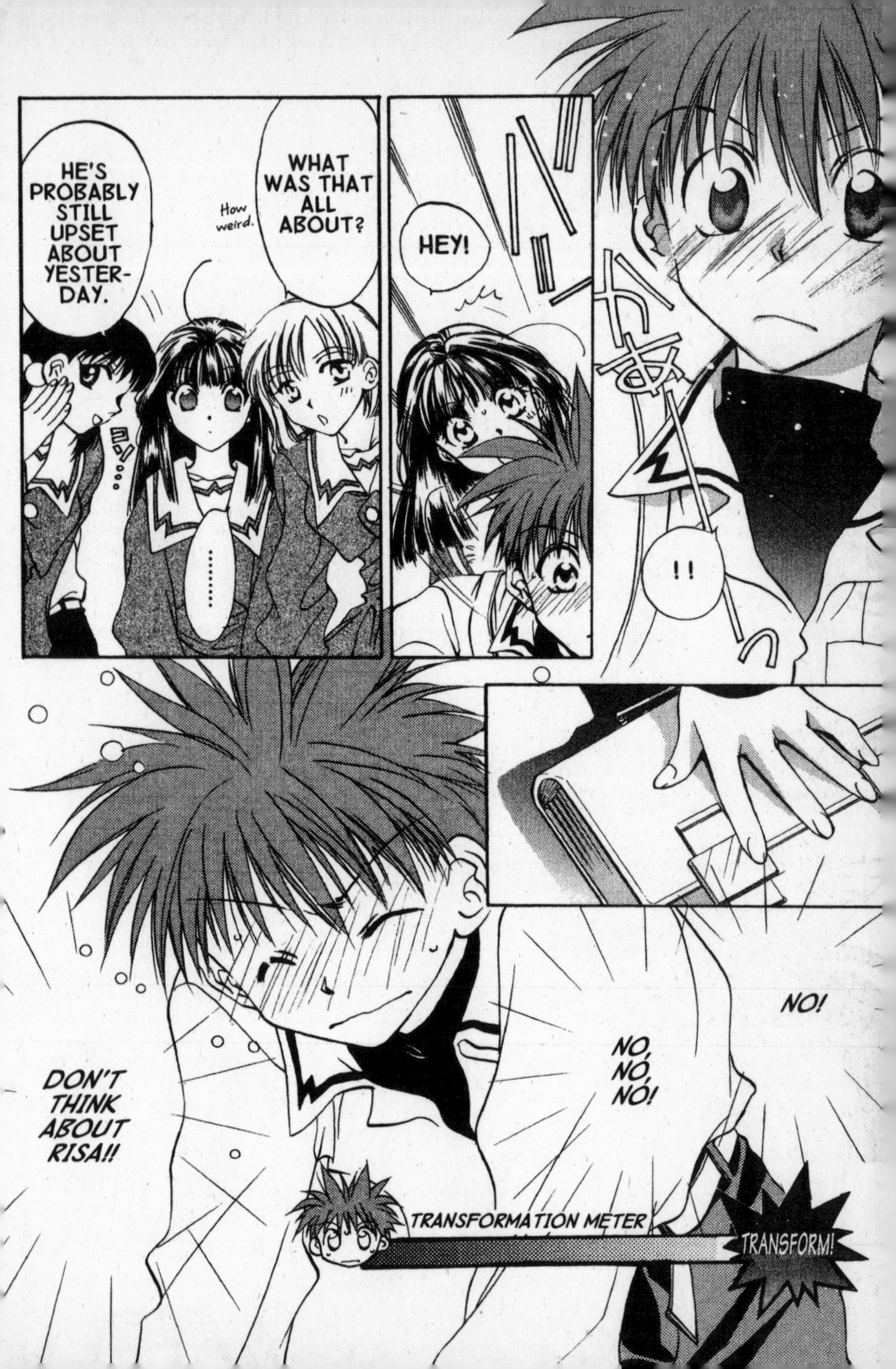
!!
HEY!
WHAT WAS THAT ALL ABOUT?
How weird.
HE'S PROBABLY STILL UPSET ABOUT YESTERDAY.
.........
NO!
NO, NO, NO!
DON'T THINK ABOUT RISA!!
TRANSFORMATION METER
TRANSFORM!

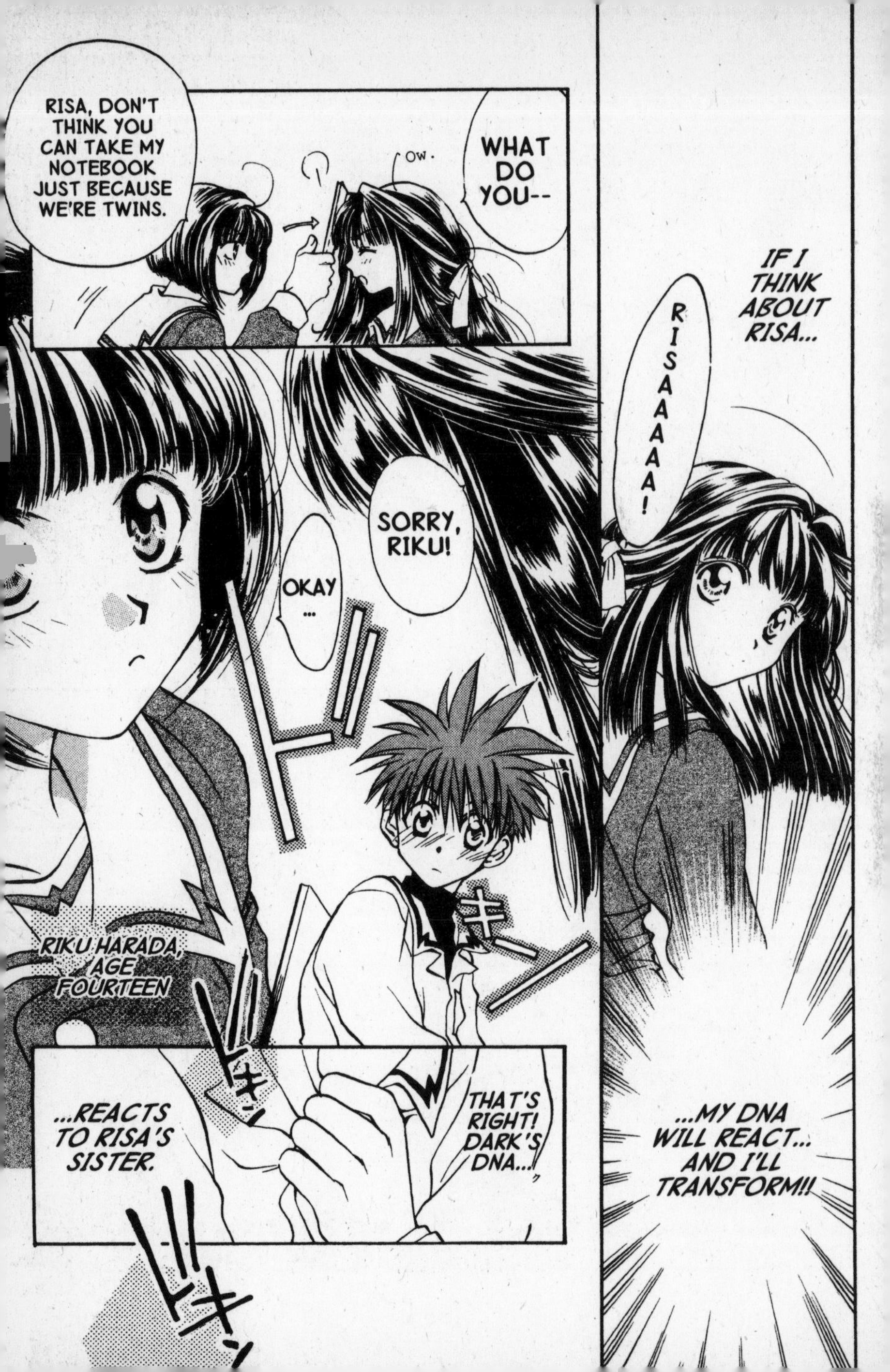
IF I THINK ABOUT RISA...
RISAAAAAA!
...MY DNA WILL REACT... AND I'LL TRANSFORM!!
WHAT DO YOU--
OW.
RISA, DON'T THINK YOU CAN TAKE MY NOTEBOOK JUST BECAUSE WE'RE TWINS.
SORRY, RIKU!
OKAY ...
RIKU HARADA, AGE FOURTEEN
THAT'S RIGHT! DARK'S DNA...
...REACTS TO RISA'S SISTER.

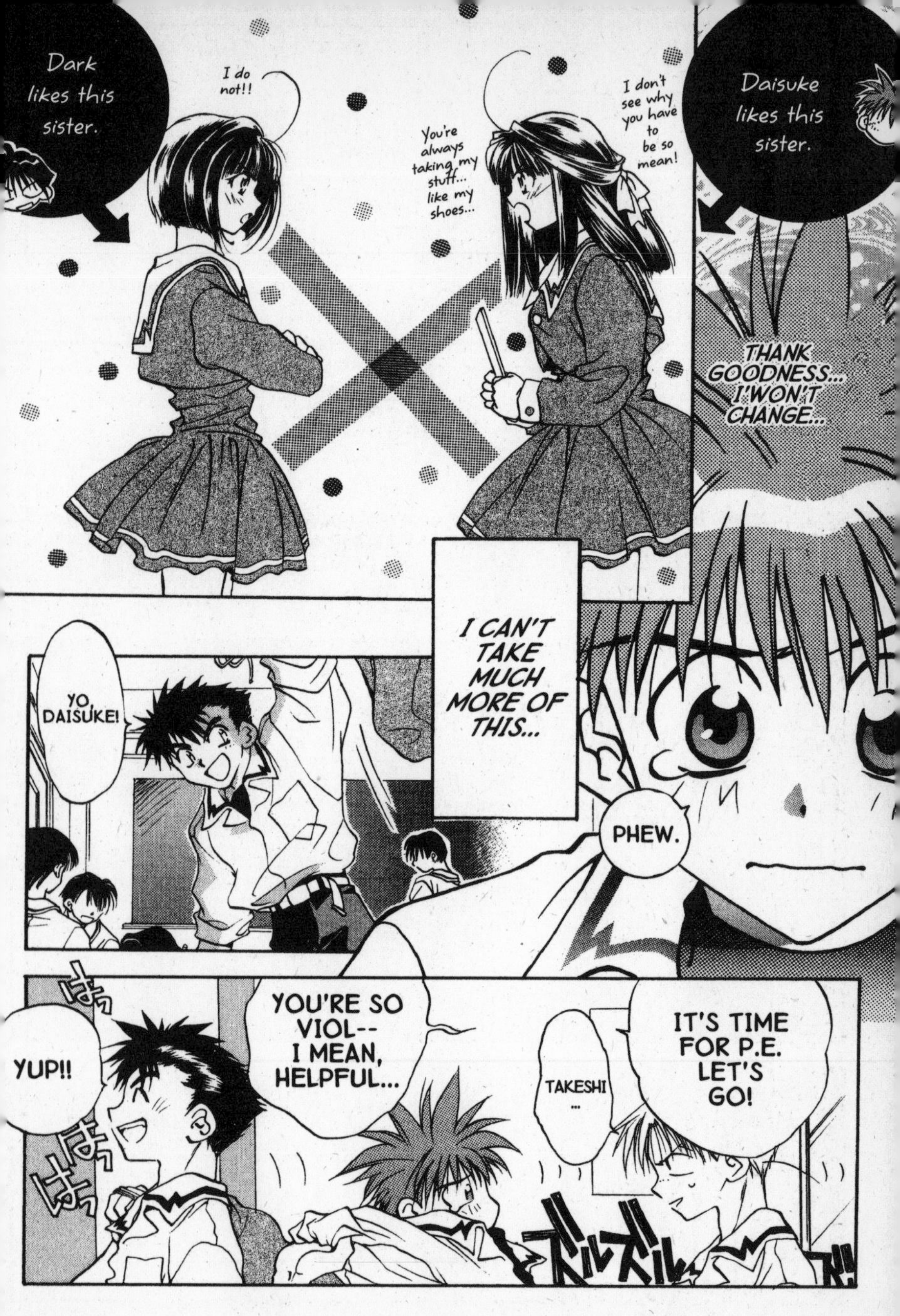
Daisuke likes this sister.
THANK GOODNESS... I WON'T CHANGE...
I CAN'T TAKE MUCH MORE OF THIS...
PHEW.
I don't see why you have to be so mean!
You're always taking my stuff... like my shoes...
I do not!!
Dark likes this sister.
YO, DAISUKE!
IT'S TIME FOR P.E. LET'S GO!
TAKESHI ...
YOU'RE SO VIOL-- I MEAN, HELPFUL...
YUP!!

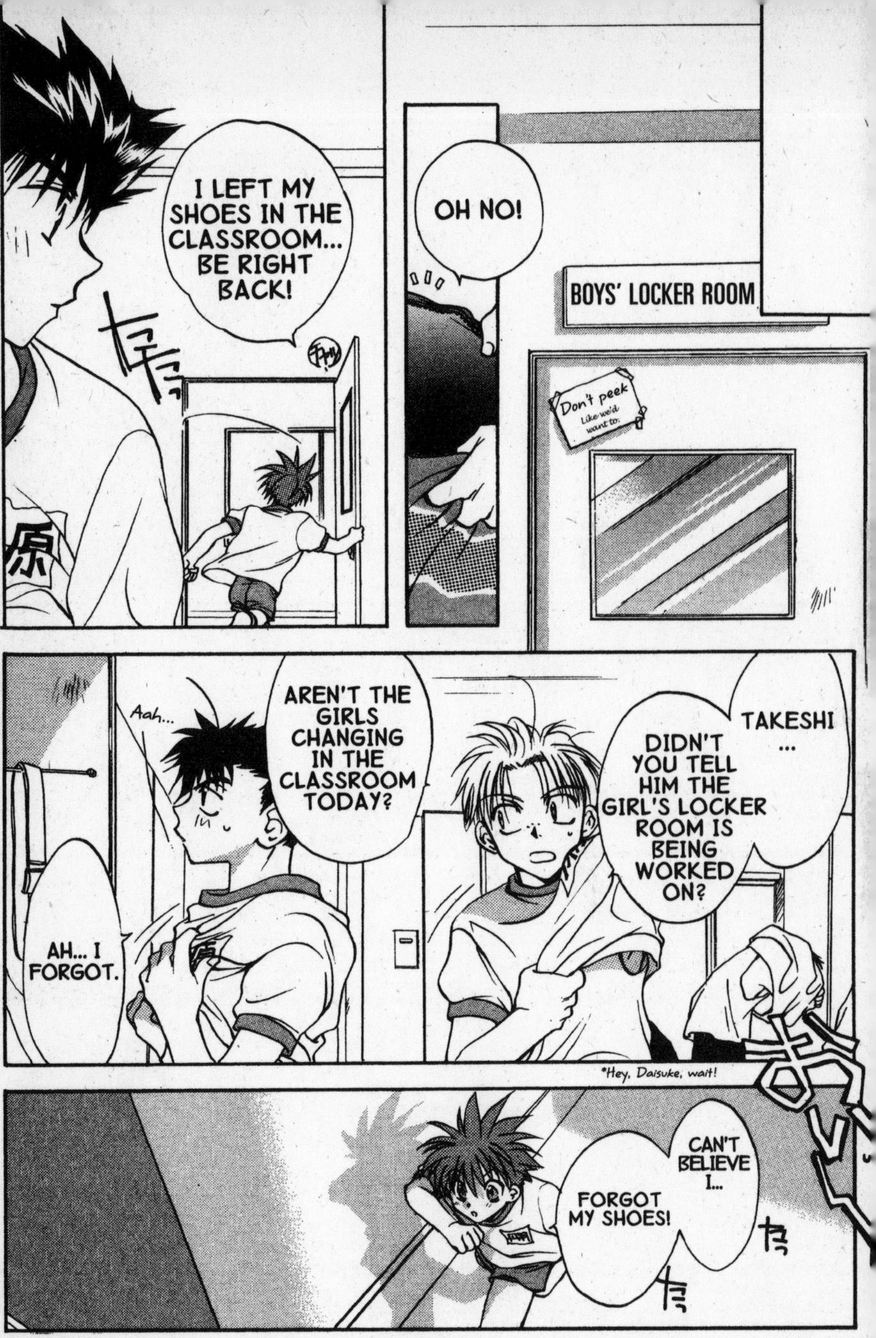
BOYS' LOCKER ROOM
Don't peek
Like we'd want to.
OH NO!
I LEFT MY SHOES IN THE CLASSROOM... BE RIGHT BACK!
TAKESHI ...
DIDN'T YOU TELL HIM THE GIRL'S LOCKER ROOM IS BEING WORKED ON?
AREN'T THE GIRLS CHANGING IN THE CLASSROOM TODAY?
Aah...
AH... I FORGOT.
*Hey, Daisuke, wait!
CAN'T BELIEVE I...
FORGOT MY SHOES!

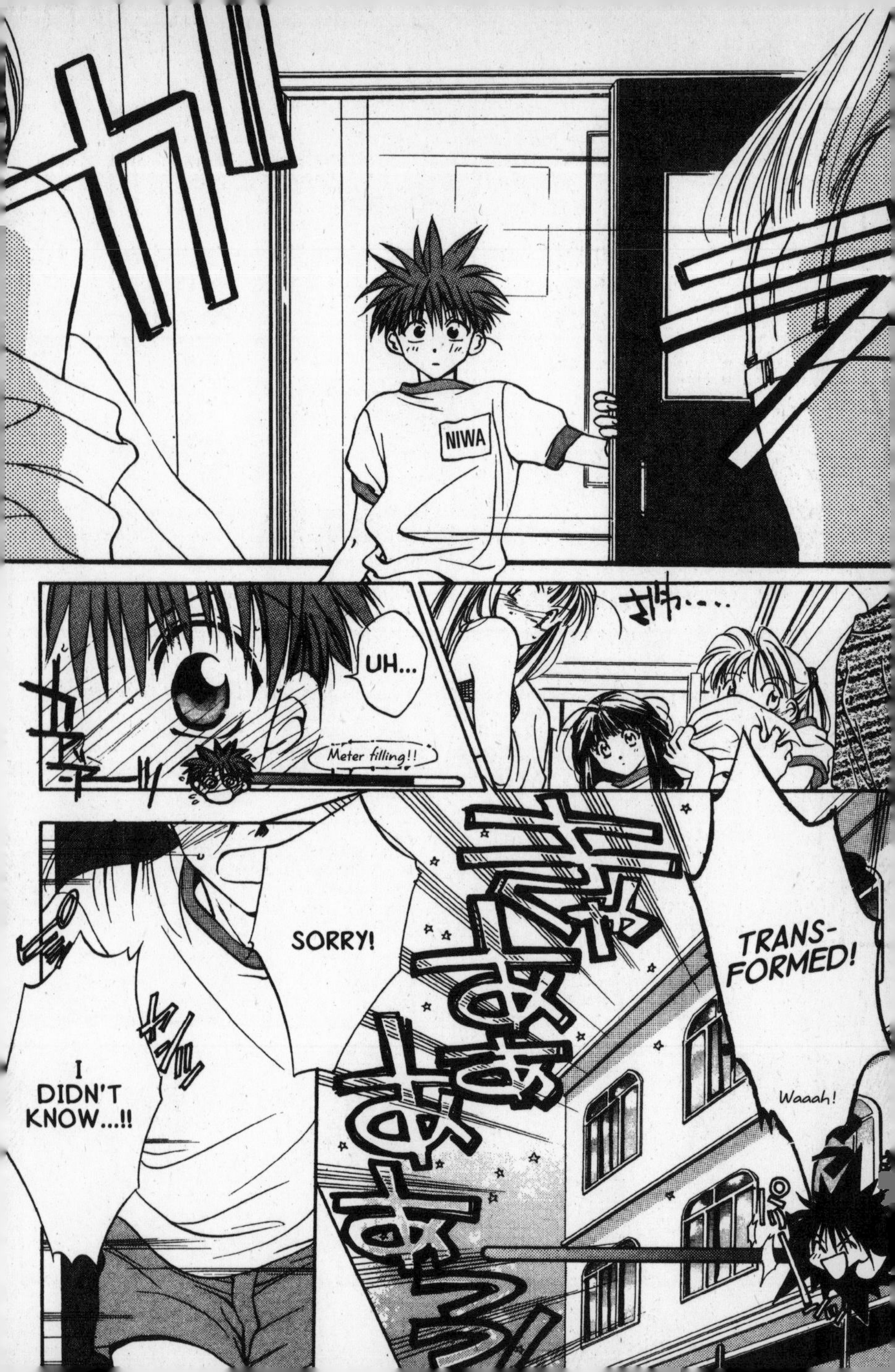
NIWA
UH...
Meter filling!!
TRANS-
FORMED!
Waaah!
SORRY!
I
DIDN'T
KNOW...!!

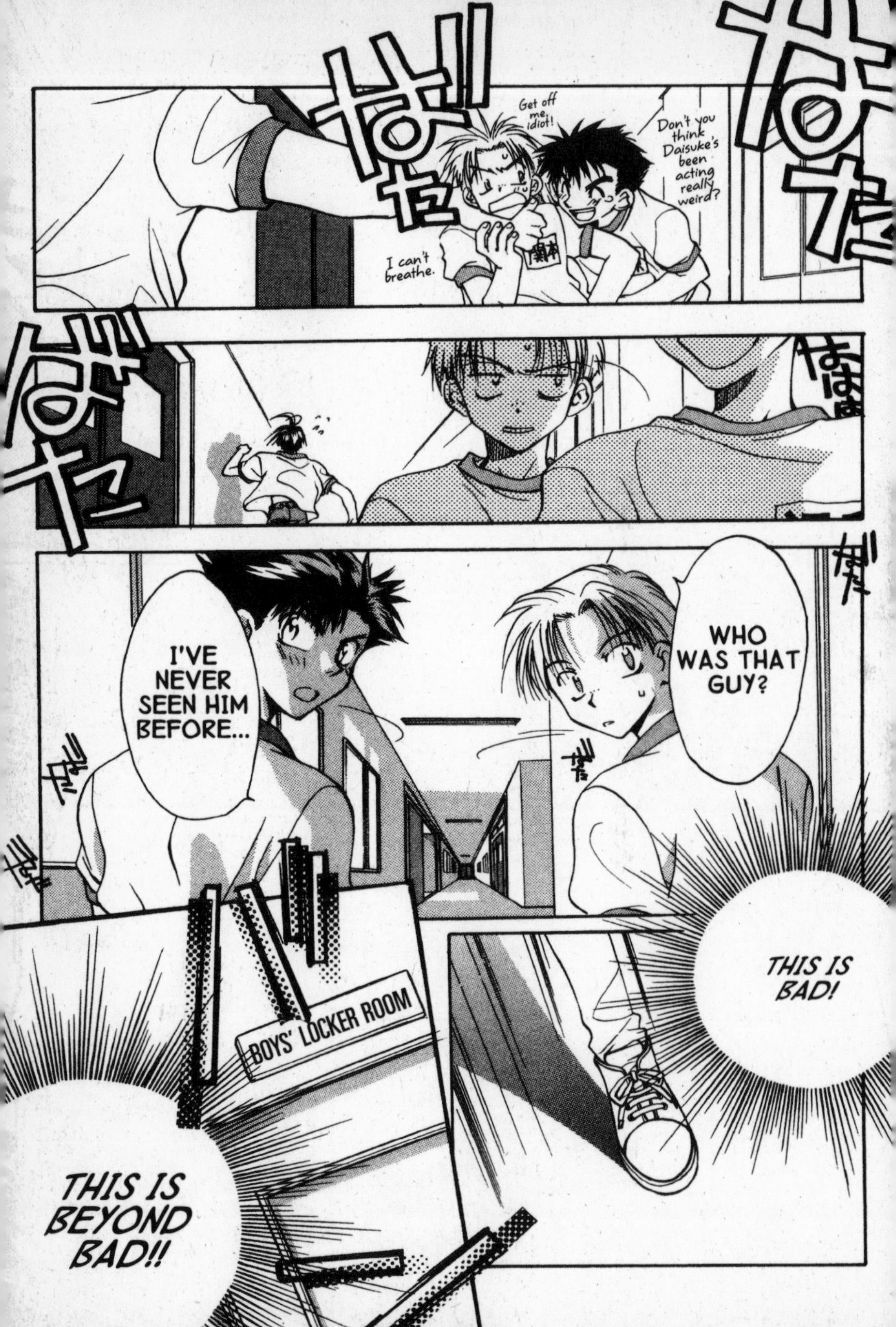
Don't you think Daisuke's been acting really weird?
Get off me, idiot!
I can't breathe.
WHO WAS THAT GUY?
I'VE NEVER SEEN HIM BEFORE...
THIS IS BAD!
BOYS' LOCKER ROOM
THIS IS BEYOND BAD!!

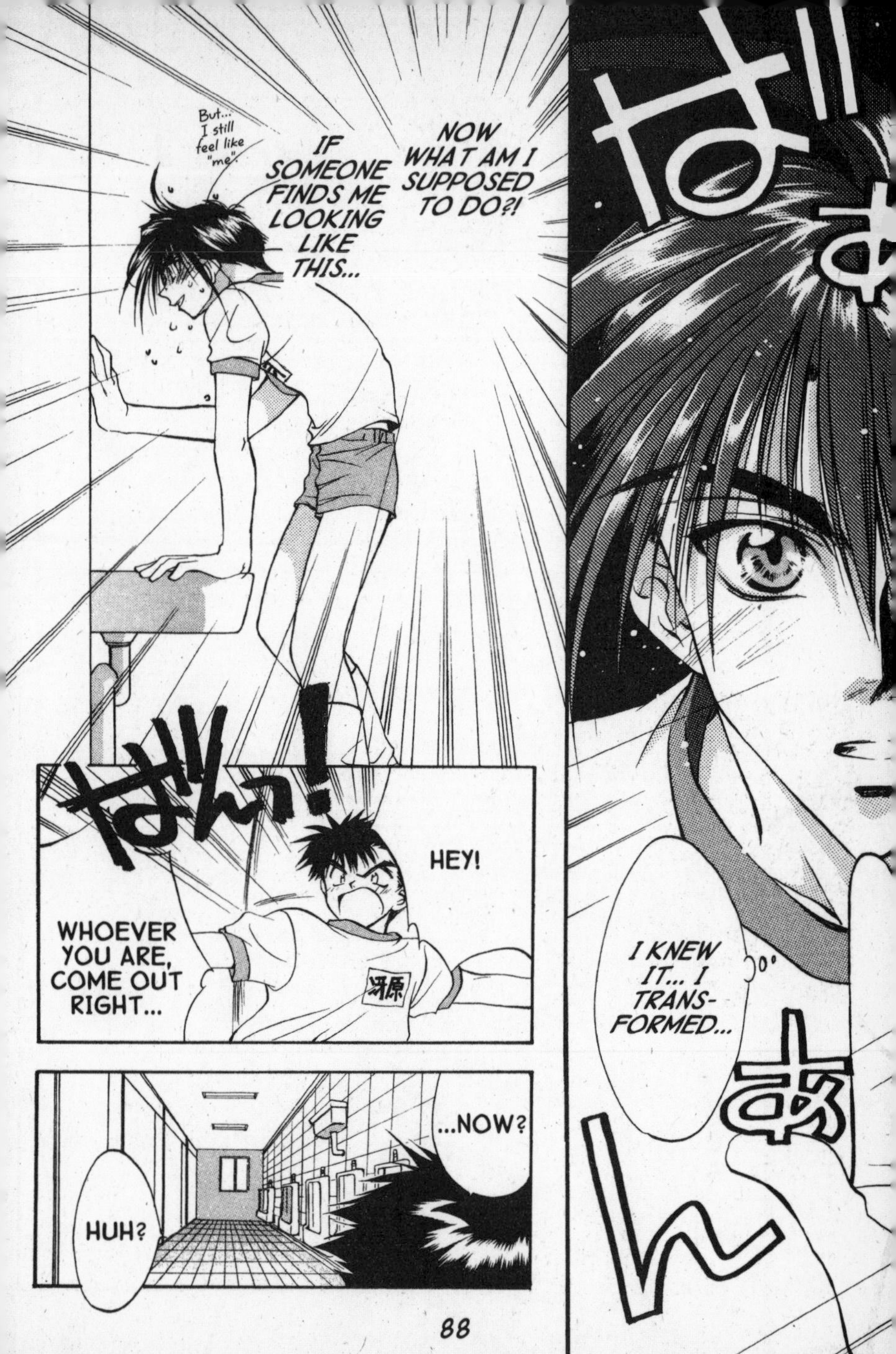
I KNEW IT... I TRANS-FORMED...
NOW WHAT AM I SUPPOSED TO DO?!
IF SOMEONE FINDS ME LOOKING LIKE THIS...
But... I still feel like "me".
ばんっ!
HEY!
WHOEVER YOU ARE, COME OUT RIGHT...
冴原
...NOW?
HUH?

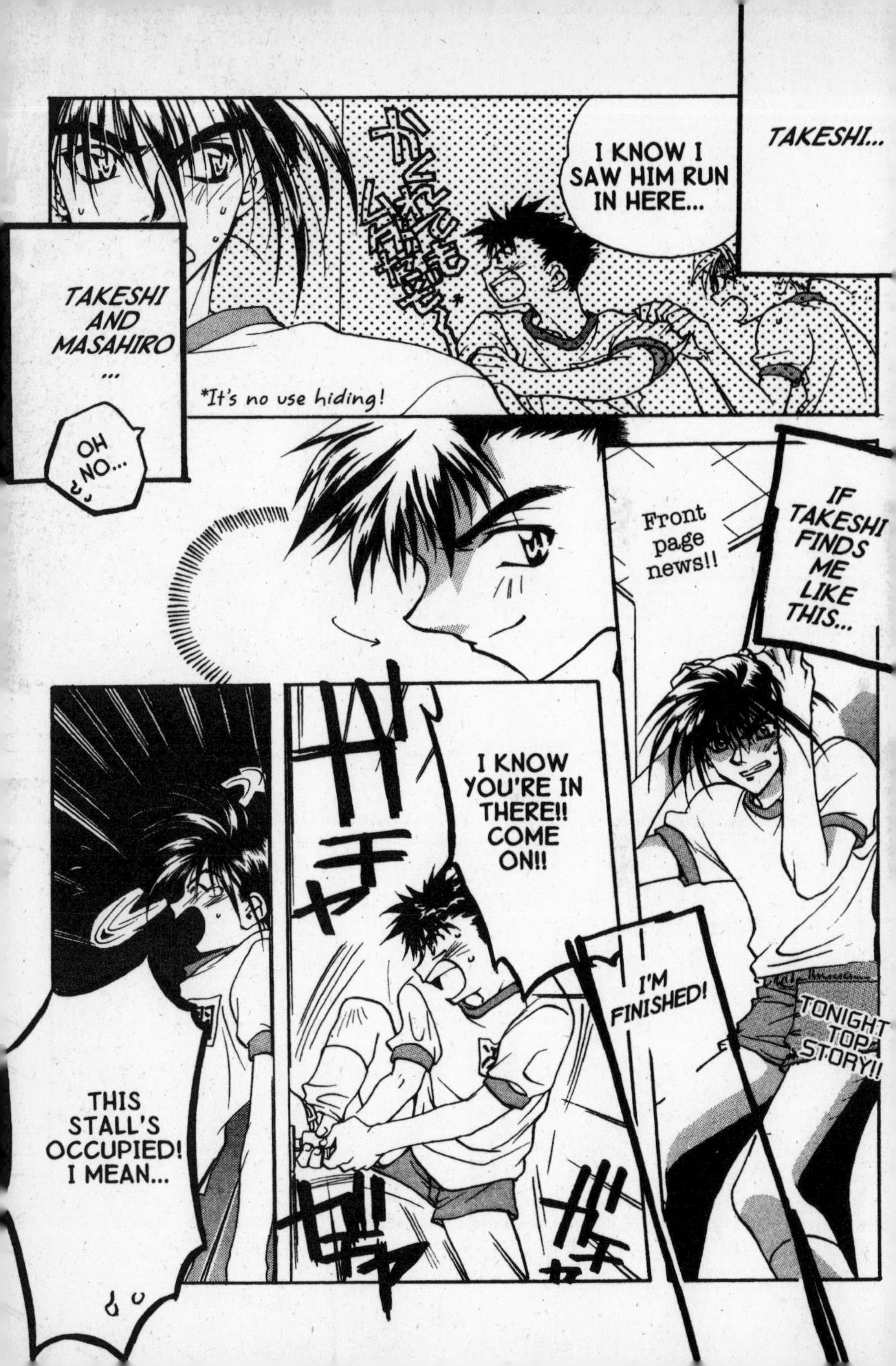

TAKESHI...
I KNOW I SAW HIM RUN IN HERE...
*It's no use hiding!
TAKESHI AND MASAHIRO ...
OH NO...
IF TAKESHI FINDS ME LIKE THIS...
Front page news!!
TONIGHT TOP STORY!!
I'M FINISHED!
I KNOW YOU'RE IN THERE!! COME ON!!
THIS STALL'S OCCUPIED! I MEAN...

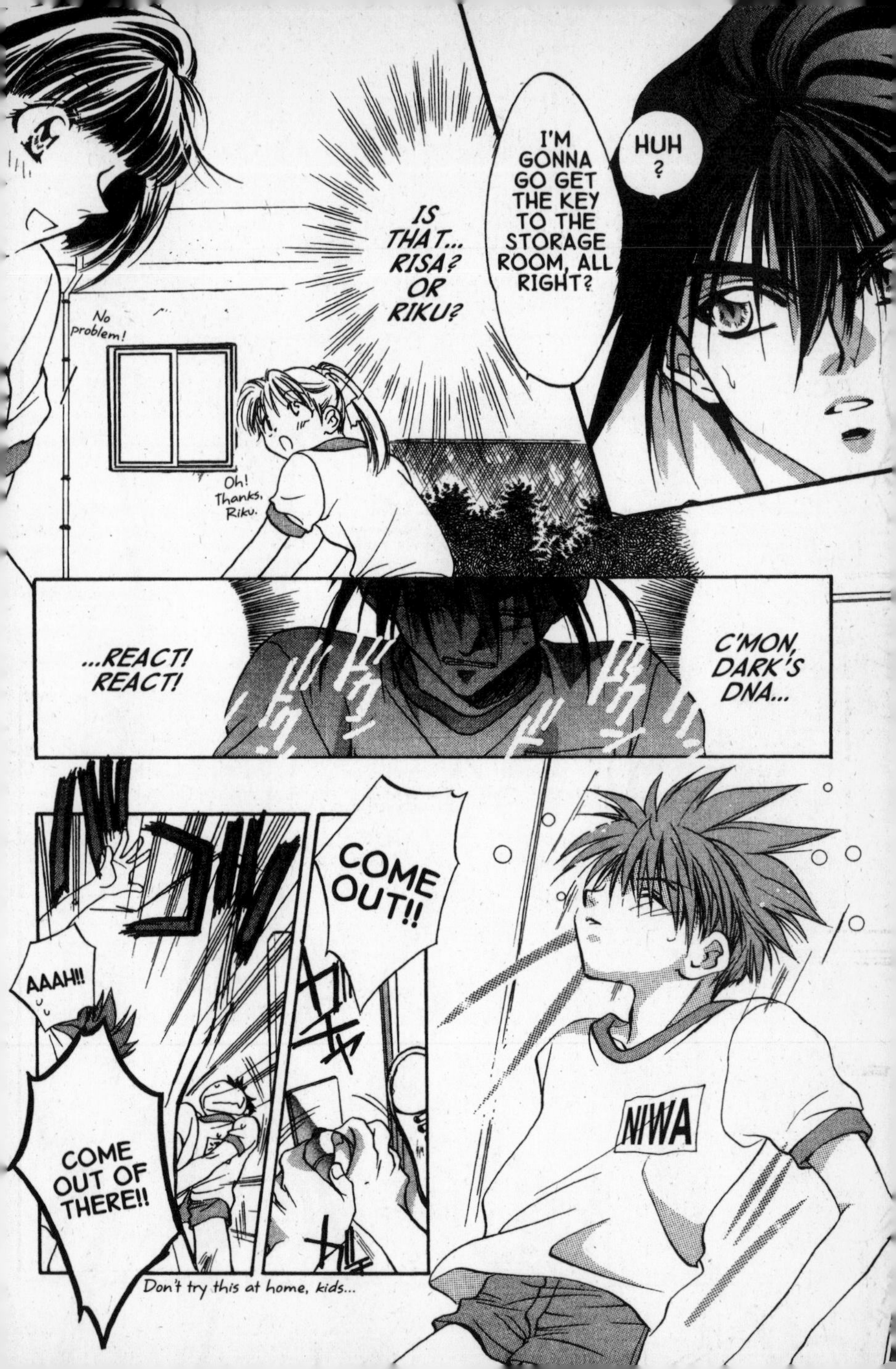
HUH?
I'M GONNA GO GET THE KEY TO THE STORAGE ROOM, ALL RIGHT?
IS THAT... RISA? OR RIKU?
No problem!
Oh! Thanks, Riku.
C'MON, DARK'S DNA...
...REACT! REACT!
NIWA
COME OUT!!
AAAH!!
COME OUT OF THERE!!
Don't try this at home, kids...

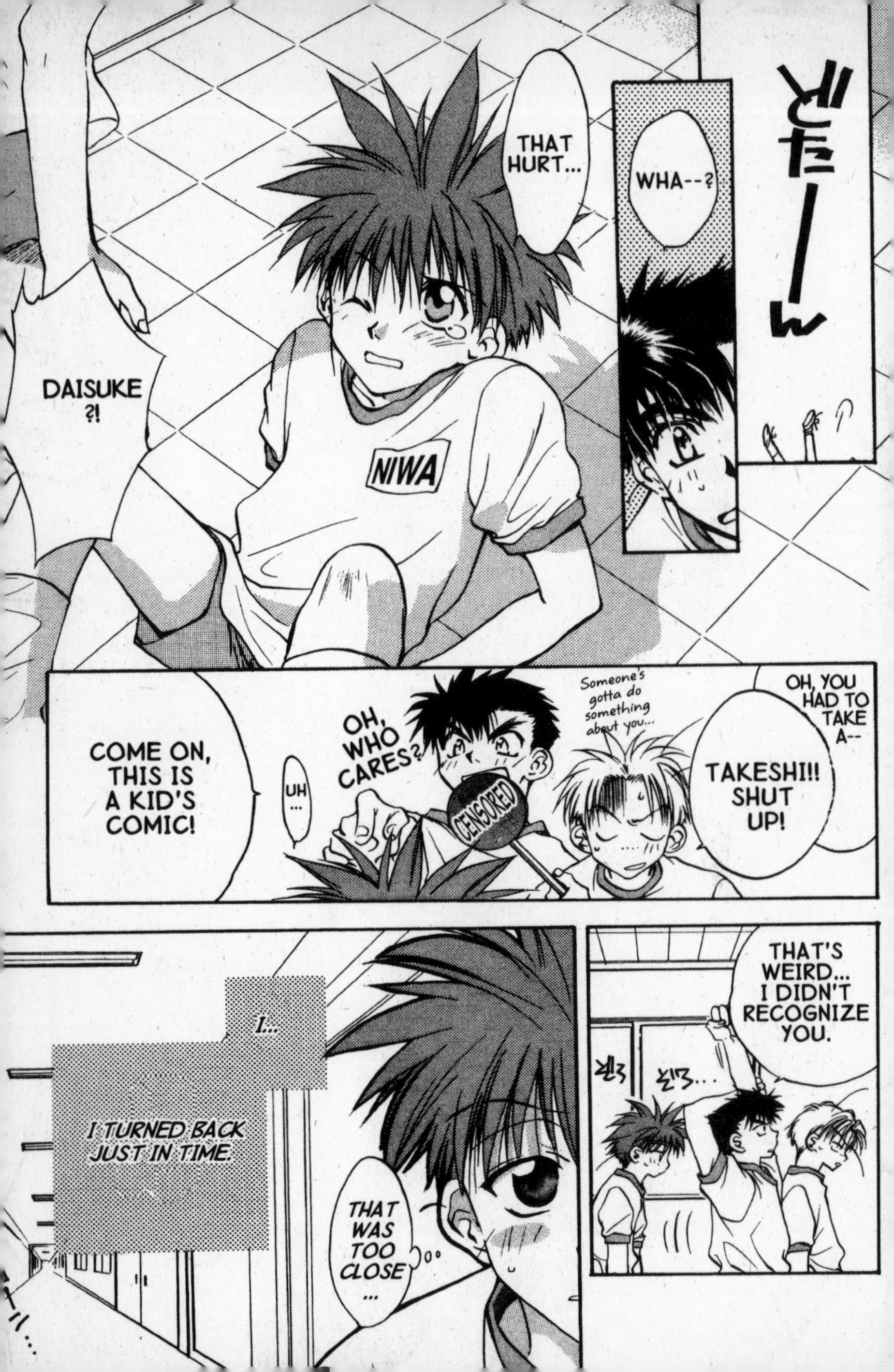

どたーん
WHA--?
THAT HURT...
DAISUKE ?!
OH, YOU HAD TO TAKE A--
TAKESHI!!! SHUT UP!
Someone's gotta do something about you...
OH, WHO CARES?
UH...
CENSORED
COME ON, THIS IS A KID'S COMIC!
THAT'S WEIRD... I DIDN'T RECOGNIZE YOU.
I...
I TURNED BACK JUST IN TIME.
THAT WAS TOO CLOSE...

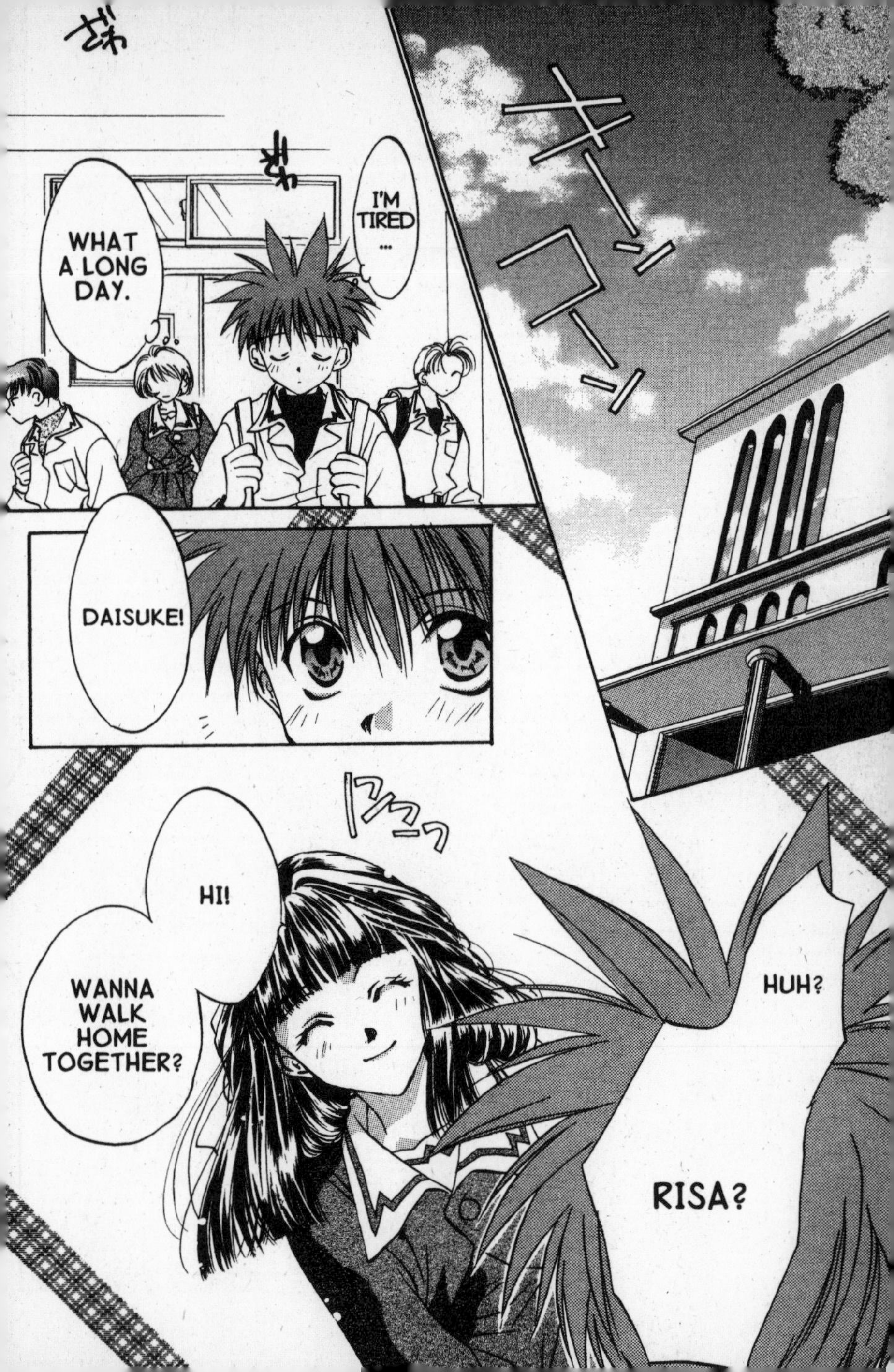
キーンコーン
ざわ
ざわ
I'M TIRED...
WHAT A LONG DAY.
DAISUKE!
HUH?
RISA?
HI!
WANNA WALK HOME TOGETHER?

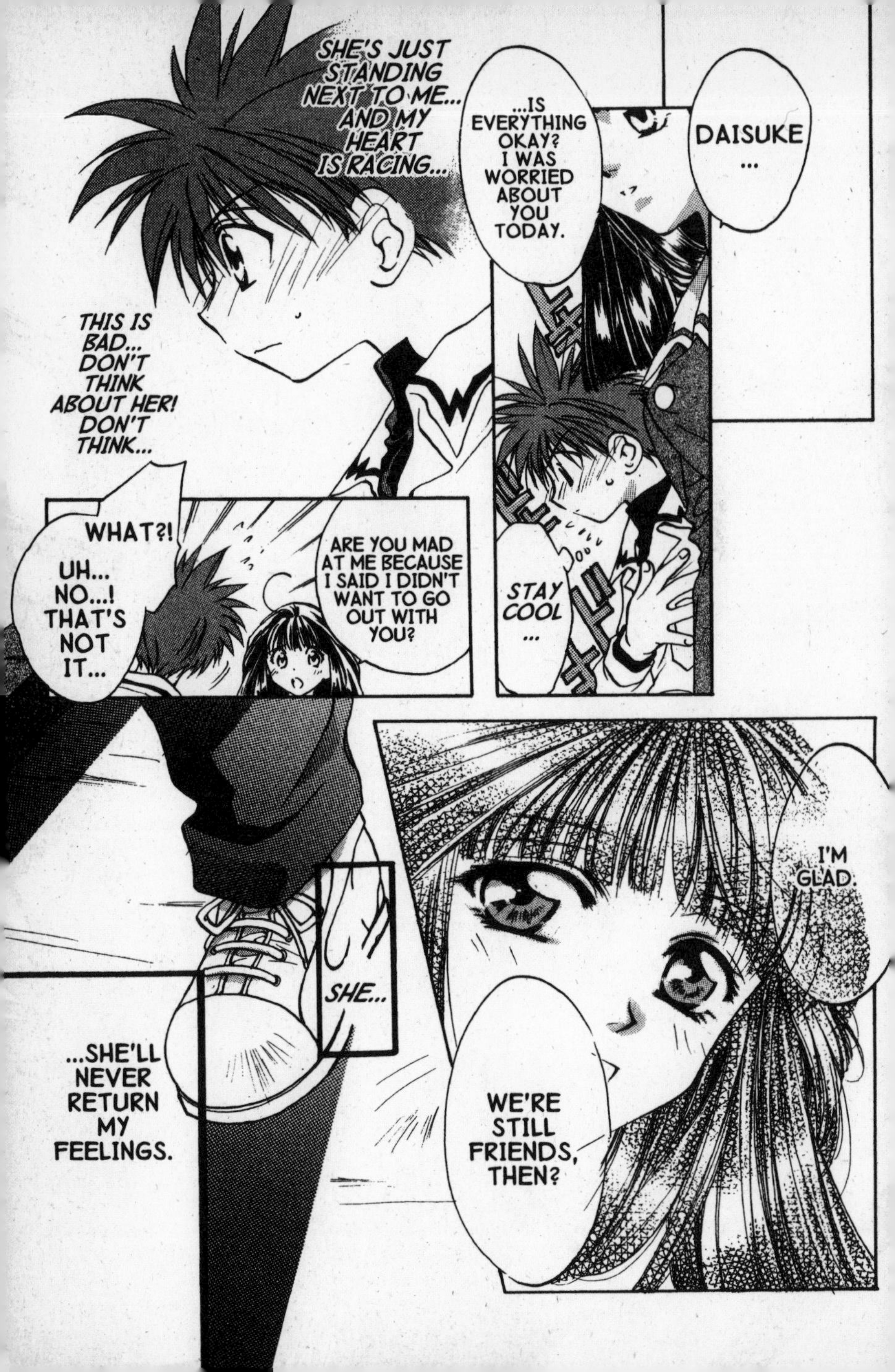
DAISUKE ...
...IS EVERYTHING OKAY? I WAS WORRIED ABOUT YOU TODAY.
STAY COOL ...
SHE'S JUST STANDING NEXT TO ME... AND MY HEART IS RACING...
THIS IS BAD... DON'T THINK ABOUT HER! DON'T THINK...
ARE YOU MAD AT ME BECAUSE I SAID I DIDN'T WANT TO GO OUT WITH YOU?
WHAT?!
UH... NO...! THAT'S NOT IT...
I'M GLAD.
WE'RE STILL FRIENDS, THEN?
SHE...
...SHE'LL NEVER RETURN MY FEELINGS.

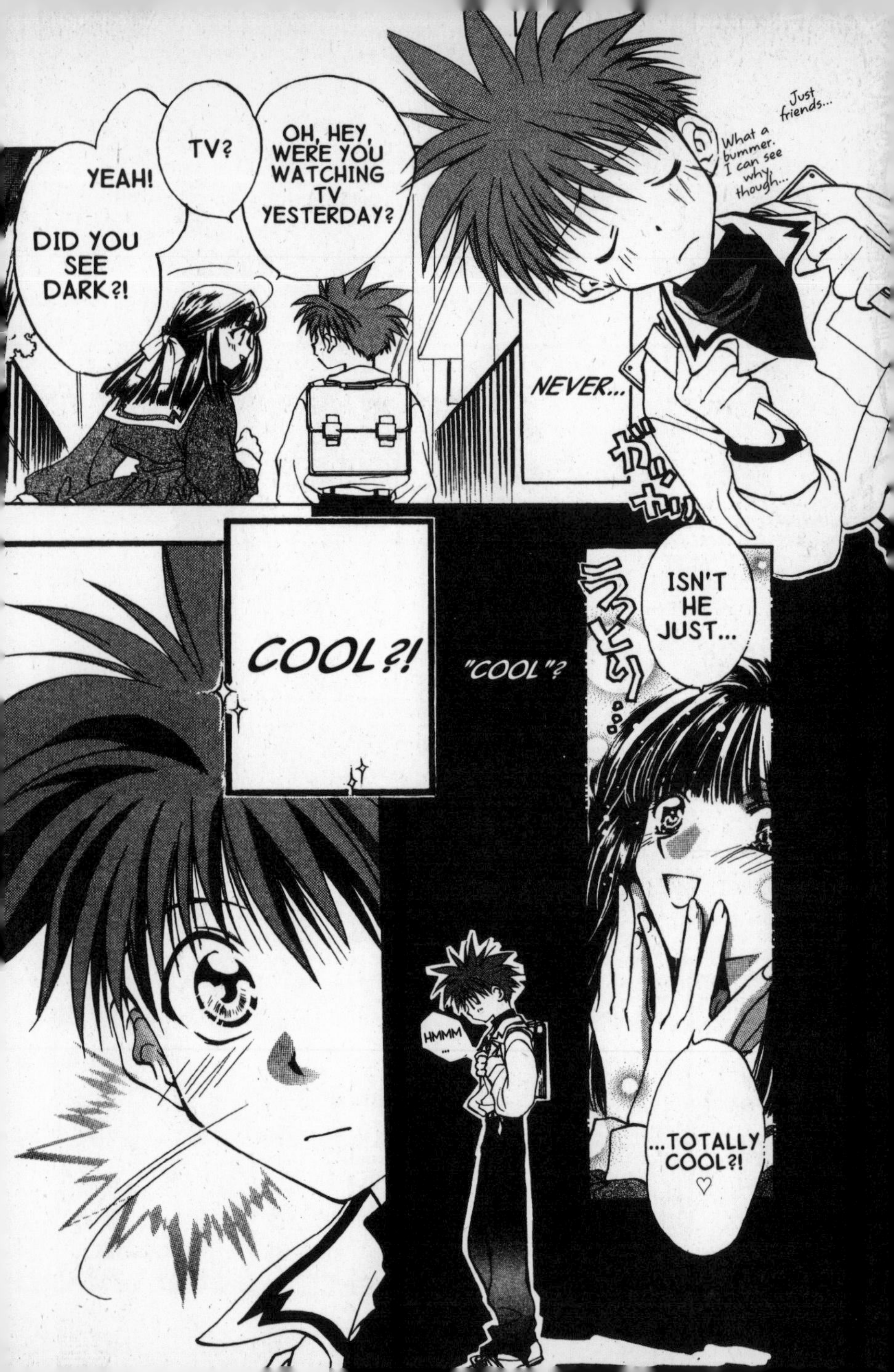

Just friends...
What a bummer. I can see why, though...
NEVER...
OH, HEY, WERE YOU WATCHING TV YESTERDAY?
TV?
YEAH!
DID YOU SEE DARK?!
ISN'T HE JUST...
...TOTALLY COOL?! ♡
"COOL"?
HMMM ...
COOL?!

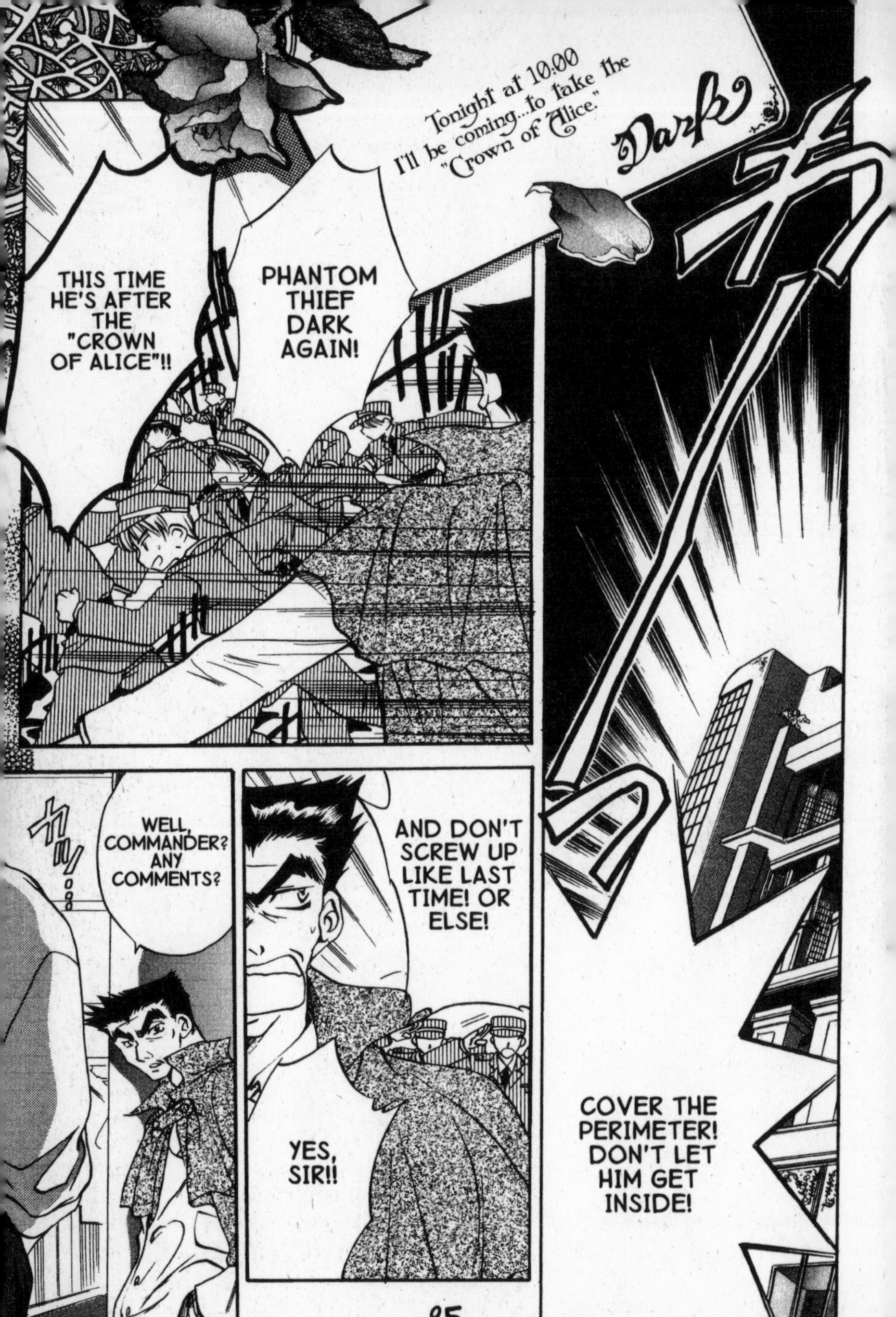

Tonight at 10:00 I'll be coming...to take the "Crown of Alice."
Dark
COVER THE PERIMETER! DON'T LET HIM GET INSIDE!
PHANTOM THIEF DARK AGAIN!
THIS TIME HE'S AFTER THE "CROWN OF ALICE"!!
AND DON'T SCREW UP LIKE LAST TIME! OR ELSE!
YES, SIR!!
WELL, COMMANDER? ANY COMMENTS?

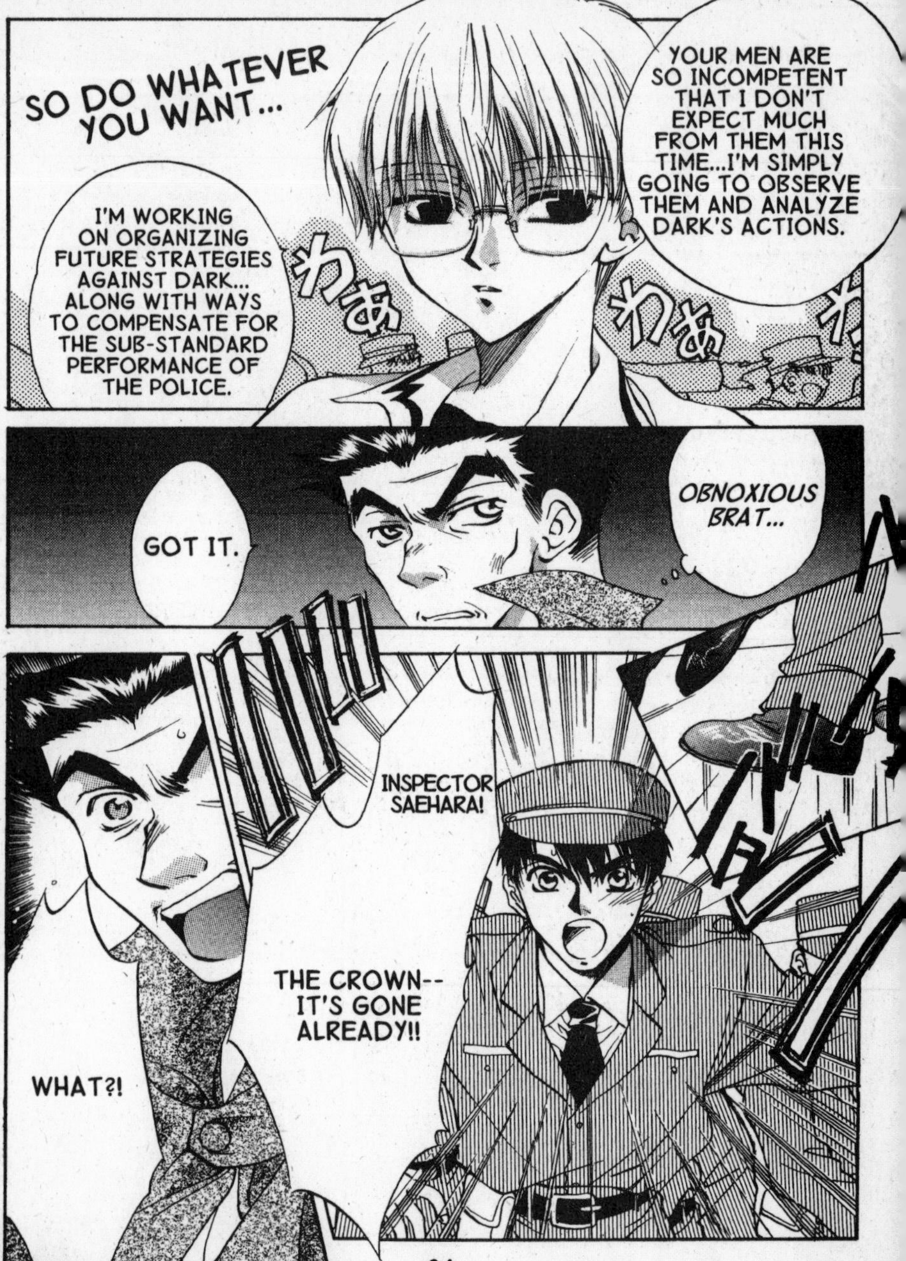
YOUR MEN ARE SO INCOMPETENT THAT I DON'T EXPECT MUCH FROM THEM THIS TIME...I'M SIMPLY GOING TO OBSERVE THEM AND ANALYZE DARK'S ACTIONS.
わぁ
わぁ
I'M WORKING ON ORGANIZING FUTURE STRATEGIES AGAINST DARK... ALONG WITH WAYS TO COMPENSATE FOR THE SUB-STANDARD PERFORMANCE OF THE POLICE.
SO DO WHATEVER YOU WANT...
OBNOXIOUS BRAT...
GOT IT.
INSPECTOR SAEHARA!
THE CROWN-- IT'S GONE ALREADY!!
WHAT?!

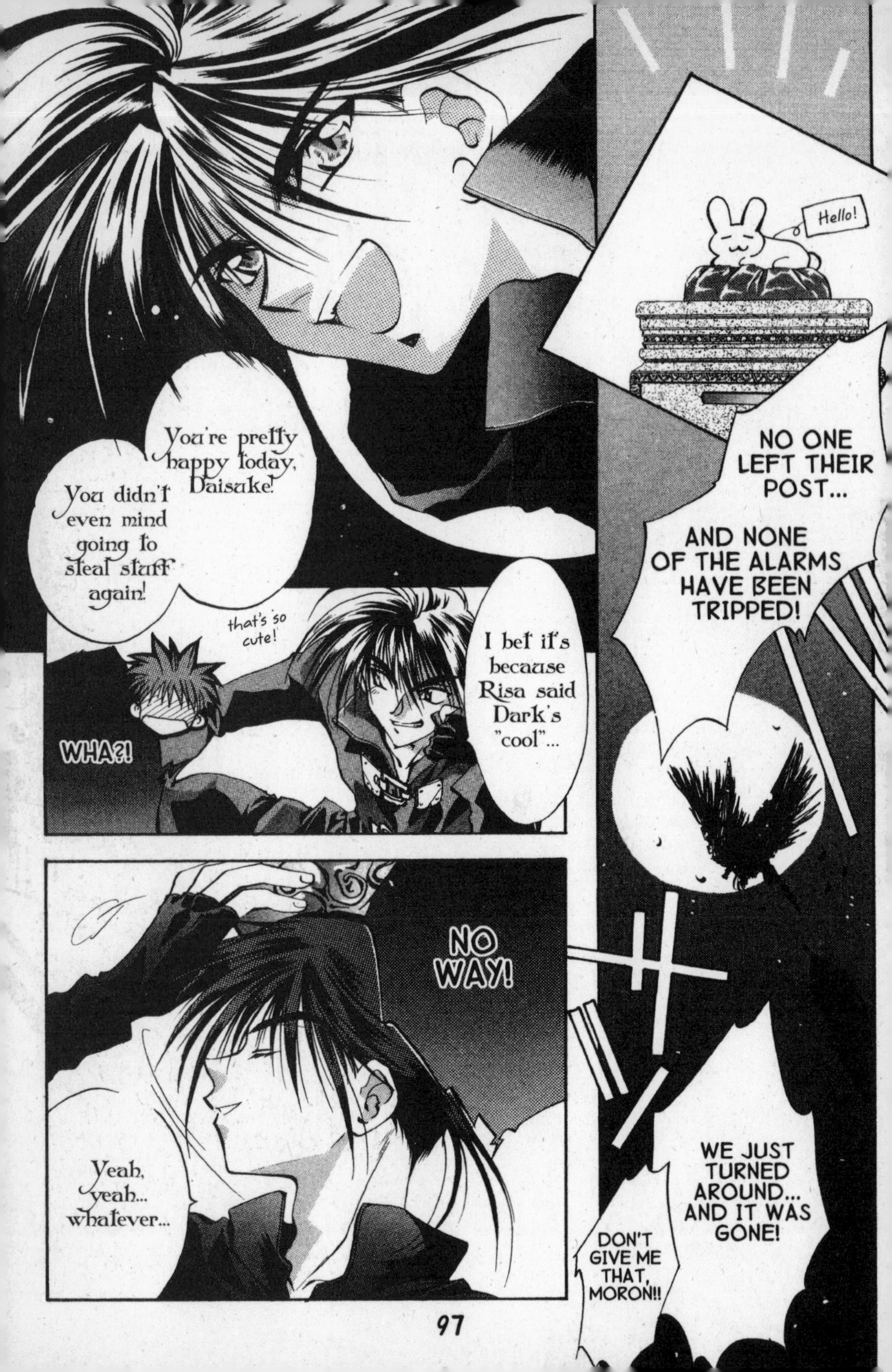
Hello!
NO ONE LEFT THEIR POST...
AND NONE OF THE ALARMS HAVE BEEN TRIPPED!
WE JUST TURNED AROUND... AND IT WAS GONE!
DON'T GIVE ME THAT, MORON!!
You're pretty happy today, Daisuke!
You didn't even mind going to steal stuff again!
I bet it's because Risa said Dark's "cool"...
that's so cute!
WHA?!
NO WAY!
Yeah, yeah... whatever...

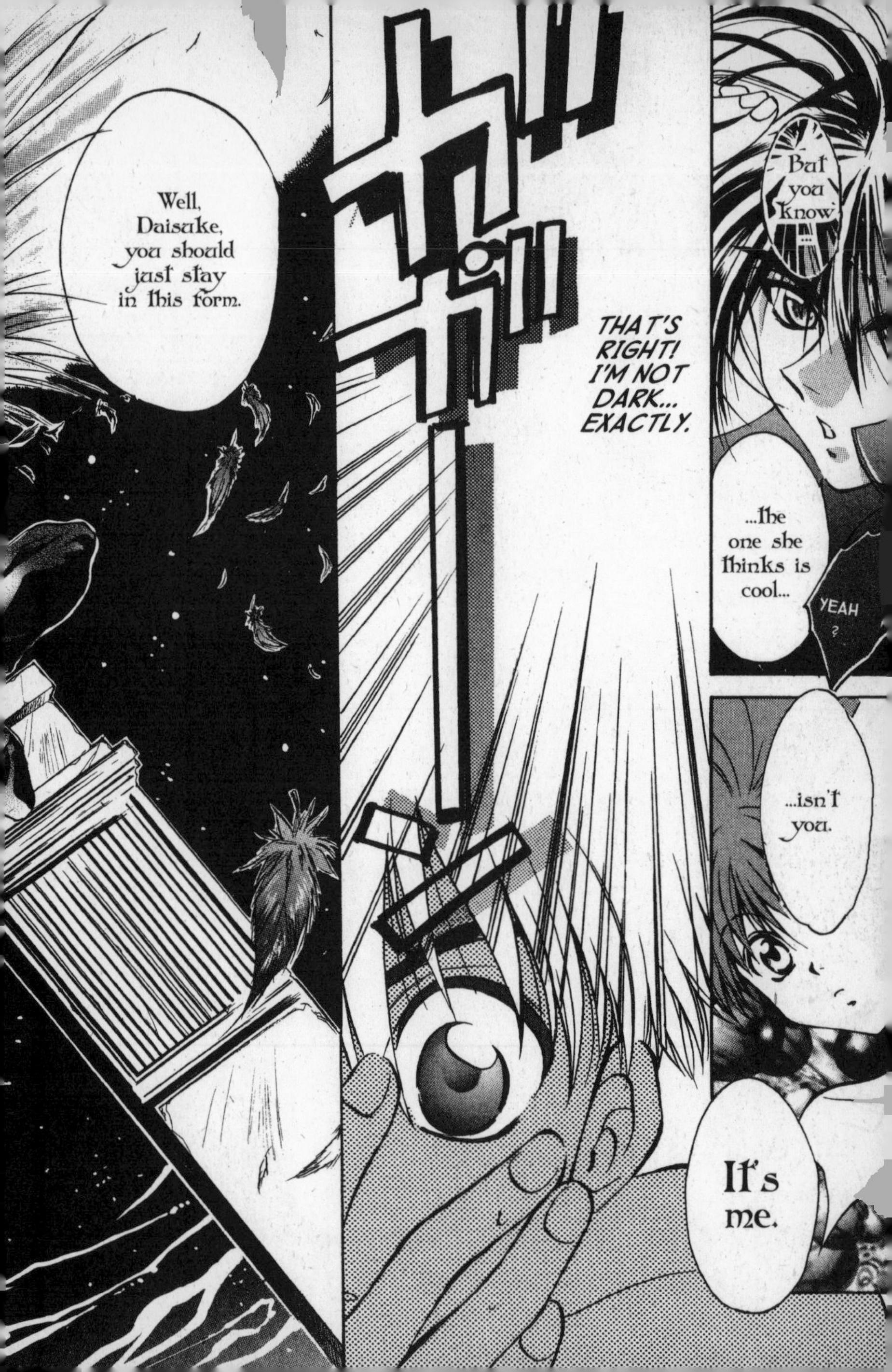
But you know...
...the one she thinks is cool...
YEAH?
...isn't you.
It's me.
THAT'S RIGHT! I'M NOT DARK... EXACTLY.
Well, Daisuke, you should just stay in this form.

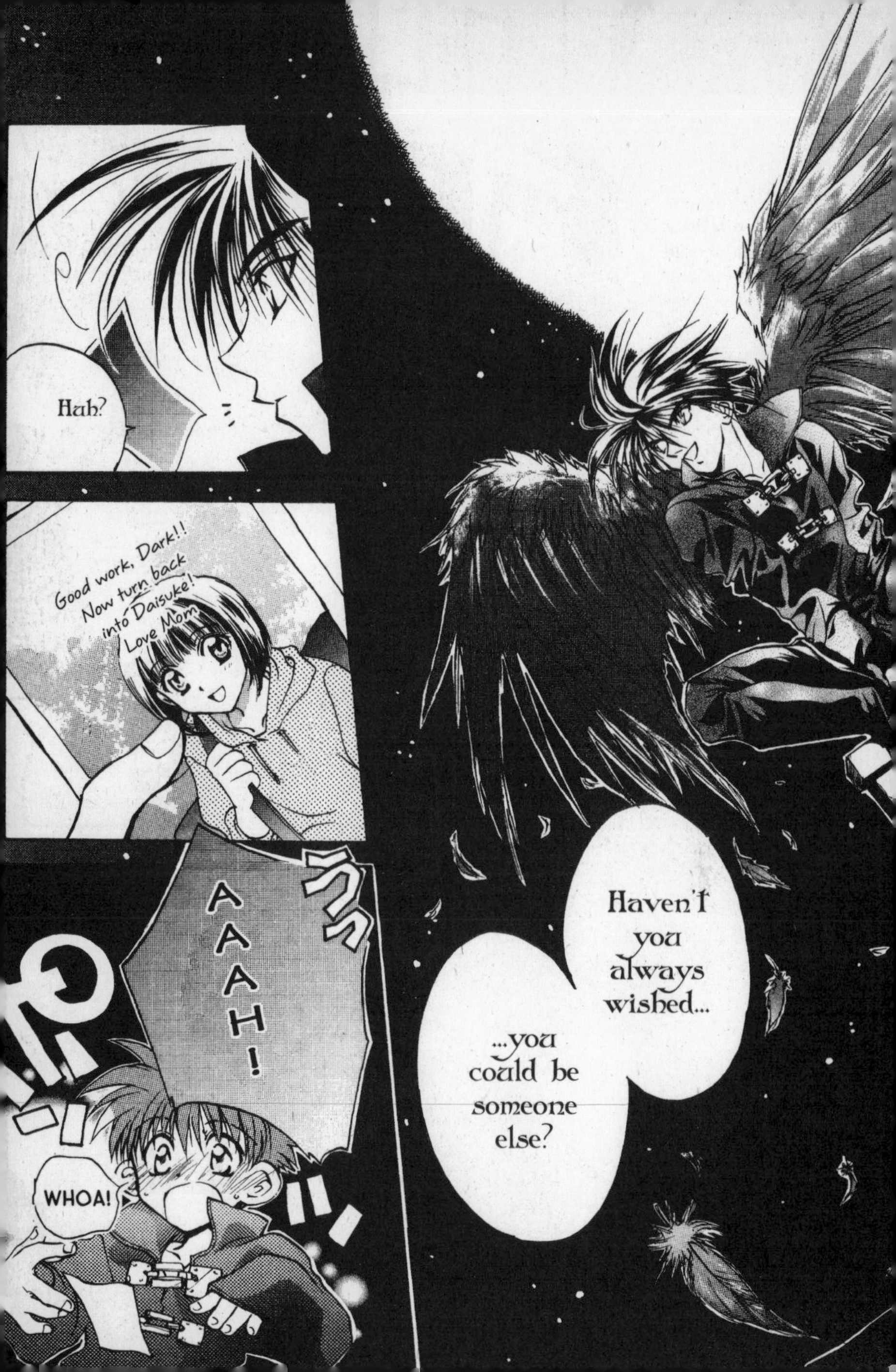
Haven't you always wished...
...you could be someone else?
Huh?
Good work, Dark!! Now turn back into Daisuke! Love Mom
AAAAH!
WHOA!

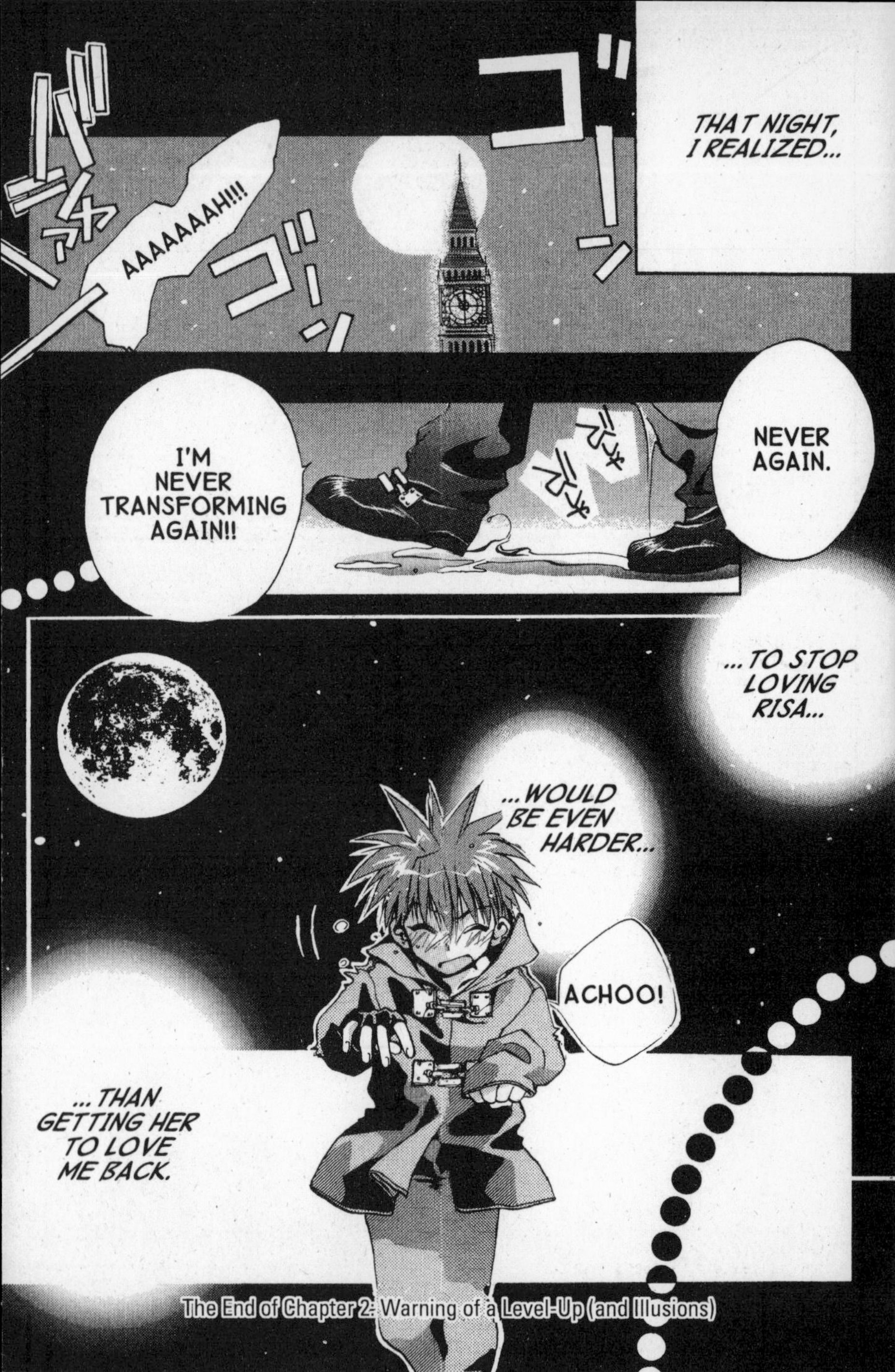
THAT NIGHT, I REALIZED...
AAAAAAAH!!!
NEVER AGAIN.
I'M NEVER TRANSFORMING AGAIN!!
...TO STOP LOVING RISA...
...WOULD BE EVEN HARDER...
ACHOO!
...THAN GETTING HER TO LOVE ME BACK.

The End of Chapter 2: Warning of a Level-Up (and Illusions)

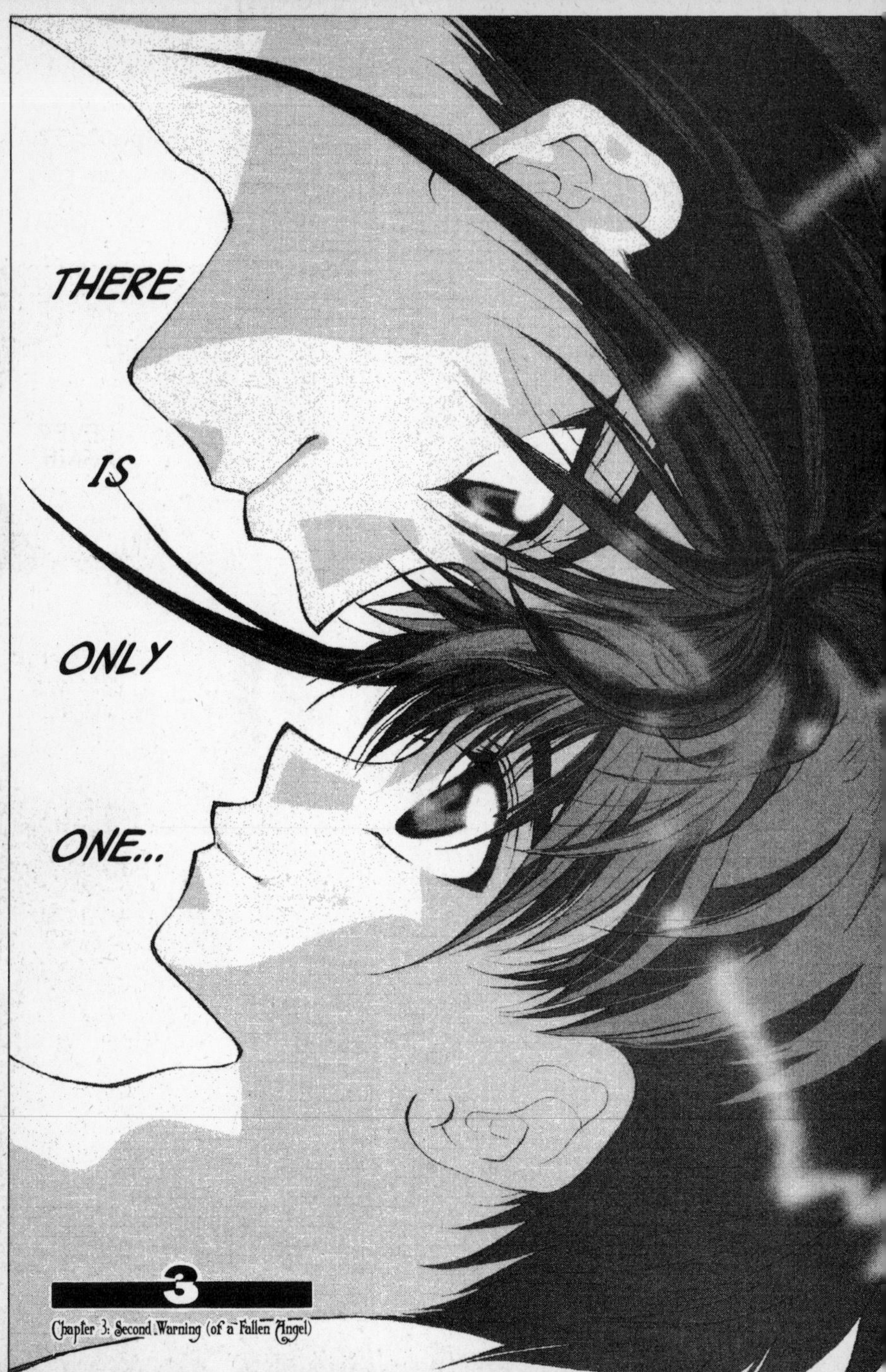
THERE IS ONLY ONE...
3
Chapter 3: Second Warning (of a Fallen Angel)

# 3

## Chapter 3: Second Warning (of a Fallen Angel)

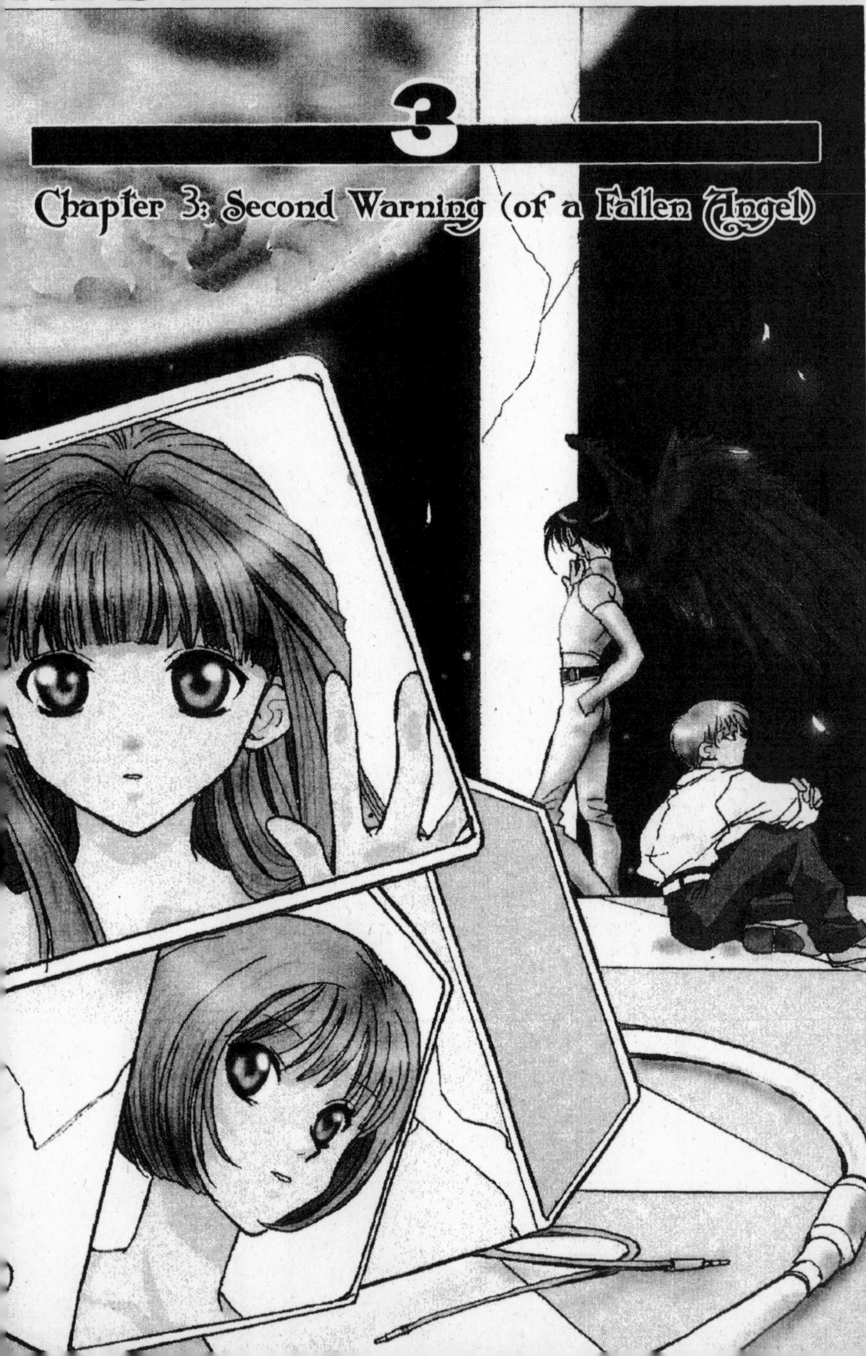
RADA·SATOSHI HI
WATARI·TAKESHI SAEHARA

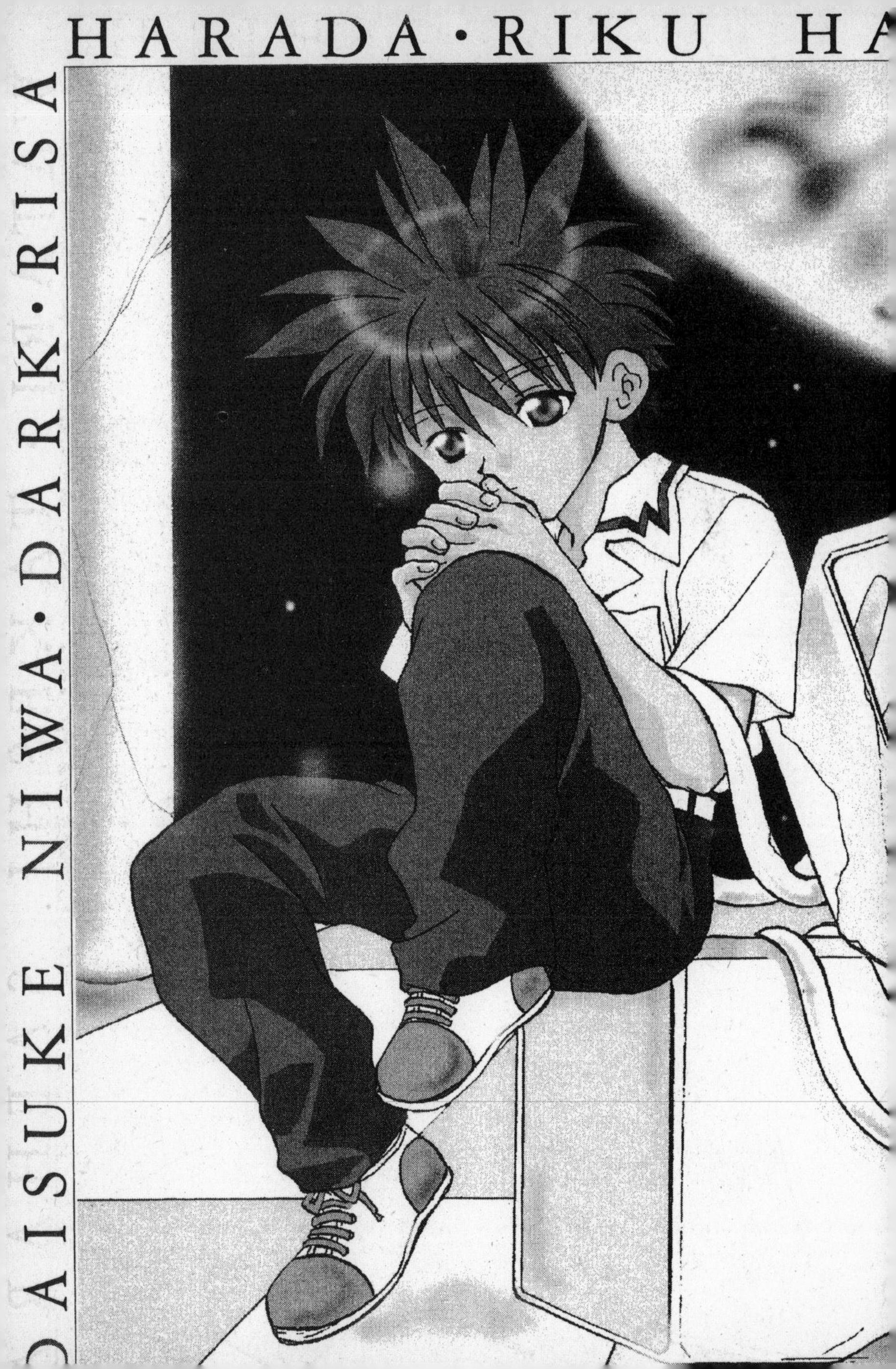
HARADA • RIKU HA
DAISUKE NIWA • DARK • RISA

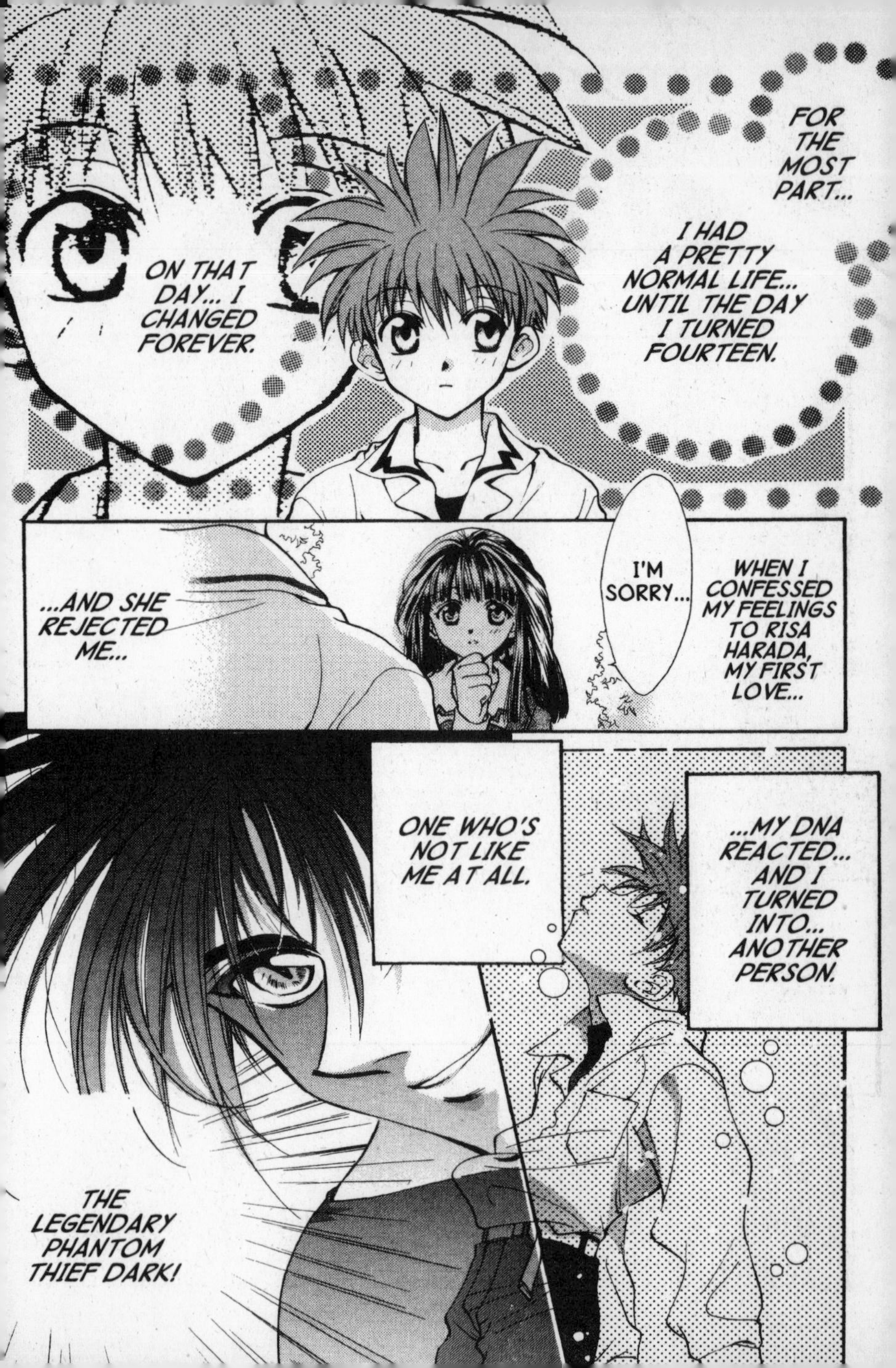
FOR THE MOST PART...
I HAD A PRETTY NORMAL LIFE... UNTIL THE DAY I TURNED FOURTEEN.
ON THAT DAY... I CHANGED FOREVER.
WHEN I CONFESSED MY FEELINGS TO RISA HARADA, MY FIRST LOVE...
I'M SORRY...
...AND SHE REJECTED ME...
...MY DNA REACTED... AND I TURNED INTO... ANOTHER PERSON.
ONE WHO'S NOT LIKE ME AT ALL.
THE LEGENDARY PHANTOM THIEF DARK!

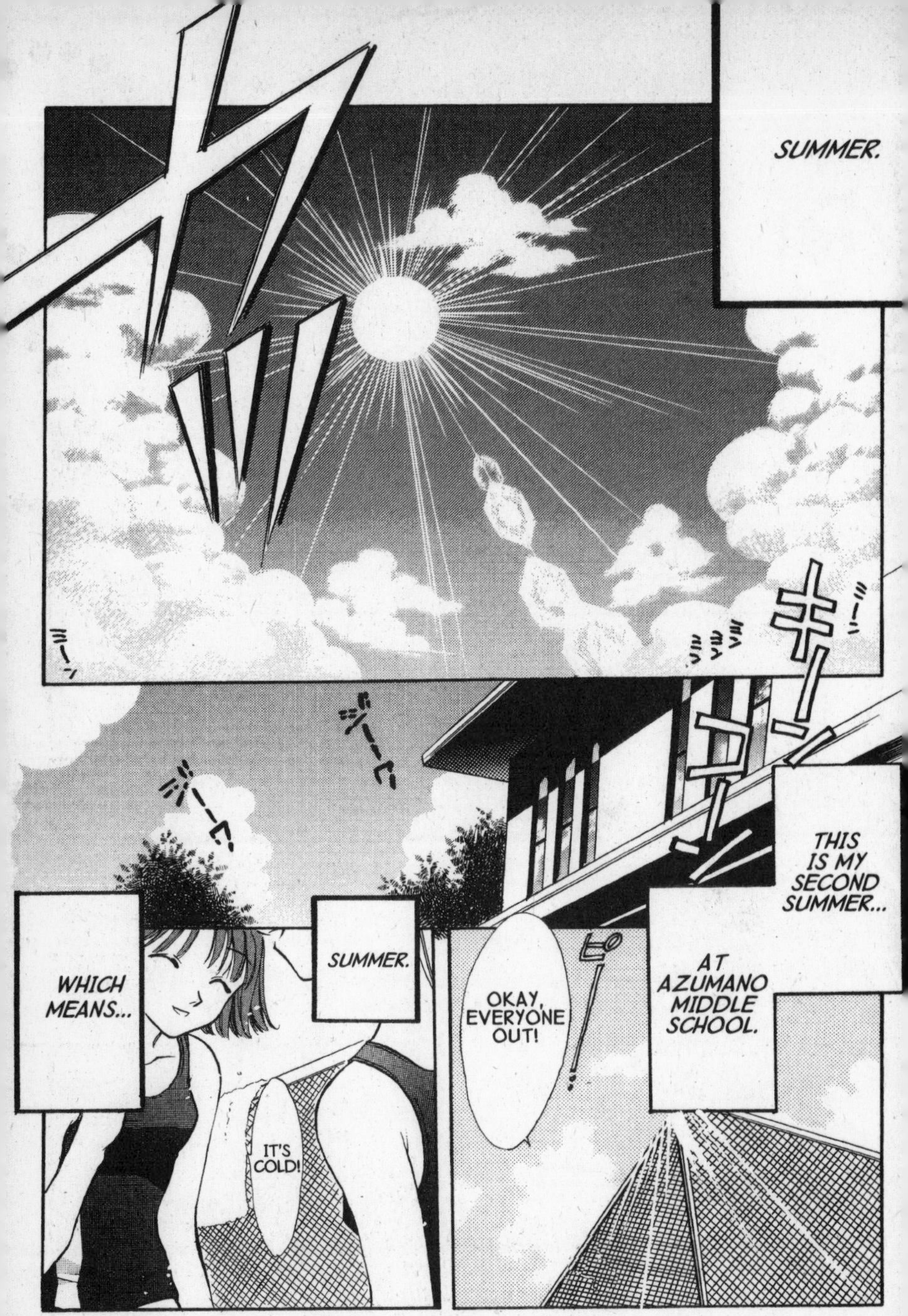
SUMMER.
THIS IS MY SECOND SUMMER...
AT AZUMANO MIDDLE SCHOOL.
OKAY, EVERYONE OUT!
SUMMER.
WHICH MEANS...
IT'S COLD!

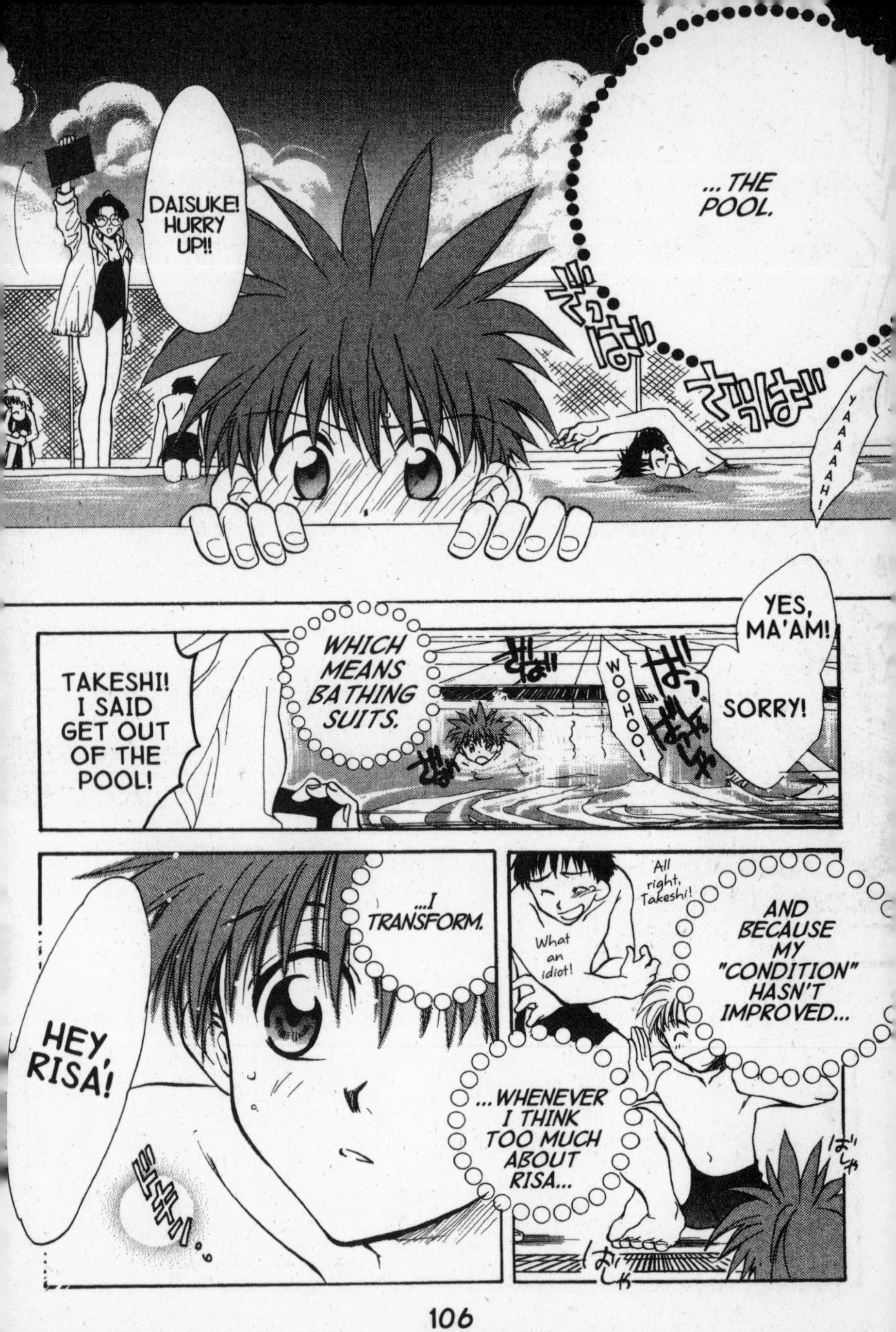
...THE POOL.
YAAAAAH!
DAISUKE! HURRY UP!!
YES, MA'AM!
SORRY!
WOOHOO!
WHICH MEANS BATHING SUITS.
TAKESHI! I SAID GET OUT OF THE POOL!
AND BECAUSE MY "CONDITION" HASN'T IMPROVED...
All right, Takeshi!
What an idiot!
...WHENEVER I THINK TOO MUCH ABOUT RISA...
...I TRANSFORM.
HEY, RISA!

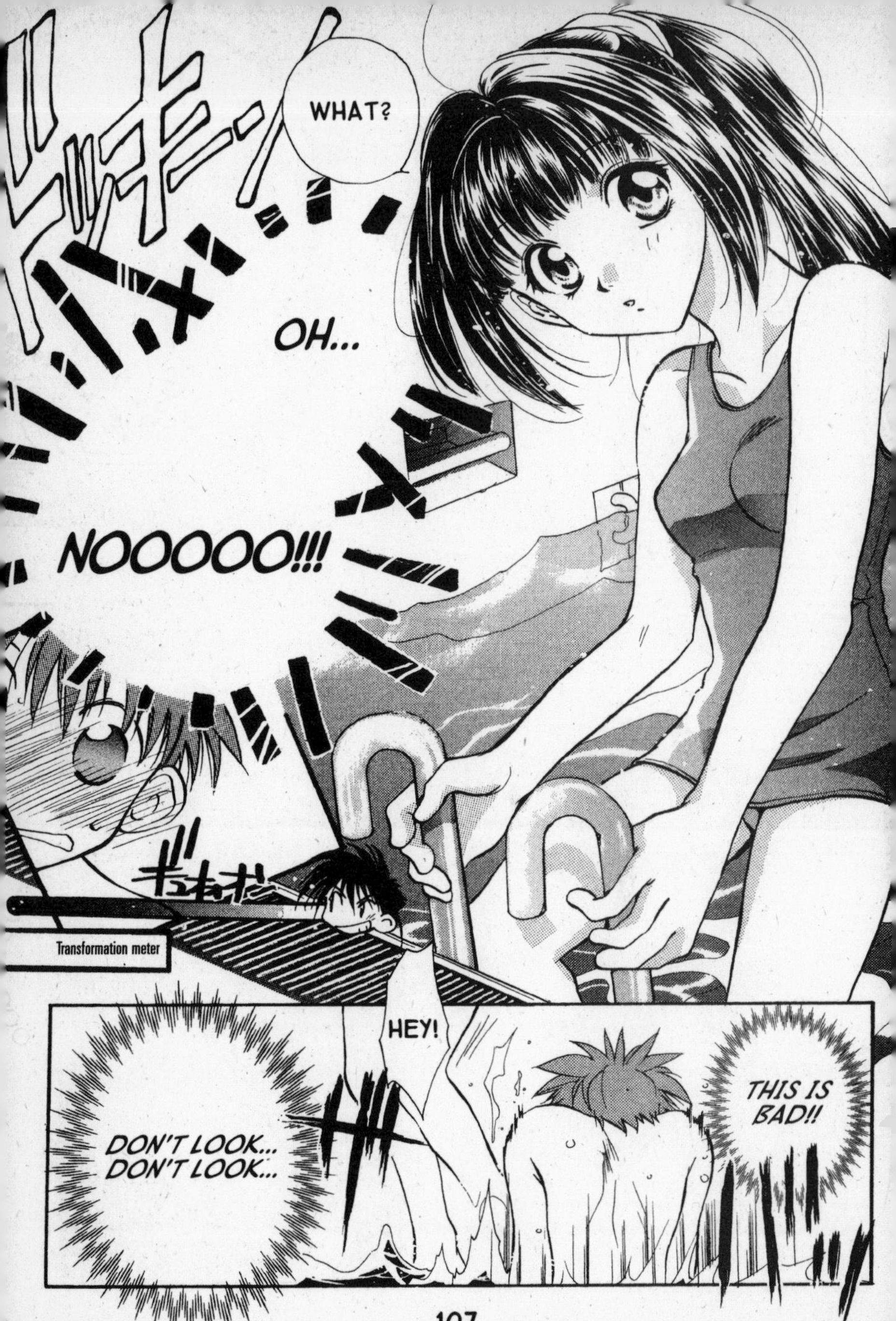
WHAT?
OH...
NOOOOO!!!
Transformation meter
THIS IS BAD!!
HEY!
DON'T LOOK...
DON'T LOOK...

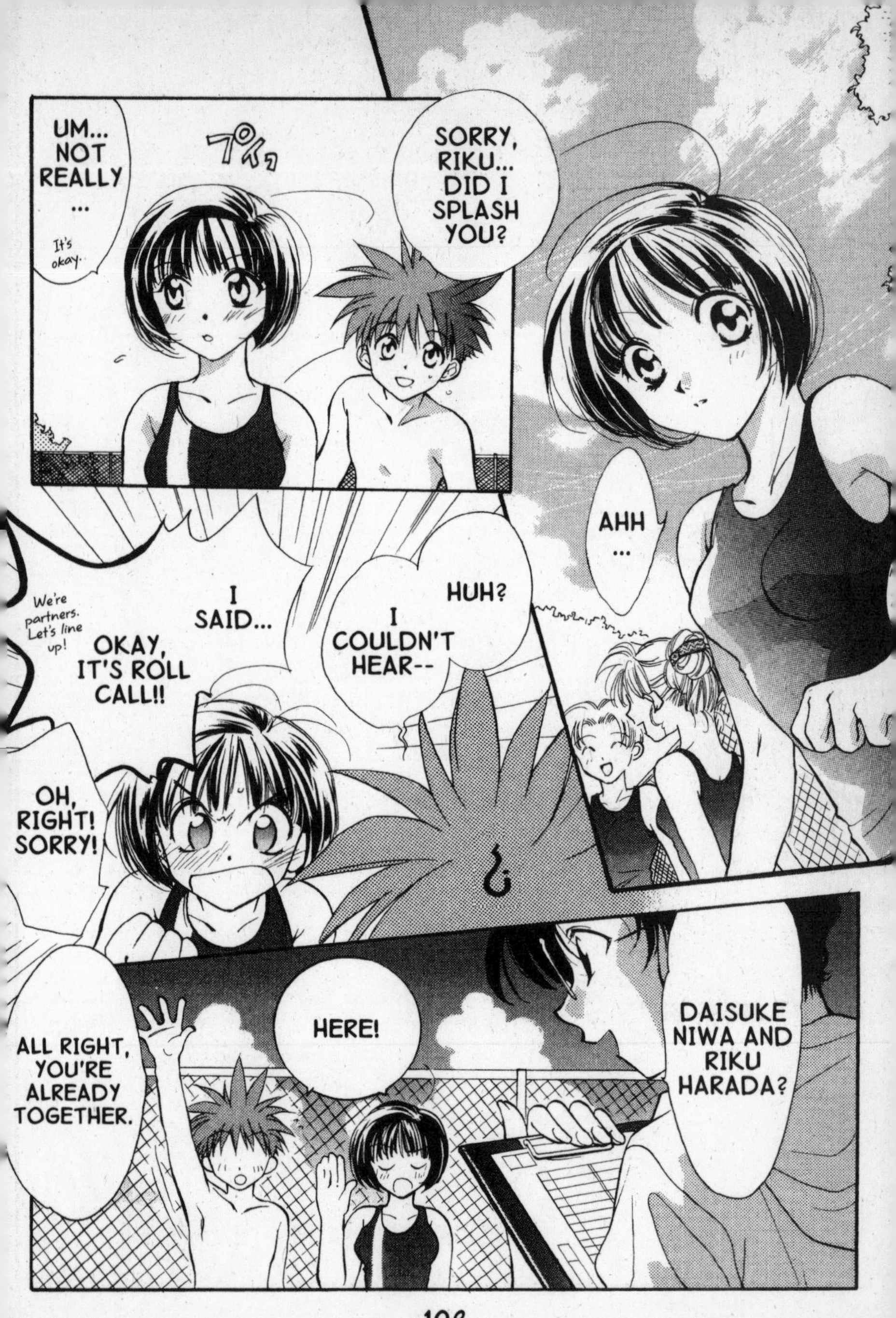
AHH ...
SORRY, RIKU... DID I SPLASH YOU?
プイッ
UM... NOT REALLY ...
It's okay.
HUH?
I COULDN'T HEAR--
I SAID...
OKAY, IT'S ROLL CALL!!
We're partners. Let's line up!
OH, RIGHT! SORRY!
DAISUKE NIWA AND RIKU HARADA?
HERE!
ALL RIGHT, YOU'RE ALREADY TOGETHER.

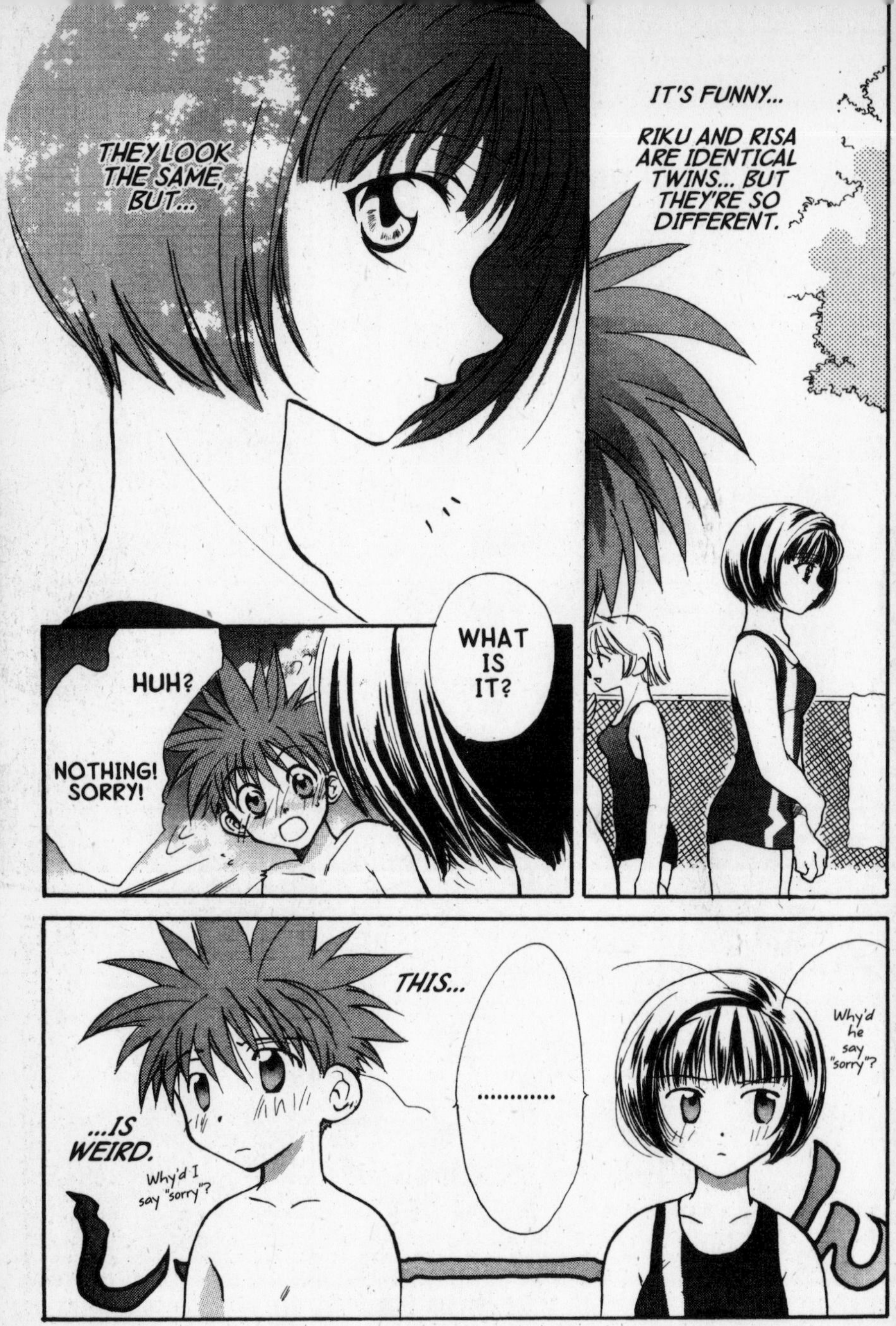
IT'S FUNNY...
RIKU AND RISA ARE IDENTICAL TWINS... BUT THEY'RE SO DIFFERENT.
THEY LOOK THE SAME, BUT...
WHAT IS IT?
HUH?
NOTHING! SORRY!
Why'd he say "sorry"?
............
THIS...
...IS WEIRD.
Why'd I say "sorry"?

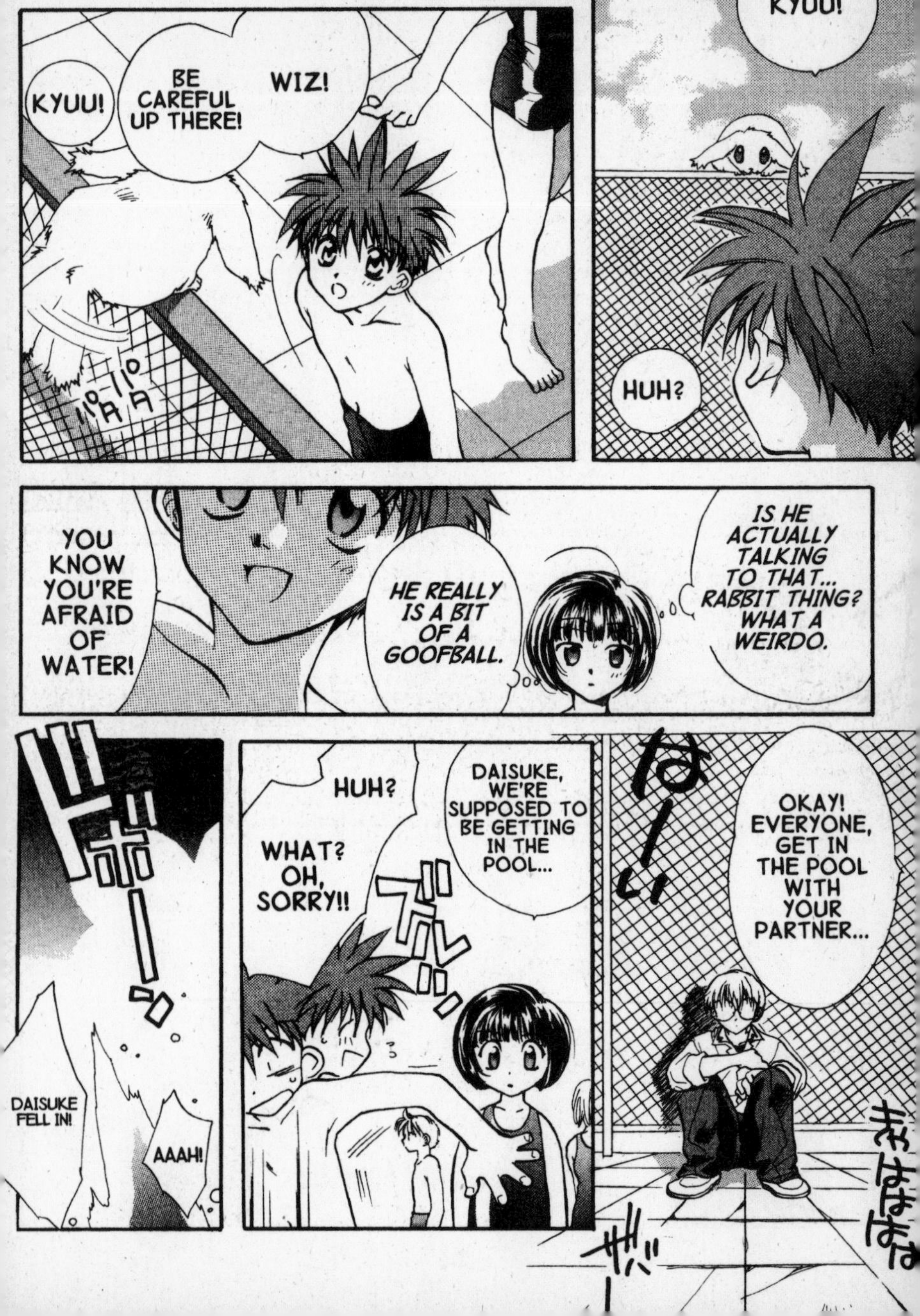
KYUU!
HUH?
WIZ!
BE CAREFUL UP THERE!
KYUU!
IS HE ACTUALLY TALKING TO THAT... RABBIT THING? WHAT A WEIRDO.
HE REALLY IS A BIT OF A GOOFBALL.
YOU KNOW YOU'RE AFRAID OF WATER!
OKAY! EVERYONE, GET IN THE POOL WITH YOUR PARTNER...
DAISUKE, WE'RE SUPPOSED TO BE GETTING IN THE POOL...
HUH?
WHAT? OH, SORRY!!
AAAH!
DAISUKE FELL IN!

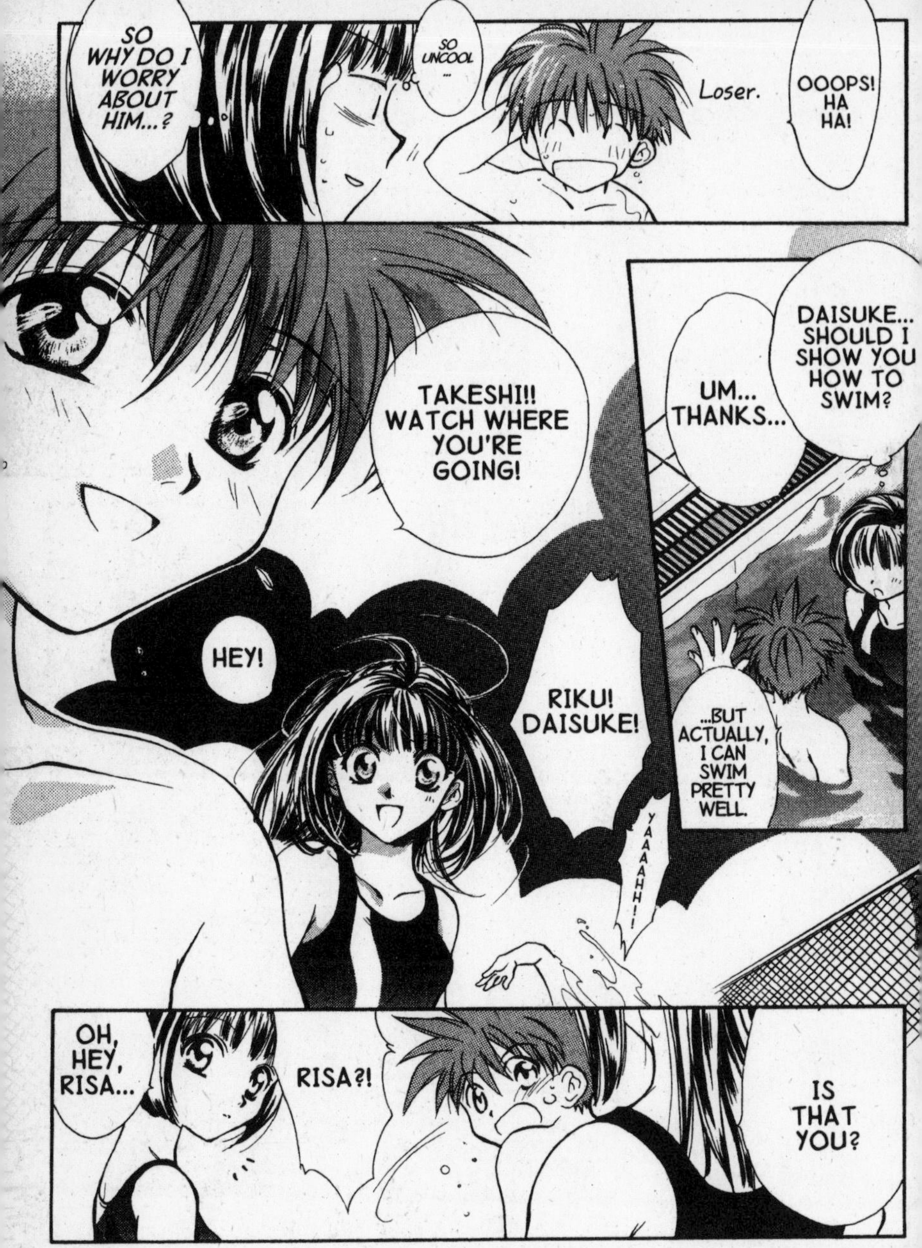
OOOPS! HA HA!
Loser.
SO UNCOOL...
SO WHY DO I WORRY ABOUT HIM...?
DAISUKE... SHOULD I SHOW YOU HOW TO SWIM?
UM... THANKS...
...BUT ACTUALLY, I CAN SWIM PRETTY WELL.
TAKESHI!!! WATCH WHERE YOU'RE GOING!
YAAAAHH!!
RIKU! DAISUKE!
HEY!
IS THAT YOU?
RISA?!
OH, HEY, RISA...

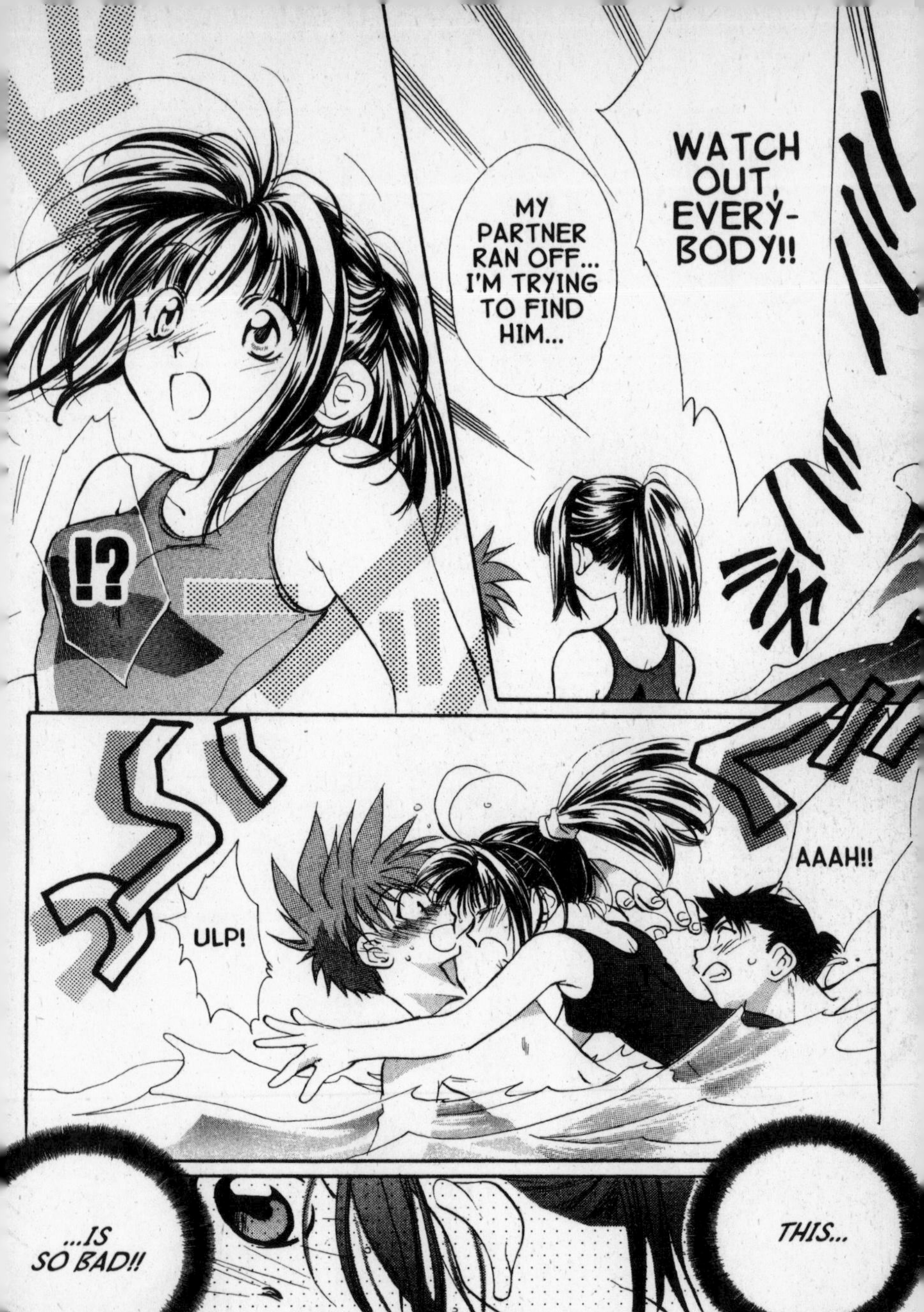
WATCH OUT, EVERY-BODY!!
MY PARTNER RAN OFF... I'M TRYING TO FIND HIM...
!?
AAAH!!
ULP!
THIS...
...IS SO BAD!!

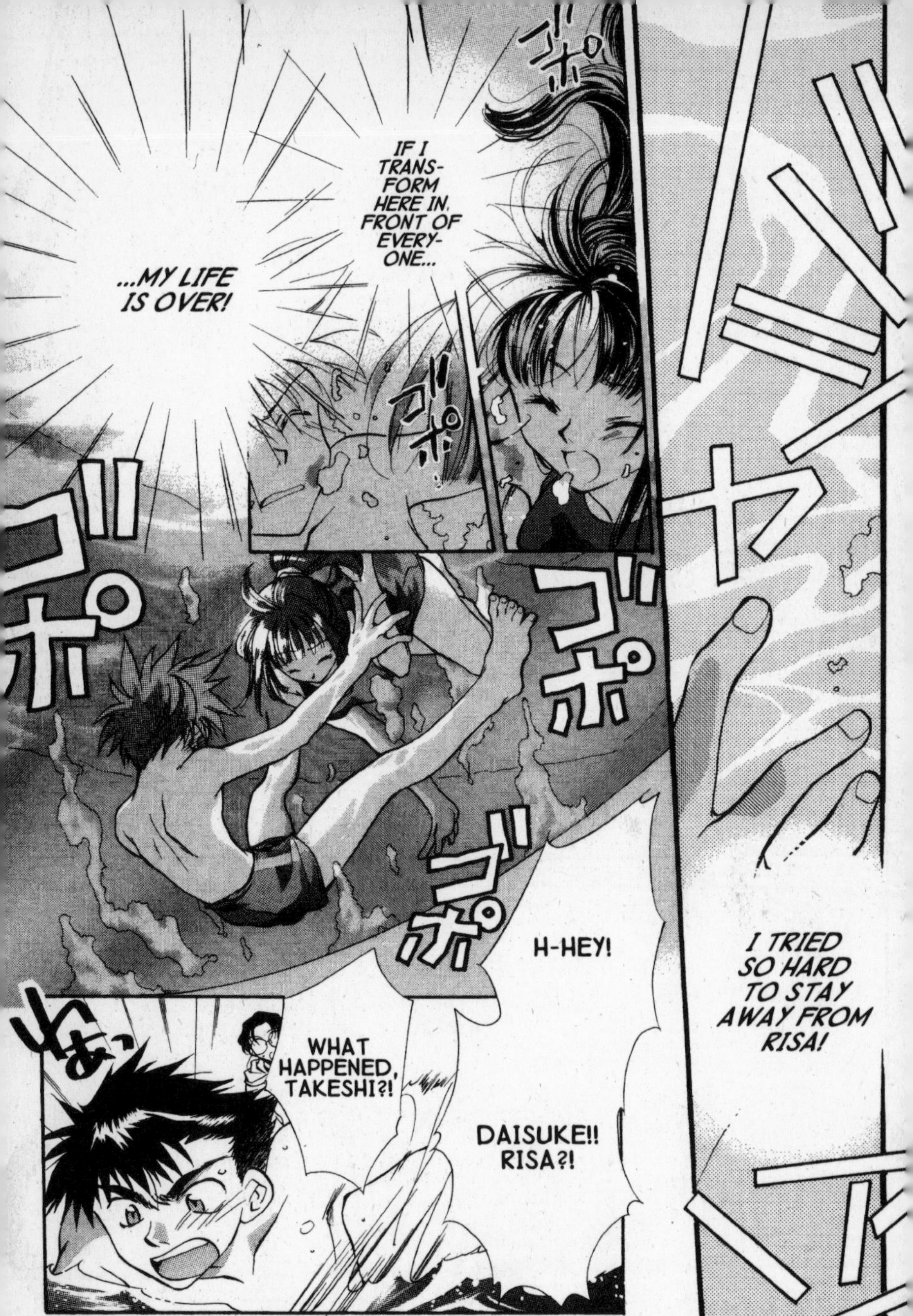
I TRIED SO HARD TO STAY AWAY FROM RISA!
IF I TRANSFORM HERE IN FRONT OF EVERYONE...
...MY LIFE IS OVER!
H-HEY!
DAISUKE!! RISA?!
WHAT HAPPENED, TAKESHI?!

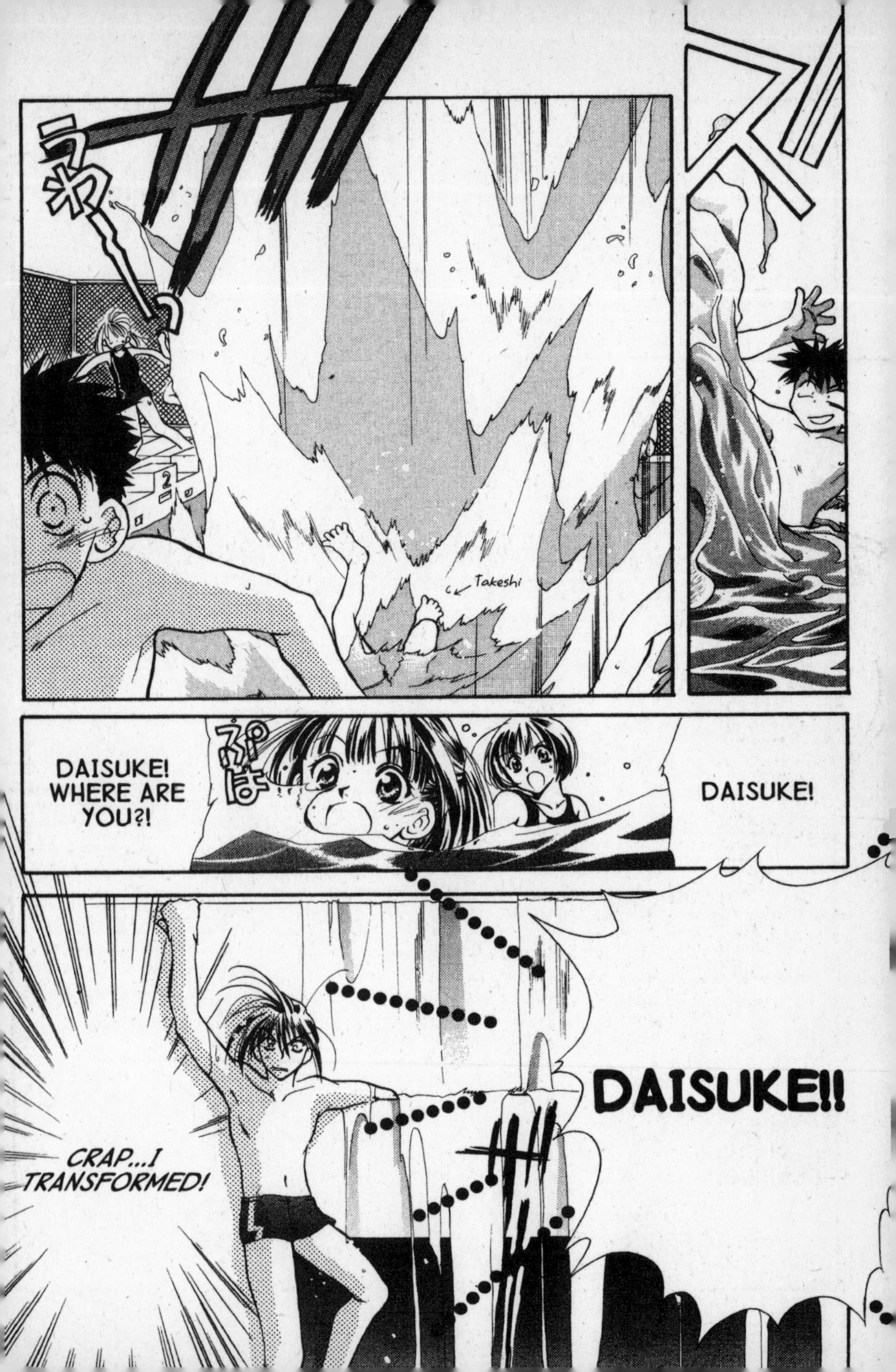

うわ〜っ
Takeshi
DAISUKE!
ぷは
DAISUKE! WHERE ARE YOU?!
DAISUKE!!
CRAP...I TRANSFORMED!

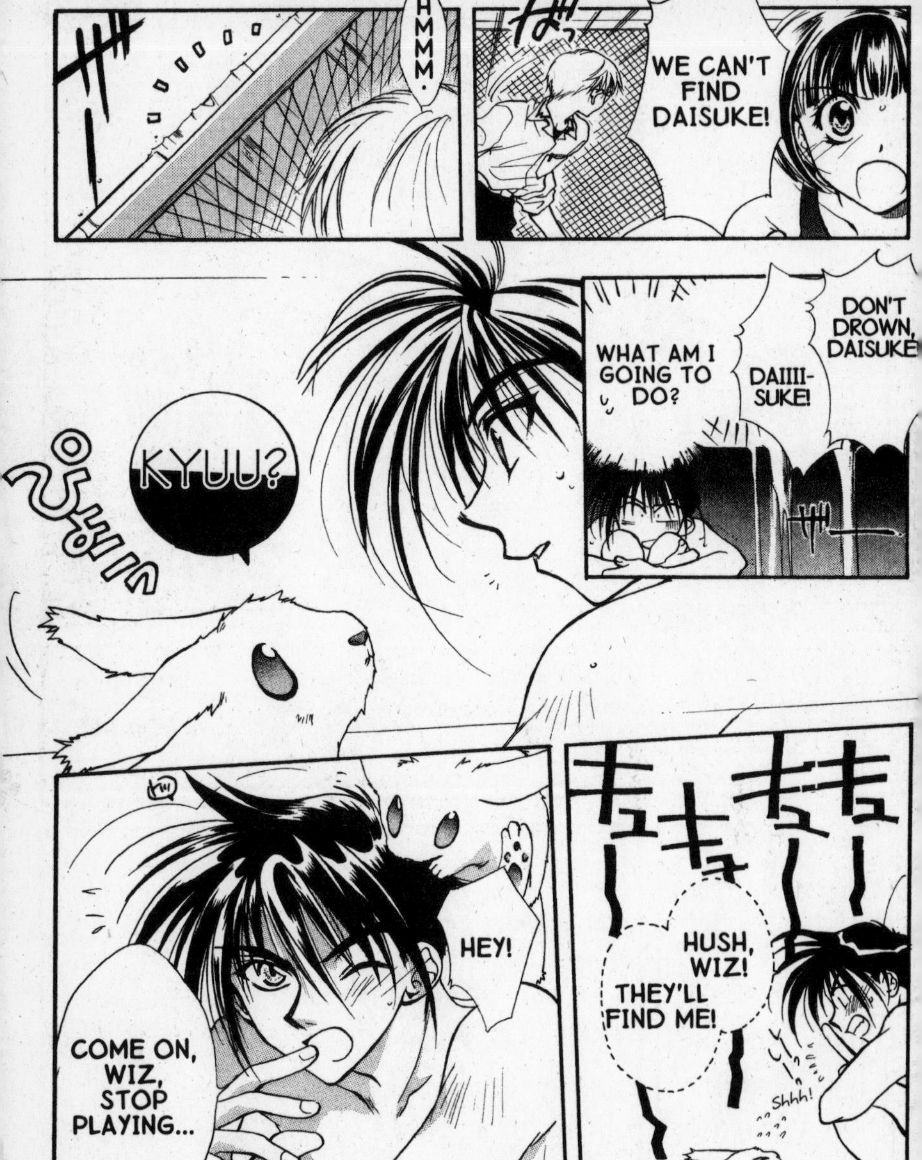
WE CAN'T FIND DAISUKE!
HMMM.
DON'T DROWN, DAISUKE
DAIIII-SUKE!
WHAT AM I GOING TO DO?
KYUU?
HUSH, WIZ!
THEY'LL FIND ME!
Shhh!
HEY!
COME ON, WIZ, STOP PLAYING...

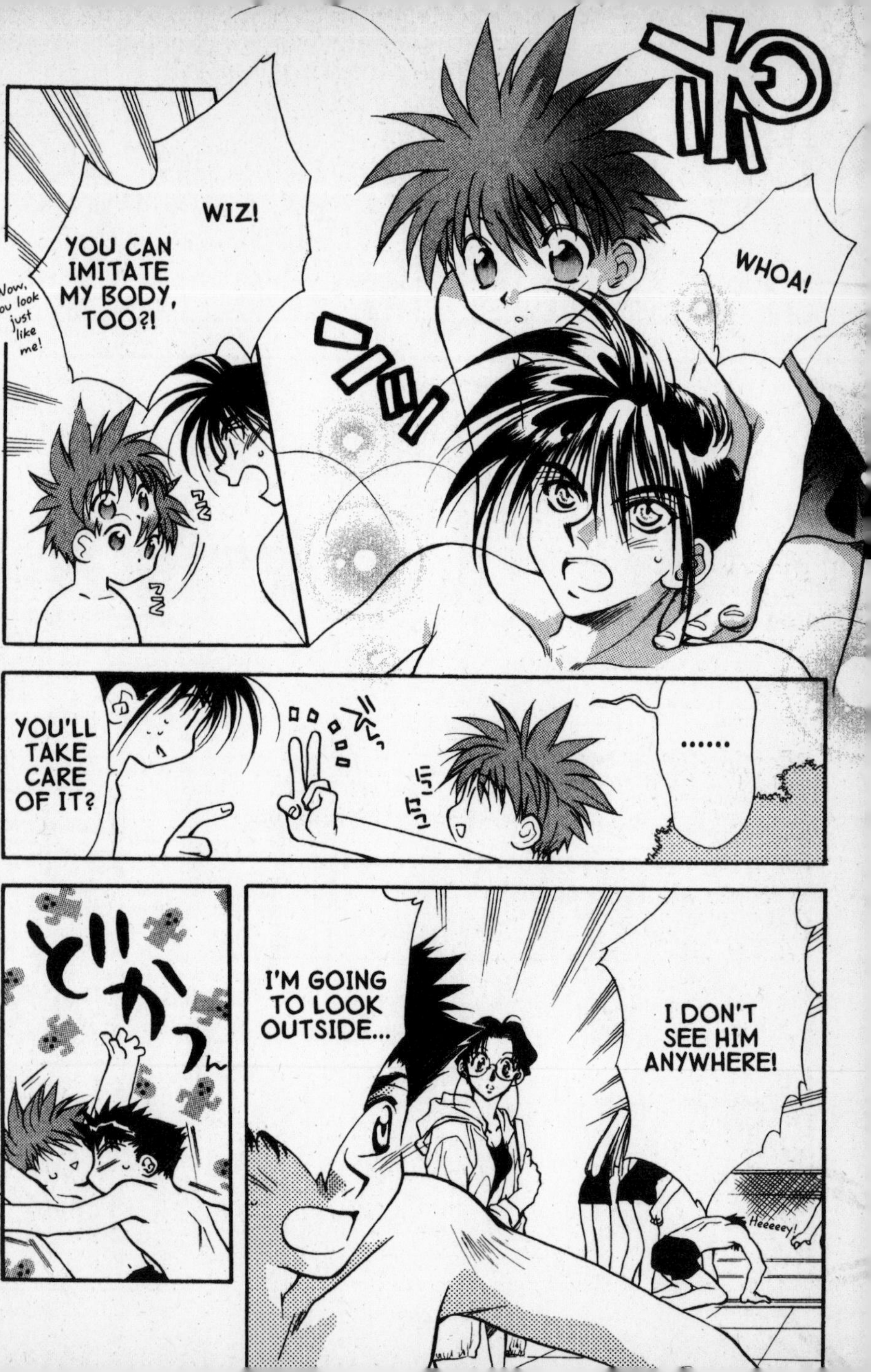
WHOA!
WIZ!
YOU CAN IMITATE MY BODY, TOO?!
Wow, you look just like me!
......
YOU'LL TAKE CARE OF IT?
I DON'T SEE HIM ANYWHERE!
Heeeeey!
I'M GOING TO LOOK OUTSIDE...

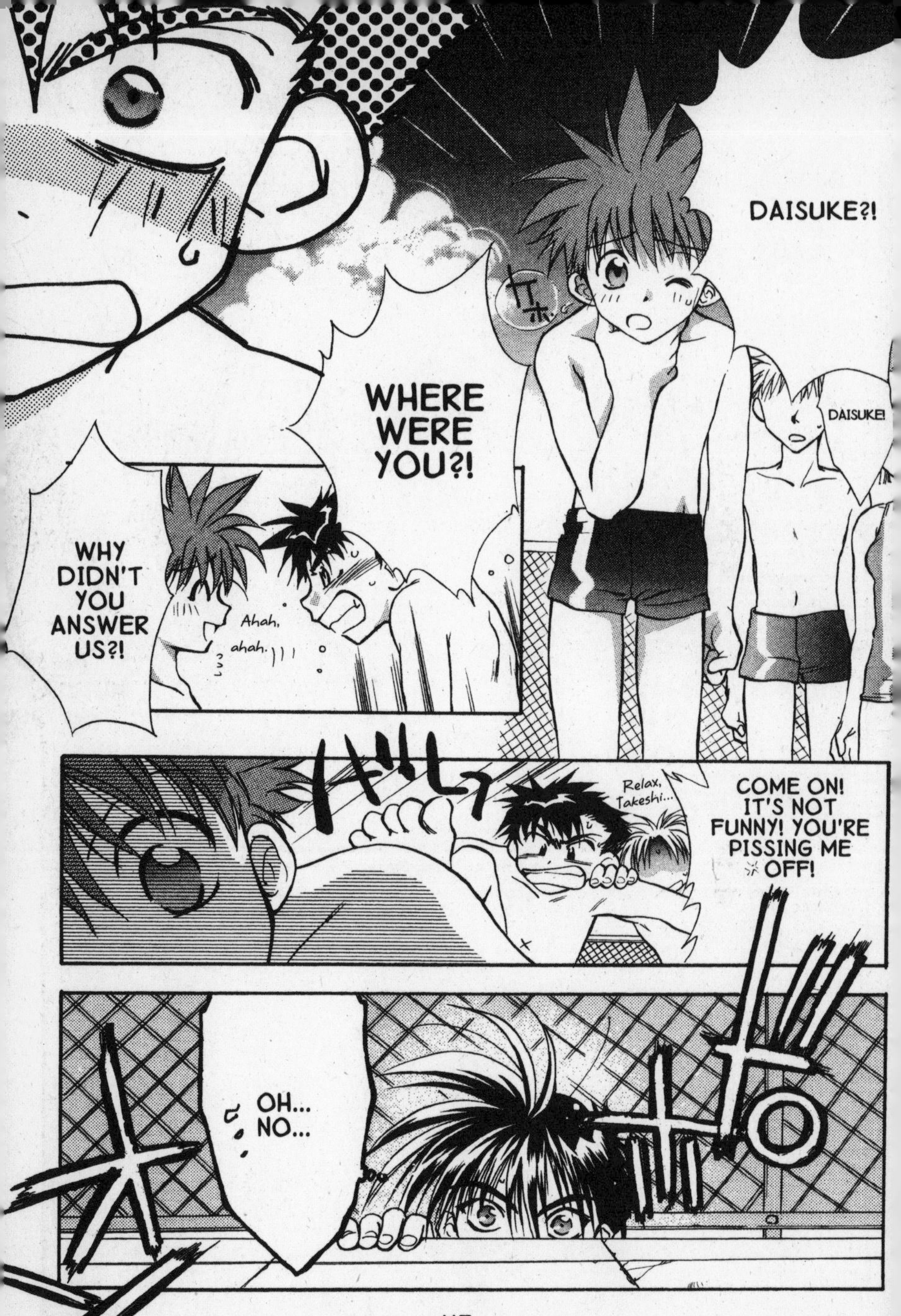
DAISUKE?!
DAISUKE!
WHERE WERE YOU?!
WHY DIDN'T YOU ANSWER US?!
Ahah, ahah.
COME ON! IT'S NOT FUNNY! YOU'RE PISSING ME OFF!
Relax, Takeshi...
OH... NO...

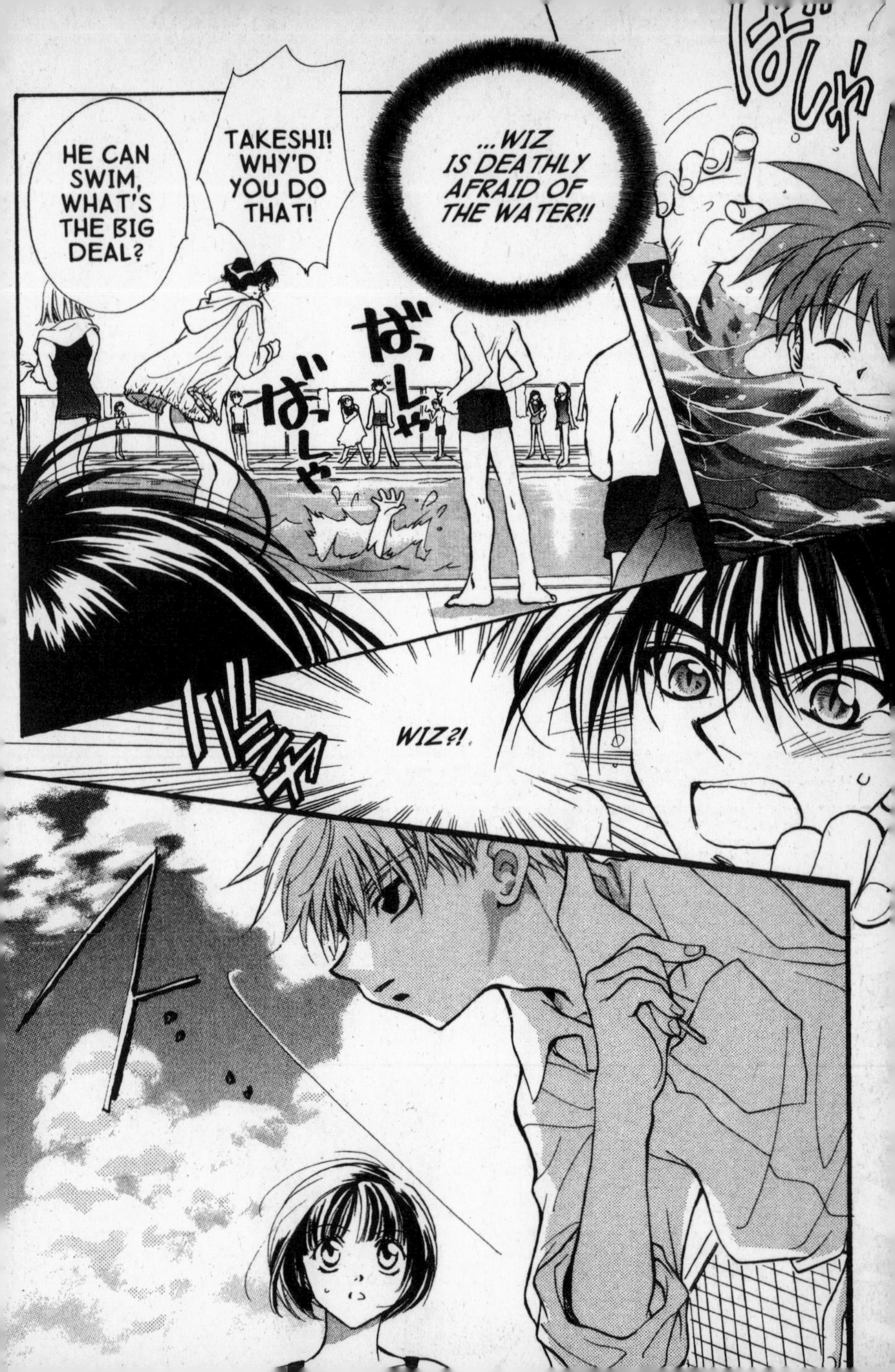
ばしゅ
...WIZ IS DEATHLY AFRAID OF THE WATER!!
TAKESHI! WHY'D YOU DO THAT!
HE CAN SWIM, WHAT'S THE BIG DEAL?
ばっしゃ
ばっしゃ
WIZ?!

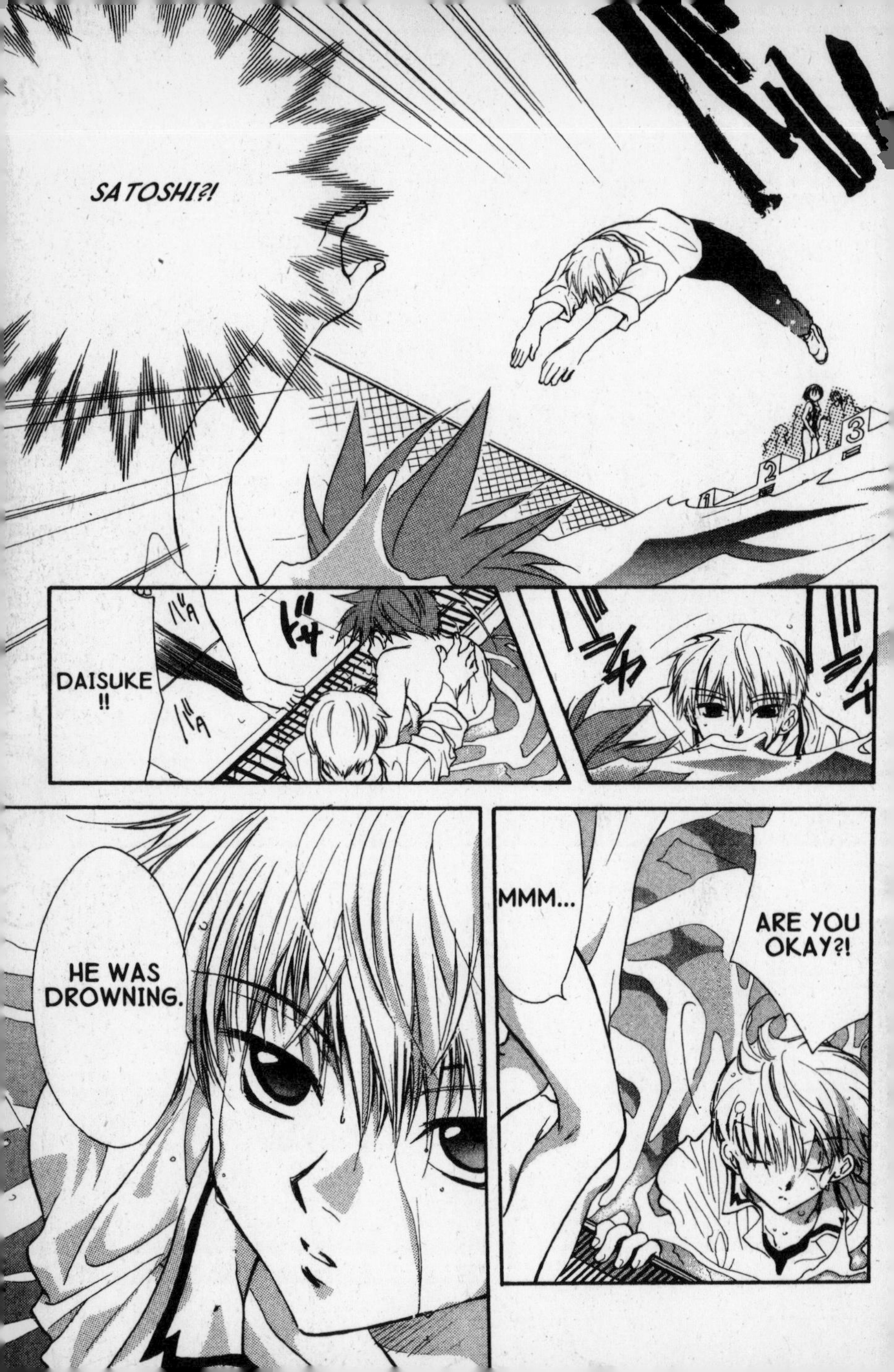
SATOSHI?!
DAISUKE !!
ARE YOU OKAY?!
MMM...
HE WAS DROWNING.

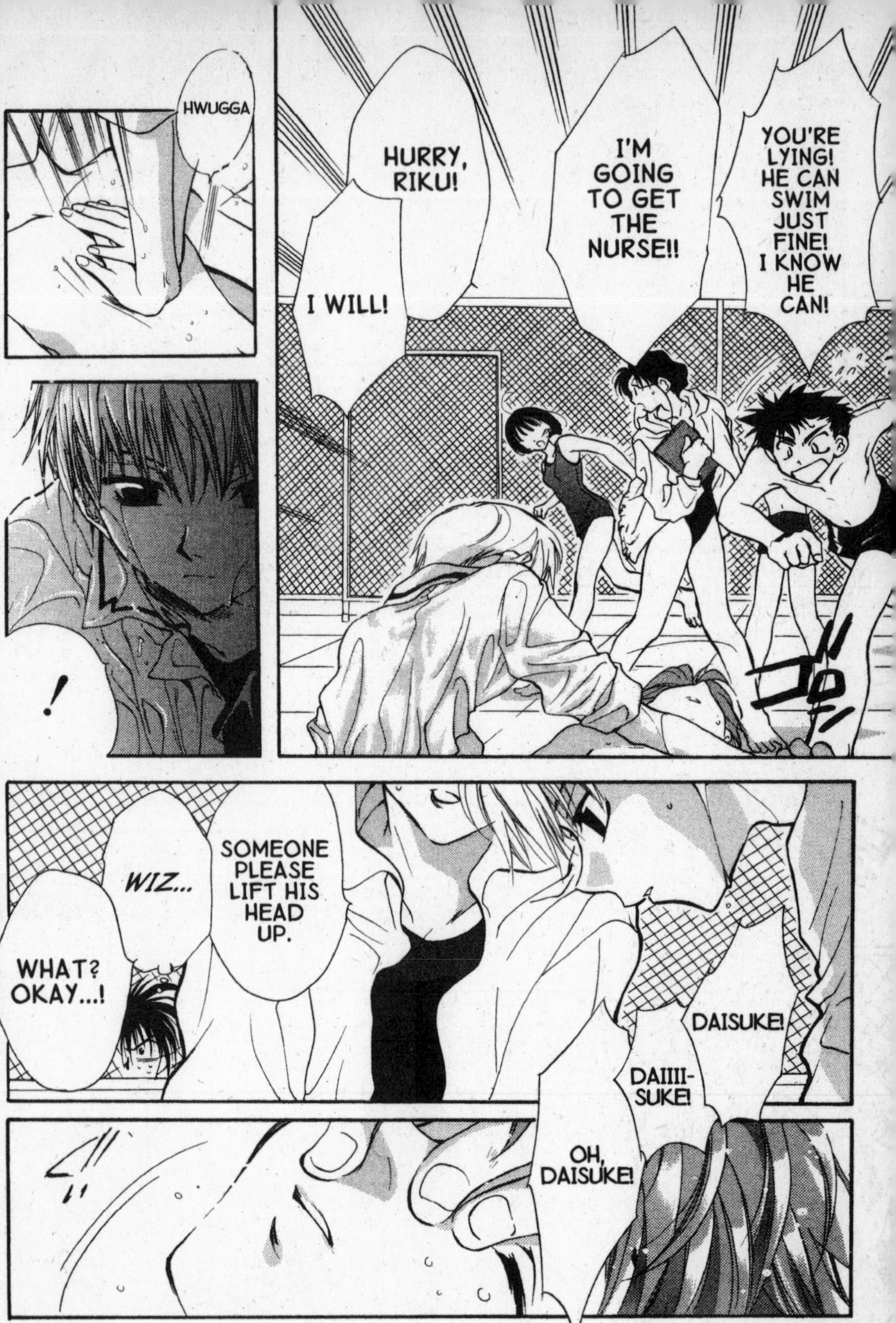
YOU'RE LYING! HE CAN SWIM JUST FINE! I KNOW HE CAN!
I'M GOING TO GET THE NURSE!!
HURRY, RIKU!
I WILL!
HWUGGA
!
DAISUKE!
DAIIII-SUKE!
SOMEONE PLEASE LIFT HIS HEAD UP.
WIZ...
WHAT? OKAY...!
OH, DAISUKE!

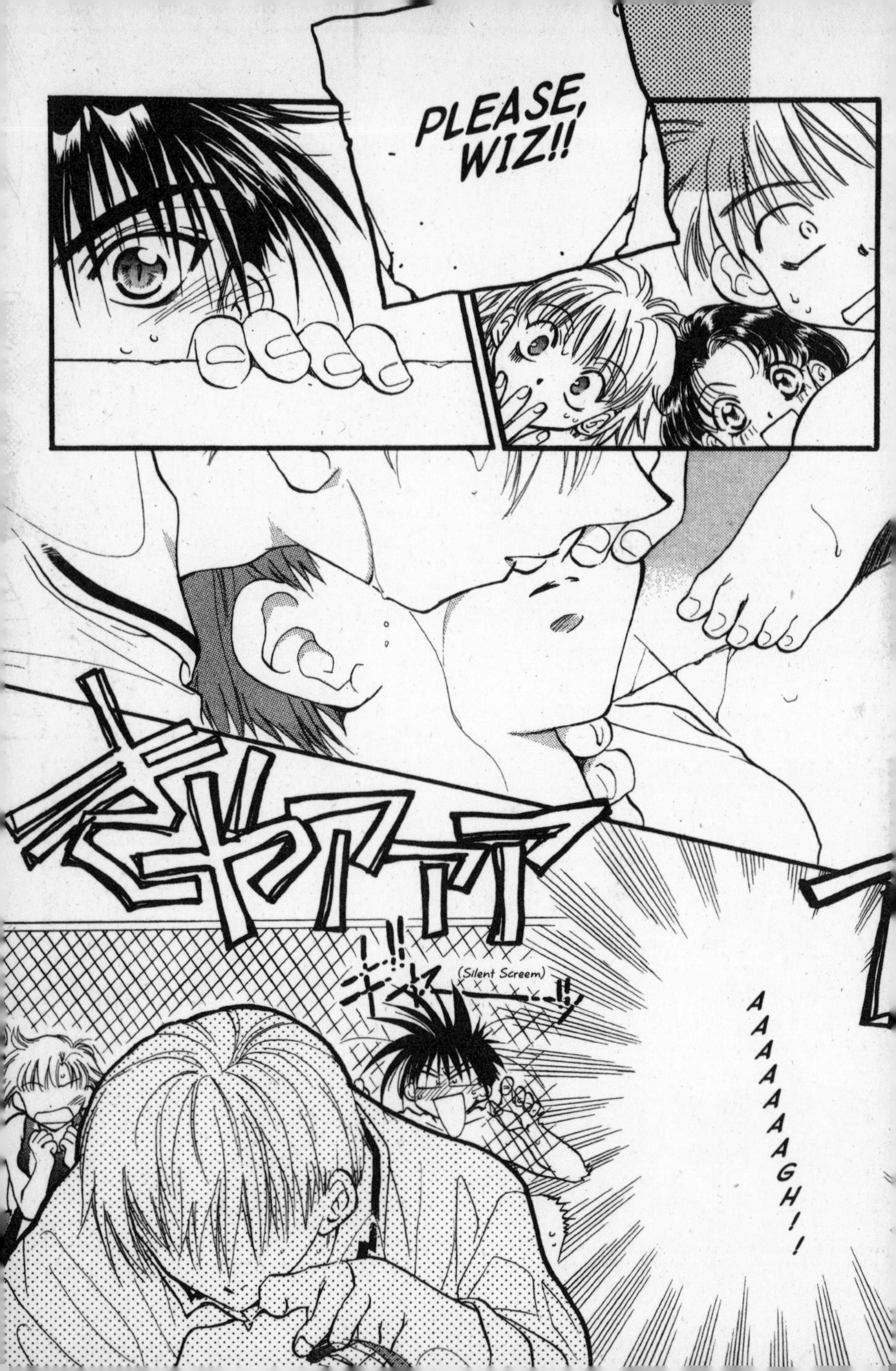
PLEASE, WIZ!!
AAAAAAAGH!!
(Silent Screem)

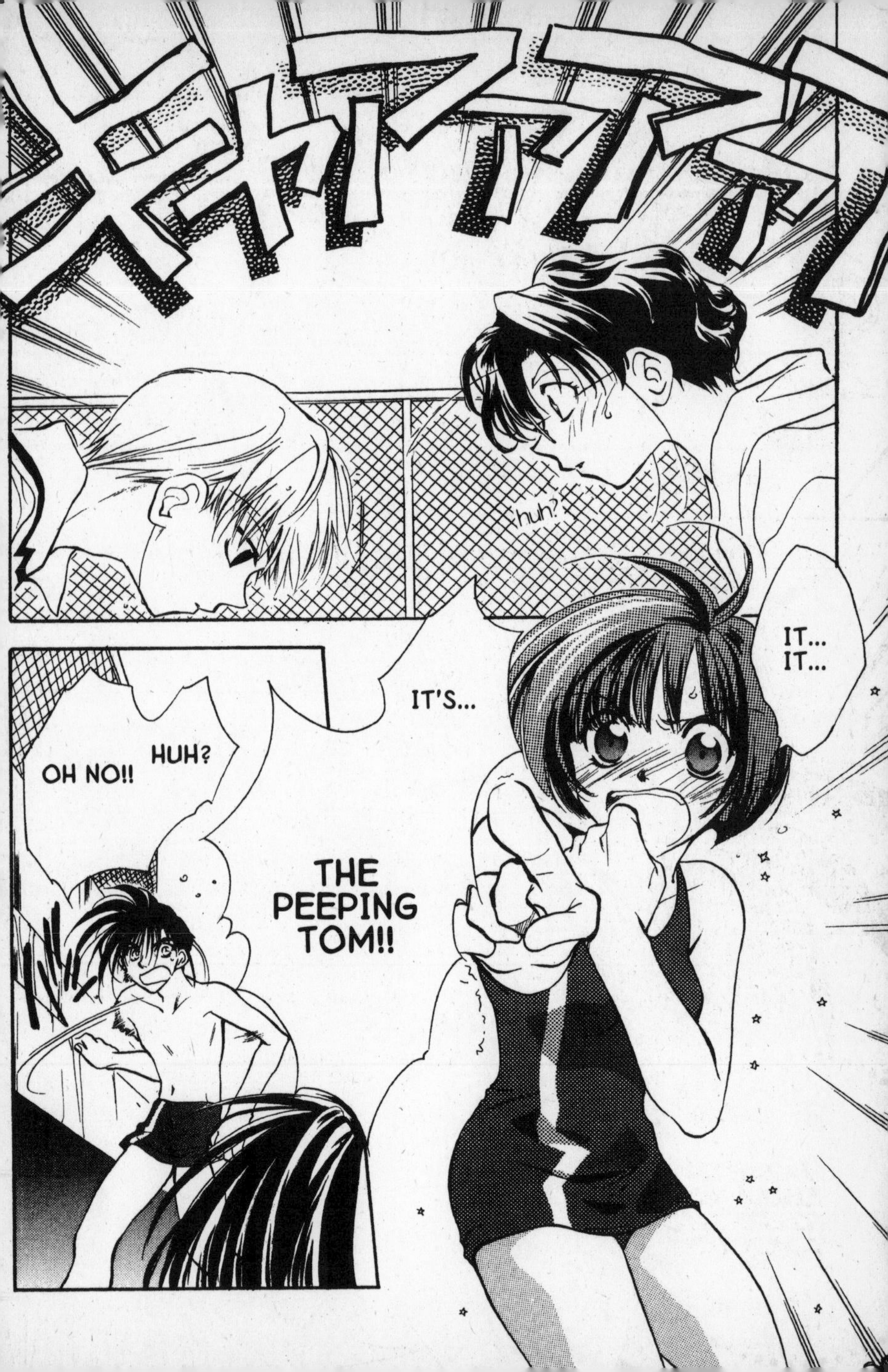
huh?
IT...
IT...
IT'S...
THE PEEPING TOM!!
HUH?
OH NO!!

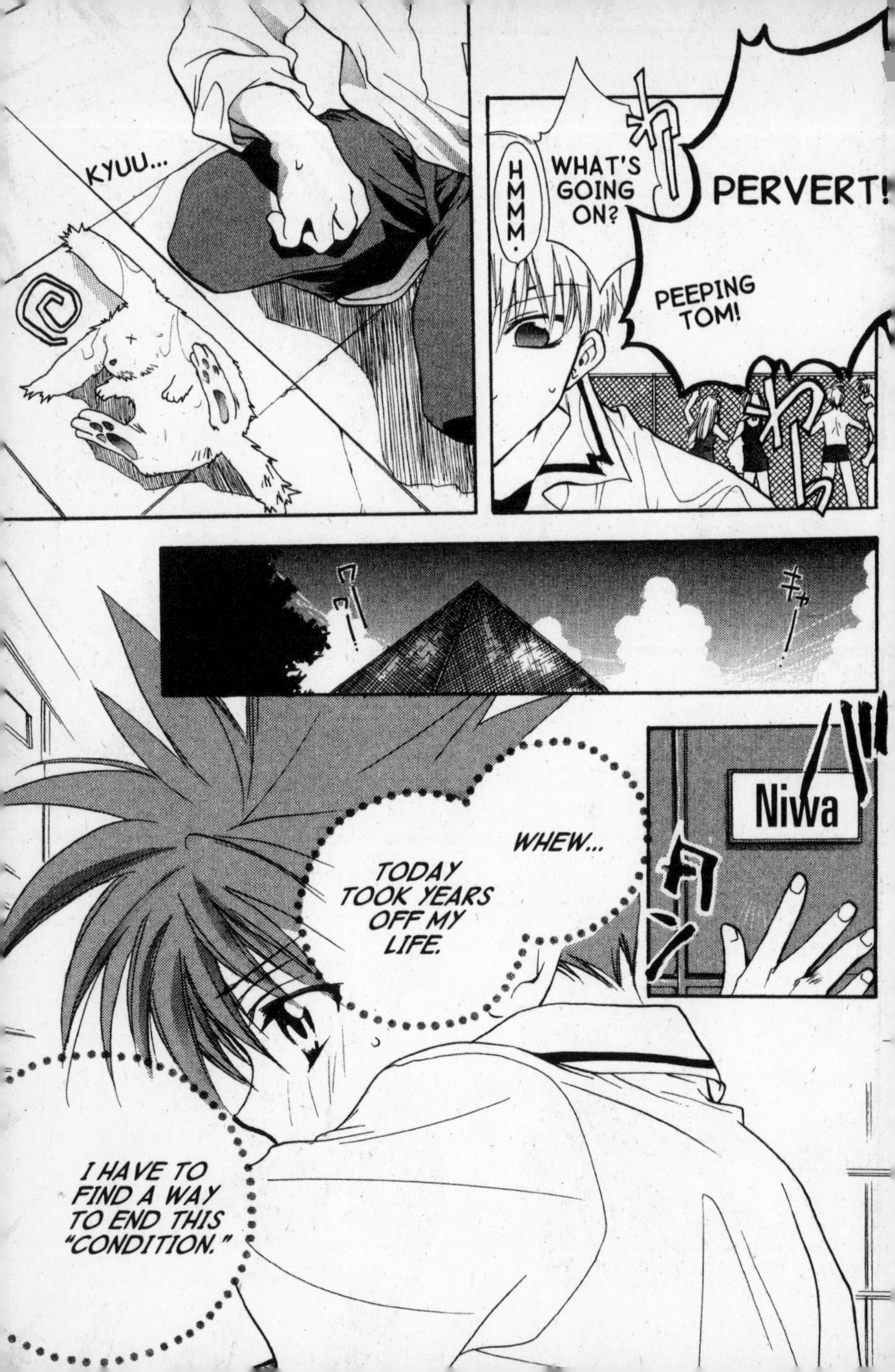
PERVERT!
PEEPING TOM!
WHAT'S GOING ON?
HMMM.
KYUU...
Niwa
WHEW...
TODAY TOOK YEARS OFF MY LIFE.
I HAVE TO FIND A WAY TO END THIS "CONDITION."

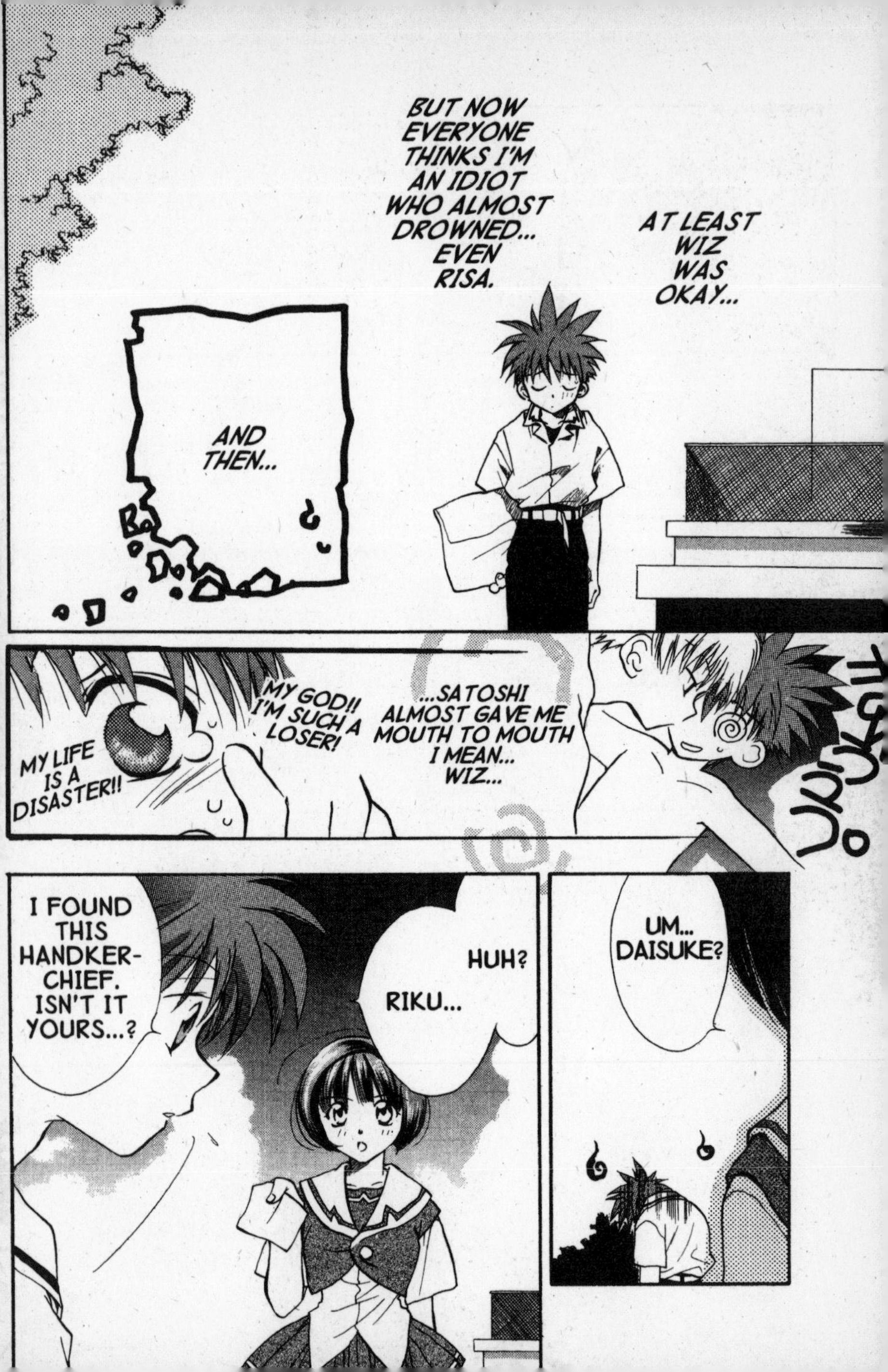
BUT NOW EVERYONE THINKS I'M AN IDIOT WHO ALMOST DROWNED... EVEN RISA.
AT LEAST WIZ WAS OKAY...
AND THEN...
...SATOSHI ALMOST GAVE ME MOUTH TO MOUTH I MEAN... WIZ...
MY GOD!! I'M SUCH A LOSER!
MY LIFE IS A DISASTER!!
UM... DAISUKE?
HUH?
RIKU...
I FOUND THIS HANDKERCHIEF. ISN'T IT YOURS...?

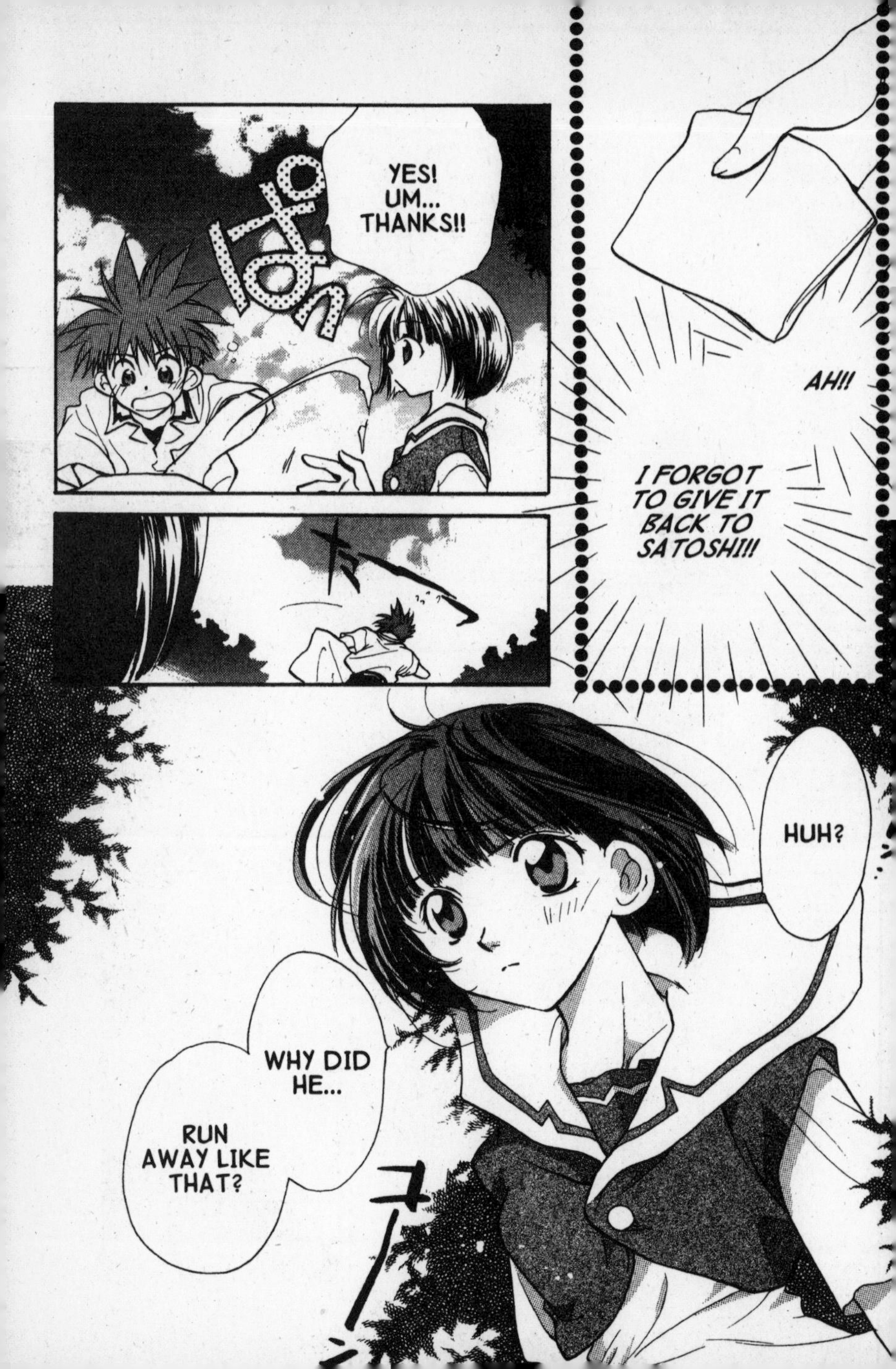
AH!!
I FORGOT TO GIVE IT BACK TO SATOSHI!!!
YES! UM... THANKS!!
HUH?
WHY DID HE...
RUN AWAY LIKE THAT?

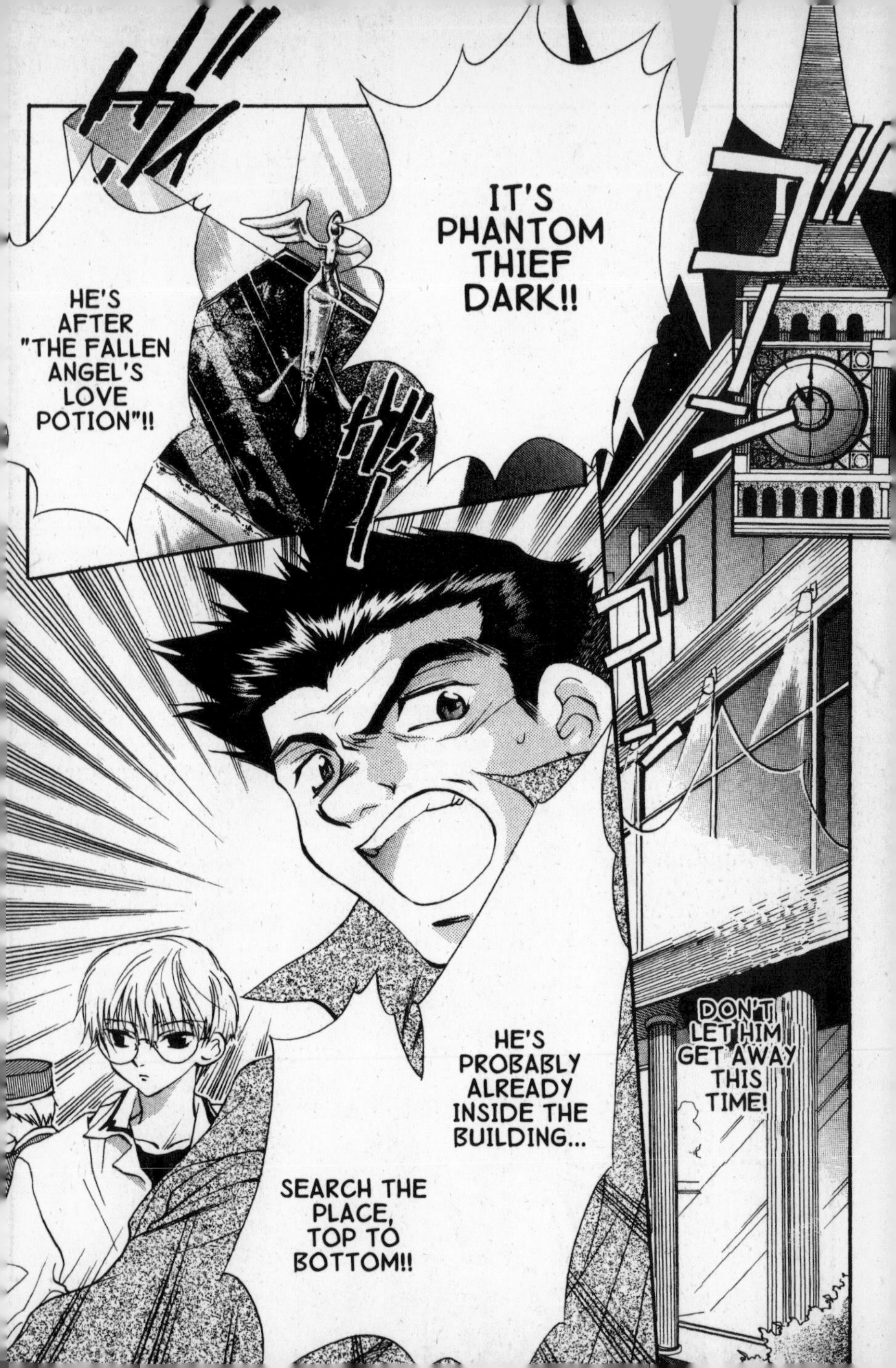
IT'S PHANTOM THIEF DARK!!
HE'S AFTER "THE FALLEN ANGEL'S LOVE POTION"!!
DON'T LET HIM GET AWAY THIS TIME!
HE'S PROBABLY ALREADY INSIDE THE BUILDING...
SEARCH THE PLACE, TOP TO BOTTOM!!

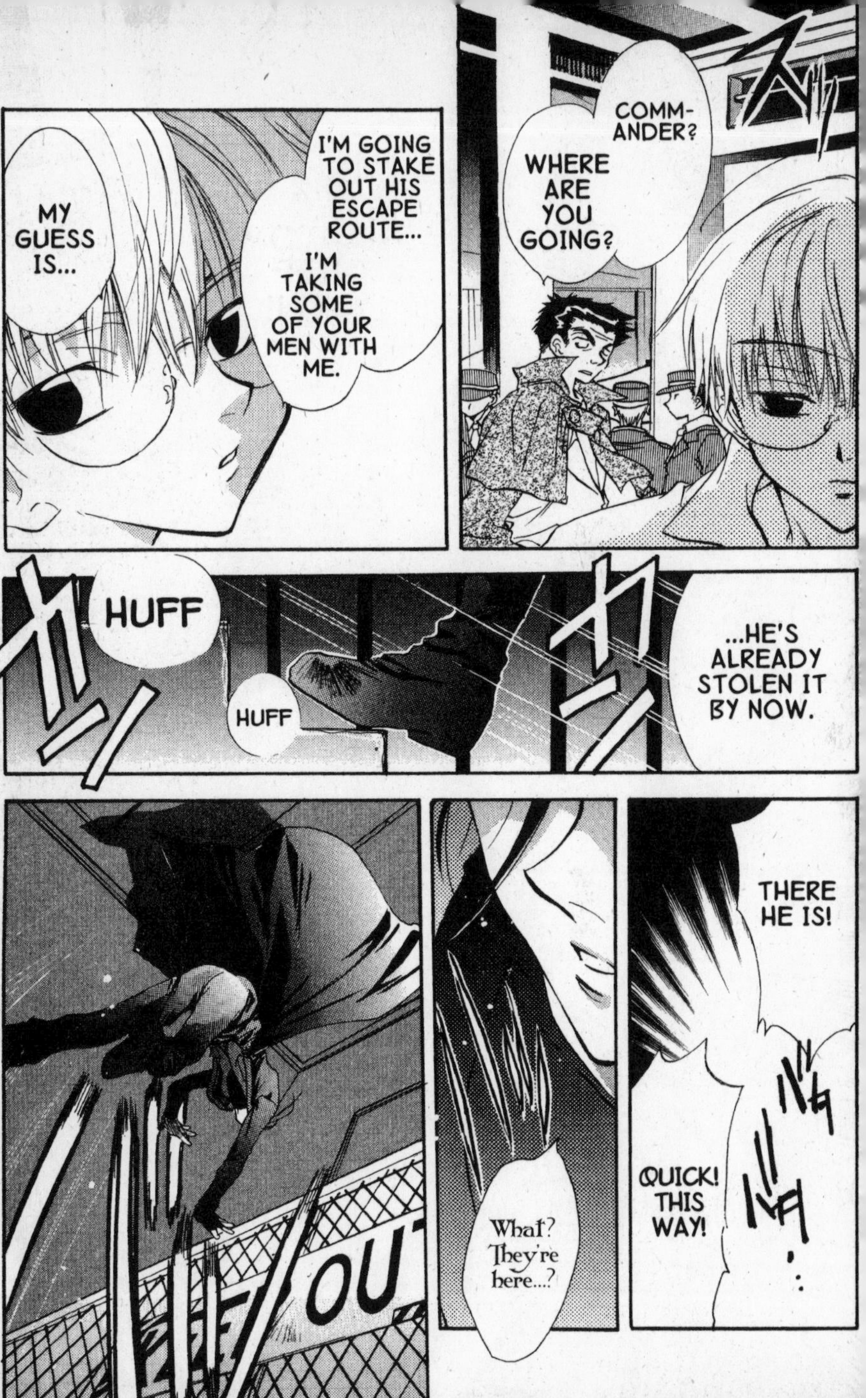
COMM-ANDER?
WHERE ARE YOU GOING?
I'M GOING TO STAKE OUT HIS ESCAPE ROUTE...
I'M TAKING SOME OF YOUR MEN WITH ME.
MY GUESS IS...
...HE'S ALREADY STOLEN IT BY NOW.
HUFF
HUFF
THERE HE IS!
QUICK! THIS WAY!
What? They're here...?
OUT

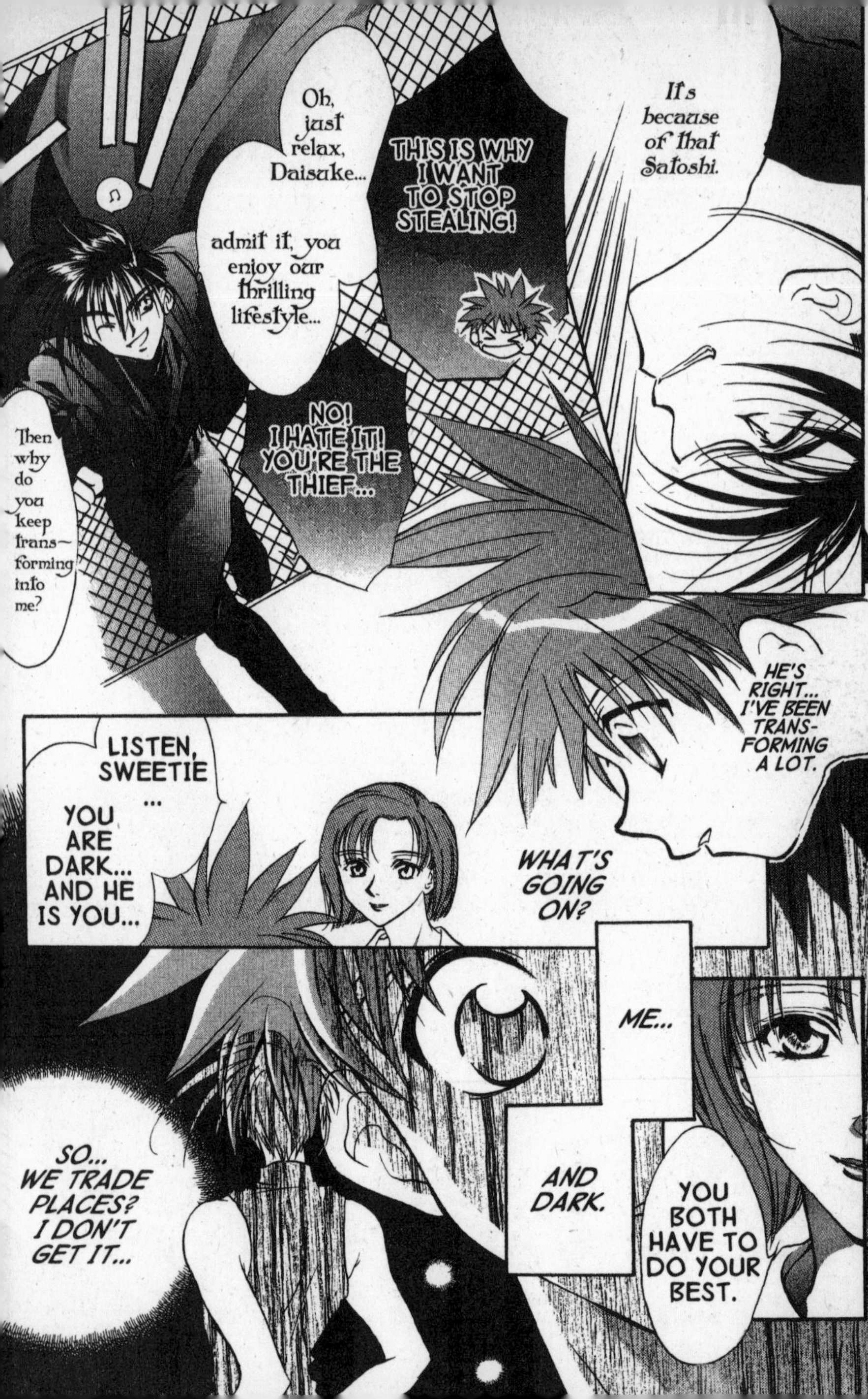
It's because of that Satoshi.
Oh, just relax, Daisuke...
THIS IS WHY I WANT TO STOP STEALING!
admit it, you enjoy our thrilling lifestyle...
NO! I HATE IT! YOU'RE THE THIEF...
Then why do you keep trans-forming into me?
HE'S RIGHT... I'VE BEEN TRANS-FORMING A LOT.
LISTEN, SWEETIE ...
YOU ARE DARK... AND HE IS YOU...
WHAT'S GOING ON?
ME...
AND DARK.
YOU BOTH HAVE TO DO YOUR BEST.
SO... WE TRADE PLACES? I DON'T GET IT...

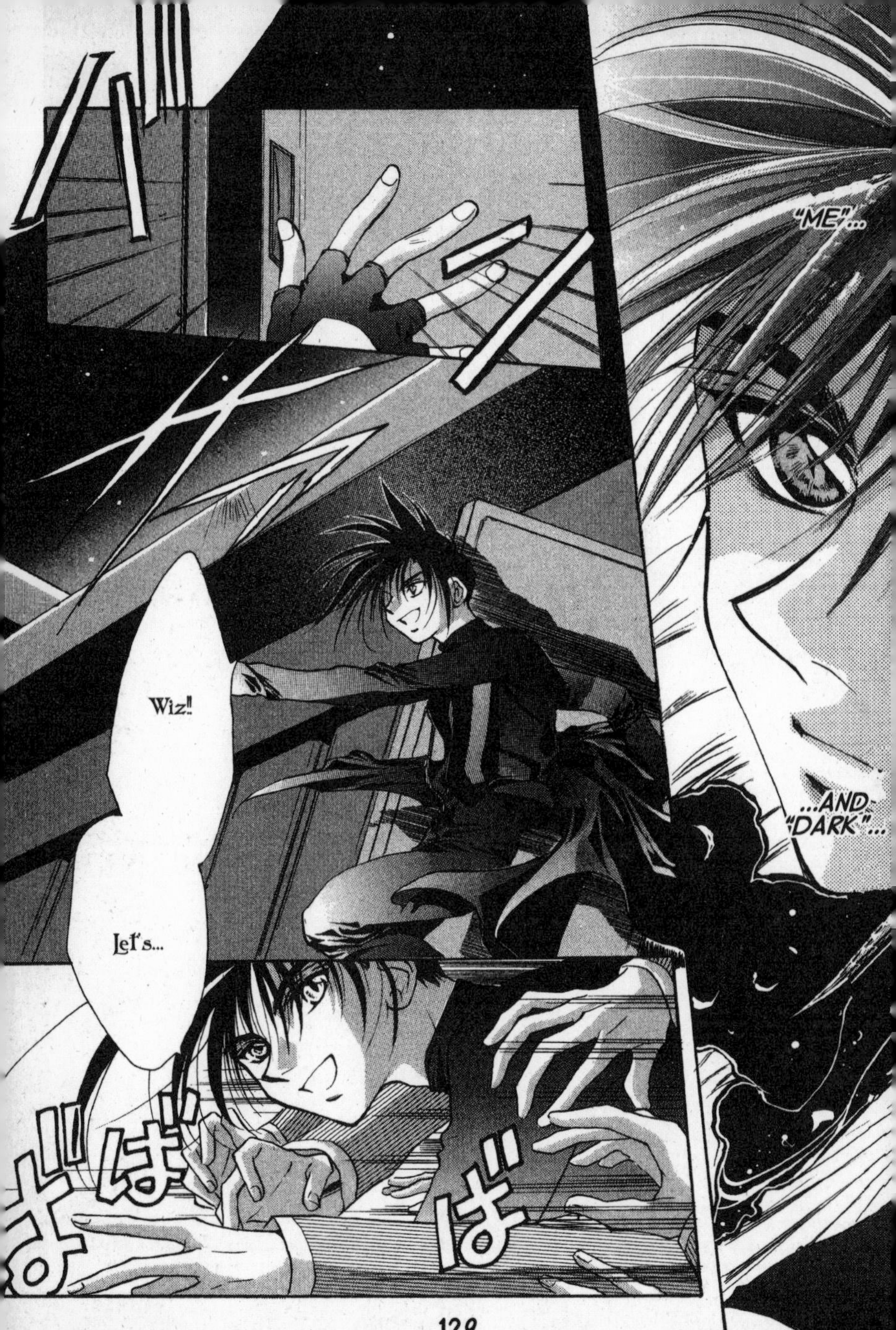
"ME"...
...AND "DARK"...
Wiz!!
Let's...

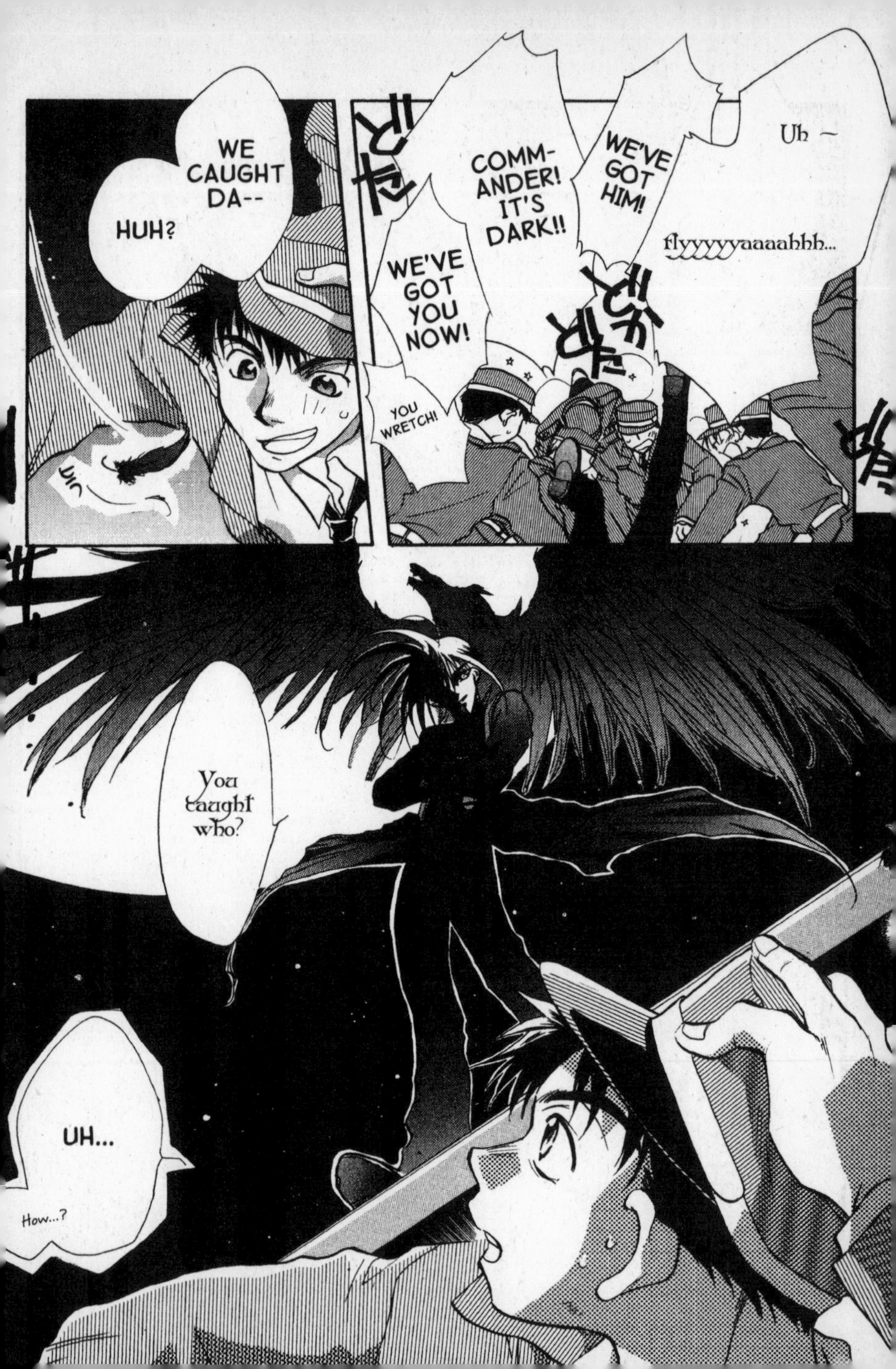
Uh ~
flyyyyyaaaahhh...
WE'VE GOT HIM!
COMM-ANDER! IT'S DARK!!
WE'VE GOT YOU NOW!
YOU WRETCH!
WE CAUGHT DA--
HUH?
You caught who?
UH...
How...?

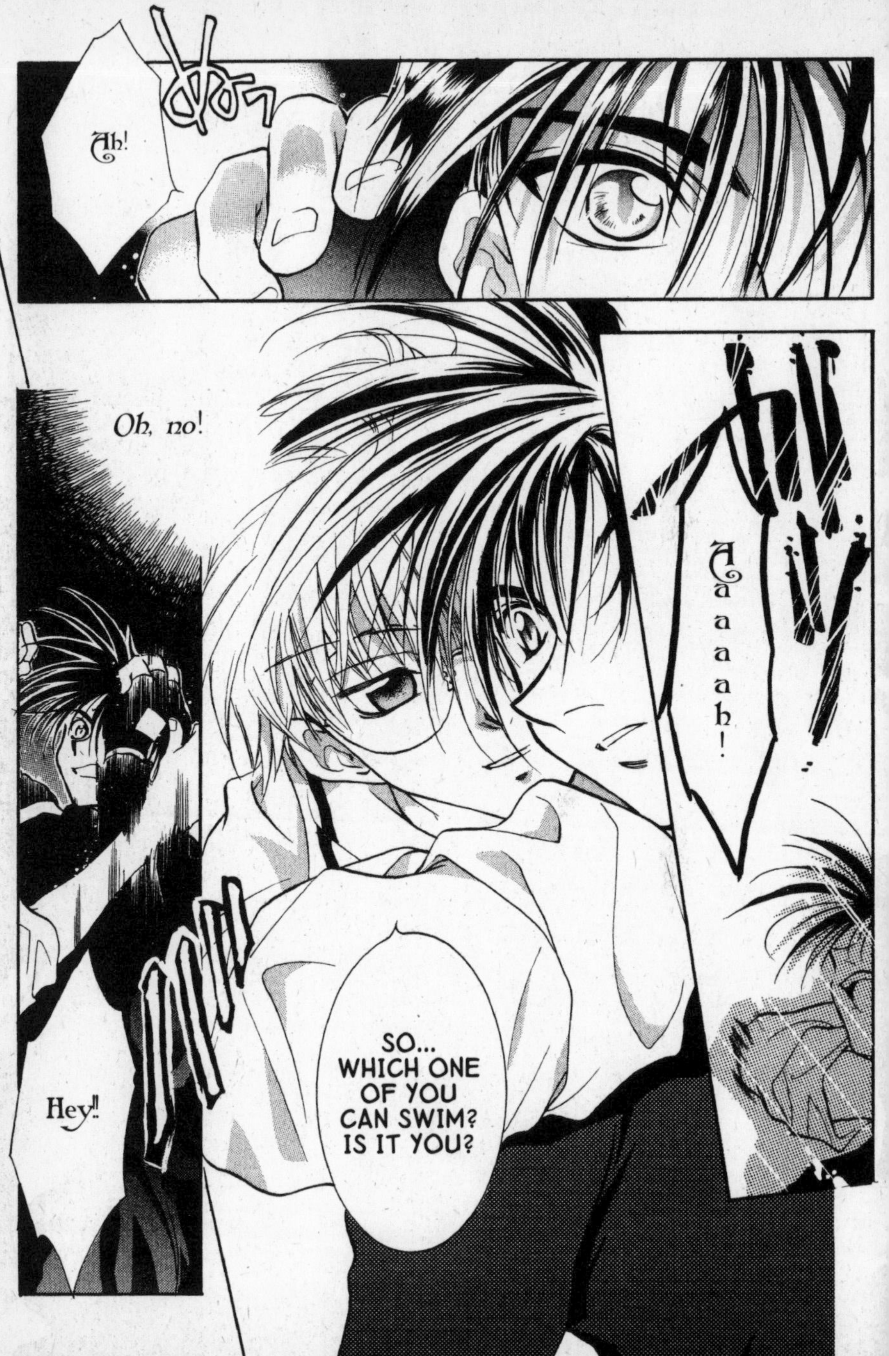
Ah!
Aaaaaah!
Oh, no!
SO... WHICH ONE OF YOU CAN SWIM? IS IT YOU?
Hey!!

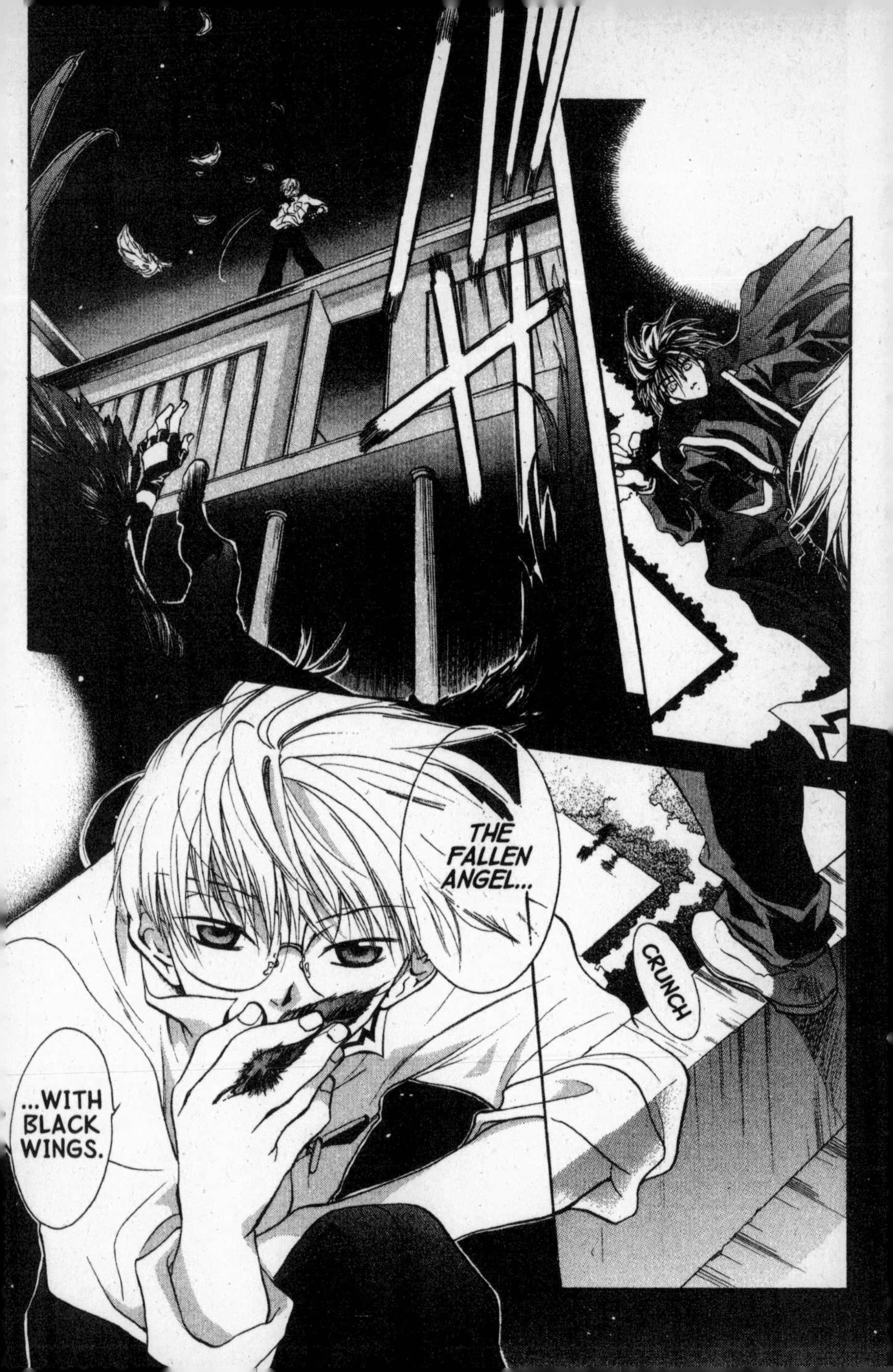
THE FALLEN ANGEL...
CRUNCH
...WITH BLACK WINGS.

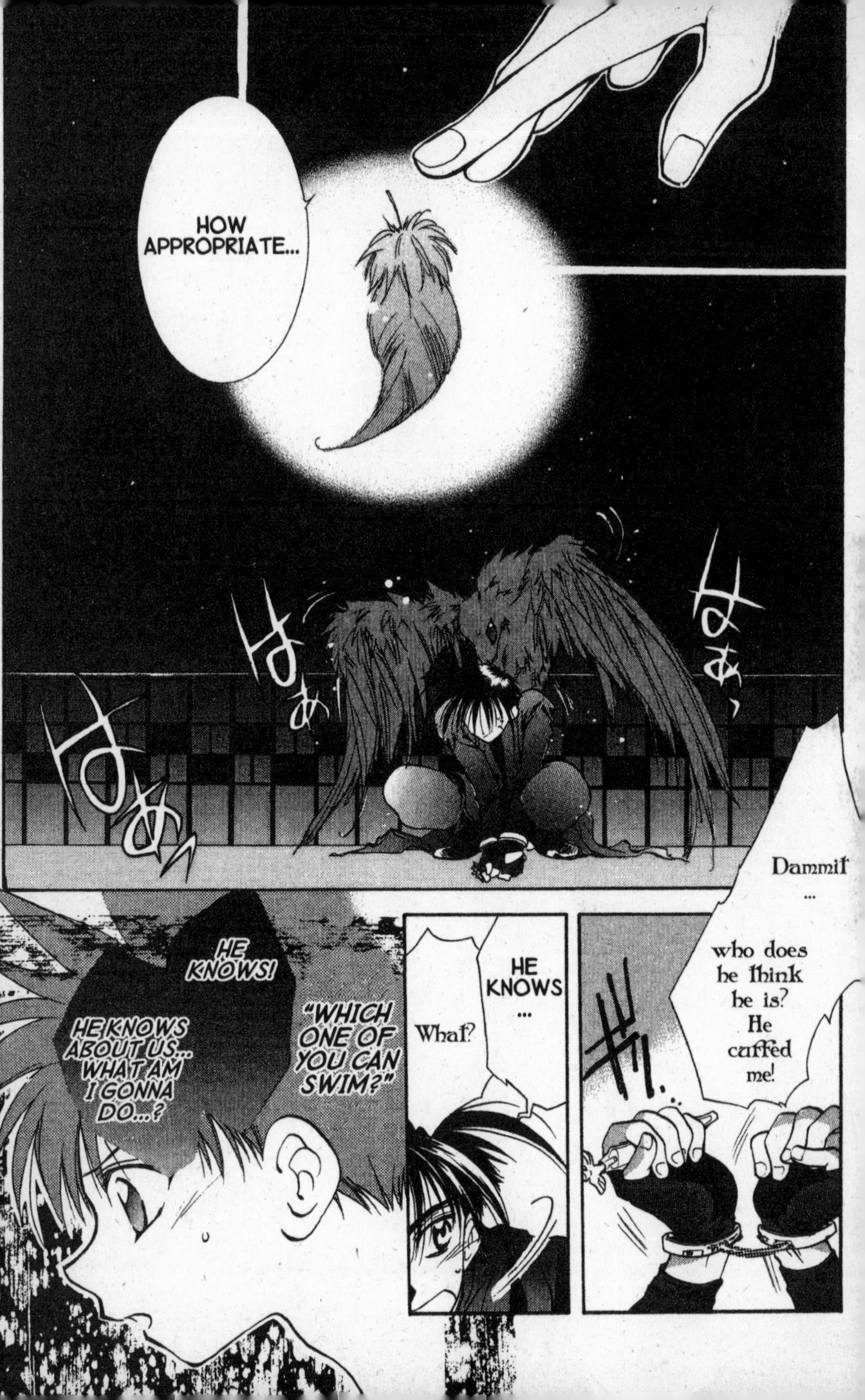
HOW APPROPRIATE...
はぁ、
はぁ
はぁ
Dammit ...
who does he think he is? He cuffed me!
ギリ...
HE KNOWS ...
What?
HE KNOWS!
"WHICH ONE OF YOU CAN SWIM?"
HE KNOWS ABOUT US... WHAT AM I GONNA DO...?

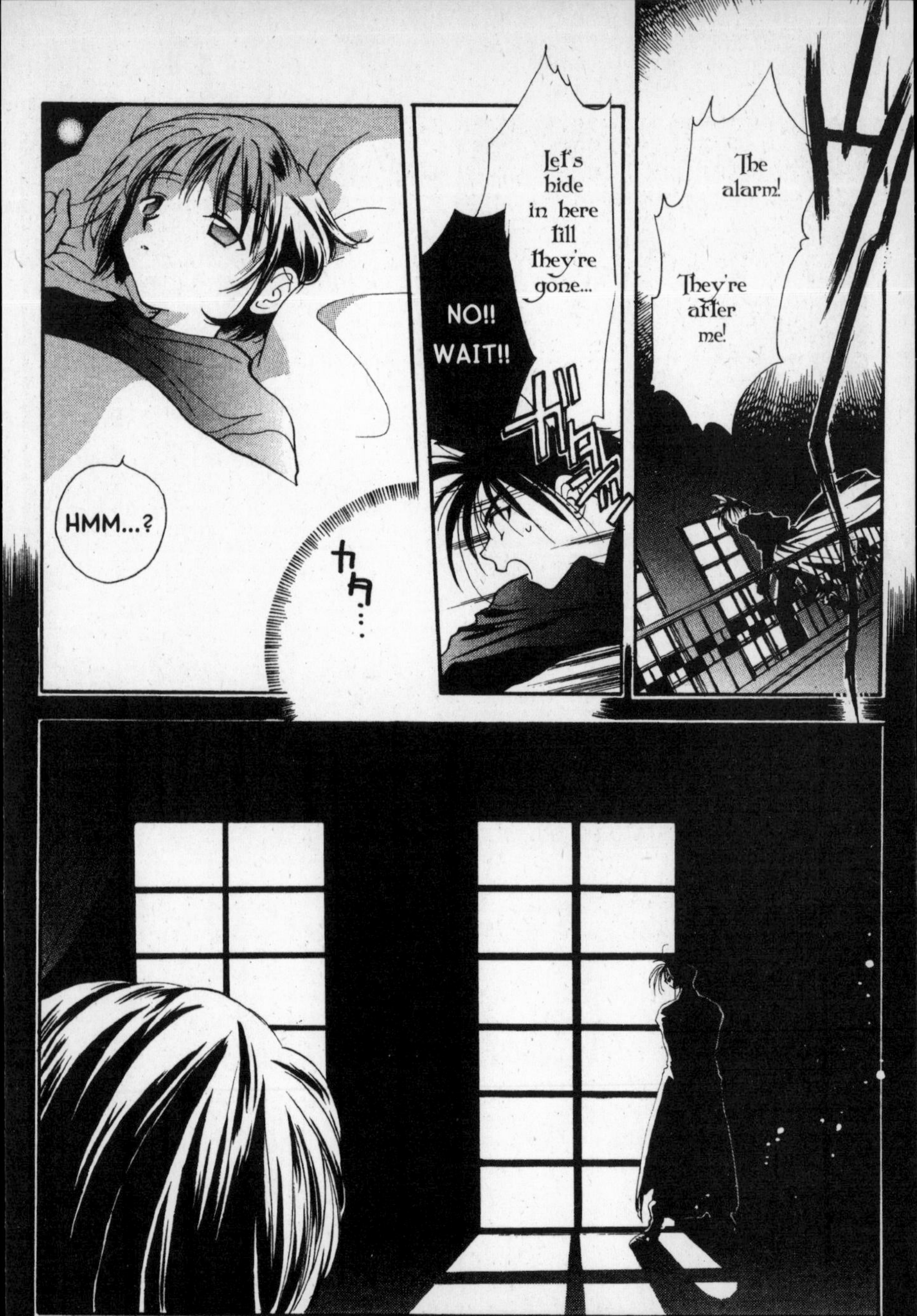
The alarm!
They're after me!
Let's hide in here till they're gone...
NO!! WAIT!!
ガタン
カタ…
HMM...?

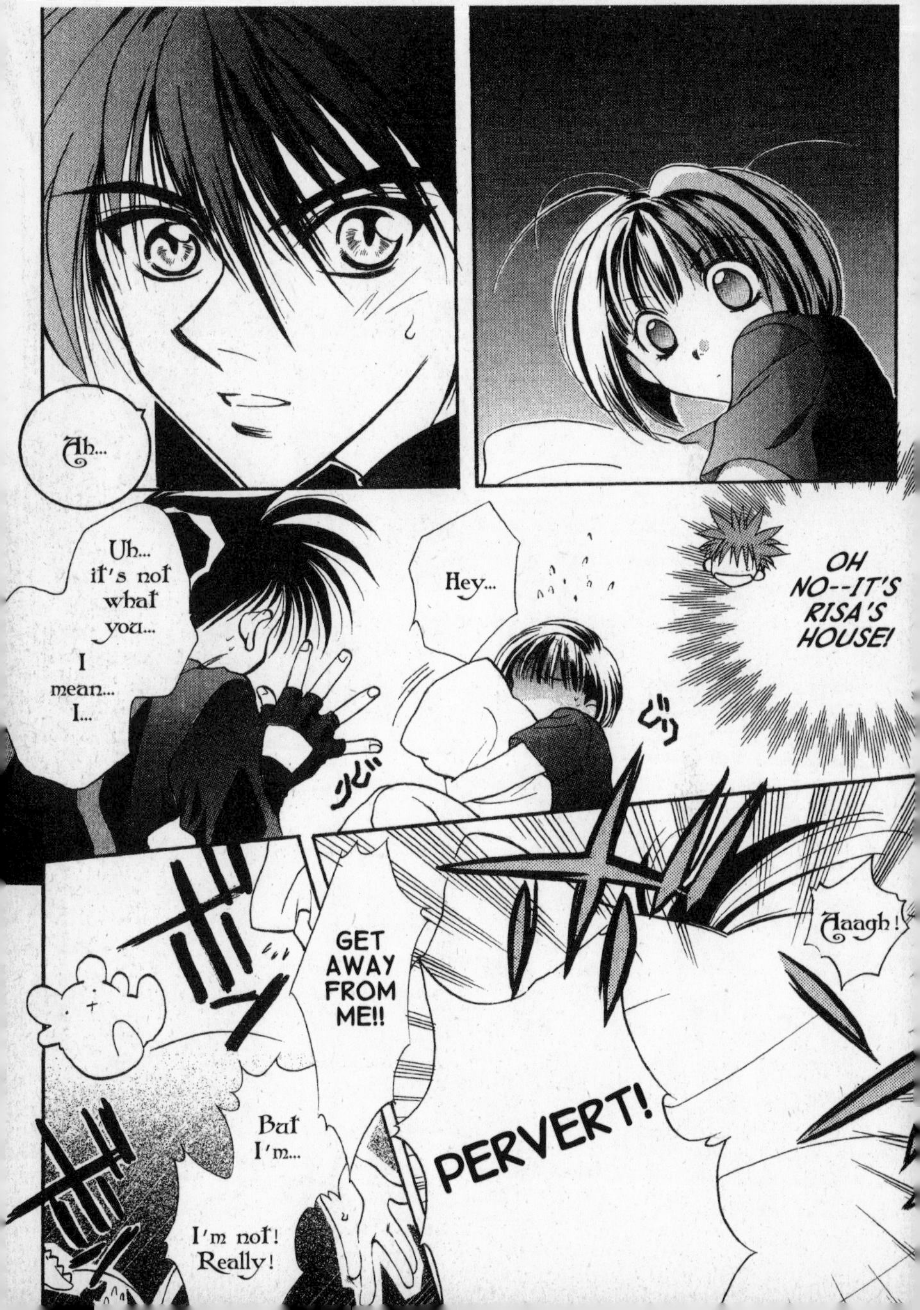
Ah...
OH NO--IT'S RISA'S HOUSE!
Hey...
Uh... it's not what you...
I mean... I...
Aaagh!
PERVERT!
GET AWAY FROM ME!!
But I'm...
I'm not! Really!

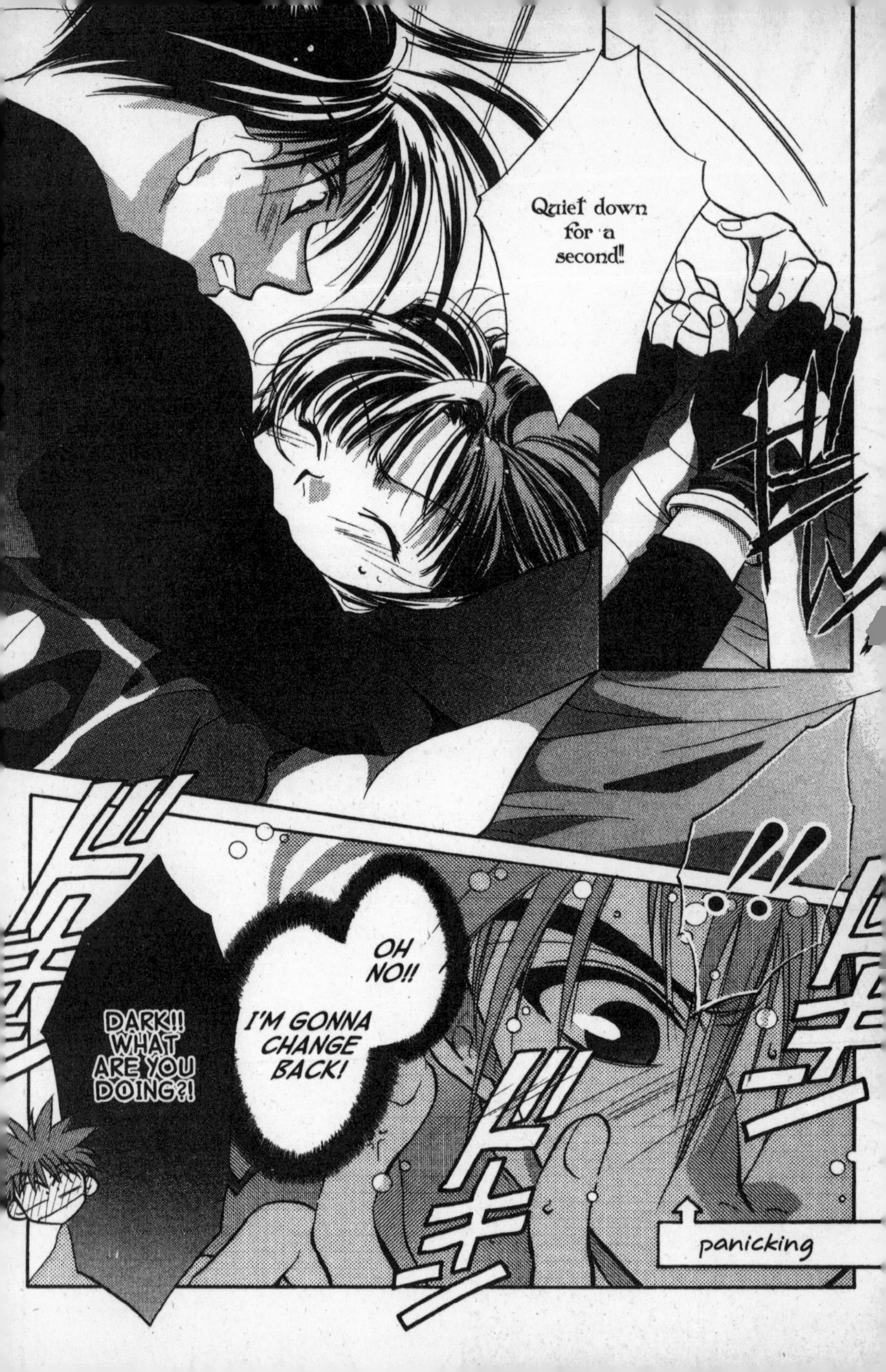
Quiet down for a second!!
OH NO!!
I'M GONNA CHANGE BACK!
DARK!! WHAT ARE YOU DOING?!
panicking

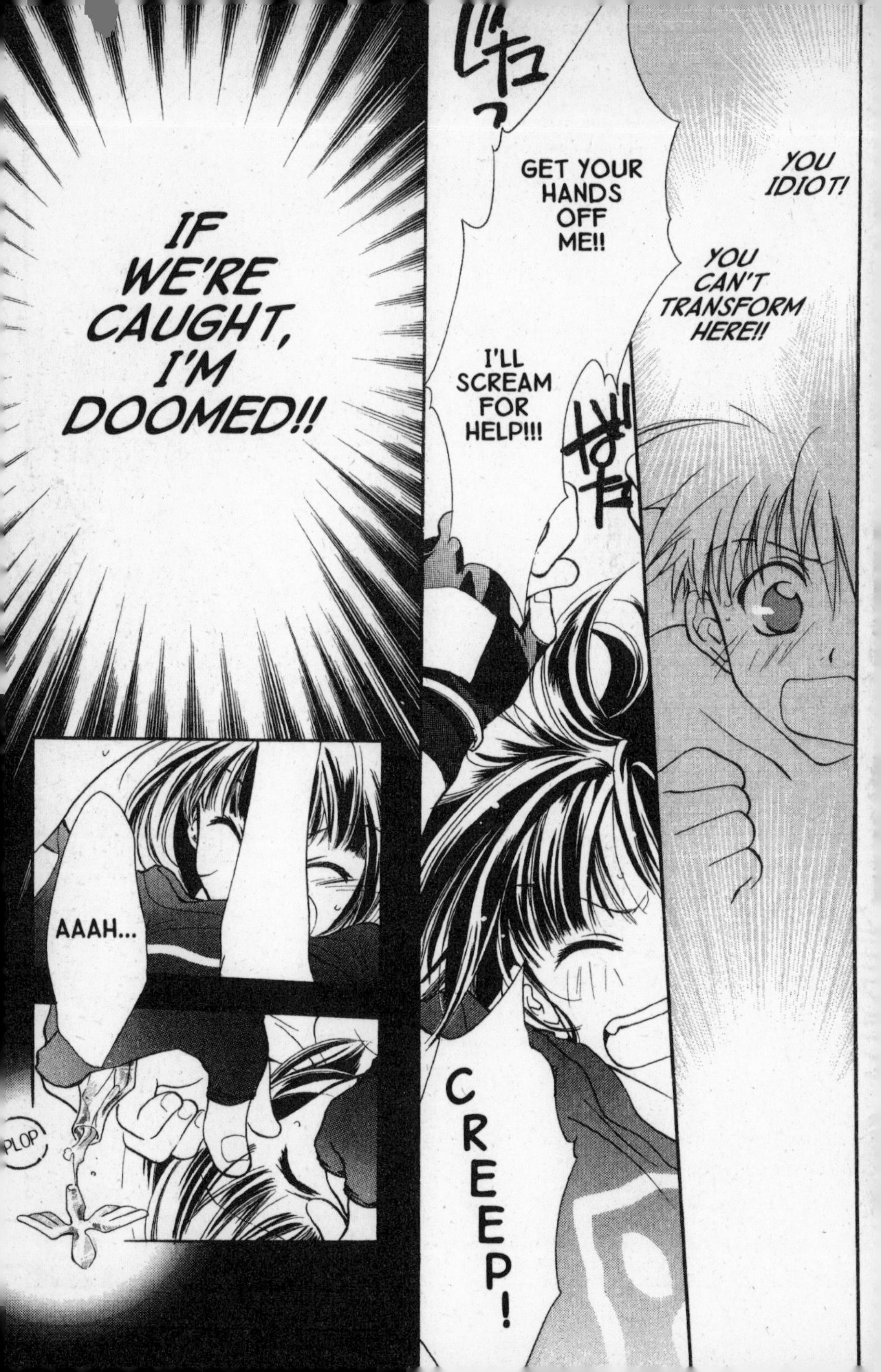
YOU IDIOT!
YOU CAN'T TRANSFORM HERE!!
GET YOUR HANDS OFF ME!!
I'LL SCREAM FOR HELP!!!
CREEP!
IF WE'RE CAUGHT, I'M DOOMED!!
AAAH...
PLOP

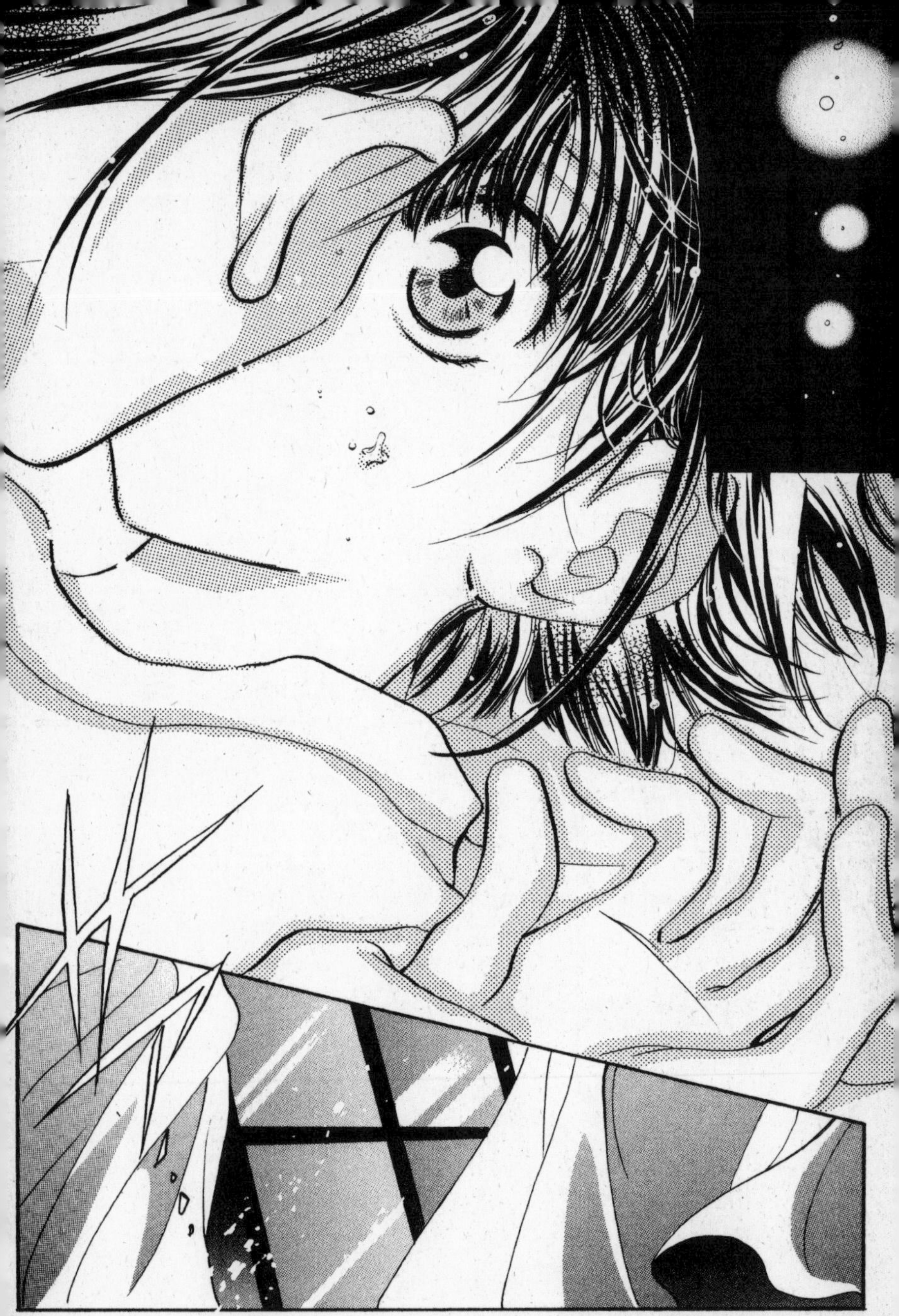

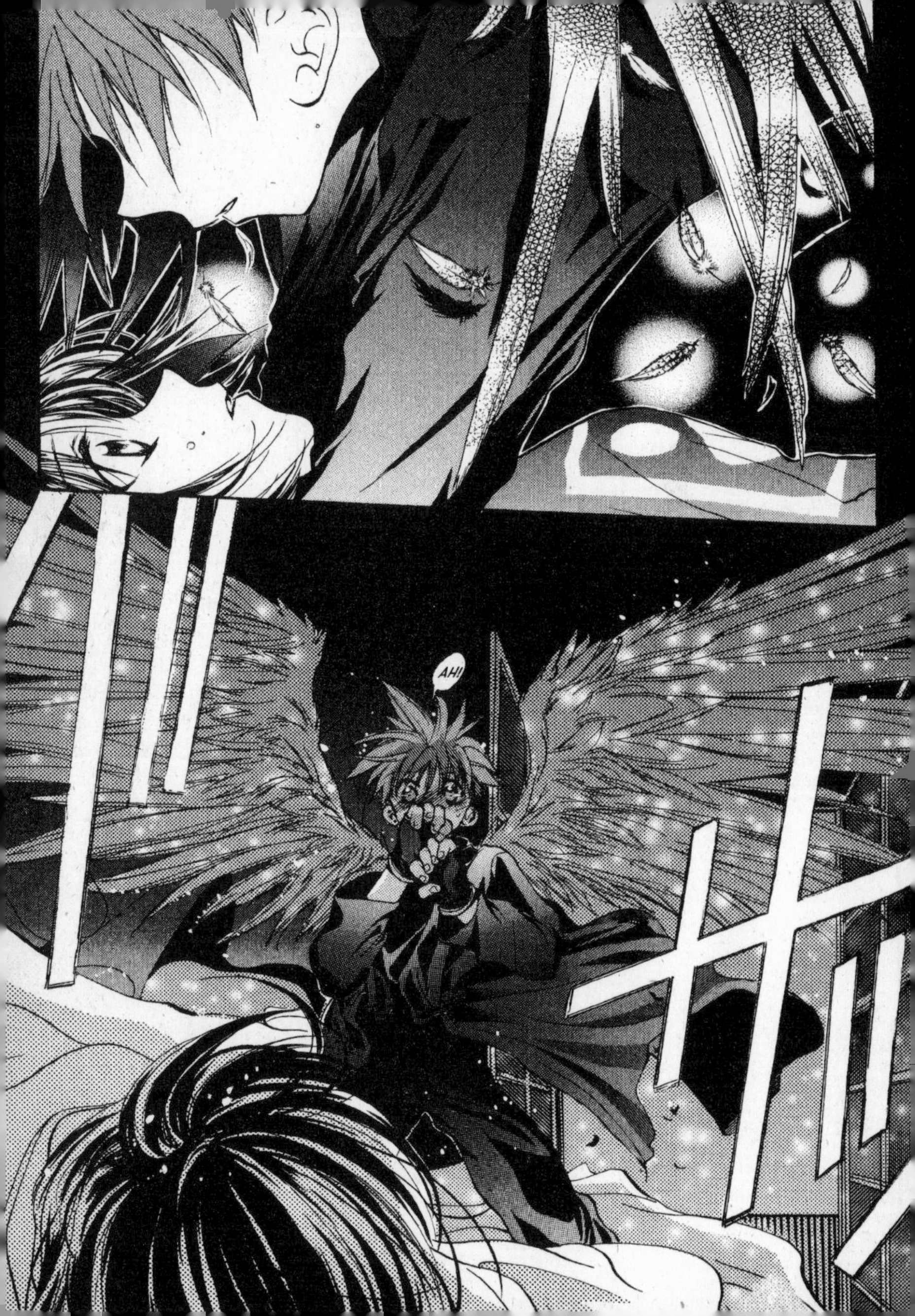
AH!

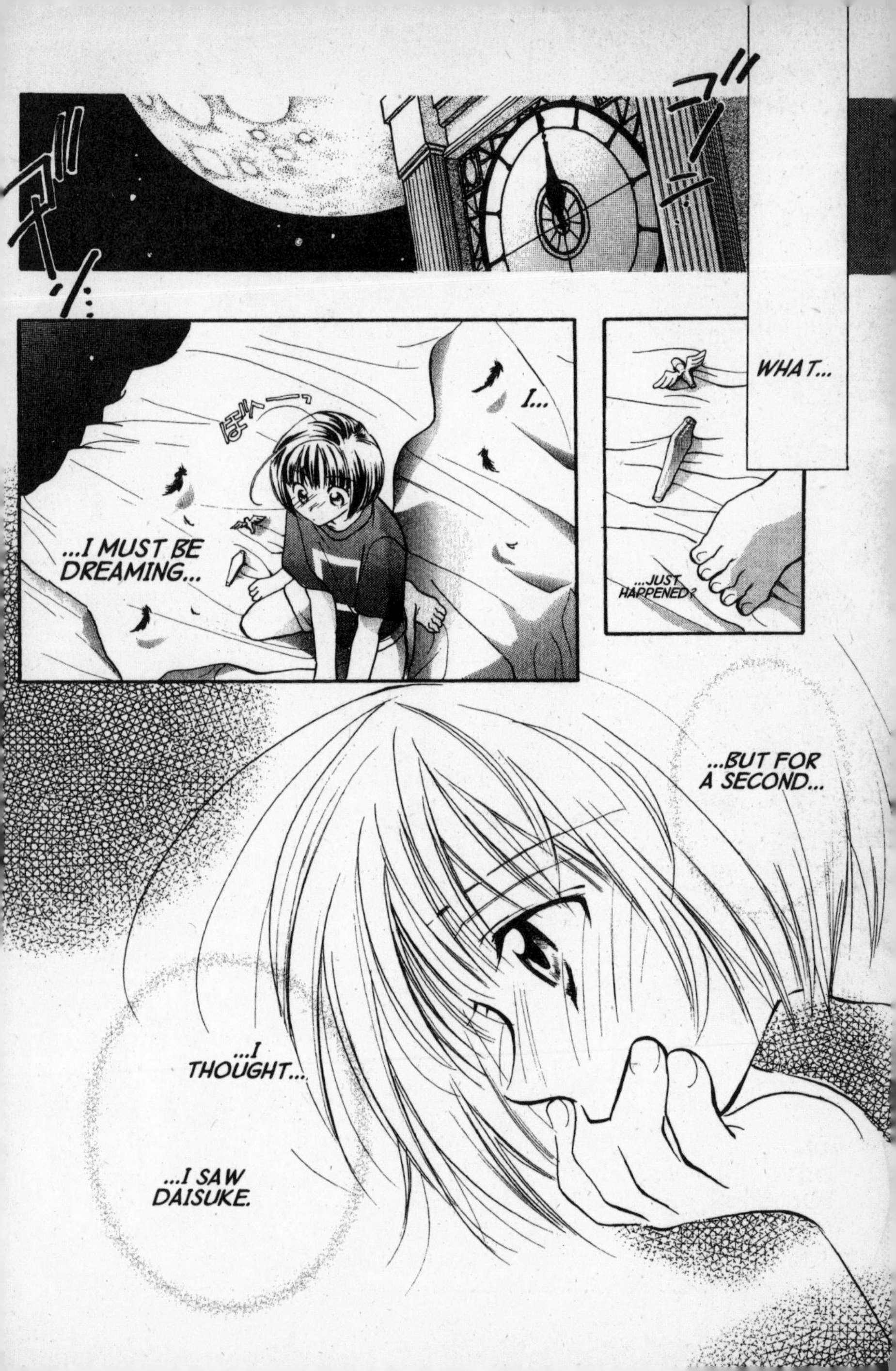
WHAT...
...JUST HAPPENED?
I...
...I MUST BE DREAMING...
...BUT FOR A SECOND...
...I THOUGHT...
...I SAW DAISUKE.

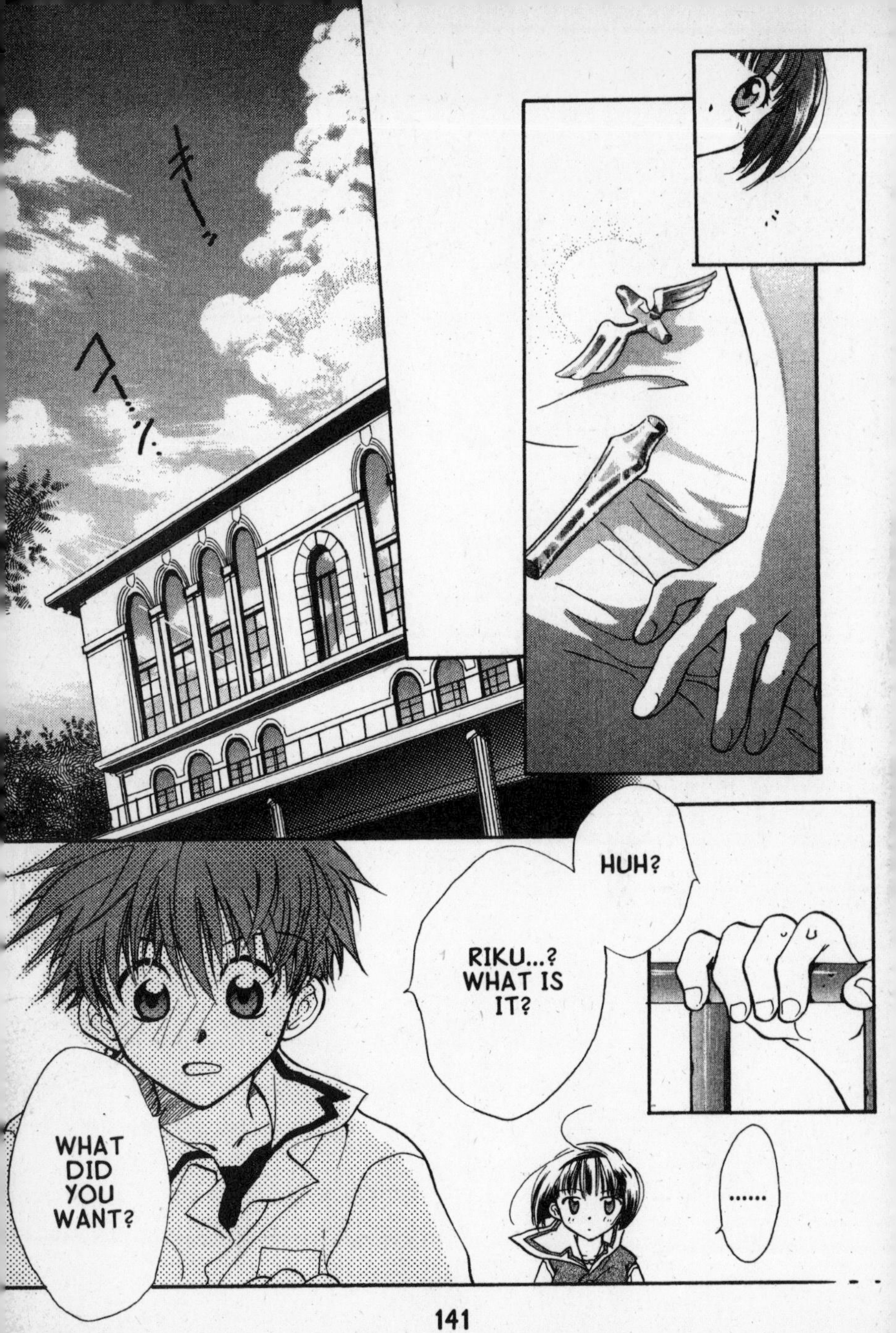
HUH?
RIKU...? WHAT IS IT?
......
WHAT DID YOU WANT?

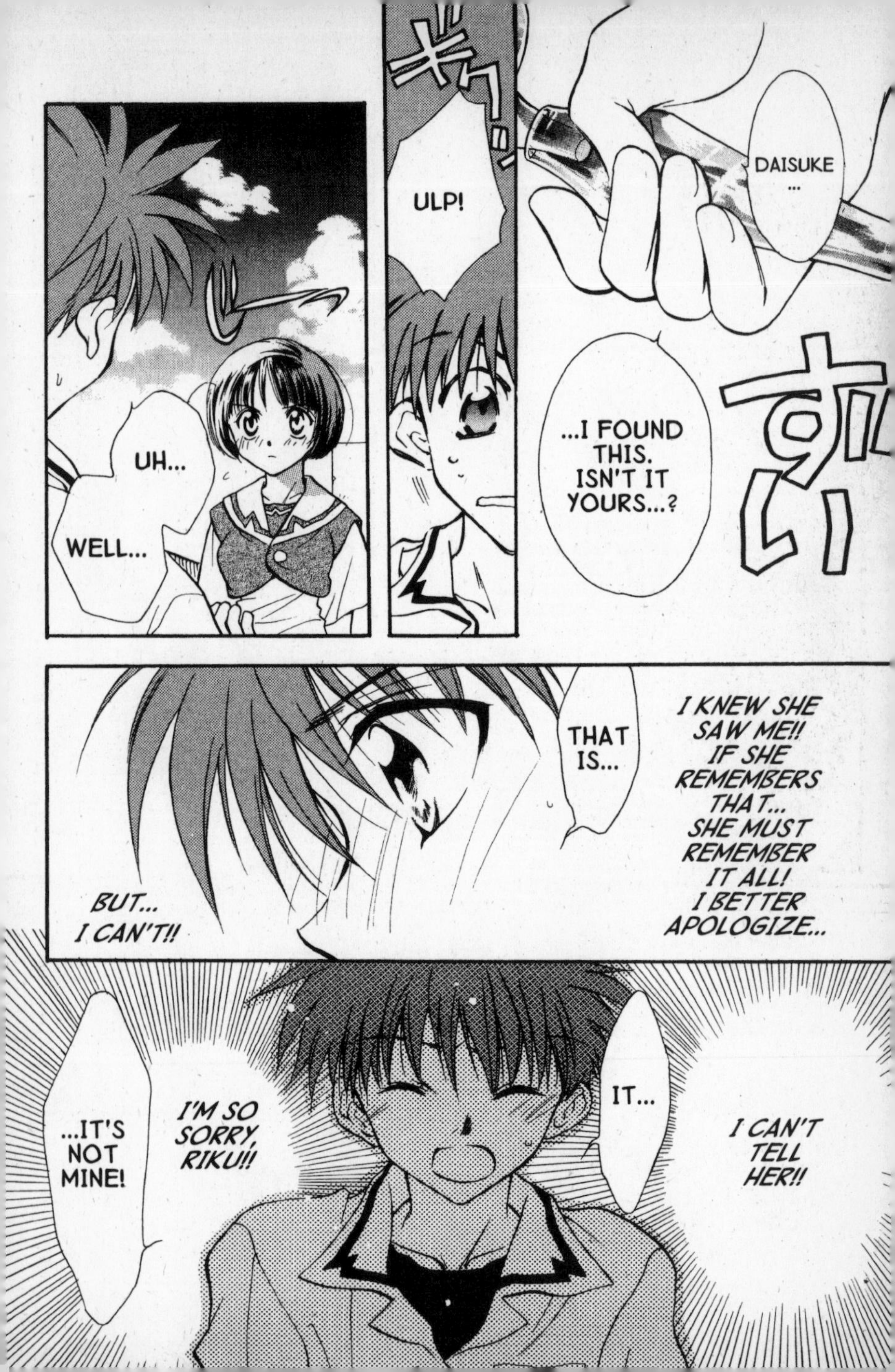
DAISUKE ...
...I FOUND THIS. ISN'T IT YOURS...?
ULP!
UH...
WELL...
THAT IS...
I KNEW SHE SAW ME!! IF SHE REMEMBERS THAT... SHE MUST REMEMBER IT ALL! I BETTER APOLOGIZE...
BUT... I CAN'T!!
IT...
I CAN'T TELL HER!!
I'M SO SORRY, RIKU!!
...IT'S NOT MINE!

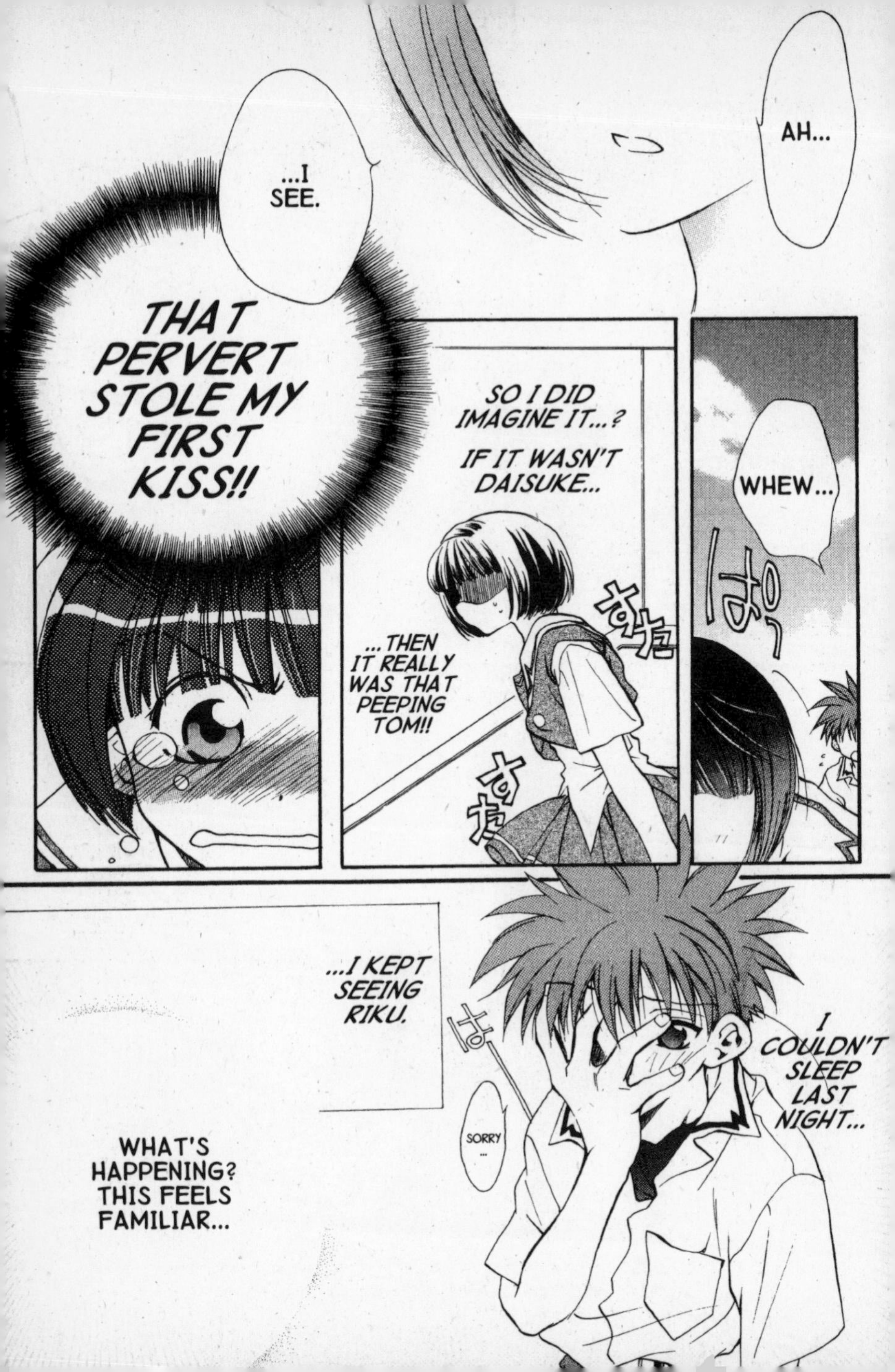

AH...
...I SEE.
WHEW...
はっ
SO I DID IMAGINE IT...?
IF IT WASN'T DAISUKE...
...THEN IT REALLY WAS THAT PEEPING TOM!!
すた
すた
THAT PERVERT STOLE MY FIRST KISS!!
I COULDN'T SLEEP LAST NIGHT...
...I KEPT SEEING RIKU.
は
SORRY...
WHAT'S HAPPENING? THIS FEELS FAMILIAR...

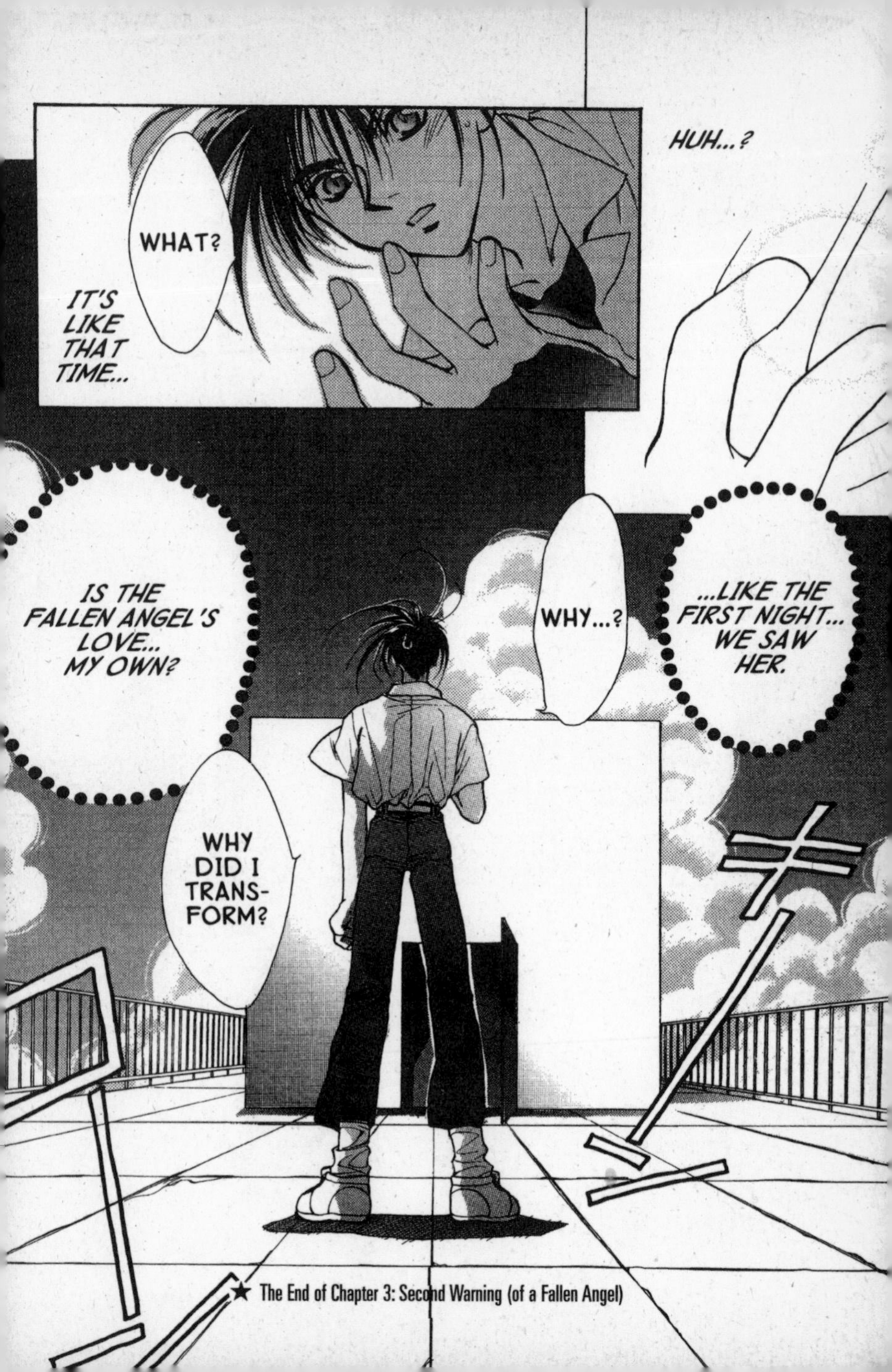
HUH...?
WHAT?
IT'S LIKE THAT TIME...
...LIKE THE FIRST NIGHT... WE SAW HER.
WHY...?
IS THE FALLEN ANGEL'S LOVE... MY OWN?
WHY DID I TRANS-FORM?

★ The End of Chapter 3: Second Warning (of a Fallen Angel)

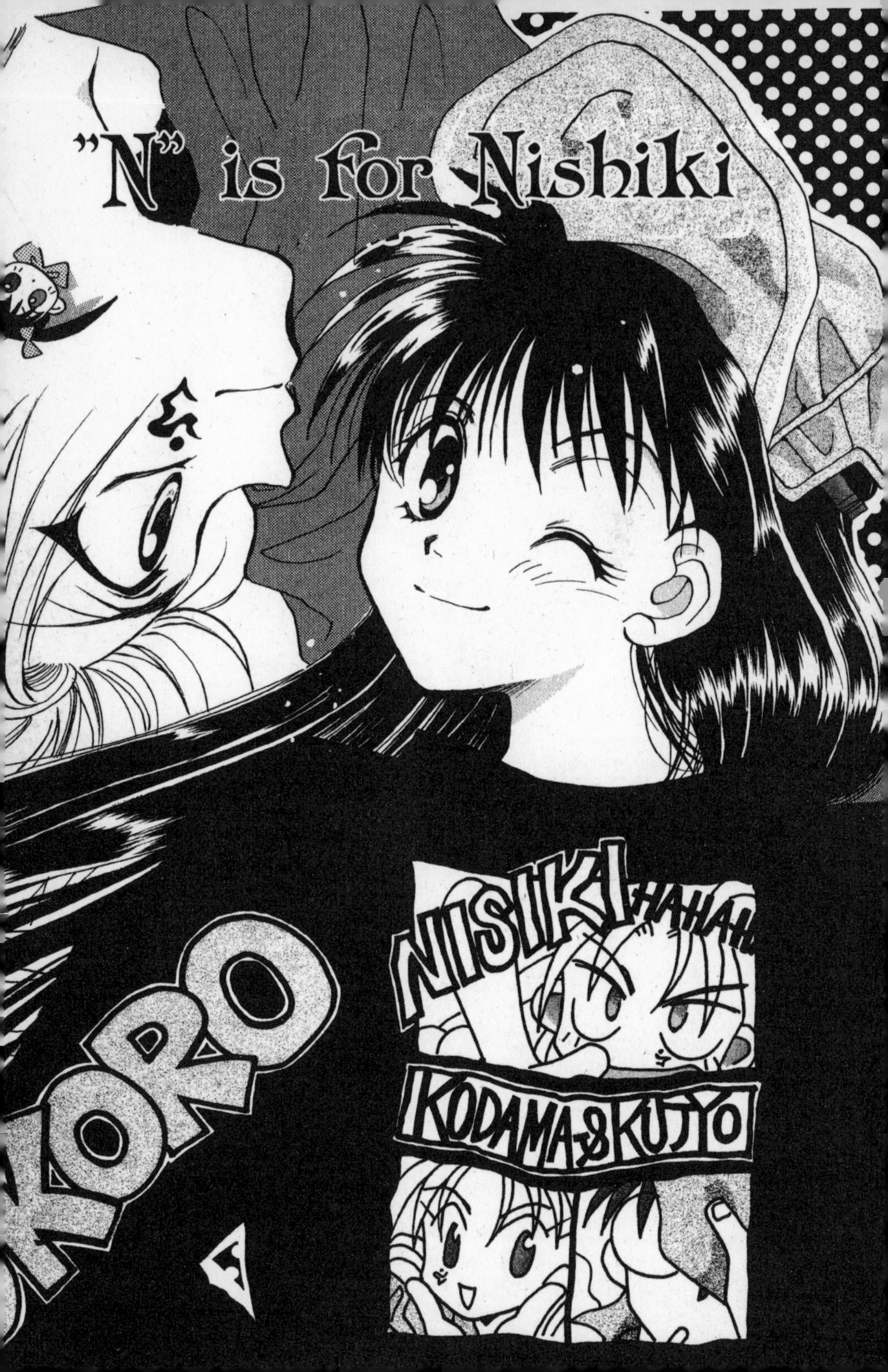
"N" is for Nishiki
NISIKI
HAHAHA
KODAMA & KUJYO
KORO

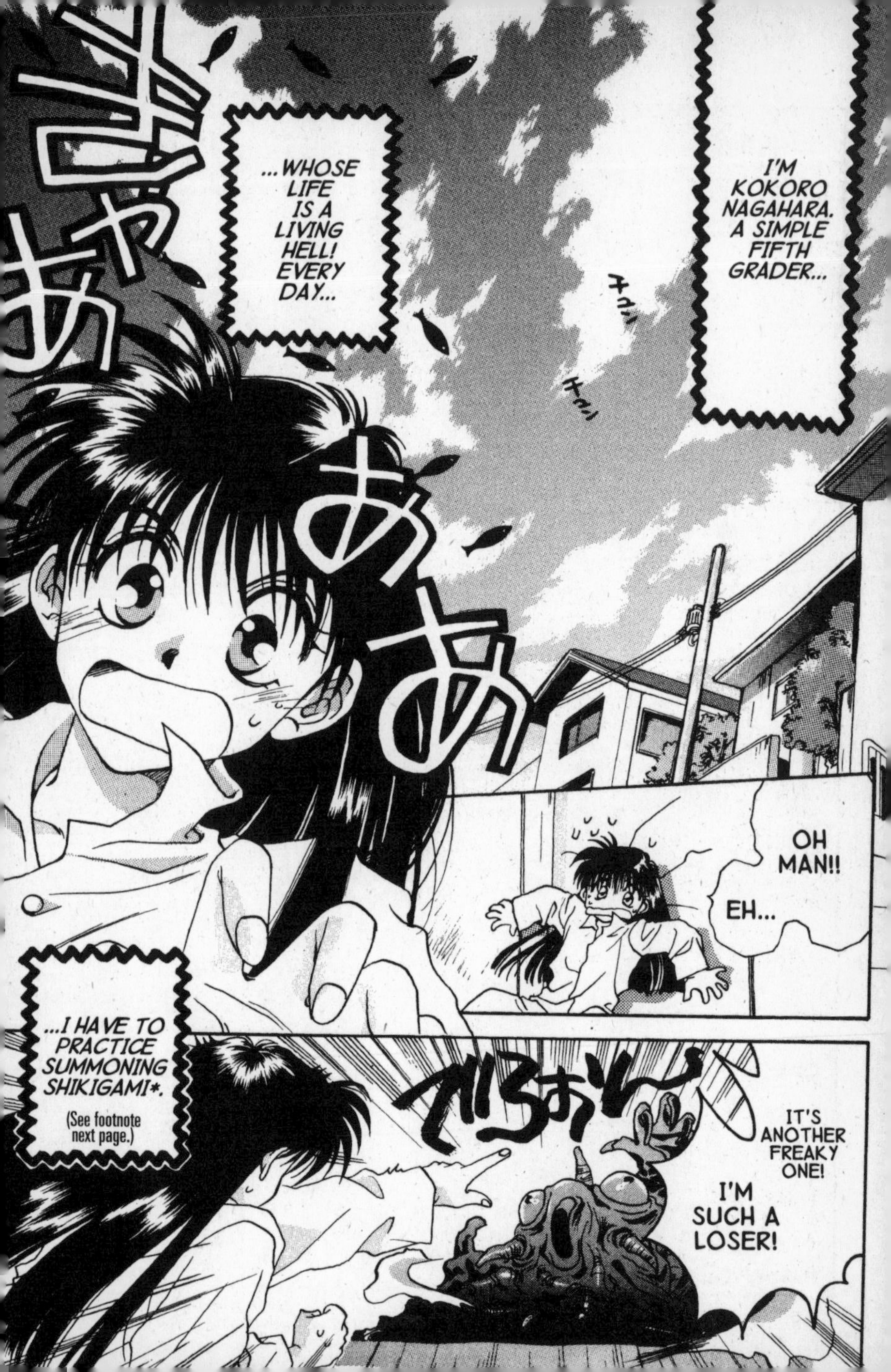
I'M KOKORO NAGAHARA. A SIMPLE FIFTH GRADER...
...WHOSE LIFE IS A LIVING HELL! EVERY DAY...
チュン
チュン
あああ
ぎゃあ
OH MAN!!
EH...
...I HAVE TO PRACTICE SUMMONING SHIKIGAMI*.
(See footnote next page.)
IT'S ANOTHER FREAKY ONE!
I'M SUCH A LOSER!

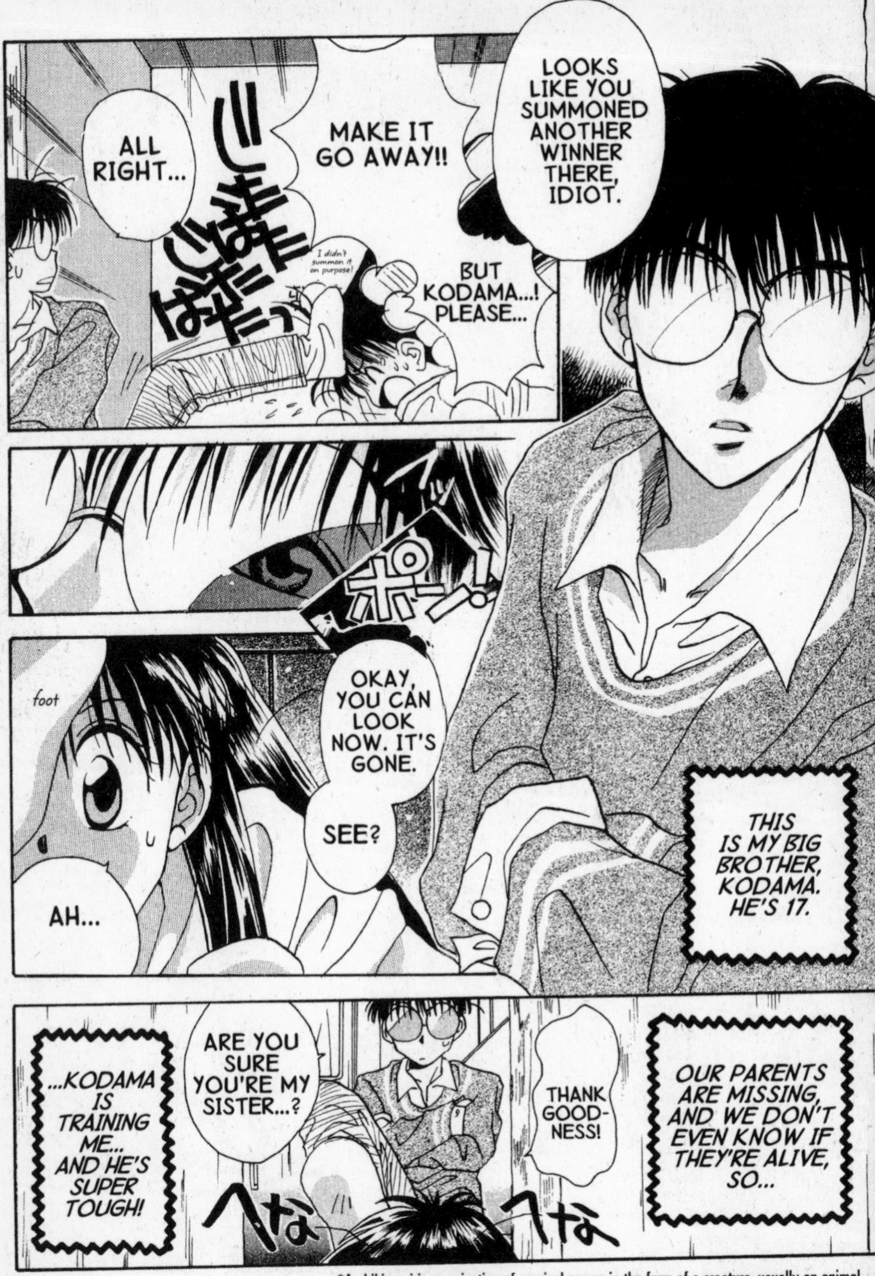
LOOKS LIKE YOU SUMMONED ANOTHER WINNER THERE, IDIOT.
I didn't summon it on purpose!
BUT KODAMA...! PLEASE...
MAKE IT GO AWAY!!
ALL RIGHT...
THIS IS MY BIG BROTHER, KODAMA. HE'S 17.
OKAY, YOU CAN LOOK NOW. IT'S GONE.
SEE?
foot
AH...
OUR PARENTS ARE MISSING, AND WE DON'T EVEN KNOW IF THEY'RE ALIVE, SO...
THANK GOODNESS!
ARE YOU SURE YOU'RE MY SISTER...?
...KODAMA IS TRAINING ME... AND HE'S SUPER TOUGH!

*A shikigami is a projection of magical power in the form of a creature, usually an animal, sort of like a familiar. The Nagahara's shikigami look like people.

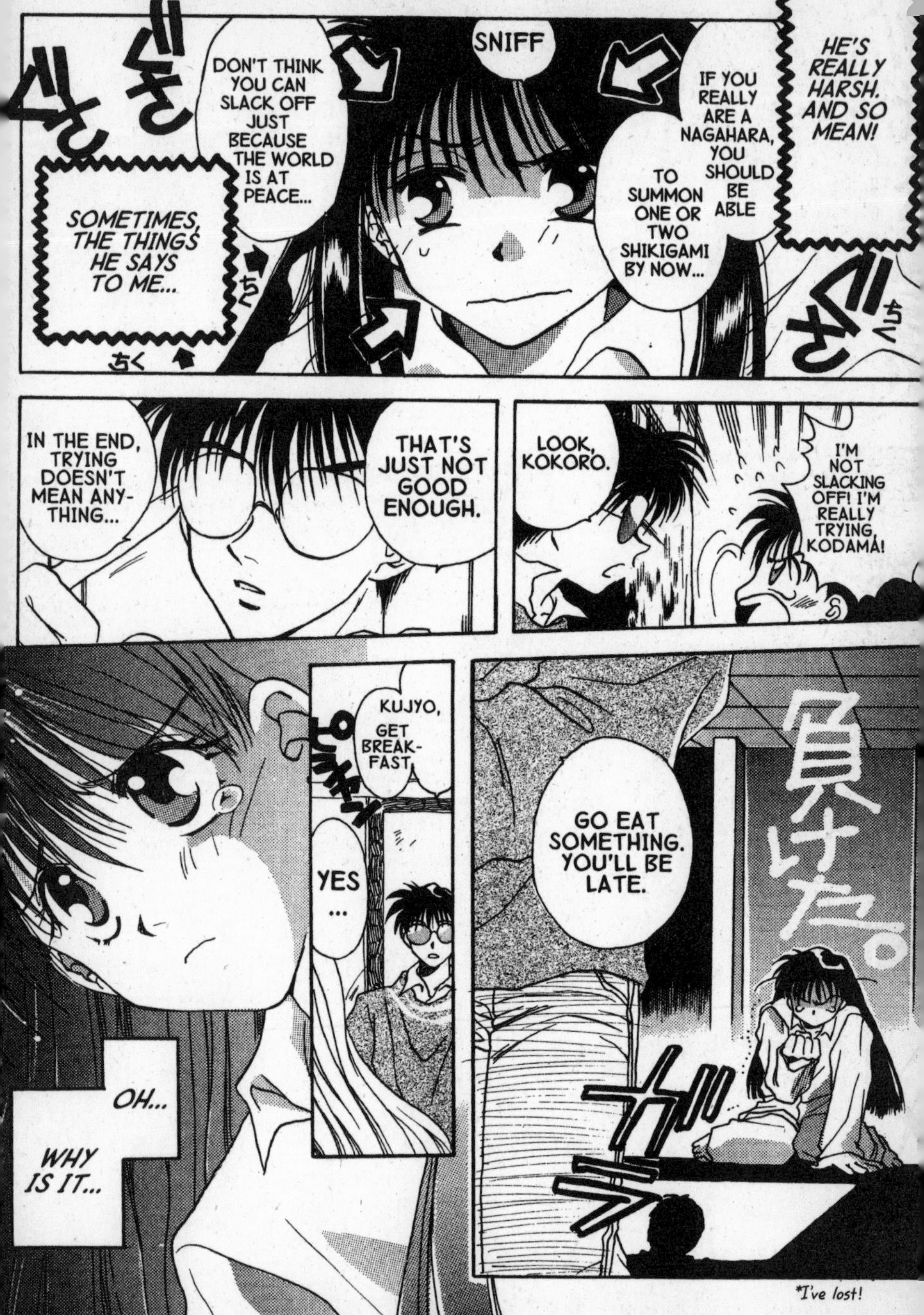
HE'S REALLY HARSH. AND SO MEAN!
IF YOU REALLY ARE A NAGAHARA, YOU SHOULD BE ABLE
TO SUMMON ONE OR TWO SHIKIGAMI BY NOW...
SNIFF
DON'T THINK YOU CAN SLACK OFF JUST BECAUSE THE WORLD IS AT PEACE...
SOMETIMES, THE THINGS HE SAYS TO ME...
I'M NOT SLACKING OFF! I'M REALLY TRYING, KODAMA!
LOOK, KOKORO.
THAT'S JUST NOT GOOD ENOUGH.
IN THE END, TRYING DOESN'T MEAN ANYTHING...
負けた。
GO EAT SOMETHING. YOU'LL BE LATE.
KUJYO, GET BREAKFAST.
YES ...
OH...
WHY IS IT...

*I've lost!

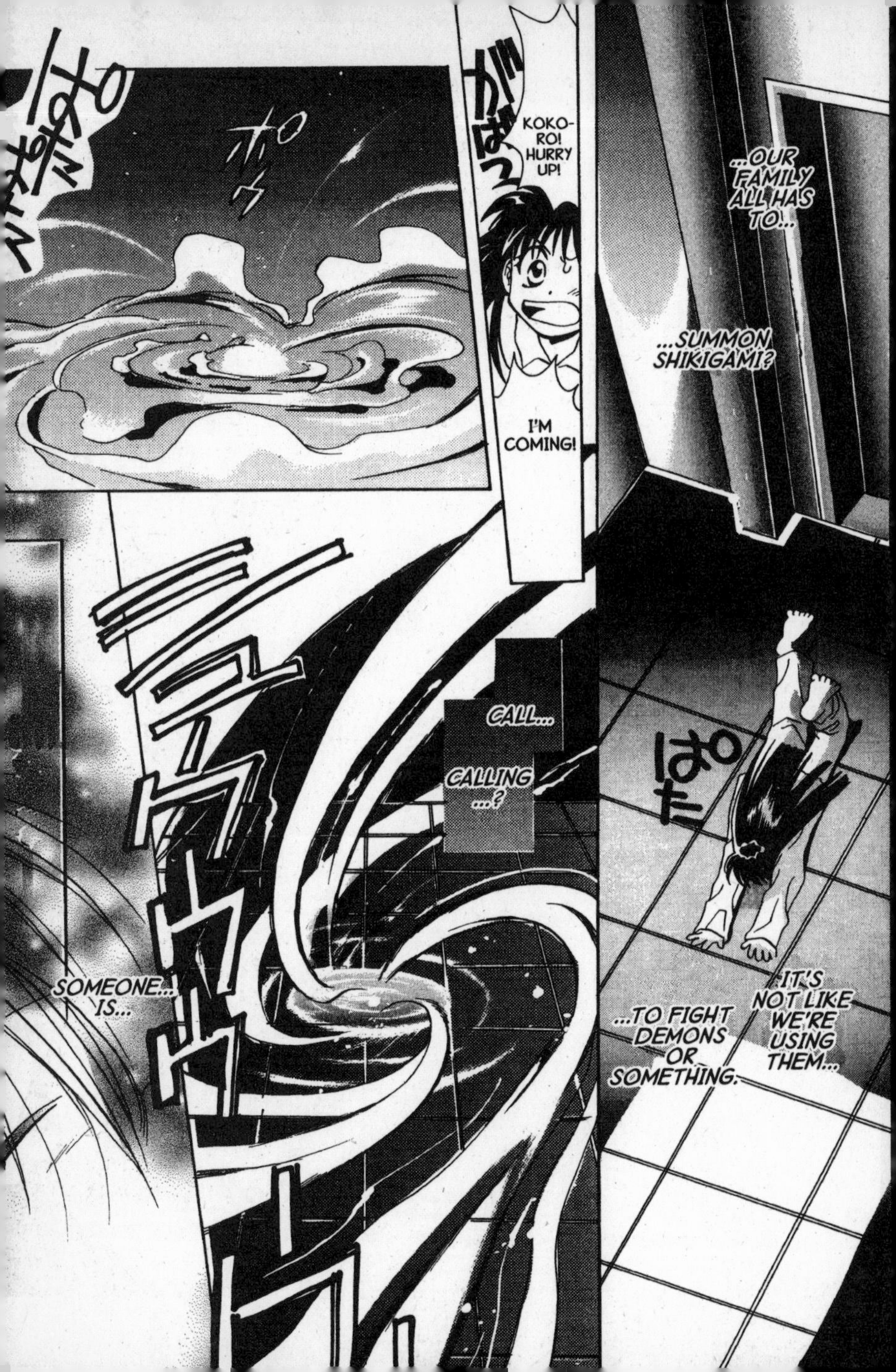
...OUR FAMILY ALL HAS TO...
...SUMMON SHIKIGAMI?
ぱた
IT'S NOT LIKE WE'RE USING THEM...
...TO FIGHT DEMONS OR SOMETHING.
がばっ
KOKO-RO! HURRY UP!
I'M COMING!
CALL...
CALLING ...?
SOMEONE... IS...

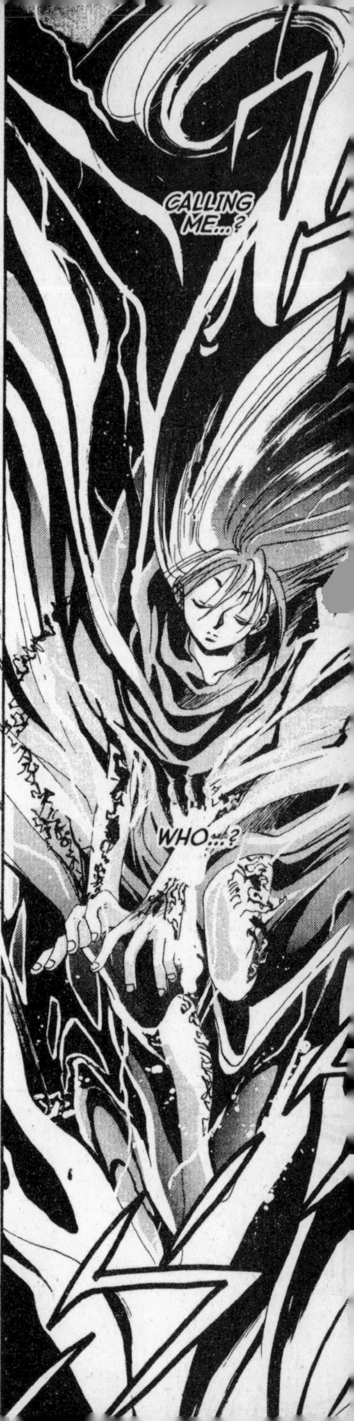
CALLING ME...?
WHO...?
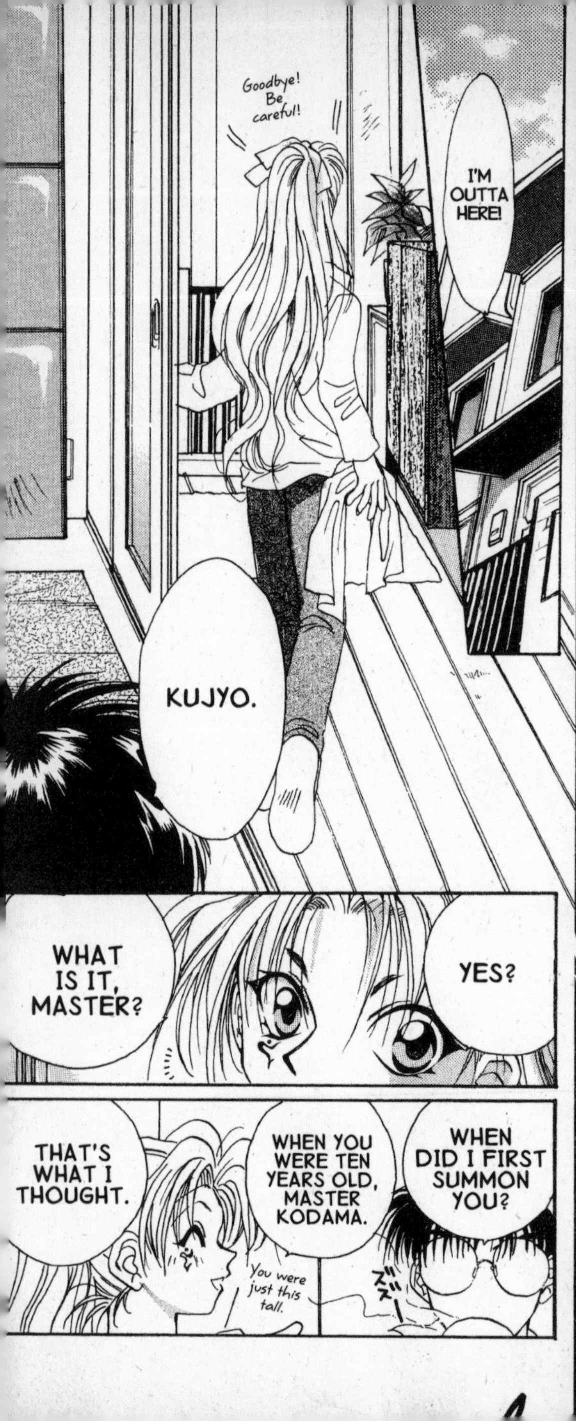
I'M OUTTA HERE!
Goodbye! Be careful!
KUJYO.
YES?
WHAT IS IT, MASTER?
WHEN DID I FIRST SUMMON YOU?
ズズー
WHEN YOU WERE TEN YEARS OLD, MASTER KODAMA.
You were just this tall.
THAT'S WHAT I THOUGHT.

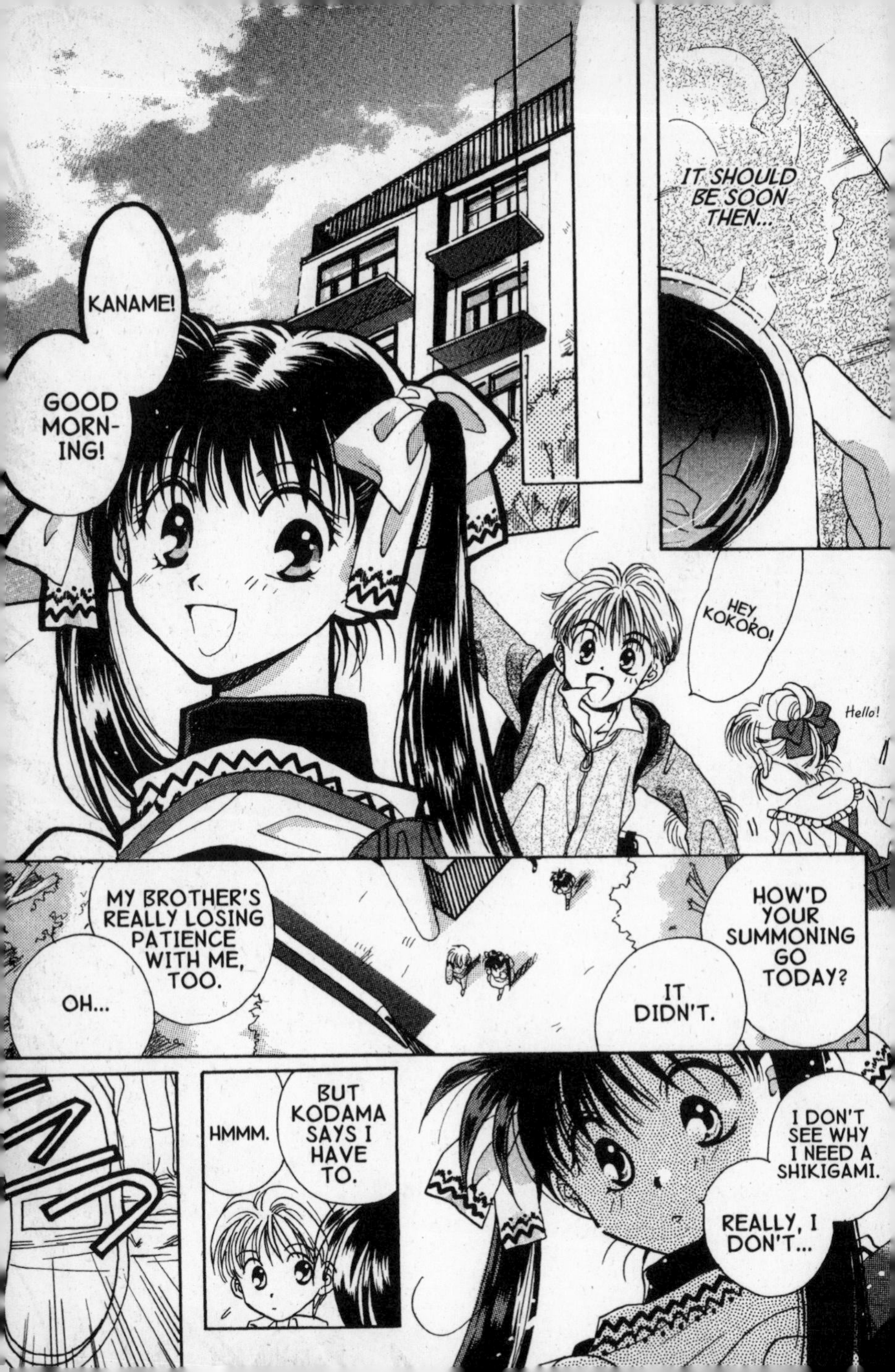
IT SHOULD BE SOON THEN...
HEY, KOKORO!
Hello!
KANAME!
GOOD MORNING!
HOW'D YOUR SUMMONING GO TODAY?
IT DIDN'T.
MY BROTHER'S REALLY LOSING PATIENCE WITH ME, TOO.
OH...
I DON'T SEE WHY I NEED A SHIKIGAMI.
REALLY, I DON'T...
BUT KODAMA SAYS I HAVE TO.
HMMM.

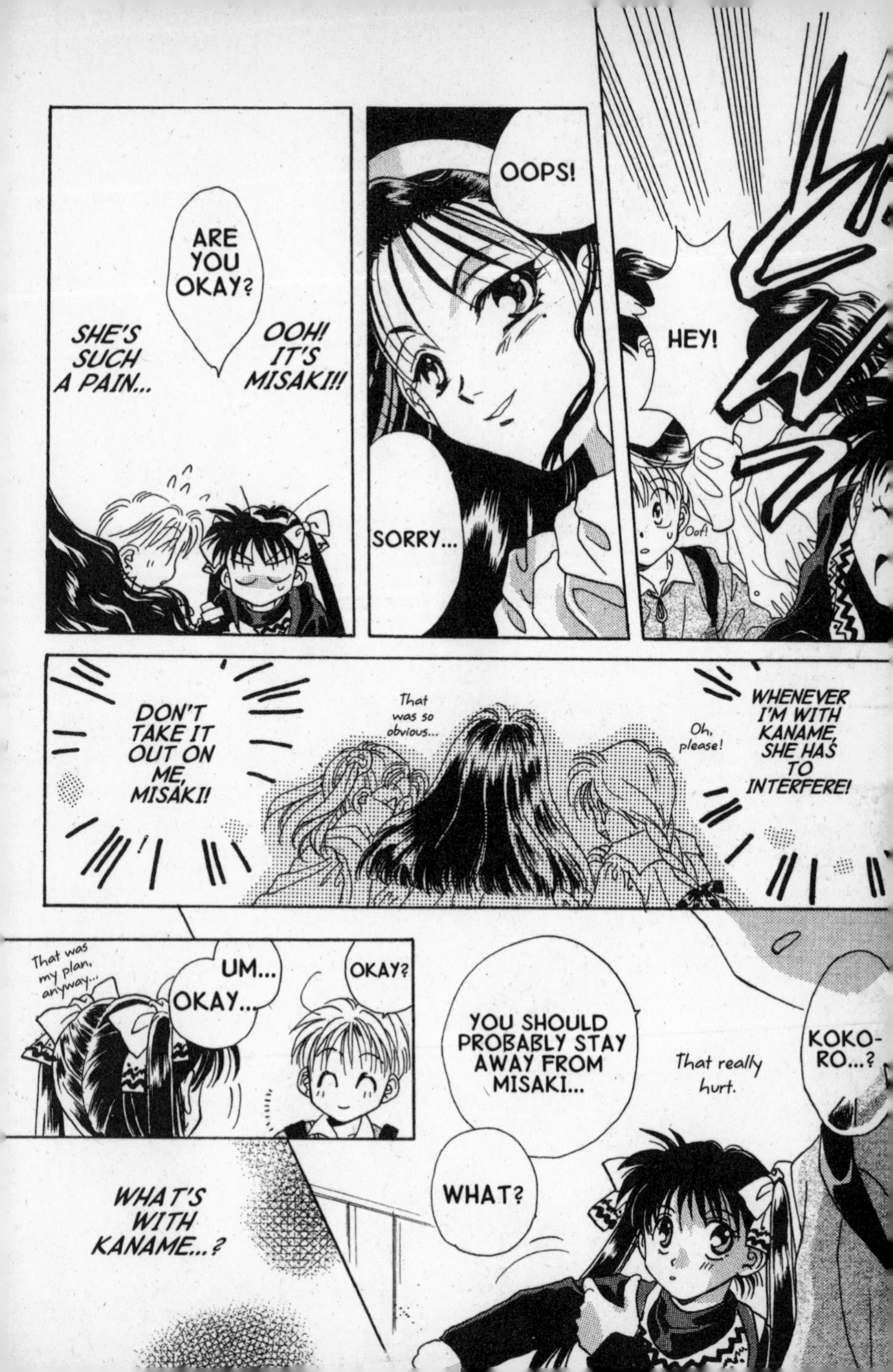
HEY!
Oof!
OOPS!
SORRY...
ARE YOU OKAY?
OOH! IT'S MISAKI!!
SHE'S SUCH A PAIN...
WHENEVER I'M WITH KANAME, SHE HAS TO INTERFERE!
Oh, please!
That was so obvious...
DON'T TAKE IT OUT ON ME, MISAKI!
KOKO-RO...?
That really hurt.
YOU SHOULD PROBABLY STAY AWAY FROM MISAKI...
WHAT?
OKAY?
UM... OKAY...
That was my plan, anyway...
WHAT'S WITH KANAME...?

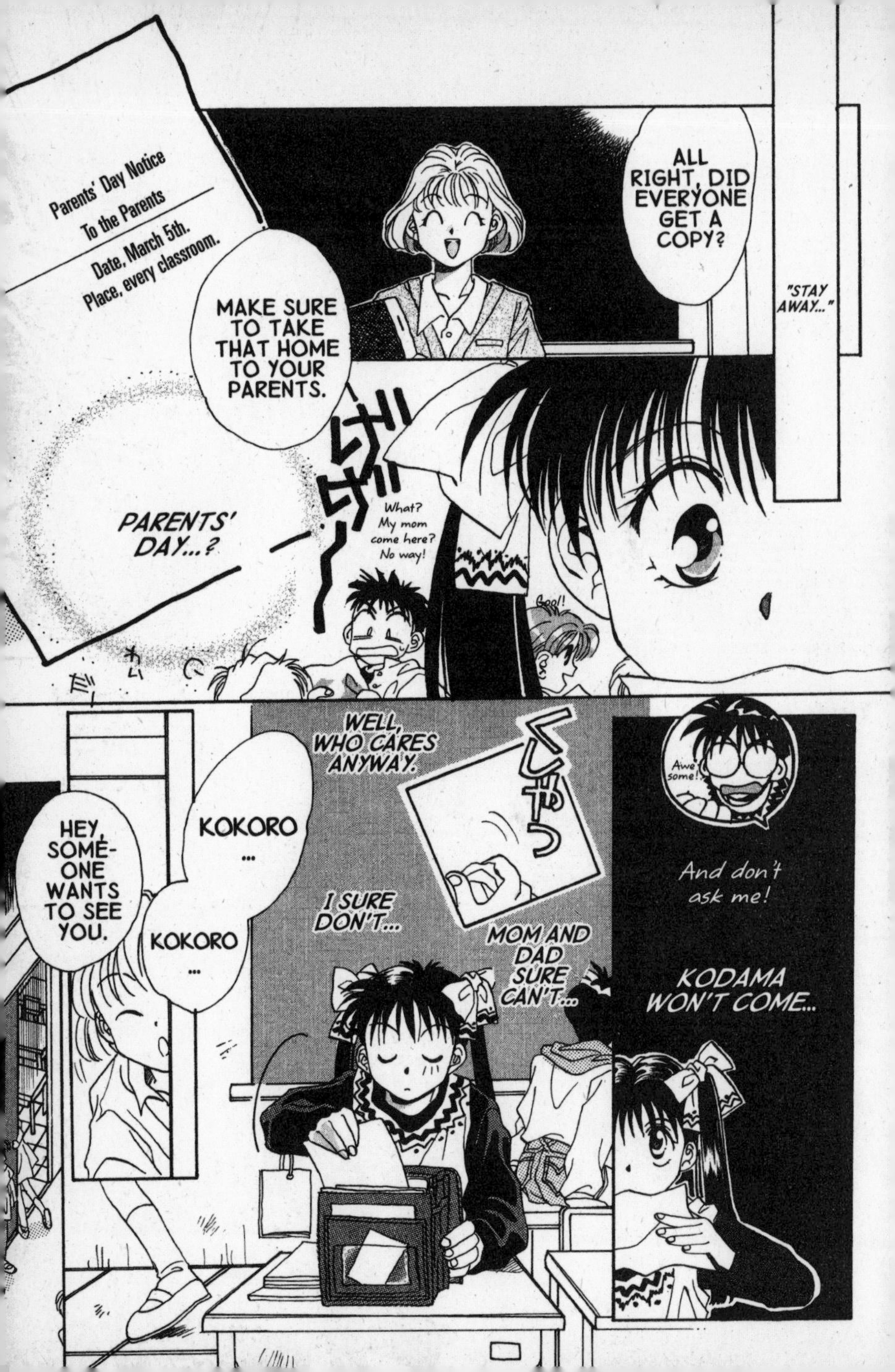
"STAY AWAY..."
ALL RIGHT, DID EVERYONE GET A COPY?
Parents' Day Notice
To the Parents
Date, March 5th.
Place, every classroom.
MAKE SURE TO TAKE THAT HOME TO YOUR PARENTS.
Cool!
What? My mom come here? No way!
PARENTS' DAY...?
Awe some!
And don't ask me!
KODAMA WON'T COME...
MOM AND DAD SURE CAN'T...
くしゃっ
WELL, WHO CARES ANYWAY.
I SURE DON'T...
KOKORO ...
KOKORO ...
HEY, SOME-ONE WANTS TO SEE YOU.

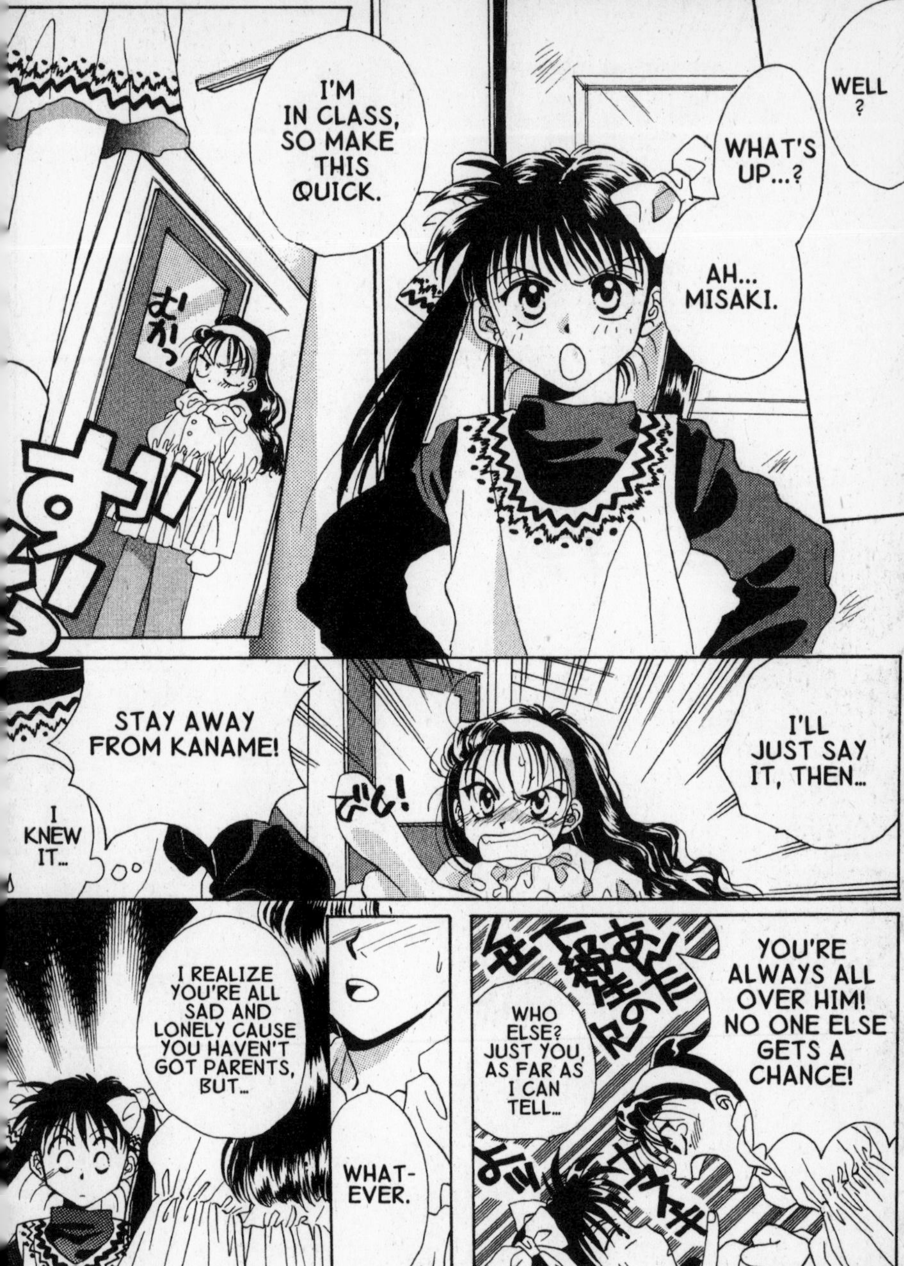
WELL?
WHAT'S UP...?
AH... MISAKI.
I'M IN CLASS, SO MAKE THIS QUICK.
むかっ
I'LL JUST SAY IT, THEN...
でん!
STAY AWAY FROM KANAME!
I KNEW IT...
YOU'RE ALWAYS ALL OVER HIM! NO ONE ELSE GETS A CHANCE!
WHO ELSE? JUST YOU, AS FAR AS I CAN TELL...
WHAT-EVER.
I REALIZE YOU'RE ALL SAD AND LONELY CAUSE YOU HAVEN'T GOT PARENTS, BUT...

*You're in a lower grade!

*You're so conceited!

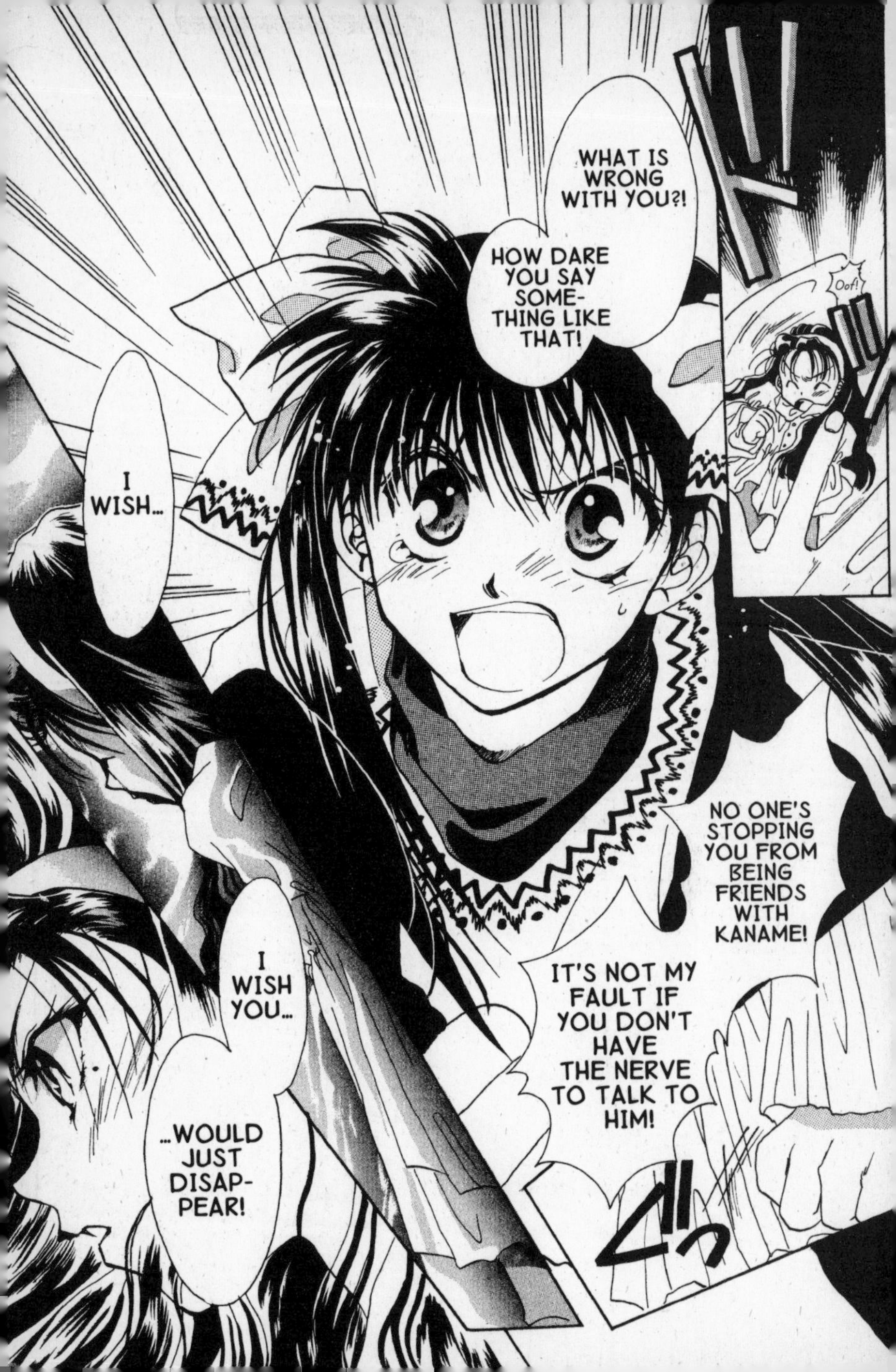
Oof!
WHAT IS WRONG WITH YOU?!
HOW DARE YOU SAY SOME-THING LIKE THAT!
I WISH...
NO ONE'S STOPPING YOU FROM BEING FRIENDS WITH KANAME!
IT'S NOT MY FAULT IF YOU DON'T HAVE THE NERVE TO TALK TO HIM!
I WISH YOU...
...WOULD JUST DISAP-PEAR!

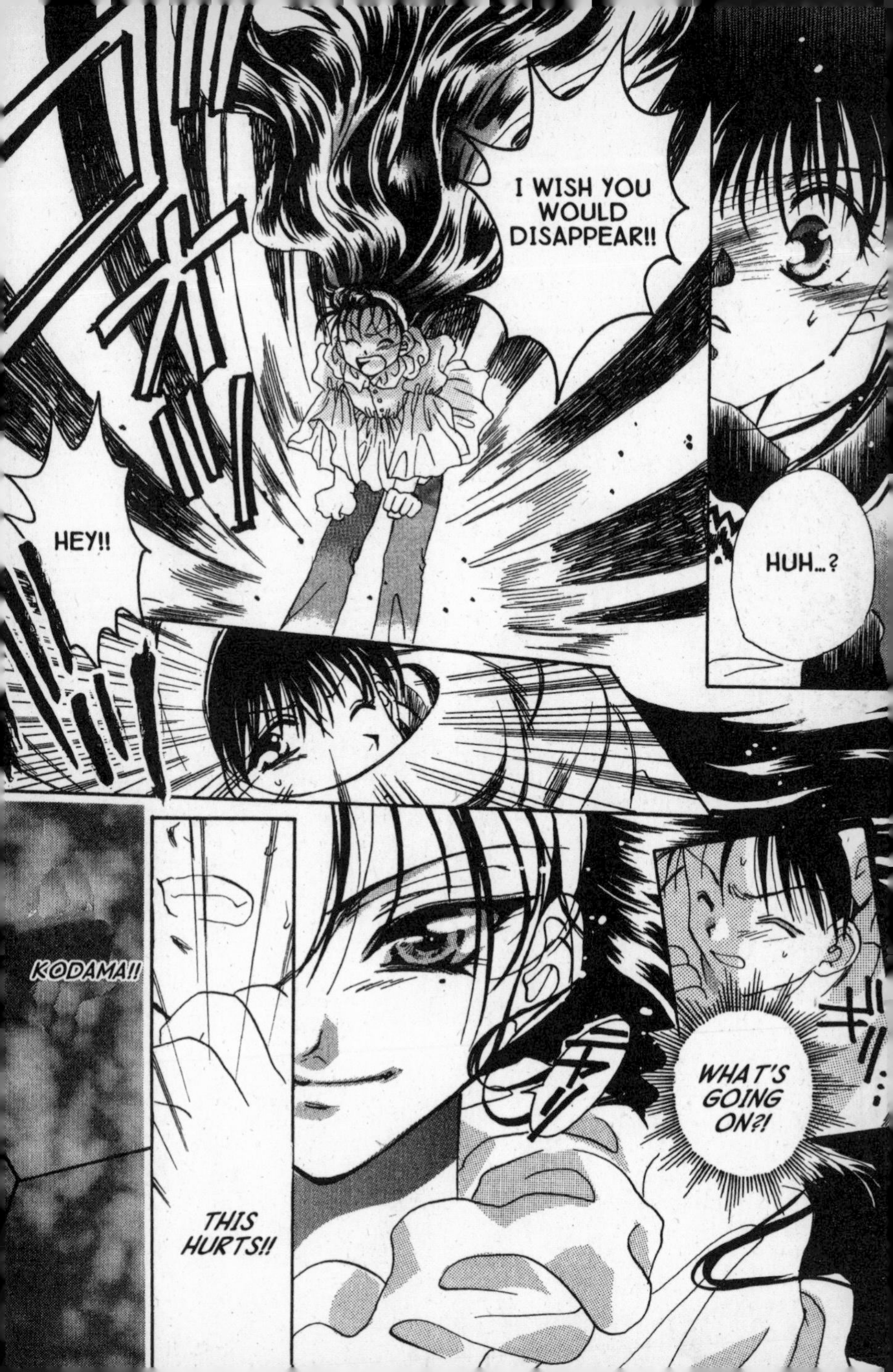
HUH...?
I WISH YOU WOULD DISAPPEAR!!
HEY!!
WHAT'S GOING ON?!
THIS HURTS!!
KODAMA!!

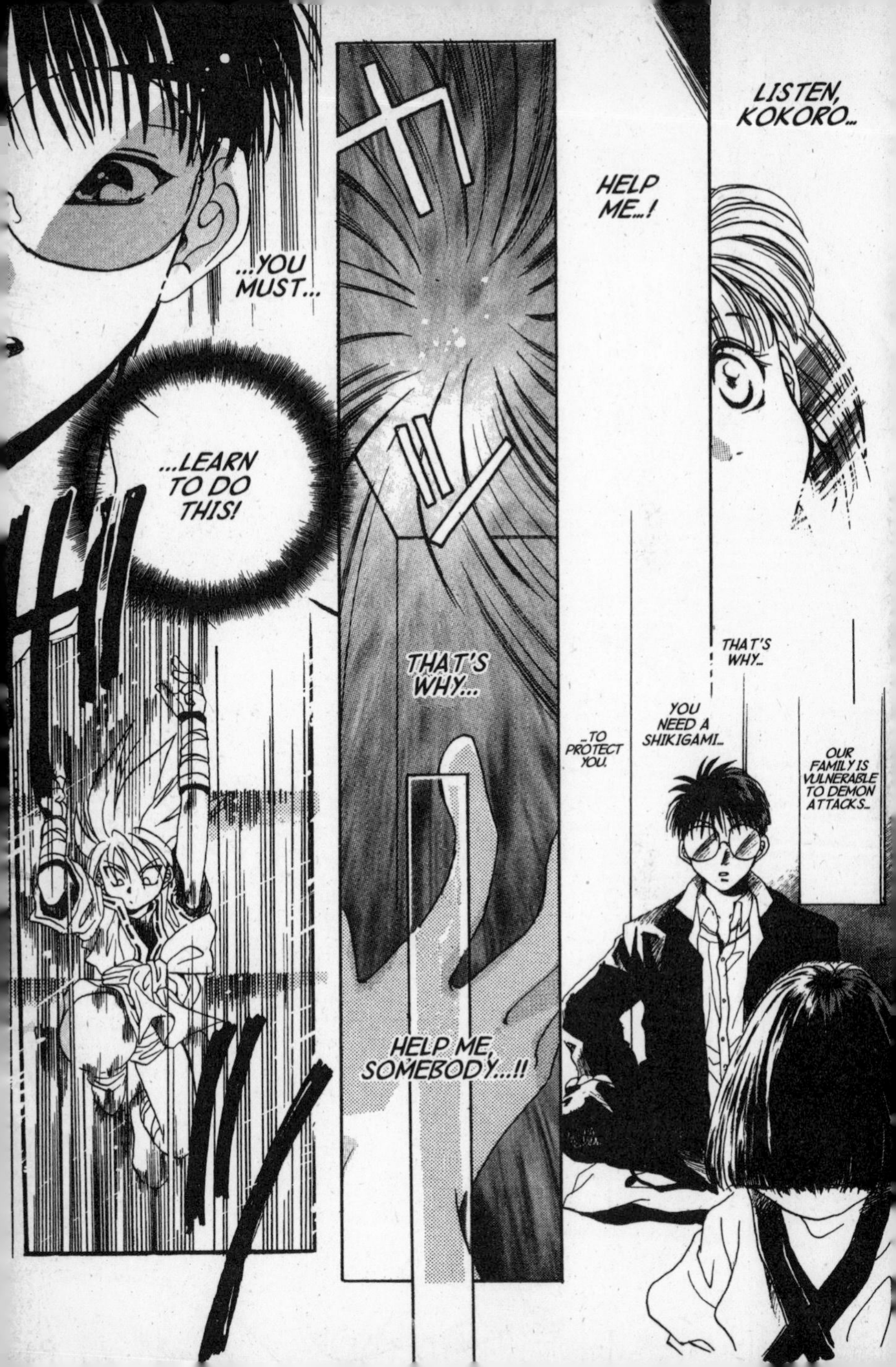
LISTEN, KOKORO...
HELP ME...!
OUR FAMILY IS VULNERABLE TO DEMON ATTACKS...
THAT'S WHY..
YOU NEED A SHIKIGAMI..
...TO PROTECT YOU.
THAT'S WHY...
HELP ME, SOMEBODY...!!
...YOU MUST...
...LEARN TO DO THIS!

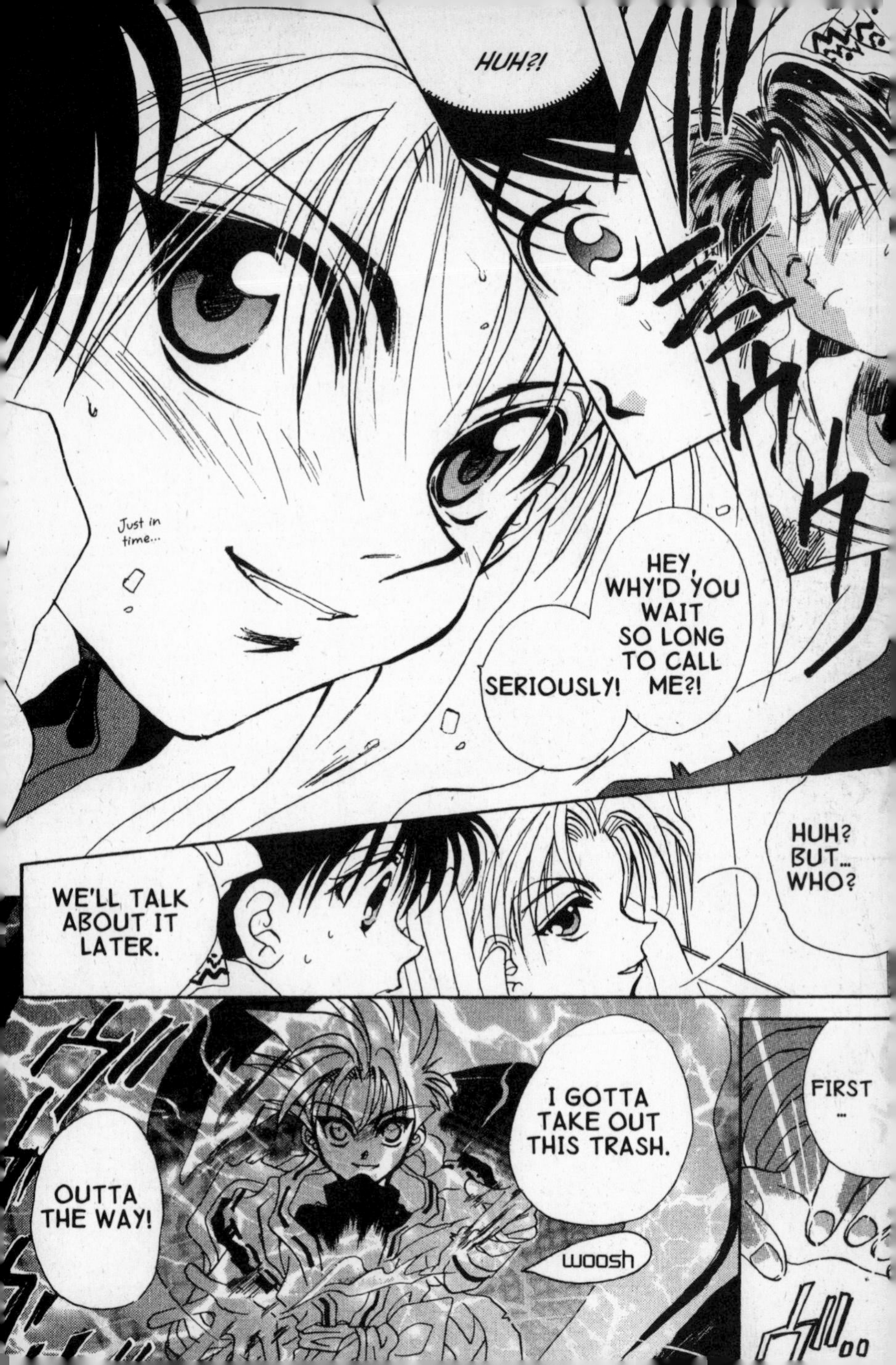
HUH?!
HEY, WHY'D YOU WAIT SO LONG TO CALL ME?!
SERIOUSLY!
Just in time...
HUH? BUT... WHO?
WE'LL TALK ABOUT IT LATER.
FIRST ...
I GOTTA TAKE OUT THIS TRASH.
woosh
OUTTA THE WAY!

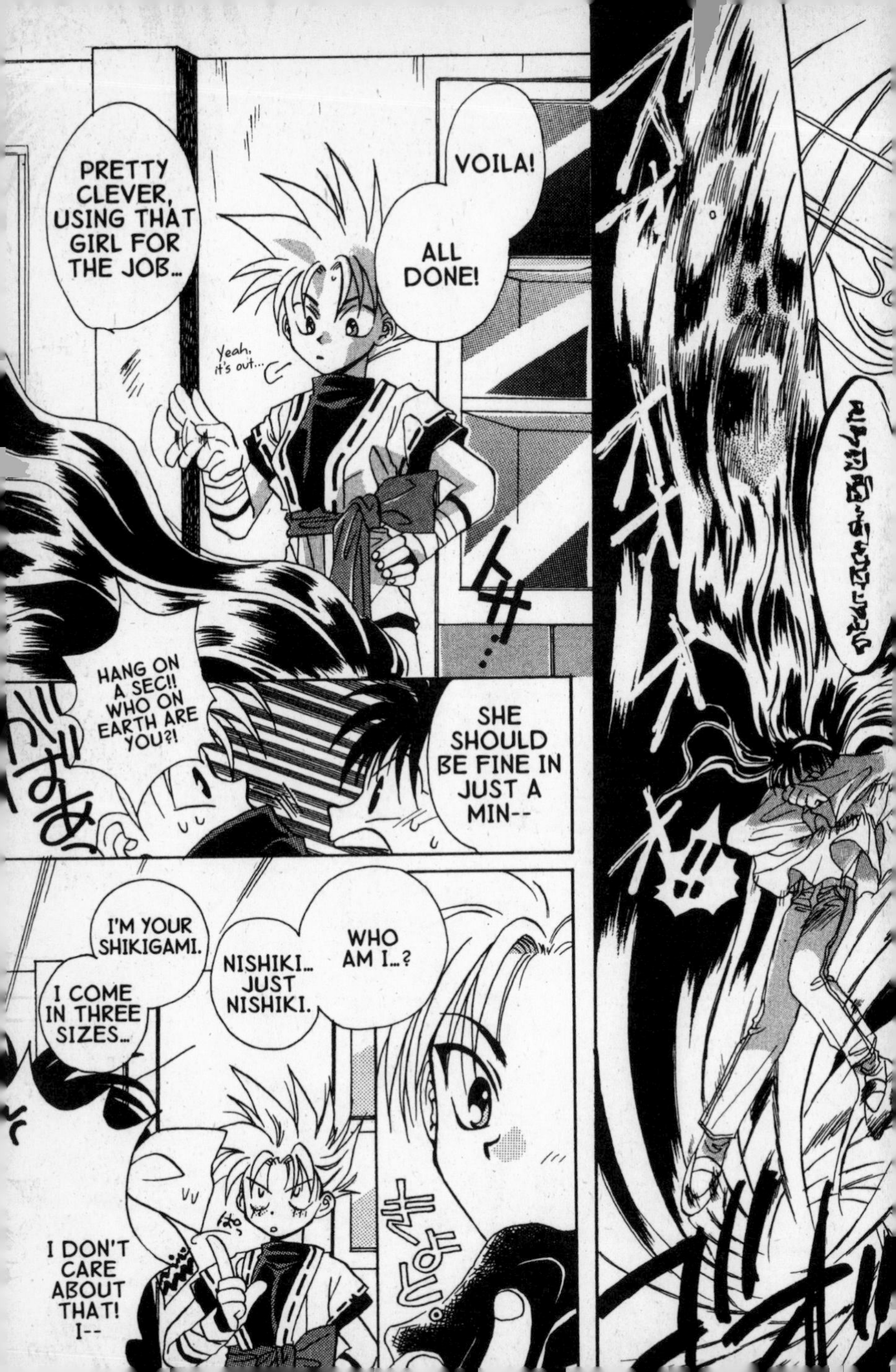
VOILA!
ALL DONE!
PRETTY CLEVER, USING THAT GIRL FOR THE JOB...
Yeah, it's out...
SHE SHOULD BE FINE IN JUST A MIN--
HANG ON A SEC!! WHO ON EARTH ARE YOU?!
がばぁっ
WHO AM I...?
NISHIKI... JUST NISHIKI.
I'M YOUR SHIKIGAMI.
I COME IN THREE SIZES...
きょと
ん
I DON'T CARE ABOUT THAT! I--

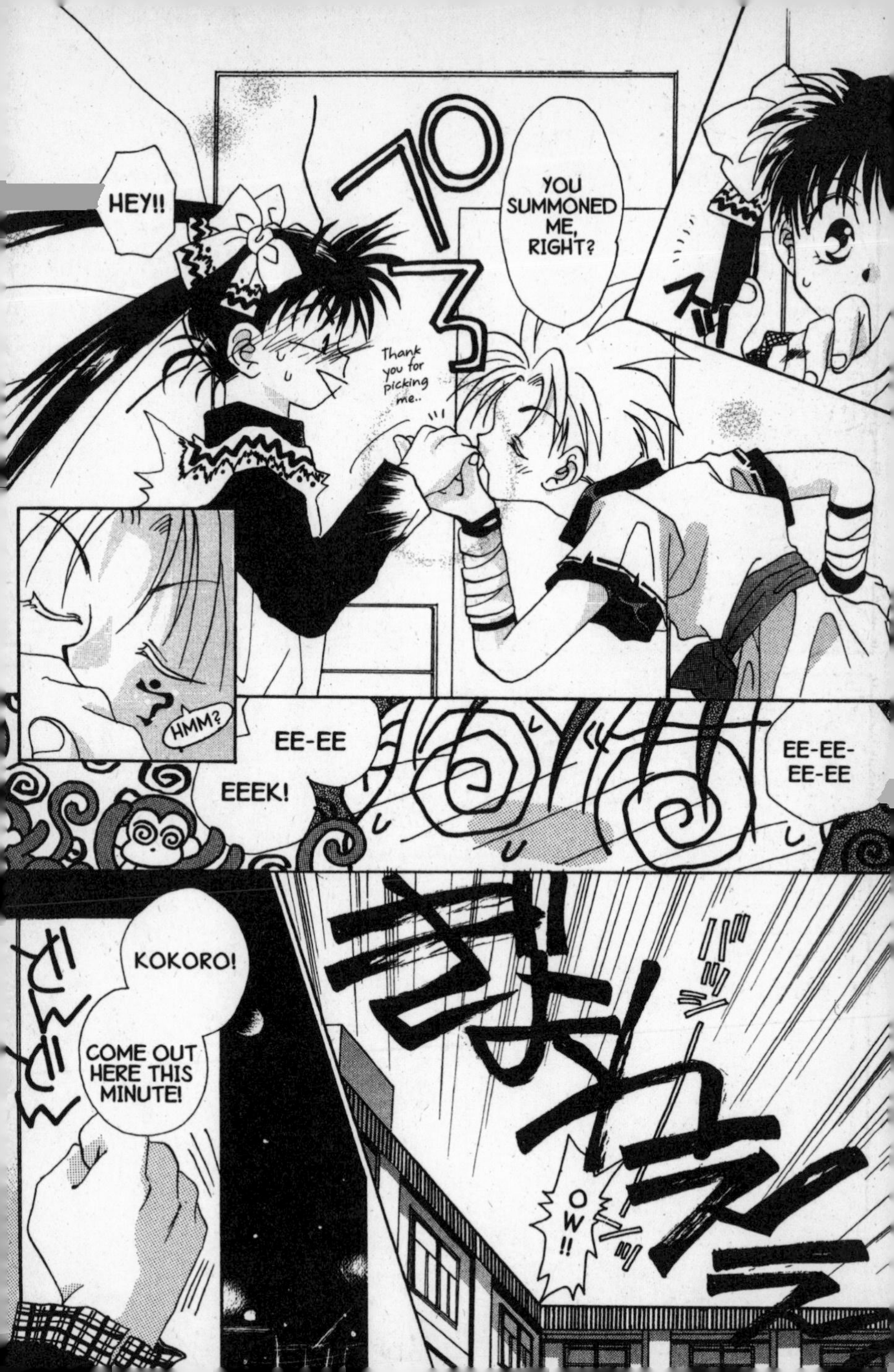
YOU SUMMONED ME, RIGHT?
HEY!!
Thank you for picking me..
HMM?
EE-EE-EE-EE
EE-EE
EEEK!
OW!!
KOKORO!
COME OUT HERE THIS MINUTE!

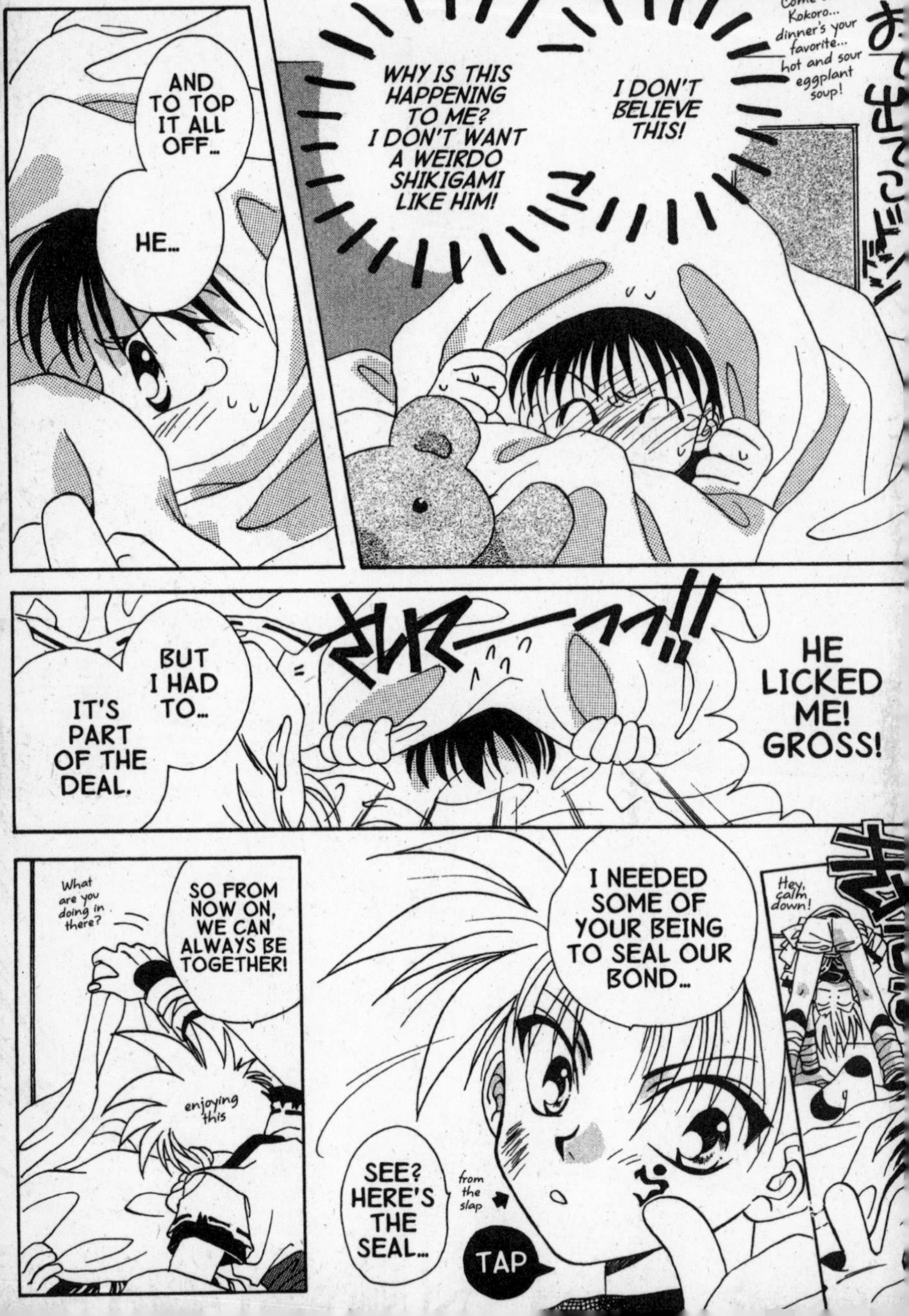
Come on, Kokoro... dinner's your favorite... hot and sour eggplant soup!
I DON'T BELIEVE THIS!
WHY IS THIS HAPPENING TO ME? I DON'T WANT A WEIRDO SHIKIGAMI LIKE HIM!
AND TO TOP IT ALL OFF...
HE...
HE LICKED ME! GROSS!
BUT I HAD TO...
IT'S PART OF THE DEAL.
Hey, calm down!
I NEEDED SOME OF YOUR BEING TO SEAL OUR BOND...
from the slap
SEE? HERE'S THE SEAL...
TAP
SO FROM NOW ON, WE CAN ALWAYS BE TOGETHER!
What are you doing in there?
enjoying this

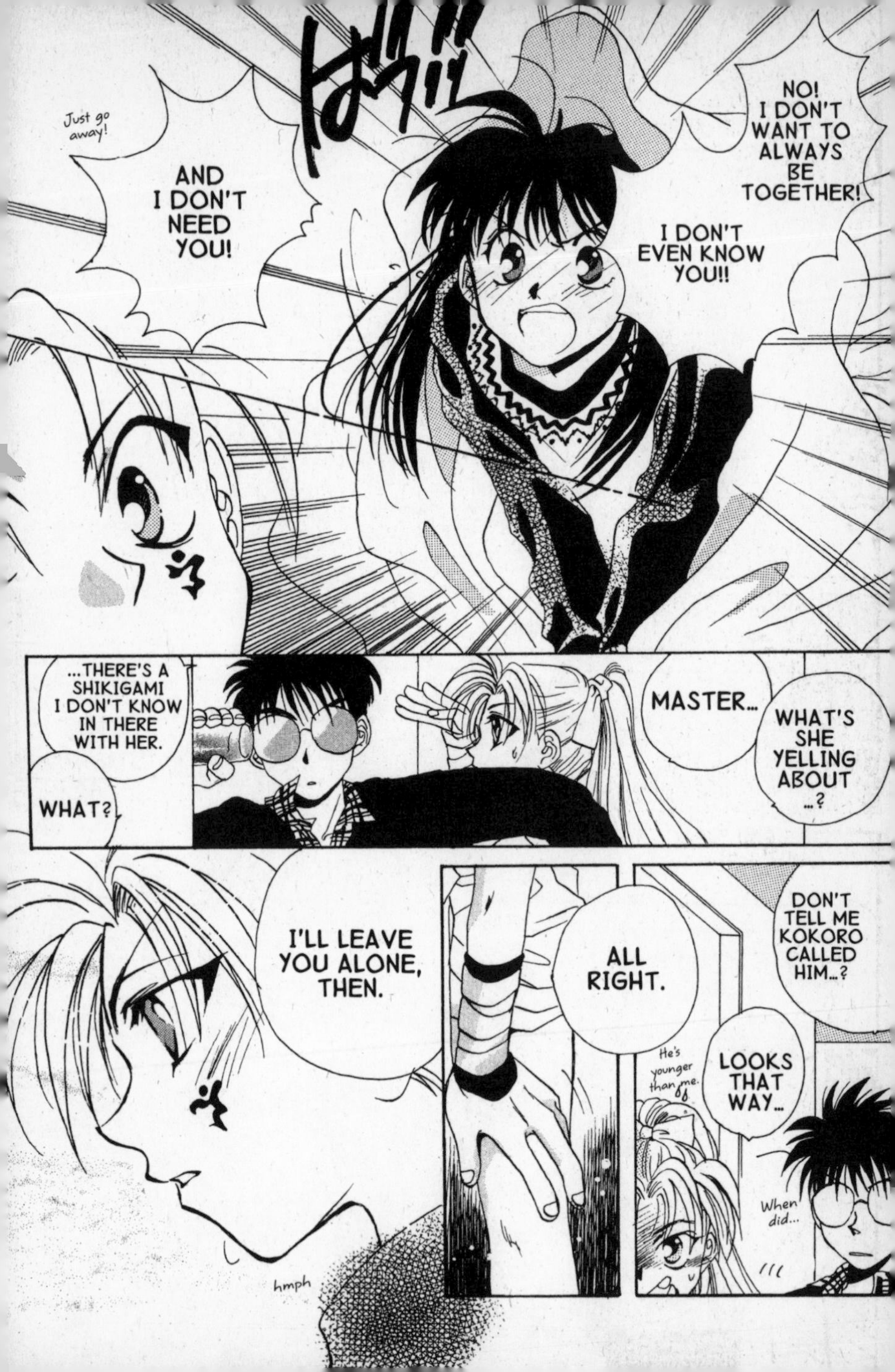
NO! I DON'T WANT TO ALWAYS BE TOGETHER!
I DON'T EVEN KNOW YOU!!
AND I DON'T NEED YOU!
Just go away!
MASTER...
WHAT'S SHE YELLING ABOUT ...?
...THERE'S A SHIKIGAMI I DON'T KNOW IN THERE WITH HER.
WHAT?
DON'T TELL ME KOKORO CALLED HIM...?
LOOKS THAT WAY...
He's younger than me.
When did...
ALL RIGHT.
I'LL LEAVE YOU ALONE, THEN.
hmph

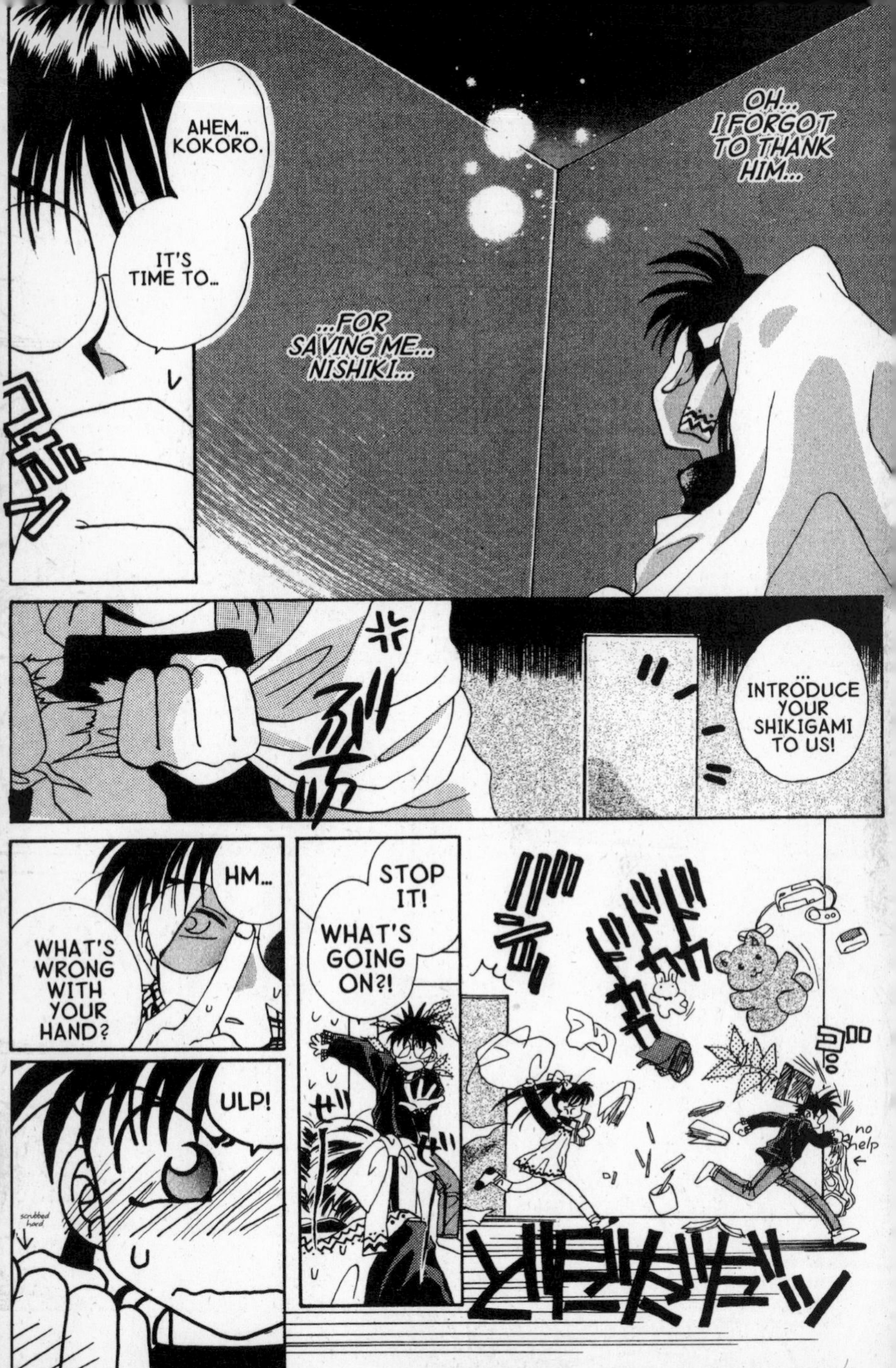
OH... I FORGOT TO THANK HIM...
...FOR SAVING ME... NISHIKI...
AHEM... KOKORO.
IT'S TIME TO...
...INTRODUCE YOUR SHIKIGAMI TO US!
no help
STOP IT!
WHAT'S GOING ON?!
HM...
WHAT'S WRONG WITH YOUR HAND?
ULP!
scrubbed hard

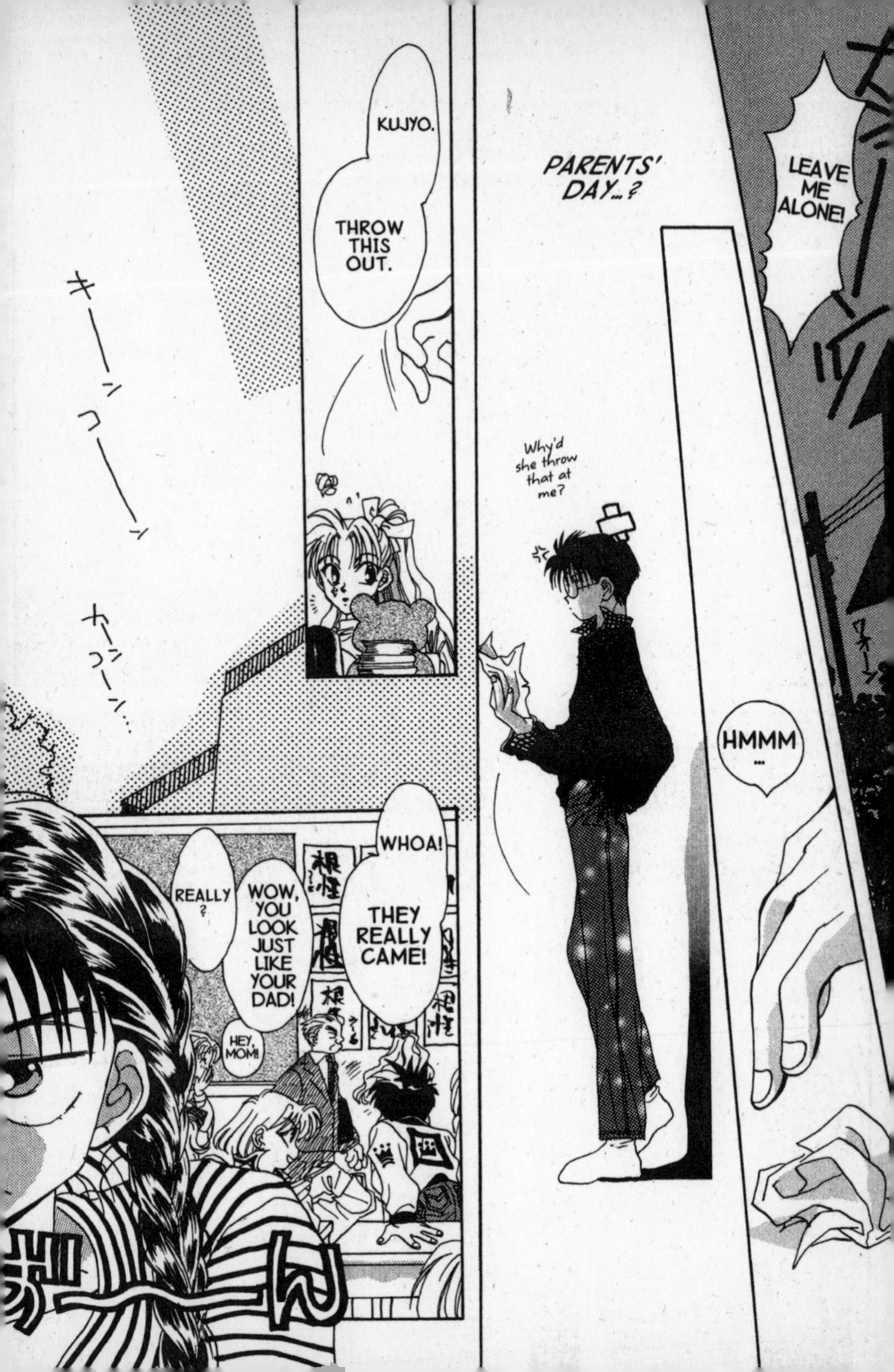
LEAVE ME ALONE!
HMMM ...
PARENTS' DAY...?
Why'd she throw that at me?
KUJYO.
THROW THIS OUT.
WHOA!
THEY REALLY CAME!
WOW, YOU LOOK JUST LIKE YOUR DAD!
REALLY?
HEY, MOM!

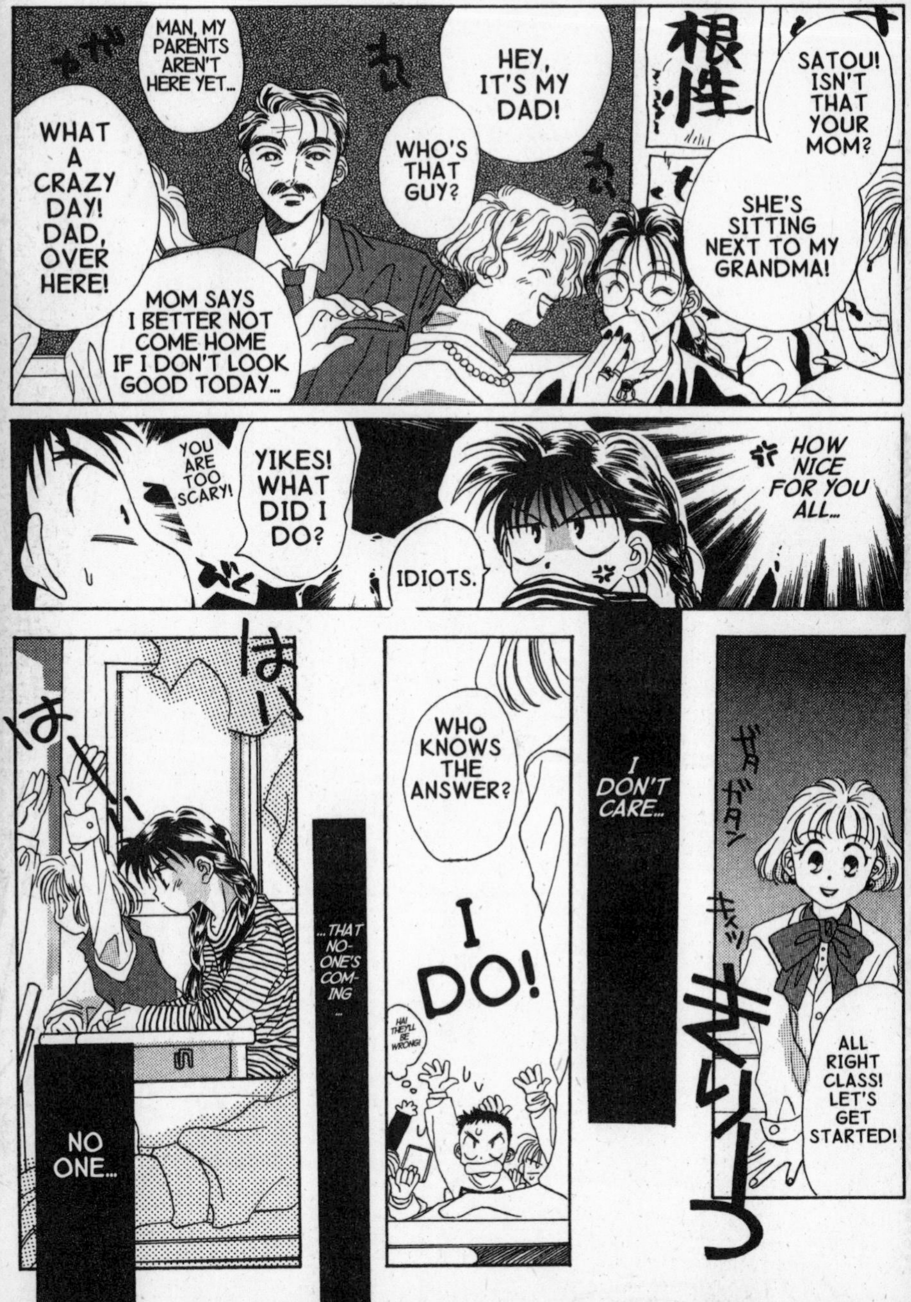
SATOU! ISN'T THAT YOUR MOM?
SHE'S SITTING NEXT TO MY GRANDMA!
HEY, IT'S MY DAD!
WHO'S THAT GUY?
MAN, MY PARENTS AREN'T HERE YET...
WHAT A CRAZY DAY! DAD, OVER HERE!
MOM SAYS I BETTER NOT COME HOME IF I DON'T LOOK GOOD TODAY...
HOW NICE FOR YOU ALL...
IDIOTS.
YIKES! WHAT DID I DO?
YOU ARE TOO SCARY!
ALL RIGHT CLASS! LET'S GET STARTED!
I DON'T CARE...
WHO KNOWS THE ANSWER?
I DO!
HA! THEY'LL BE WRONG!
...THAT NO-ONE'S COMING-ING ...
NO ONE...

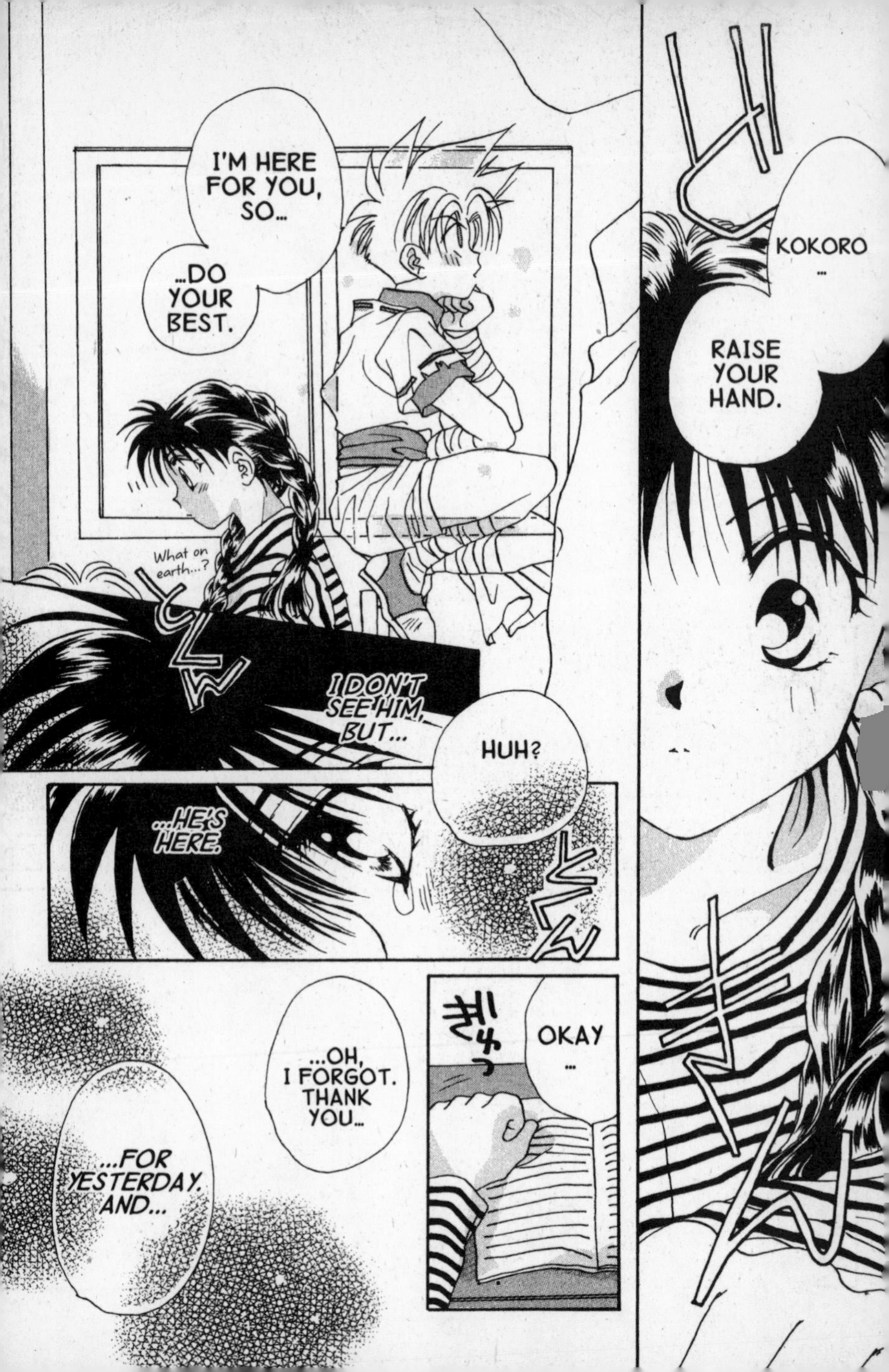
KOKORO ...
RAISE YOUR HAND.
I'M HERE FOR YOU, SO...
...DO YOUR BEST.
What on earth...?
I DON'T SEE HIM, BUT...
HUH?
...HE'S HERE.
OKAY ...
...OH, I FORGOT. THANK YOU...
...FOR YESTERDAY. AND...

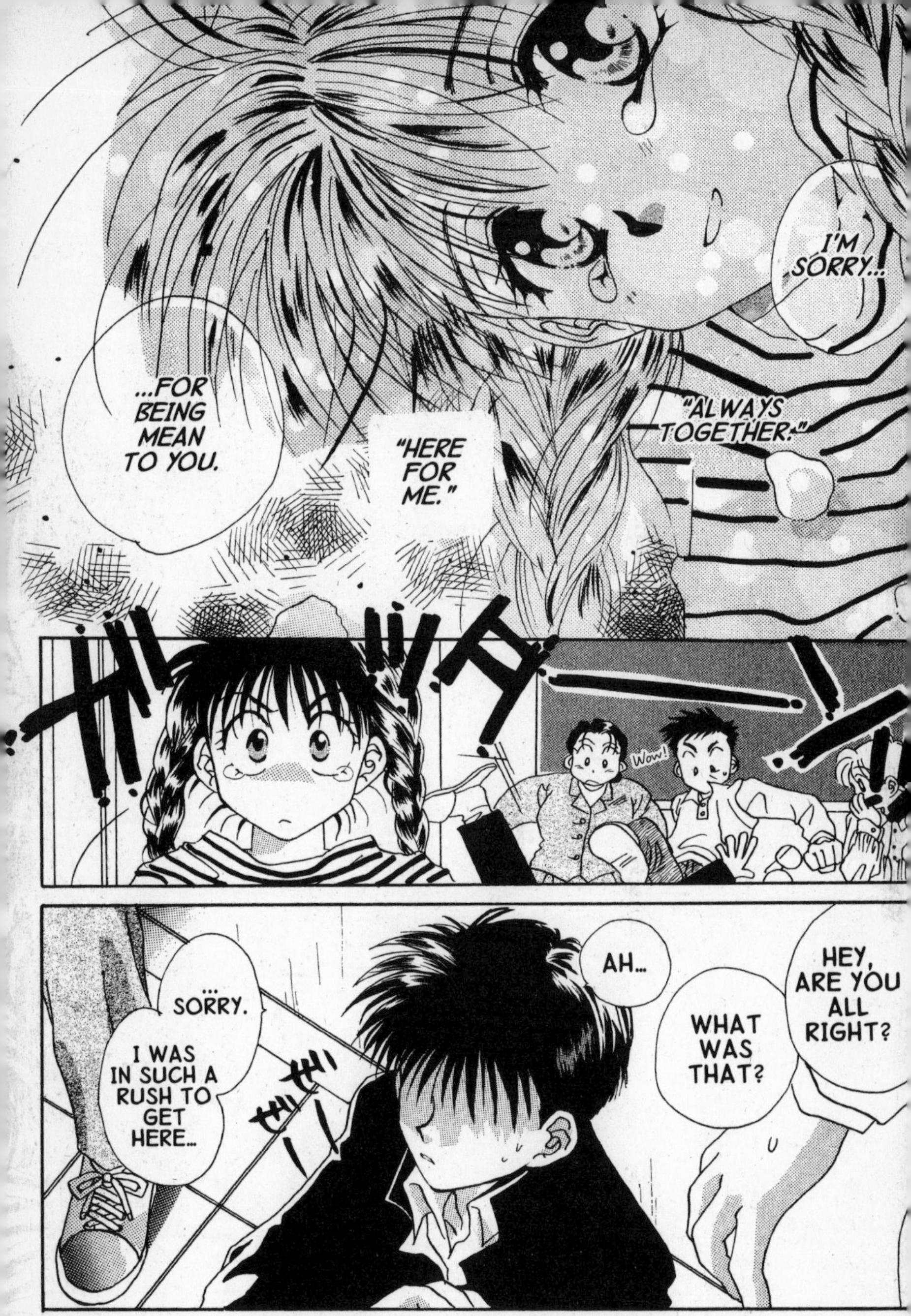
I'M SORRY...
"ALWAYS TOGETHER."
"HERE FOR ME."
...FOR BEING MEAN TO YOU.
Wow!
HEY, ARE YOU ALL RIGHT?
WHAT WAS THAT?
AH...
... SORRY.
I WAS IN SUCH A RUSH TO GET HERE...

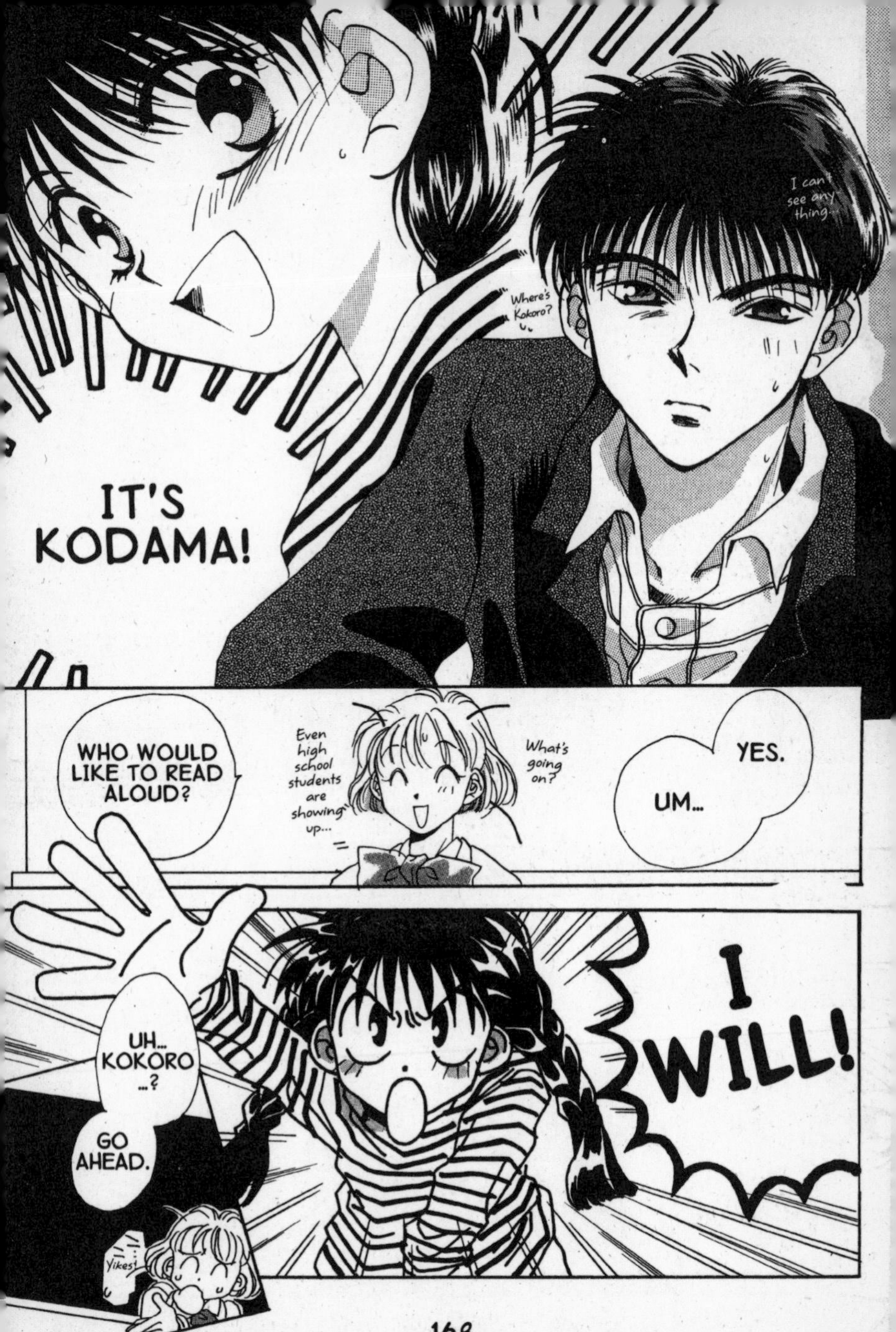
I can't see any thing...
Where's Kokoro?
IT'S KODAMA!
YES.
UM...
What's going on?
Even high school students are showing up...
WHO WOULD LIKE TO READ ALOUD?
I WILL!
UH... KOKORO ...?
GO AHEAD.
Yikes!

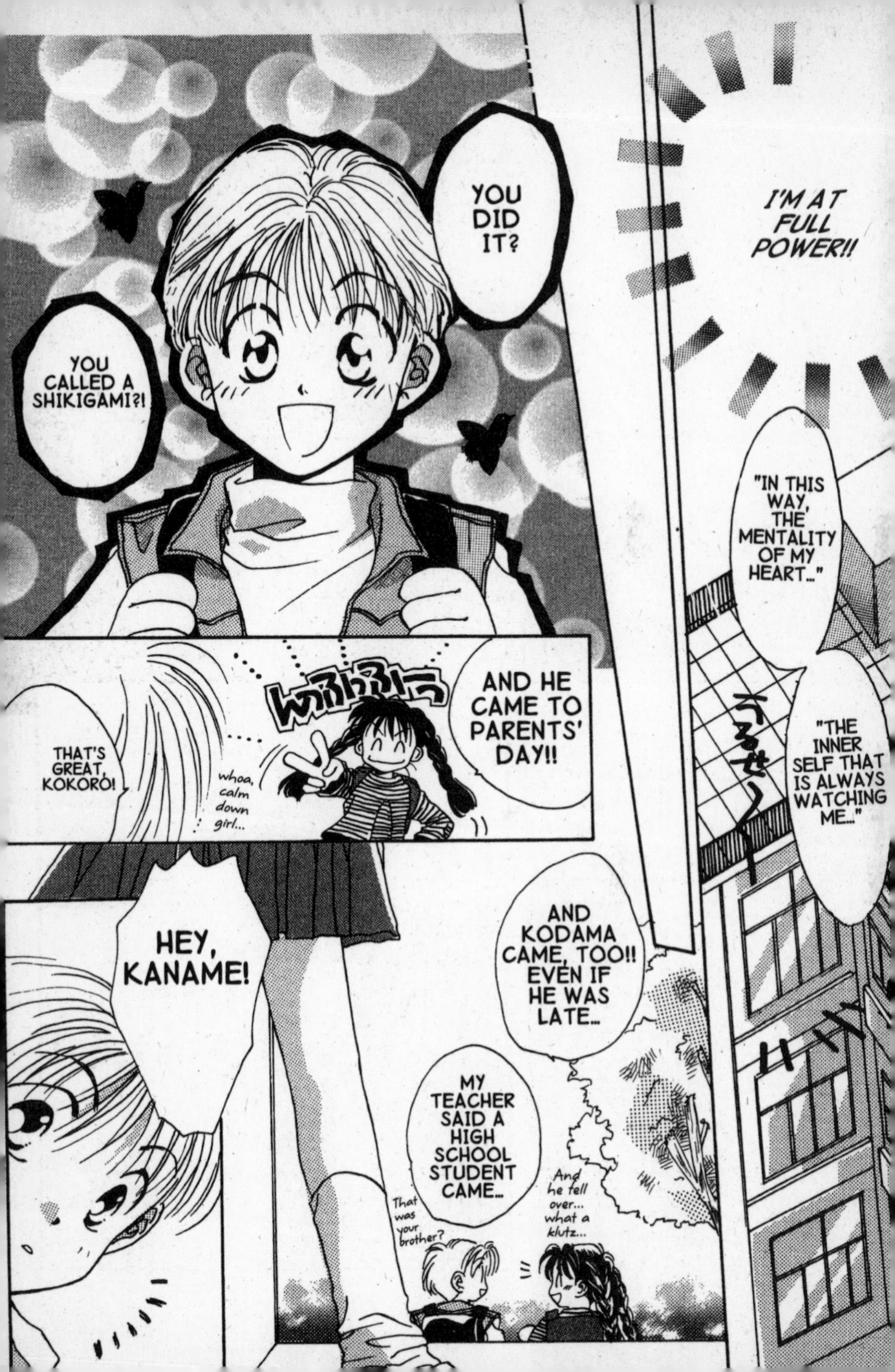
I'M AT FULL POWER!!
"IN THIS WAY, THE MENTALITY OF MY HEART..."
"THE INNER SELF THAT IS ALWAYS WATCHING ME..."
YOU DID IT?
YOU CALLED A SHIKIGAMI?!
AND HE CAME TO PARENTS' DAY!!
whoa, calm down girl...
THAT'S GREAT, KOKORO!
AND KODAMA CAME, TOO!! EVEN IF HE WAS LATE...
MY TEACHER SAID A HIGH SCHOOL STUDENT CAME...
And he fell over... what a klutz...
That was your brother?
HEY, KANAME!

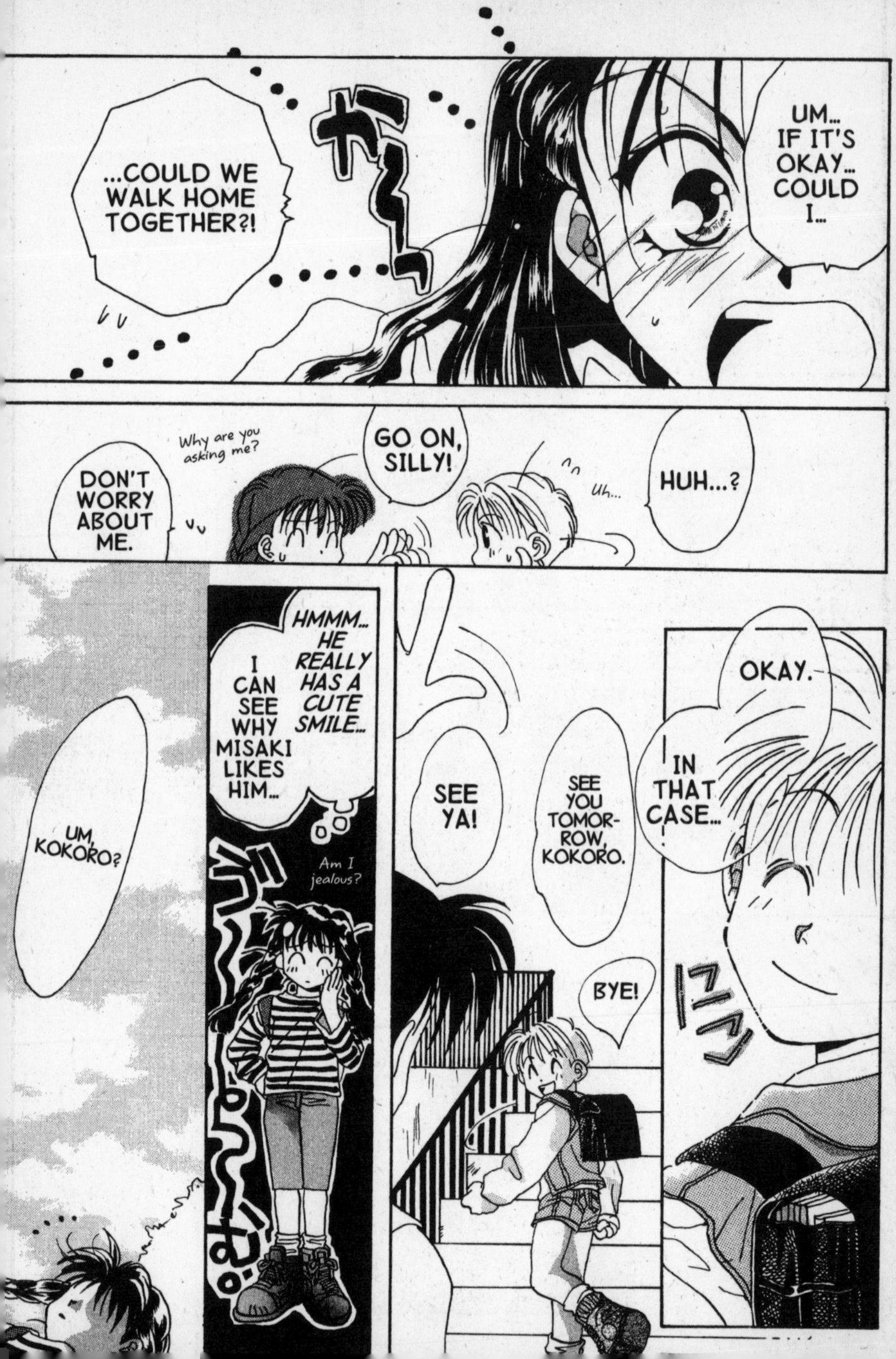
UM... IF IT'S OKAY... COULD I...
...COULD WE WALK HOME TOGETHER?!
HUH...?
Uh...
GO ON, SILLY!
Why are you asking me?
DON'T WORRY ABOUT ME.
OKAY.
IN THAT CASE...
SEE YOU TOMORROW, KOKORO.
SEE YA!
BYE!
HMMM... HE REALLY HAS A CUTE SMILE...
I CAN SEE WHY MISAKI LIKES HIM...
Am I jealous?
UM, KOKORO?

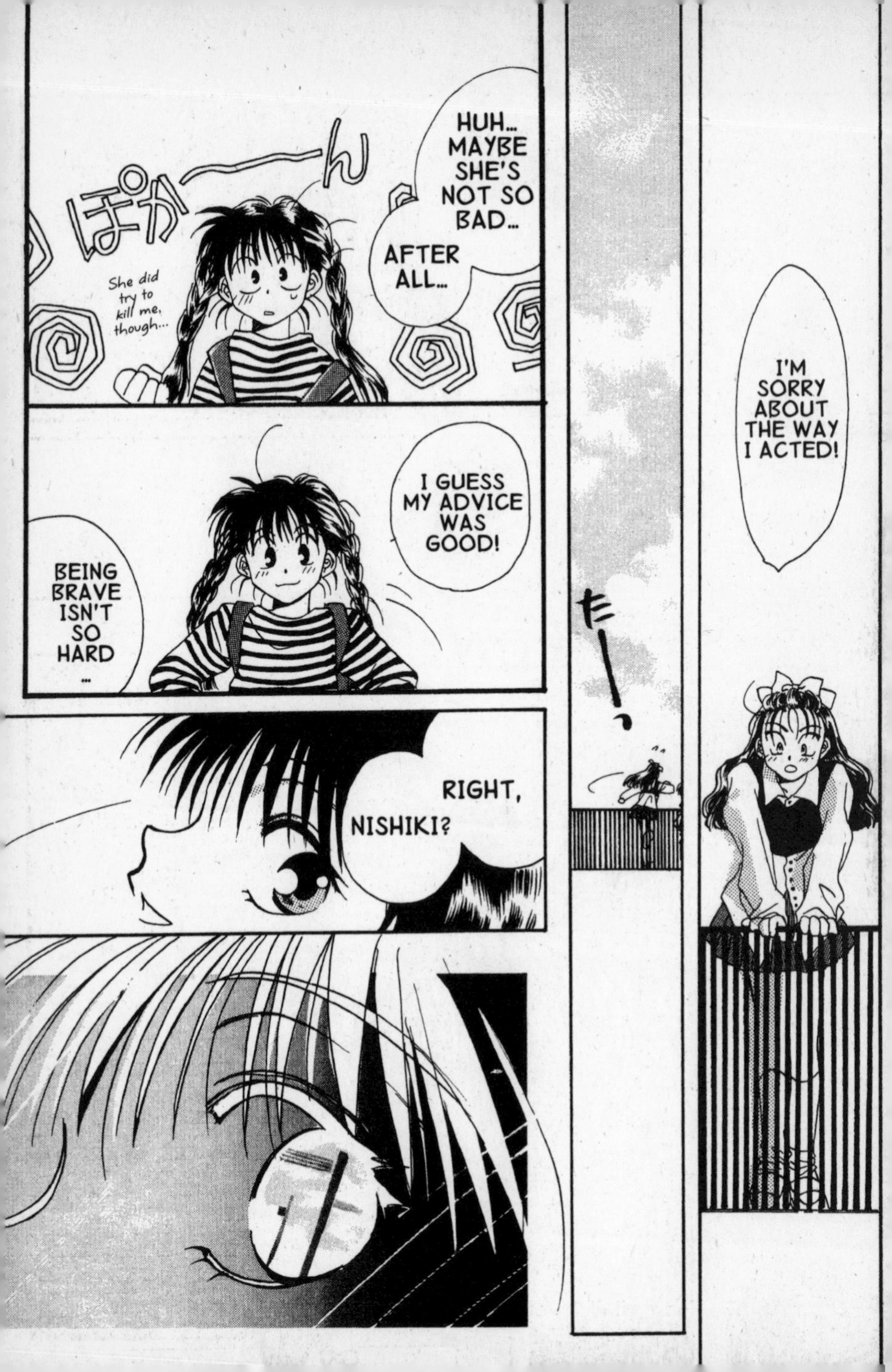
I'M SORRY ABOUT THE WAY I ACTED!
たー!
ぽか〜〜ん
HUH... MAYBE SHE'S NOT SO BAD...
AFTER ALL...
She did try to kill me, though...
I GUESS MY ADVICE WAS GOOD!
BEING BRAVE ISN'T SO HARD ...
RIGHT, NISHIKI?

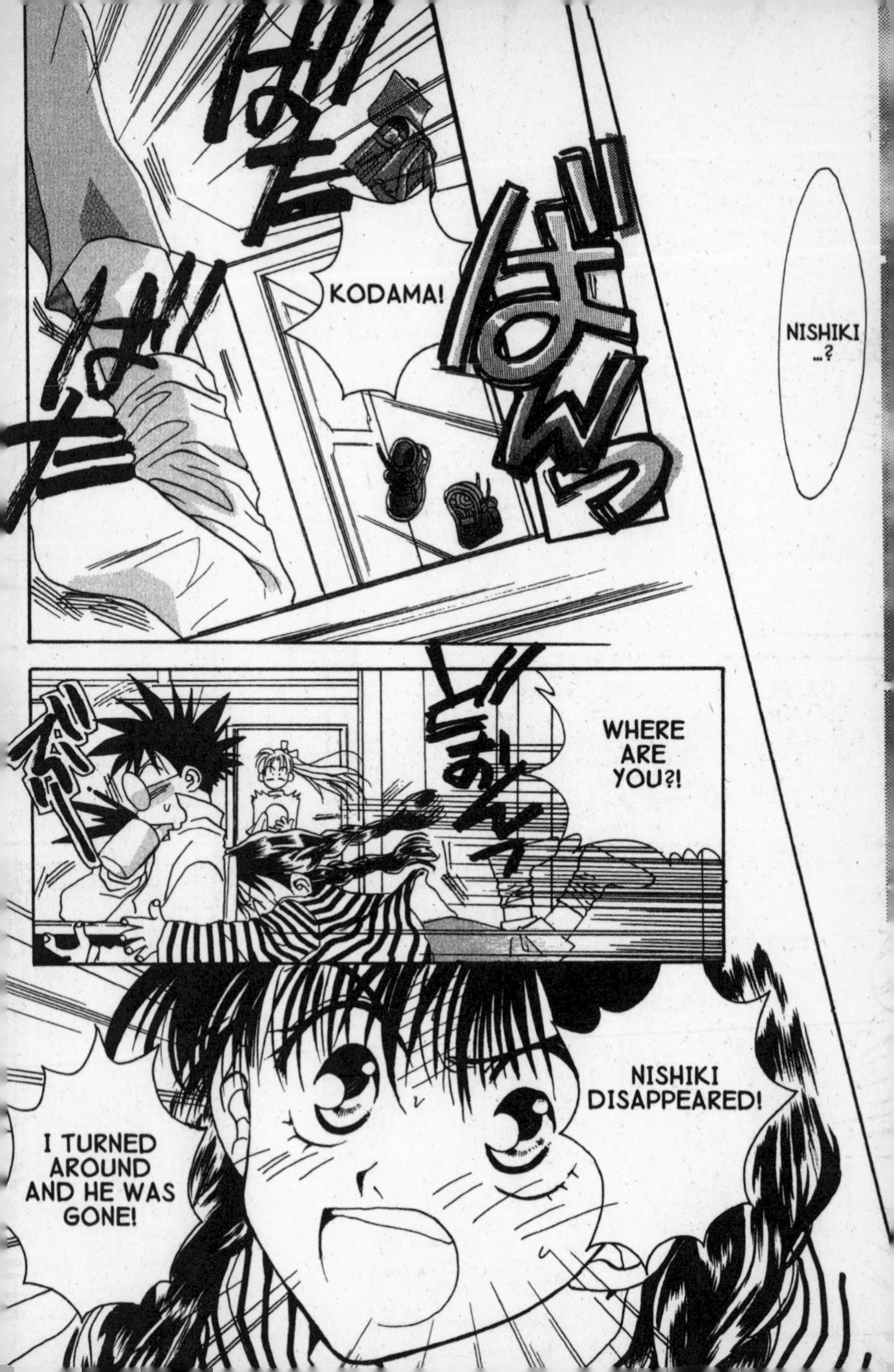
NISHIKI ...?
KODAMA!
WHERE ARE YOU?!
NISHIKI DISAPPEARED!
I TURNED AROUND AND HE WAS GONE!

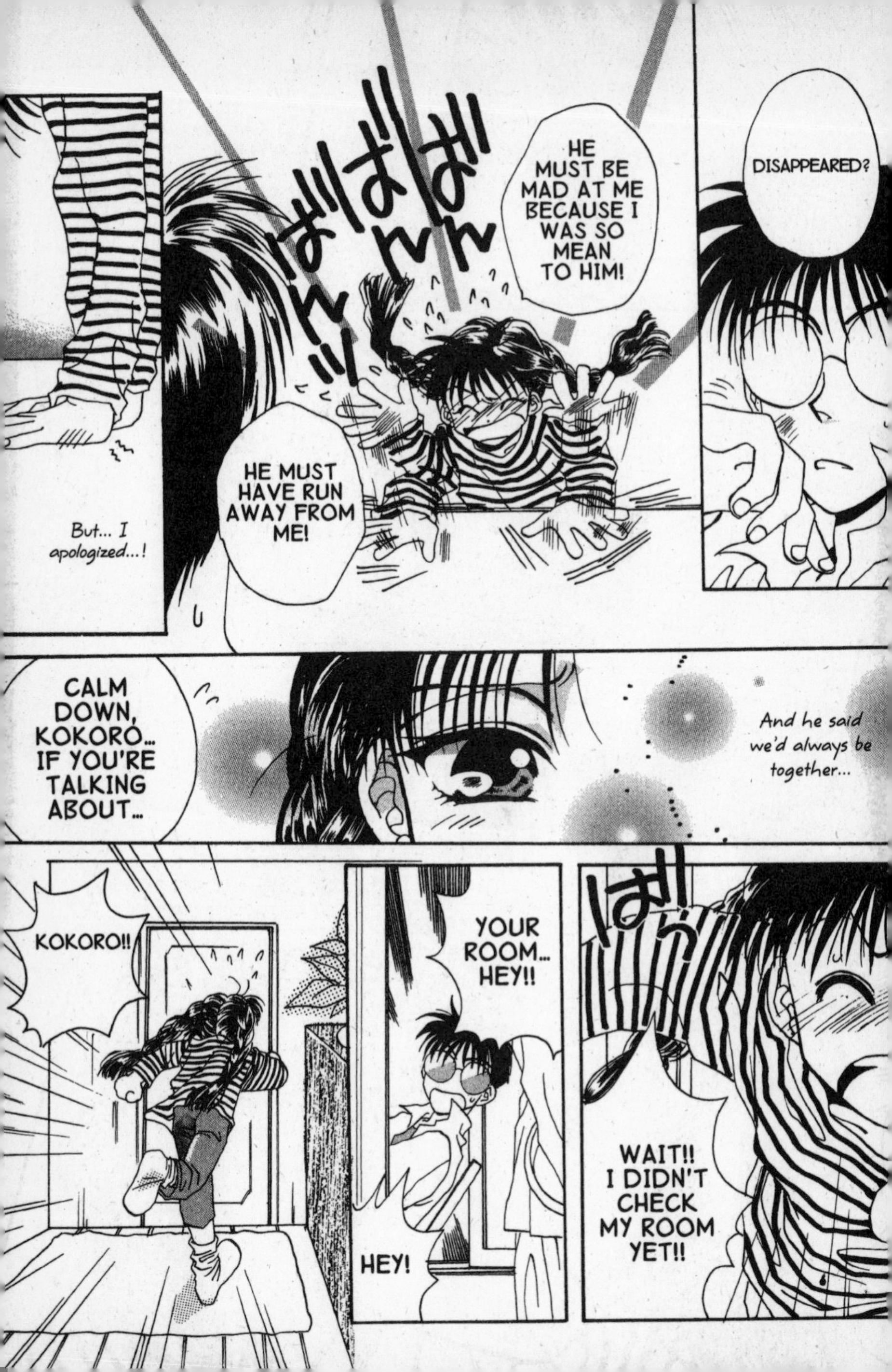
DISAPPEARED?
HE MUST BE MAD AT ME BECAUSE I WAS SO MEAN TO HIM!
HE MUST HAVE RUN AWAY FROM ME!
But... I apologized...!
And he said we'd always be together...
CALM DOWN, KOKORO... IF YOU'RE TALKING ABOUT...
WAIT!! I DIDN'T CHECK MY ROOM YET!!
YOUR ROOM... HEY!!
HEY!
KOKORO!!

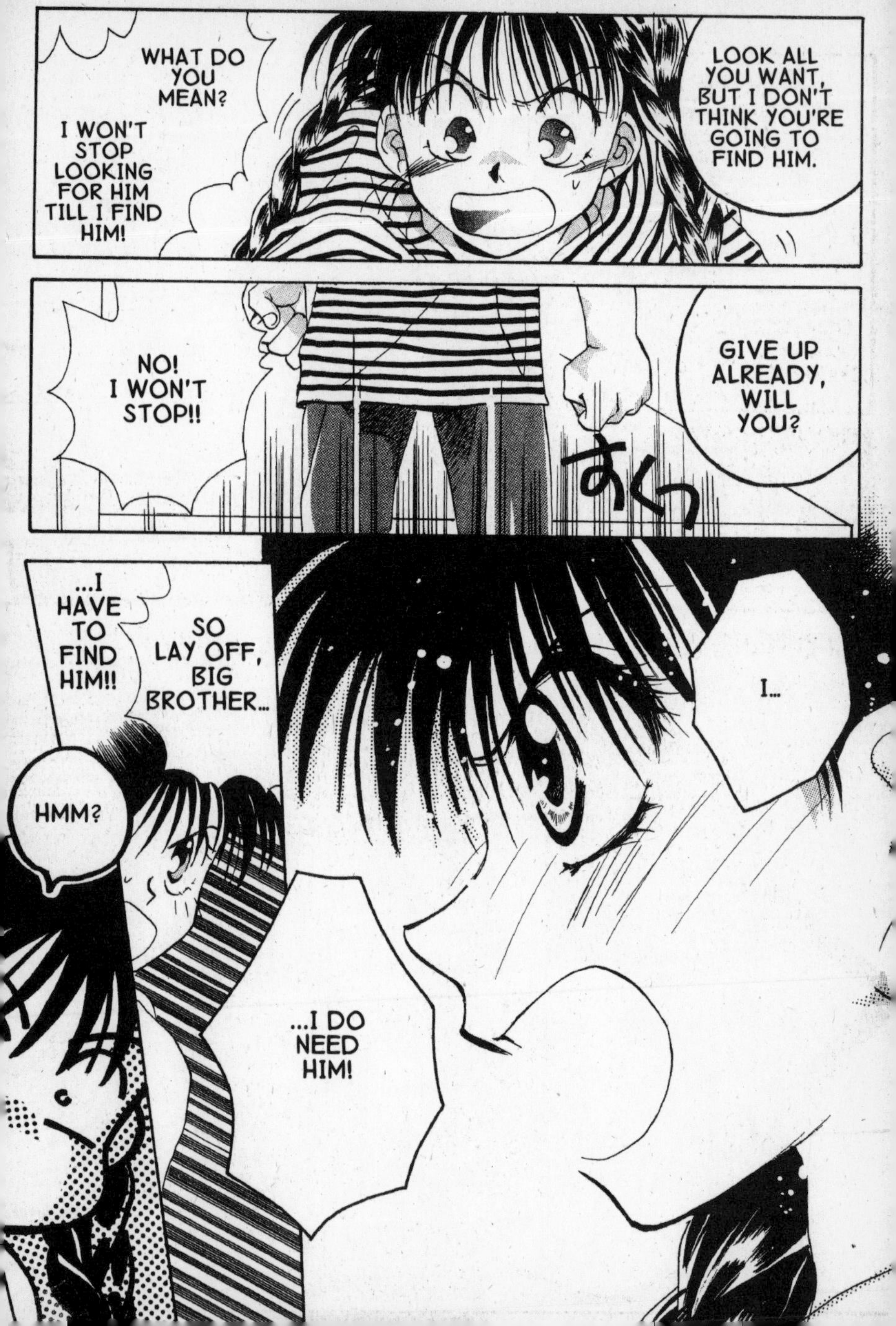

LOOK ALL YOU WANT, BUT I DON'T THINK YOU'RE GOING TO FIND HIM.
WHAT DO YOU MEAN?
I WON'T STOP LOOKING FOR HIM TILL I FIND HIM!
GIVE UP ALREADY, WILL YOU?
すくっ
NO! I WON'T STOP!!
I...
...I DO NEED HIM!
...I HAVE TO FIND HIM!!
SO LAY OFF, BIG BROTHER...
HMM?

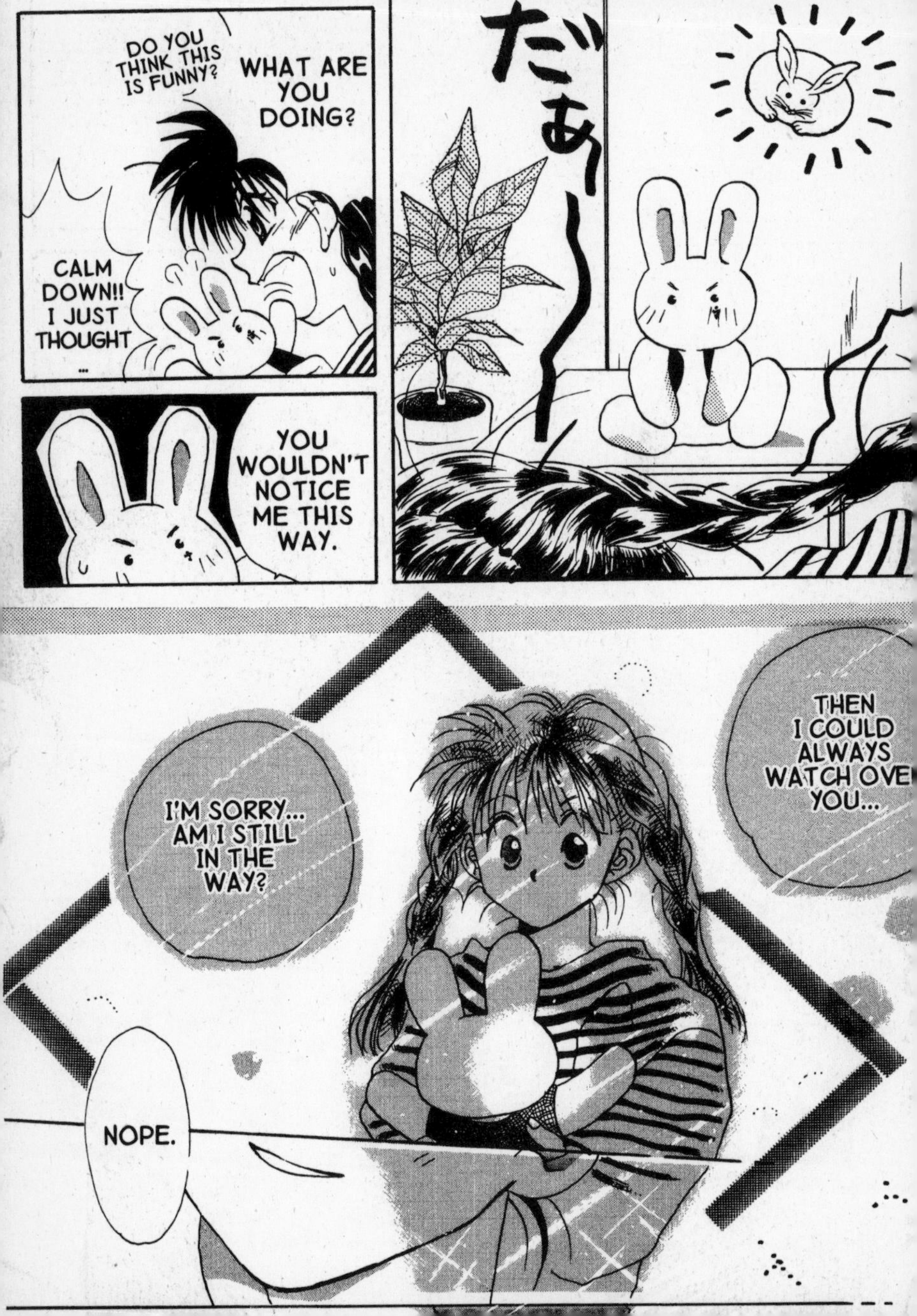
だあ〜
WHAT ARE YOU DOING?
DO YOU THINK THIS IS FUNNY?
CALM DOWN!! I JUST THOUGHT ...
YOU WOULDN'T NOTICE ME THIS WAY.
THEN I COULD ALWAYS WATCH OVE YOU...
I'M SORRY... AM I STILL IN THE WAY?
NOPE.

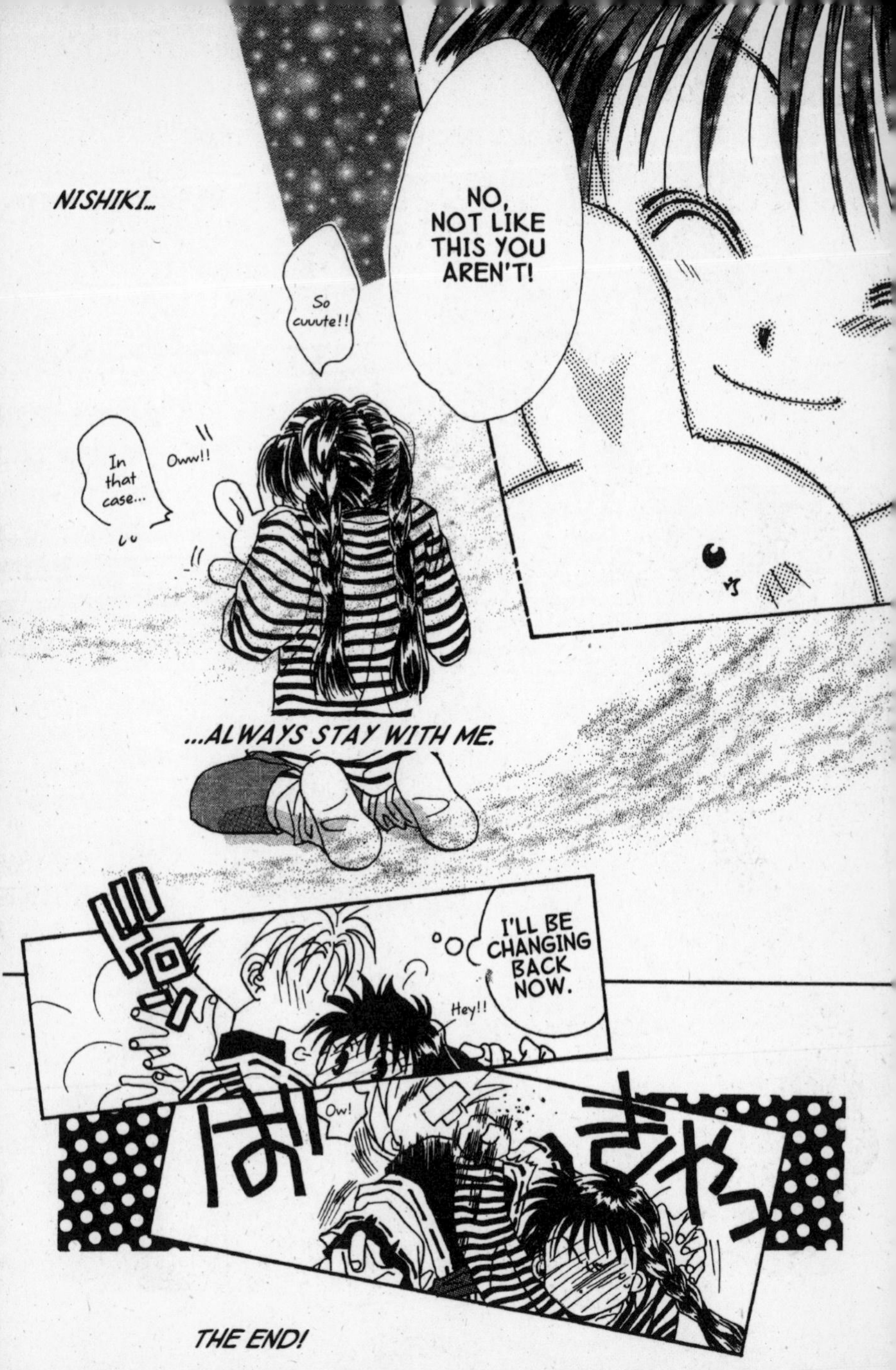
NO, NOT LIKE THIS YOU AREN'T!
So cuuute!!
NISHIKI...
Oww!!
In that case...
...ALWAYS STAY WITH ME.
I'LL BE CHANGING BACK NOW.
Hey!!
Ow!
THE END!

# AFTERWORD

A FEW WORDS ABOUT "N" IS FOR NISHIKI:

THIS IS THE FIRST COMIC I DID FOR ASUKA COMICS (WHO PUBLISH D.N.ANGEL IN JAPAN). I NEVER THOUGHT IT WOULD END UP COLLECTED IN A BOOK, BUT A LOT OF PEOPLE SAID THEY WANTED TO SEE IT...SO HERE IT IS. I WROTE AND DREW IT OVER THREE YEARS BEFORE D·N·ANGEL, SO PLEASE FORGIVE ME FOR THE PARTS THAT AREN'T SO GOOD!! I HOPE YOU ENJOY IT, AND I HOPE SOMEDAY I CAN CONTINUE THE STORY...

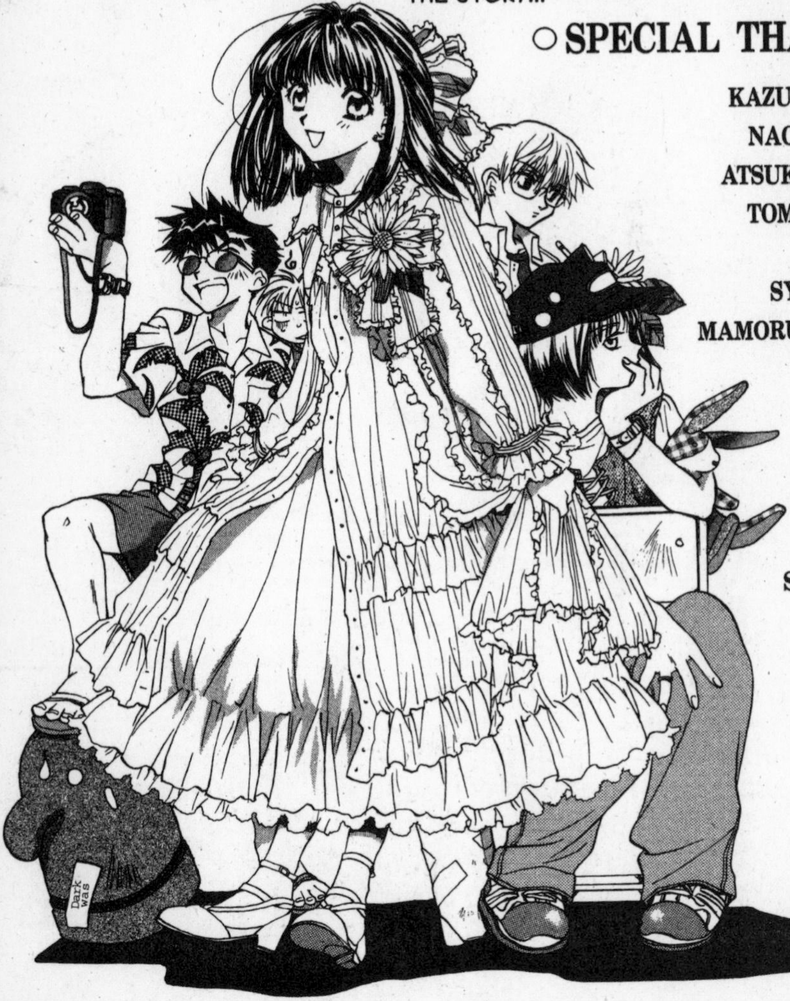

Dark was


○ SPECIAL THANKS ○

KAZUMA JINNA
NAOKO ISHID
ATSUKO KUWAT
TOMO HANED
Mt. HIG
SYO ASAGI
MAMORU SUGISA

YUKIR
SUGISA
199

○

○

○

SEE YO
NEXT

THE END!

# D·N·ANGEL

## THINGS TO COME...

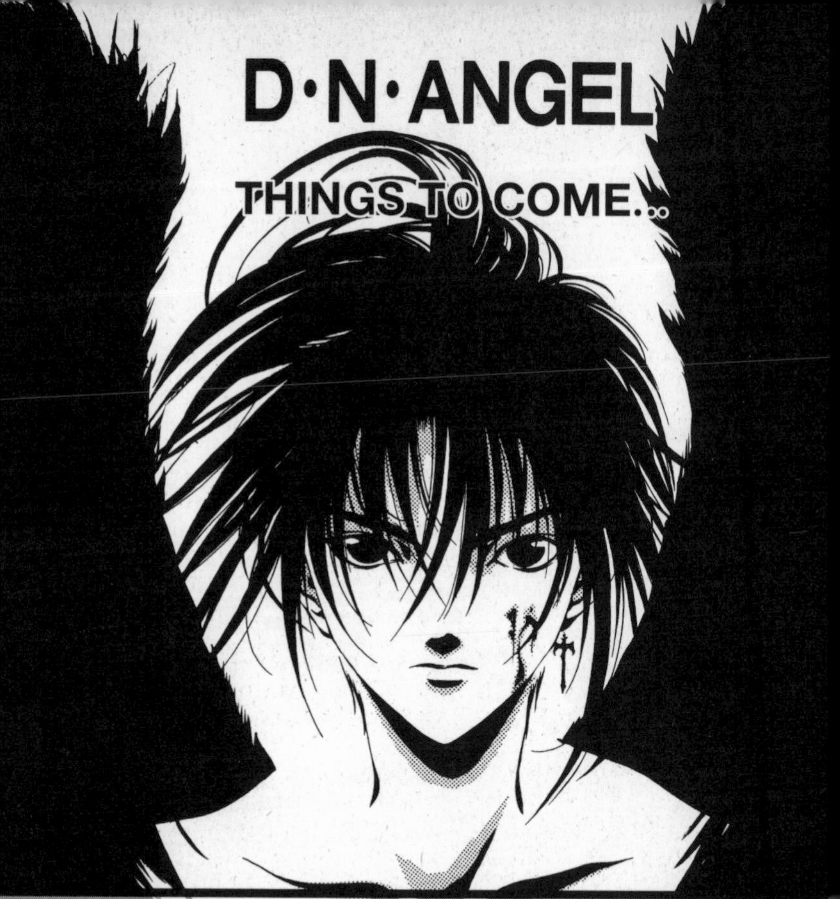

It's that time again—time for everyone to suffer the midwinter hike imposed upon all the students at Azumano Middle School. While Daisuke has been dreading this all year, he can't really say he's unhappy about it, as this year he gets to go mountain climbing with his beloved Risa. But when Daisuke and Riku find themselves lost and alone on the frigid mountainside, it's Dark to the rescue. Can the Phantom Thief save the day without blowing Daisuke's cover? And is Risa finally warming up to our young hero?

**Find out in D.N. Angel volume 2!**

# Crazy Love Story

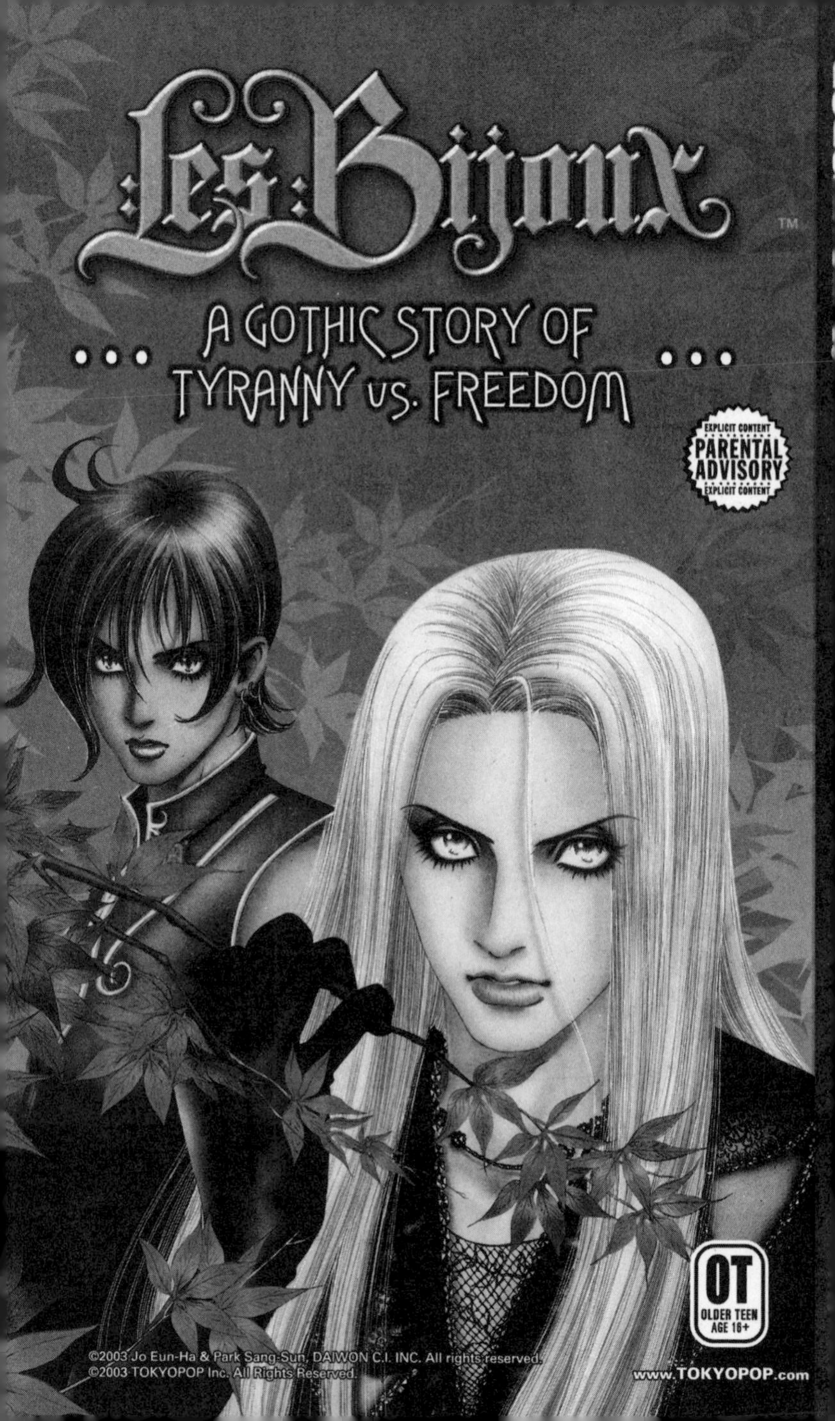
Les Bijoux™
... A GOTHIC STORY OF TYRANNY vs. FREEDOM ...
EXPLICIT CONTENT PARENTAL ADVISORY EXPLICIT CONTENT
OT OLDER TEEN AGE 16+
©2003 Jo Eun-Ha & Park Sang-Sun, DAIWON C.I. INC. All rights reserved.
©2003 TOKYOPOP Inc. All Rights Reserved.
www.TOKYOPOP.com

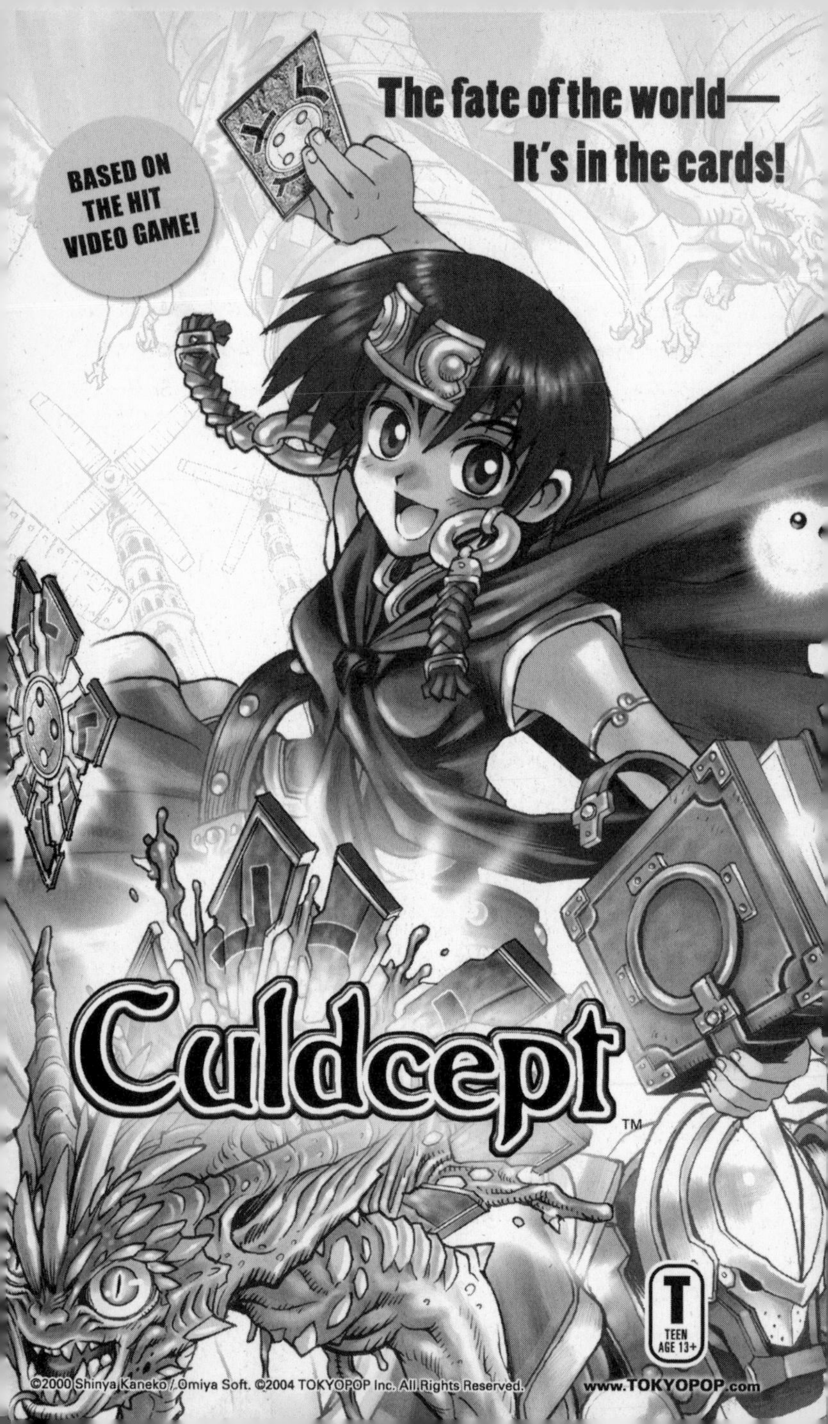
The fate of the world—
It's in the cards!
BASED ON THE HIT VIDEO GAME!
Culdcept™
T TEEN AGE 13+
©2000 Shinya Kaneko / Omiya Soft. ©2004 TOKYOPOP Inc. All Rights Reserved.
www.TOKYOPOP.com

# kare kano
*his and her circumstances*
Story by Masami Tsuda

## Life Was A Popularity Contest For Yukino.
## Somebody Is About To Steal Her Crown.

Available Now At Your Favorite Book And Comic Stores!

| Rank | Name | Class | Points |
|------|------|-------|--------|
| 1 | ??? | | |
| 2 | ??? | | |
| 3 | Tomohiko Ta | B | |
| 4 | Takumi | A | |
| 5 | Mieko T | E | |
| 6 | Nijo Watana | C | |
| 7 | Akemi Imafuku | | |
| 8 | Mizue Tanaka | | |
| 9 | Yuki Honjo | | |
| 10 | Reiko Yokoo | | |
| 11 | Hiroki Sato | | |
| 12 | Akira Oshima | | |
| 13 | Eri Yugawa | | |
| 14 | Aiko Yamac | | |
| 15 | Shogo Ka | | |
| 16 | Masami H | | |
| 17 | Mizuho On | | |

HEH
HEH

100% AUTHENTIC MANGA

T
TEEN
AGE 13+

www.TOKYOPOP.c

# STOP!

## This is the back of the book.
## You wouldn't want to spoil a great ending!

This book is printed "manga-style," in the authentic Japanese right-to-left format. Since none of the artwork has been flipped or altered, readers get to experience the story just as the creator intended. You've been asking for it, so TOKYOPOP® delivered: authentic, hot-off-the-press, and far more fun!

# DIRECTIONS

If this is your first time reading manga-style, here's a quick guide to help you understand how it works.

It's easy... just start in the top right panel and follow the numbers. Have fun, and look for more 100% authentic manga from TOKYOPOP®!

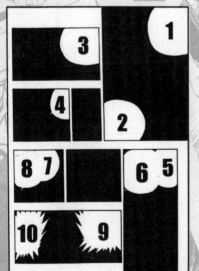